THE LETTERS OF MARGARET FULLER

Giovanni Angelo Ossoli, husband of Margaret Fuller. By permission of the Houghton Library, Harvard University.

THE LETTERS OF
Margaret Fuller

Edited by

ROBERT N. HUDSPETH

VOLUME V · 1848–49

Cornell University Press

ITHACA AND LONDON

PUBLICATION OF THIS BOOK WAS ASSISTED BY A GRANT
FROM THE PUBLICATIONS PROGRAM OF THE NATIONAL ENDOWMENT
FOR THE HUMANITIES, AN INDEPENDENT FEDERAL AGENCY.

First published 1988 by Cornell University Press.

International Standard Book Number 0-8014-2174-8
Library of Congress Catalog Card Number 82-22098
Printed in the United States of America
*Librarians: Library of Congress cataloging information appears
on the last page of the book.*

*The paper in this book is acid-free and meets the guidelines for
permanence and durability of the Committee on Production Guidelines
for Book Longevity of the Council on Library Resources.*

PREFACE

Readers of previous volumes of Margaret Fuller's letters will remember that she left the United States in 1846 on a long-delayed trip to Europe, whose literature and art had engrossed her for twenty years. Eighteen months later, as 1848 began amid incessant rain in Rome, Margaret Fuller was intellectually and emotionally committed to Italy in a more complex way than her American correspondents could know. She had, to be sure, championed the growing revolutionary movement in her essays in the *New-York Daily Tribune* and in her personal correspondence. What her family and friends did not know was that she was pregnant by Giovanni Angelo Ossoli, the younger son of a noble family, a man devoted to republican ideas. No one, perhaps even Fuller herself, could understand how far she had traveled from New England.

After an eclectic, distinguished public career as a translator, critic, editor, journalist, and feminist theoretician, Fuller had left New England in 1844—left Boston and Cambridge with their writers, abolitionists, and Unitarian radicals; left her easy access to Concord, where she frequently visited with Emerson, Thoreau, and Hawthorne—and had gone to New York City, where she became a writer for Horace Greeley's Whig *Tribune*. In New York, Fuller had developed an interest in social reform which came to all but replace her earlier enthusiasm for literary topics. In England she naturally sought out Victorian reformers and in France she cultivated socialists. Throughout late 1846 and early 1847 she met notable intellectuals who shared her ideas: Thomas Carlyle, Giuseppi Mazzini, George Sand, and Félicité-Robert de Lamennais.

In the spring of 1847 she toured Italy: from Naples to Rome, to

Venice, over to Milan, and back to Rome. She wrote for the *Tribune*, filling her essays with views on art, statues, and personalities. And she increasingly reported the public events that were making a revolution seem possible.

In 1846 Giovanni Maria Mastai-Ferretti, Pius IX, succeeded Pope Gregory XVI. Pius quickly embarked on a series of reforms that heartened the liberals both in and out of Italy. To Fuller, the pontiff was the Great Man, the genius who would lead a revolution that was increasingly imminent, for Italy had become a restless prize in European struggles for power. France, Spain, and, most important, Austria dominated parts of the peninsula, while the pope ruled as a temporal prince over the Papal States. Piedmont-Sardinia (called also simply Piedmont or Sardinia) was perhaps the strongest of the independent states, but its king, Charles Albert, could not challenge the Austrian army that occupied Lombardy and Venetia, nor was he sympathetic to liberalism. Measured against contemporary princes, the new pope was a welcome change to Fuller. Although she doubted his ability to control the cardinals, Fuller understood that Pius was the single ruler who might free and unite Italy.

This political world that offered the possibility of change was offset for Fuller by her pregnancy, which bound her to an uncomfortable secrecy. Here, as before in her life, her outward existence masked compelling intimate realities. Most recently, as readers of her letters remember, she had kept her love for James Nathan to herself in New York City. As far as we can tell, Fuller took no one into her confidence save Ossoli, to whom she was probably not yet married.[1]

Little wonder that she was depressed during the weeks of constant rain at the beginning of 1848. She could not talk in her letters about what was most on her mind—her love for Ossoli and her coming motherhood. She was short of money, and no resolution to her dilemma was in sight. Fuller kept up her correspondence with family and friends in the United States, and she keenly felt her separation from them. Emerson was in England, but he might as well have been in Concord. Never wholly sympathetic to her aspirations or warm in his responses to her, he had no interest in the political forces that gave her hope. Elizabeth Hoar, Emerson's neighbor and Fuller's close friend, stopped writing completely; Caroline Sturgis married William Aspinwall Tappan but did not tell Fuller (a reticence that later led

---

1. For a summary of the questions surrounding Fuller's marriage, see Madeleine B. Stern, *The Life of Margaret Fuller* (New York: Dutton, 1942), pp. 430–31, and Joseph Jay Deiss, *The Roman Years of Margaret Fuller: A Biography* (New York: Crowell, 1969).

Fuller into the ironic position of chiding Tappan for a secrecy that she herself practiced).

Although her private life become ever more complicated and dangerous, Fuller grew increasingly enthusiastic about the political events that were developing up and down Italy. On 1 January the citizens of Milan began an antismoking campaign designed to cut the Austrian excise tax on tobacco. Marshal Josef Wenzel Radetzky harshly quelled the Milanese, but the city was restive under its military occupation. In the south, the cruelest of all Italian monarchs, Ferdinand, the Bourbon monarch of Naples (called also the Kingdom of the Two Sicilies), was threatened with revolt when, on 12 January, Palermo erupted in fighting.[2]

Then, with an unforeseen suddenness, monarch after monarch began to grant constitutions in response to popular pressures. A land that had little experience with such open documents began to have them everywhere: on 29 January Ferdinand granted one; Tuscany was next on 17 February, followed by Piedmont on 5 March, despite Charles Albert's fear of republics. Finally, Pius proclaimed a *statuto* on 14 March, thus completing a movement that bode well for even further changes.[3] If constitutions were granted, could constituent assemblies be far behind? Might not the several small nations become a united Italy?

The dream of a united nation was very much alive despite formidable political obstacles: Lombardy and Venetia were occupied by Austria; Charles Albert in Piedmont had the largest army and the biggest dream of national leadership, but he was weak and ineffective when action was needed; the Grand Duke of Tuscany was allied to Austria by marriage and cowed by its military power; Ferdinand was a despot whose only goal was to retain absolute power over Naples. Lying astride the peninsula were the Papal States, ruled by the temporal power of Pius IX, whose reputation as a liberal reformer was beginning to frighten him. The pope was coming to understand a fact that many Italians did not see: the responsibilities of his temporal power directly clashed with his role as the spiritual head of the church.

The year 1848, however, is remembered for far more than the revolutionary movements in Italy. It was a year of upheaval throughout Europe: on 24 February (in the midst of the Italian drive for constitutions) a French revolution deposed Louis-Philippe. On 13

2. G. F.-H. Berkeley and J. Berkeley, *Italy in the Making: January 1st 1848 to November 16th 1848* (Cambridge: Cambridge University Press, 1940), pp. 18–24.
3. Bolton King, *A History of Italian Unity* (London: J. Nisbet, 1899), 1:191–212.

March, Austria revolted and forced the resignation and flight of Prince Klemens Wenzel Metternich, the architect of Austrian domination in eastern and southern Europe. By the end of March the liberals in the German states could openly talk of a German federation.[4]

Thus, while Fuller contended with her need for secrecy and with her lack of money, she could turn her attention to the political upheavals in both her private correspondence and her *Tribune* essays. The political situation was improving more rapidly than even she had predicted. Italy was creating constitutions; Austria was weakened, perhaps fatally; Louis-Philippe and Metternich were forced into exile; and, most important to her, for she had many friends among the Milanese republicans and liberals, Milan revolted.

On 18 March, the day after Metternich left Vienna, Milan engaged Radetzky in open street warfare. By the end of the now-famous "five days of Milan," the almost unarmed citizens had forced the exhausted Austrians out of Milan and made Radetzky retreat toward his home base near Verona. For the first time, the Austrians seemed vulnerable to the neighboring Piedmontese. A decisive monarch might have exploited such an opportunity, but Charles Albert delayed his move until Radetzky was clear of Milan and had regrouped his army into an orderly retreat. On 25 March, Charles Albert declared war on Austria, crossed the Tincio River, and pursued Radetzky. The badly equipped and poorly led Piedmontese army offered no immediate threat to Radetzky's rear or flank, so the Austrians made their way to their fortified positions in the "quadrilateral" of north-central Lombardy.[5]

Meanwhile, volunteers soon formed units that left from Naples, Tuscany, and Rome to make, the liberals thought, a national war of liberation against Austria. Even their distrust of Charles Albert and their fear of his dynastic ambition did not keep them from rushing to aid his army. Now Pius had to make a decision. Pressed vigorously to commit Roman troops against Austria, the pope could no longer evade his dual role. As head of the church, he could declare war on a Catholic country only if attacked; as a prominent Italian prince, he could hardly refuse to aid a war of Italian freedom. His temporal power, on which the liberals had to rely, directly countered his duty as supreme pontiff, the duty Pius chose.[6] Throughout 1847 his acts, markedly more humane and enlightened than those of his predeces-

---

4. A. W. Ward et al., *The Cambridge Modern History* (New York: Macmillan, 1909), 11:151–64.
5. Berkeley and Berkeley, *Italy in the Making*, pp. 97–110.
6. Ibid., pp. 169–80.

sor, were thought to be made deliberately to establish himself as the liberal Italian pope that the Piedmontese philosopher Vincenzo Gioberti had envisioned. Not only had Pius no wish to supplant Austria, however, he abhorred the liberals. On 29 April he issued an allocution that satisfied the conservatives and outraged the liberals, Margaret Fuller among them. Pius declared that he had not intended to foment revolution through his reforms, that he would not wage war on Austria, and that he repudiated the idea of an Italian republic.[7] Unmistakably the reformers had lost the pope. Fuller's outrage and disillusionment were characteristic of those who had thought they had found a revolutionary pontiff.

By early May the pope was no longer a factor in the situation; Radetzky was reinforced by a second Austrian army, and Charles Albert was unable to pierce the Austrian defenses. Fuller reported the situation in detail for the *Tribune*, but she was coming to the time when she had to leave Rome in order to conceal the approaching birth of her child. She took farewell of her readers and told her family merely that she was going to the better climate of the mountains. It was galling, however, to have to leave Rome just as a crisis was approaching.

She left in mid-May for Aquila, in the kingdom of Naples. There she felt too cut off from Ossoli (their letters suggest that they had been married in April) and undoubtedly she disliked being under Neapolitan rule. On 29 July she moved to Rieti, a small town in the Abruzzi Mountains, in the Papal States. In the letters of this summer the reader sees clearly the nature of her double life: to friends in the United States she wrote accounts of her rustication in the Umbrian hills, but to Ossoli she complained of bad teeth, sleeplessness, and a sore shoulder. The normal anxieties of approaching motherhood were compounded by her isolation, both from Ossoli and from her American world. For the first time we can see what her life in Rieti was like and see at the same time how she created another reality for her family and friends.

As she had feared it would, the war for independence failed. Charles Albert attacked Radetzky at Custoza, only to suffer a decisive defeat on 25 July. On 9 August the Piedmontese and Austrians signed the treaty of Salasco, an act that Fuller called a cowardly betrayal of all Italy. Charles Albert retreated to Milan, where his life was threatened before he escaped to Turin. Radetzky reoccupied Milan and crushed the liberal dream of a free and united Italy.[8]

7. For excerpts from the allocution, see Denis Mack Smith, ed., *The Making of Italy, 1796–1870* (New York: Walker, 1968), pp. 151–52.
8. Berkeley and Berkeley, *Italy in the Making*, pp. 352–94.

Shortly after this political failure, Fuller gave birth to a son, Angelo Eugene Ossoli, on 5 September 1848. Ossoli hurried to Rieti to join his family, and Fuller began her long convalescence, during which she had to deal by post with financial problems, a lack of trustworthy political news, and an inability to get smallpox serum to vaccinate the child. It was an exhausting autumn, for Fuller had to balance her love for the baby against the necessity to leave him and return to Rome.

Finally, the first week in November, Fuller had to leave Angelino with the family of his wetnurse as she returned to the capital, where the political situation suddenly became tense. In September, Pius had asked Pelligrino Rossi, a veteran diplomat who had served France during an exile from Italy, to head the government. Although a man of undoubted talent, Rossi was abrasive and haughty. He enraged both right and left, but it was the radical reformers who hated him most deeply. When Pius announced the re-formation of the constituent assembly for 15 November, a group of radicals led by Pietro Sturbini, a prominent politician, and Angelo Brunetti (known as Ciceruacchio), the workingman leader of the most extreme political "club," hatched an assassination plot against Rossi. Shortly after Fuller returned to Rome, the assembly met. As Rossi started up the steps of the building, an assassin stabbed him mortally.[9]

The following day a crowd gathered outside the pontiff's palace to demand that he appoint a more liberal ministry. Shots were exchanged between the guards and the people, who then started a small fire in the palace. In both her private letters and an essay for the *Tribune*, Fuller discussed the event, which had occurred close to her apartment, and bitterly denounced the pope.[10]

Pius fled the turmoil in Rome on 24 November, disguised as a common priest. He and the cardinals took residence in Gaeta, just over the border in the kingdom of Naples. By the end of 1848 Rome seemed to Margaret Fuller to be liberated—rid of a useless pope, free to become a republican center of a genuine Italian revolution now that Charles Albert had failed to defeat the Austrians.[11]

Fuller took a Christmas trip to Rieti to be with Angelino but was back in Rome to greet 1849. Though again separated from her son, Fuller was secure with Ossoli. Rome voted to create a republic, a move that would undoubtedly draw to the city Giuseppi Mazzini, the one Italian leader whom Fuller trusted. She continued her essays for the

9. Ibid., pp. 416–33.
10. See Fuller's letter of 2 December 1848, *New-York Daily Tribune*, 19 January 1849.
11. Berkeley and Berkeley, *Italy in the Making*, p. 460.

Tribune and kept up a flow of commentary on the political situation for her family and American friends. Then, on 9 February, the Roman republic was created; the Romans voted for a constituent assembly and called on Mazzini to come to Rome to lead the republic.[12]

The first week in March 1849, Fuller was reunited with the man who dominated her political imagination. Since their meetings in London in 1846, she had seen Italy through Mazzini's political ideals: a nation unified (not federated) under a republic. Neither the federal ideals of Gioberti nor the royalist ambitions of Charles Albert were valid to Fuller. Now, in 1849, the goal of unification might not be attainable, but a republic of Rome came into existence under Mazzini's leadership. In her *Tribune* essays she says clearly that both Charles Albert and Pius had physical bravery and personal integrity but that each lacked political vision and the courage to risk his throne. To be a good man was necessary but not sufficient at a time of national crisis. Only Mazzini, Fuller thought, had the capacity to rally Italians of all the states.

As the republic was founded, Charles Albert made his last attempt to influence events. On 12 March he attacked the Austrians. The renewed war lasted only eleven days. After he was defeated at Novara on 23 March, he abdicated in favor of his son and went into exile.[13] The Italian monarch who at one time had the best chance to defeat Austria and to unite Italy lost his opportunity for the last time and left Italy to the extremes of revolution and reaction.

And yet, for Fuller, this was a time of completion. She was contemptuous of Boston and she had never felt at ease in New York, but in Rome, in the democratic republic with which she identified, she made a home. Here she found nearly universal suffrage, a level of political participation that far outstripped that in the United States, and a genuine civility. Although Rome had a past, although it had art, architecture, and sculpture, although it was a center of the high culture to which Fuller had devoted her life, it was the Roman self-confidence and honor that most impressed Fuller, not the museums and statues. When she had lived in New England, Margaret Fuller might have overvalued the relics of history, but by mid-century she had come to terms with the present and claimed her kinship with a people who, like an earlier generation of Americans, had taken their destiny into their own hands and created a free government.

At the head of this new creation stood Giuseppi Mazzini, the living

12. King, *Italian Unity*, 1:292.
13. Ibid., 1:297–306.

embodiment of the genius so important to Fuller and her friends. His presence fused the ideal of a united Italian republic with a spiritual commitment: the Roman people inscribed Mazzini's slogan, "Dio e popolo"—"God and the people"—on their coins as a symbol of both a secular and a sacred faith.

Fuller understood the inevitable European reaction to a republic at Rome, the city that was the literal and emotional center of Catholicism. Neither the Austrians, the Neapolitans, the Spaniards, nor the French (as Fuller predicted) were willing to see the pope forced into exile and a republican virus flourish in Rome. Fuller had expected the open hostility of Naples and Vienna, but she was outraged by the French. A government created only months earlier by revolution against Louis-Philippe should, she thought, welcome a sister republic. But Fuller had no illusions about Louis Napoleon, who in December 1848 rose to leadership on a wave of reaction in France. When a French army commanded by Nicolas-Charles-Victor Oudinot landed at Civitavecchia on 25 April and announced that they had come in republican fraternity, Fuller knew what was ahead: the French were determined to crush the Roman republic and to restore the pope.

The Roman army under Giuseppe Garibaldi soon showed that it would fight General Oudinot's troops rather than submit to an occupation, so the French general withdrew to see what would happen after the arrival of Ferdinand de Lesseps, whom Paris sent to arrange a peaceful capitulation. The Romans, however, were no more willing to negotiate than they were to surrender, so Oudinot brushed Lesseps aside and laid seige to Rome on 3 June.[14]

By now, after a two-year residence in Italy and after the birth of her son, Fuller was committed to her adopted city in body and soul. Rome was to undergo a bloody test of its political destiny in which the possibilities of democracy and freedom were to be tested against the power of Catholic Europe. More than her family or American friends could know, Fuller had ceased to regard herself primarily as a reporter for the *Tribune*; she was a Roman defending her home. She took charge of a hospital under the direction of Cristina Belgioioso, a liberal Milanese noblewoman who the year before had raised troops to fight for Piedmont against Austria. While Fuller nursed the wounded, Ossoli fought with the Roman army. They were in physical danger, trapped in a besieged city, far from their son, who, Fuller knew, might be orphaned at any time.

The Romans were no match for the military power Oudinot com-

14. Ibid., 1:333–37.

manded. Despite a dogged resistance, the Romans were unable to prevent the French from breaking through the city walls. By 30 June the French had ensured their victory, but they could not prevent Garibaldi from evacuating his army intact.[15] Mazzini went into exile. Fuller got an American passport for Ossoli from Lewis Cass, Jr., the sympathetic American chargé d'affaires who had become a close friend.

For the first time in her life, Margaret Fuller left a city that she felt to be a home. Other removals—from Boston to New York City and from there to Europe—had been choices made at the promptings of a restless, unfulfilled spirit. Her flight from Rome in 1849 was commanded by events over which she had no control. Her decision in 1850 to leave Italy entirely was not nearly so significant as her forced removal from Rome, the only genuine home of her life.

By the end of June, Fuller knew that Mazzini's wisdom and Garibaldi's skill could not preserve the Republic of Rome, but she developed a vision of heroism that would sustain the Italians in their defeat.[16] Mazzini had not conquered Oudinot, but he had shown that the ideal of nationalism was not mere fancy. To Fuller, the defeats that Charles Albert suffered at Custoza and Novara were ruinous; the military loss of Rome did not, however, impeach the ideal of "Dio e popolo," for Mazzini had accomplished what Charles Albert, Gioberti, and Pius had been unable to do: he made an idea live.

Fuller lived in Italy for only thirty-eight months; the pope left Rome for barely more than seven months; the republic lasted only five months. Yet, judged against Fuller's early life, these three years marked a triumph, a high-water mark in her existence. She brought to Italy her acquaintance with art and books; she brought a practiced critic's eye that was not easily impressed and that knew the difference between an art that was transitory and one that lasted. More important, she brought a willingness to change, to love, to risk her life. Instead of leaving Rome, as Emerson had urged her to do in 1848, or standing aside as an observer, Fuller made Italy her home. As she herself said, it was in Italy that an American could best be an American.[17] It was here that the ideals of freedom were to be tested. The test took courage and faith, ideals that she had valued in Goethe almost three decades earlier and that she now had a chance to test for herself.

As soon as they could after the French entered Rome, Fuller and Ossoli left for Rieti, where they found Angelino half dead from ne-

15. Ibid., 1:339–40.
16. See Fuller's letter of 21 June 1849, *New-York Daily Tribune*, 23 July 1849.
17. See Fuller's letter, *New-York Daily Tribune*, 1 January 1848.

glect. After nursing the child back to health, they moved to Florence, the most lenient of the Italian states in the aftermath of the complete failure of the revolutions. By midsummer 1849 all of Italy had reverted to the status quo ante: the great promises and bloody battles of 1848–49 appeared to have had no effect: the pope was back in Rome; Grand Duke Leopold returned to Florence; Radetzky's Austrian army controlled not only Lombardy and Venetia but the northern part of the Papal States as well. Ossoli had to explain to the Florentine police why he had an American passport, but otherwise he and Fuller were ignored in Florence (an Italian Boston, she scornfully called it). As it had done so often, Fuller's life changed dramatically, but this time it swung from turmoil to calm. As her political hopes were shattered, Fuller came to value the calm of her family life. If Mazzini and the republic were gone, she had Ossoli and their son, both of whom she now openly introduced to her friends and described to her family.

It is impossible at this distance to measure the pain it caused Fuller to end her secret life, but we know that it was intense. She knew she would be the object of gossip and speculation, and she chafed at the need to explain. Refusing to admit error, she was firm in her belief that her true friends would accept the fact that silence had been necessary. She first told Caroline Tappan, then her mother, who apparently had already heard, then Costanza Arconati Visconti, her closest Italian friend.

Once past the painful revelations, Fuller settled into a quiet life in Florence. She took Angelino for walks along the Arno, visited the Brownings, whom she liked very much, and tried unsuccessfully to find an English publisher for her history of the Italian revolutions. Her American home seemed farther away than ever after these years of war and turmoil and after the changes in the lives of family and friends. She had nieces in the United States whom she had never seen; death had claimed several loved ones: Aunt Mary Rotch died in New Bedford, Ellen Sturgis Hooper in Boston, and little Pickie Greeley in New York. Pickie's death was especially terrible to Fuller, for it not only brought back the memory of Waldo Emerson's death but forcibly called to mind the peril that her own son faced.

Other changes in America were less traumatic but had a special poignancy for Fuller. Both Carrie Sturgis and Richard Fuller married, not unusual events in themselves, but reminders of Fuller's previous inability to be open about her own marriage. Her mother's comment that she had never been present at the marriage of one of her children made the hurt worse, the guilt more intense. Not until late in this volume of letters can Fuller relax with her friends and speak openly of her love for Ossoli and their son. In fact, not since she lived in New England had Fuller been able to be so unguarded in her letters. Her secret involvements with James Nathan in 1845–46 and with Ossoli in 1847–49 had caused Fuller to use her letters as a shield against revelations even to her most intimate friends. Now for the first time in years she could be open.

The letters of 1848 and 1849 trace a great emotional ebb and flow in Fuller's life. As she said to Emerson, "One dont want deep calling unto deep always, the shallows with their gold and silver fishes may take their turn."[18] She had heard the deeps in the wars, in the pope's flight, and in Angelino's birth, but in Florence as this volume closes, Margaret Fuller could finally take delight in the "gold and silver fishes."

Though several of these letters exist only in fragments or in copies and other important letters to and from Italian and American friends have been lost, this penultimate volume of Fuller letters presents her world in its complex doubleness. Here the Italian war of independence and the Roman struggle for life are recorded by a woman who knew what was at stake and who understood the pressures influencing public events. Here, too, is a woman almost alone, almost destitute, who was called on to give birth to her first child among strangers. Through her letters we understand the strength she brought to both parts of her life and the success she had in fulfilling the responsibilities she faced.

As this volume closes, Fuller just begins to plan her departure from Italy to remake an American home and to reclaim her vocation. As the final volume of her letters will show, she had few illusions about either possibility. She was all too conscious of her inability to regain the security that Rome had offered for one luminous spring.

ROBERT N. HUDSPETH

State College, Pennsylvania

18. See Fuller's letter to Ralph Waldo Emerson, 21 January 1849.

CONTENTS

Preface 5

Acknowledgments 25

Editorial Method 29
    Format, 30; Text, 30; Annotation and Index, 31

Editorial Apparatus 33
    Textual Devices, 33; Descriptive Symbols, 33; Location
    Symbols, 34; Short Titles and Abbreviations, 34

1848

700. 1 January, to Richard F. Fuller 39
701. 10 January, to Frederic H. Hedge 41
702. 11 January, to Caroline Sturgis Tappan 41
703. 12 January, to Ellen Fuller Channing 45
704. 12 January, to Richard F. Fuller 48
705. 14 January, to Costanza Arconati Visconti 49
706. 8 February, to Richard F. Fuller 49
707. 9 February, to Margaret Fuller Channing 52
708. 8 March, to Jane Stirling 53
709. 8 March, to Frederic H. Hedge 54
710. 14 March, to Ralph Waldo Emerson 55
711. 17 March, to Richard F. Fuller 56
712. 29 March, to William H. Channing 58
713. April, to Jane Tuckerman King 59

Contents

714. 7 April, to Henry Colman   60
715. 22 April, to Ann Waln Rotch   61
716. ca. May, to Mr. Page   62
717. ca. May, to Ralph Waldo Emerson   63
718. 14 May, to Elizabeth De Windt Cranch   64
719. 17 May, to Thomas Hicks   66
720. 19 May, to Ralph Waldo Emerson   66
721. 20 May, to Richard F. Fuller   67
722. 27 May, to Costanza Arconati Visconti   69
723. 29 May, to Mary Rotch   70
724. 22 June, to Costanza Arconati Visconti   73
725. 22 June, to Emelyn Story   74
726. 22 June, to Charles King Newcomb   76
727. 27 June, to Giovanni Angelo Ossoli   78
728. 29 June, to Giovanni Angelo Ossoli   79
729. 1 July, to Richard F. Fuller   81
730. 3 July, to Richard F. Fuller   82
731. 8 July, to Giovanni Angelo Ossoli   84
732. 11 July, to Ralph Waldo Emerson   85
733. 13 July, to Giovanni Angelo Ossoli   86
734. 15 July, to Giovanni Angelo Ossoli   88
735. 18 July, to Giovanni Angelo Ossoli   89
736. 18 July, to James C. Hooker   90
737. 22 July, to Giovanni Angelo Ossoli   92
738. 27 July, to Giovanni Angelo Ossoli   94
739. 30 July, to Giovanni Angelo Ossoli   95
740. 30 July, to James C. Hooker   96
741. 2 August, to Giovanni Angelo Ossoli   97
742. 13 August, to Giovanni Angelo Ossoli   99
743. ca. 15 August, to ?   100
744. 15 August, to Giovanni Angelo Ossoli   101
745. 16 August, to Richard F. Fuller   103
746. 17 August, to Giovanni Angelo Ossoli   105
747. 18 August, to Giovanni Angelo Ossoli   106
748. 20 August, to Giovanni Angelo Ossoli   108
749. 22 August, to Giovanni Angelo Ossoli   108
750. 25 August, to Giovanni Angelo Ossoli   110
751. 7 September, to Giovanni Angelo Ossoli   111
752. 9 September, to Giovanni Angelo Ossoli   112
753. 10 September, to Giovanni Angelo Ossoli   112

Contents

754. 13 September, to Giovanni Angelo Ossoli 114
755. 15 September, to Giovanni Angelo Ossoli 115
756. 17 September, to Giovanni Angelo Ossoli 116
757. 19 September, to Giovanni Angelo Ossoli 118
758. 21 September, to Giovanni Angelo Ossoli 119
759. 23 September, to Giovanni Angelo Ossoli 120
760. 26 September, to Giovanni Angelo Ossoli 122
761. 28 September, to Giovanni Angelo Ossoli 123
762. 7 October, to Giovanni Angelo Ossoli 124
763. 8 October, to Giovanni Angelo Ossoli 126
764. 11 October, to Giovanni Angelo Ossoli 127
765. 13 October, to Giovanni Angelo Ossoli 129
766. 15 October, to Giovanni Angelo Ossoli 130
767. 18 October, to Giovanni Angelo Ossoli 132
768. 20 October, to Giovanni Angelo Ossoli 134
769. 25 October, to Giovanni Angelo Ossoli 136
770. 27 October, to Giovanni Angelo Ossoli 138
771. 28 October, to Giovanni Angelo Ossoli 139
772. 29 October, to Giovanni Angelo Ossoli 142
773. 1 November, to Giovanni Angelo Ossoli 144
774. 16 November, to Margarett C. Fuller 145
775. 17 November, to Richard F. Fuller 151
776. 23 November, to Marcus Spring 152
777. 23 November, to ? 153
778. 23 November, to William H. Channing 155
779. 24 November, to Charles King Newcomb 156
780. 28 November, to Emelyn Story 157
781. 7 December, to Richard F. Fuller 160
782. 9 December, to William Wetmore Story 161
783. 22 December, to Giovanni Angelo Ossoli 163
784. 24 December, to Giovanni Angelo Ossoli 165
785. 27 December, to Giovanni Angelo Ossoli 167

1849

786. January, to Jane Tuckerman King 168
787. 7 January, to Emelyn Story 168
788. 18 January, to Sarah Ann Clarke 171
789. 19 January, to James F. Clarke 173

Contents

790. 19 January, to Margarett C. Fuller   176
791. 19 January, to Richard F. Fuller   179
792. 20 January, to Arthur B. Fuller   185
793. 21 January, to Ralph Waldo Emerson   187
794. 27 January, to Emelyn Story   188
795. 3 February, to Maria Rotch   191
796. 5 February, to Costanza Arconati Visconti   192
797. 23 February, to Richard F. Fuller   193
798. ca. early March, to Emelyn Story   195
799. 3 March, to Giuseppe Mazzini   196
800. 8 March, to Caroline Sturgis Tappan   198
801. 9 March, to Marcus Spring   201
802. 9 March, to Margarett C. Fuller   202
803. 9 March, to Elizabeth De Windt Cranch   203
804. 10 March, to William H. Channing   205
805. 13 March, to Ellen Fuller Channing   206
806. 16 March, to Caroline Sturgis Tappan   207
807. 17 March, to Richard F. Fuller   211
808. 18 March, to Sarah Shaw   214
809. 18 March, to Anna Barker Ward   216
810. 27 March, to Giovanni Angelo Ossoli   218
811. 30 March, to Giovanni Angelo Ossoli   219
812. 1 April, to Giovanni Angelo Ossoli   221
813. 4 April, to Giovanni Angelo Ossoli   222
814. 6 April, to Giovanni Angelo Ossoli   224
815. 13 April, to Giovanni Angelo Ossoli   225
816. 15 April, to Giovanni Angelo Ossoli   226
817. 4 May, to Giovanni Angelo Ossoli   226
818. ca. 6 May, to Giovanni Angelo Ossoli   227
819. 20 May, to Lewis Cass, Jr.   228
820. 22? May?, to Lewis Cass, Jr.   228
821. 22 May, to Richard F. Fuller   229
822. 24? May?, to Lewis Cass, Jr.   231
823. 28 May, to Richard F. Fuller   231
824. 29 May, to Emelyn Story   232
825. ca. June, to Emelyn Story   234
826. June, to Giovanni Angelo Ossoli   235
827. June? to Arthur Hugh Clough   236
828. 4 June, to Giovanni Angelo Ossoli   237
829. 6 June, to Emelyn Story   238

Contents

830. 10 June, to Ralph Waldo Emerson   239
831. 17 June, to Elizabeth Hoar   241
832. ca. 17 June, to Lewis Cass, Jr.   242
833. 19 June, to Ellen Fuller Channing   242
834. ca. 8 July, to Lewis Cass, Jr.   243
835. 8 July, to Richard F. Fuller   243
836. 10 July, to Lewis Cass, Jr.   244
837. 19 July, to Lewis Cass, Jr.   245
838. ca. late July, to William H. Channing   246
839. 30 July, to Lewis Cass, Jr.   249
840. August, to Costanza Arconati Visconti   249
841. ca. August, to Ellen Fuller Channing   251
842. 8 August, to Lewis Cass, Jr.   252
843. 9 August, to Giovanni Angelo Ossoli   253
844. 13 August, to Lewis Cass, Jr.   254
845. 25 August, to Horace Greeley   255
846. 28 August, to William H. Channing   258
847. 28 August, to Caroline Sturgis Tappan   258
848. 31 August, to Margarett C. Fuller   259
849. 31 August, to Emelyn Story?   262
850. 31 August, to Edgar T. Welby   263
851. September, to Lewis Cass, Jr.   264
852. 21 September, to Edgar T. Welby   264
853. 30 September, to Lewis Cass, Jr.   265
854. ca. Autumn, to ?   265
855. ca. Autumn, to Elizabeth Hoar?   266
856. ca. Autumn, to William H. Channing?   266
857. 4 October, to Lewis Cass, Jr.   267
858. 8 October, to Lewis Cass, Jr.   267
859. 16 October, to Costanza Arconati Visconti   269
860. 21 October, to Samuel G. and Anna Barker Ward   271
861. 25 October, to George W. Curtis   274
862. 31 October, to Samuel G. Ward   278
863. ca. November, to Emelyn Story   279
864. 8 November, to Miss Erbeau   281
865. 18 November, to Sarah Ann Clarke   281
866. 29 November, to ?   282
867. 30 November, to Emelyn Story   284
868. 2 December, to William Wetmore Story   286
869. 6 December, to Elizabeth Barrett Browning   289

Contents

870. 11 December, to Ellen Fuller Channing   290
871. 12 December, to Marcus and Rebecca Buffum Spring   294
872. 15? December, to Margarett C. Fuller   298
873. 17 December, to William H. Channing   300
874. ca. 17 December, to Caroline Sturgis Tappan   301

Index   309

ILLUSTRATIONS

GIOVANNI ANGELO OSSOLI   *frontis*
COSTANZA ARCONATI VISCONTI   50
BASILICA OF SANTA MARIA MAGGIORE, ROME   162
PIAZZA DI SPAGNA, ROME   183
PIAZZA DEL POPOLO, ROME   184
GIUSEPPI MAZZINI   197
HORACE GREELEY   256
SAMUEL GRAY WARD   272
GEORGE WILLIAM CURTIS   276

Acknowledgments

I am grateful to John C. Fuller, Willard P. Fuller, Elizabeth Channing Fuller, Richard E. Fuller, and Willard P. Fuller, Jr., for permission to publish Margaret Fuller's letters. I also thank the following institutions and individuals for permission to publish the Fuller letters in their possession which appear in this volume: the Bodleian Library, Oxford University; the Trustees of the Boston Public Library; the James Fraser Gluck Collection, the Buffalo and Erie County Library; the Butler Library of Columbia University; the Fruitlands Museums, Harvard, Massachusetts; Mary Lillian Haight; the Trustees of the Ralph Waldo Emerson Memorial Association, the Harvard College Library, and the Houghton Library, Harvard University; the Massachusetts Historical Society; the Middlebury College Library; the Pierpont Morgan Library; the Princeton University Library; the Arthur and Elizabeth Schlesinger Library, Radcliffe College; the Humanities Research Center, the University of Texas; the Sarah Margaret Fuller Collection, the Barrett Library, University of Virginia Library; and Nelson C. White.

Letters to Fuller are quoted by permission of the Harvard College Library and the Houghton Library, Harvard University; the letter from George Curtis to William Wetmore Story is quoted by permission of the Humanities Research Center, the University of Texas.

The following librarians have generously aided me in the preparation of this volume: John Alden of the Boston Public Library; Edmund Berkeley, Jr., and Barbara Bettcher of the University of Virginia Library; William H. Bond of the Houghton Library, Harvard University; Robert Buckeye of the Middlebury College Library; Herbert Cahoon of the Pierpont Morgan Library; John Cushing of the Massachusetts Historical Society; Rodney G. Dennis of the Houghton Library, Harvard University; Ellen S. Dunlap of the Humanities Research Center, the University of Texas; Rudolph Ellenbogen of the Columbia University Library; William Henry Harrison of the Fruitlands Museums; Patricia King of the Schlesinger Library, Radcliffe College; Carl Lane of the New Jersey Historical Society; James Lawton of the Boston Public Library; Kenneth A. Lohf of the Columbia University Library; William H. Loos of the Buffalo and Erie County Library; Richard M. Ludwig of the Princeton University Library; Charles Mann of the Pennsylvania State University Library; Marian Marx of the Schlesinger Library, Radcliffe College; June Moll of the Humanities Research Center, the University of Texas; E. J. S. Parsons of the Bodleian Library, Oxford University; Jean F. Preston and Wanda M. Randall of the Princeton University Library; Richard S. Reed of the Fruitlands Museums; Stephen T. Riley of the Massachusetts Historical Society; Elizabeth Ryall of the University of Virginia Library; C. A. Ryskamp of the Pierpont Morgan Library; Elizabeth Shenton of the Schlesinger Library, Radcliffe College; Cornelia Starks of the Bodleian Library, Oxford University; Sandra Stelts of the Pennsylvania State University Library; Louis L. Tucker of the Massachusetts Historical Society; Jane Van Arsdale of the Buffalo and Erie County Library.

I am grateful to the following individuals for help in securing illustrations for this volume: Suzanne Embree of the National Portrait Gallery, Smithsonian Institution; Ann S. Gwyn of the Milton S. Eisenhower Library, the Johns Hopkins University; Charles Mann of the Pennsylvania State University Library; Theresa Witt of the National Portrait Gallery, Smithsonian Institution.

Among the scholars who have answered my many queries are Patricia Barber, Charles Blackburn, Paula Blanchard, Arthur W. Brown, Lynn Cadwallader, Joseph Jay Deiss, Russell E. Durning, Alfred R. Ferguson, Elizabeth Maxfield-Miller, Howard N. Meyer, Margaret Nussendorfer, Bruce A. Ronda, Carl F. Strauch, and Richard P. Wunder. I am particularly grateful for the generous advice of Eleanor M. Tilton and Madeleine B. Stern. Kathy Fuller of the Division of Research Programs at the National Endowment for the Humanities was generous with her help. Mary Lillian Haight extended me many kindnesses in making available to me the Fuller letters in her possession. I am glad to be able to acknowledge the patient support extended me by my departmental chairmen: Robert B. Heilman and Robert D. Stevick of the University of Washington, and David Stewart, Arthur O. Lewis, Robert Worth Frank, Jr., Wendell V. Harris, and Christopher Clausen of the Pennsylvania State University. The two deans of the College of the Liberal Arts at Penn State under whom I have served, Stanley Paulson and Hart Nelsen, have supported my work in several ways; Irene Johnston Petrick has efficiently overseen the details of my grants. My colleagues Wilma R. Ebbitt, James Rambeau, and Philip Young have given freely of their advice and expertise. Charles Mann, the Rare Books and Manuscripts Librarian of the Pennsylvania State University, has helped me gather manuscripts and illustrations for this edition. It is a pleasure again to acknowledge the assistance I have received for several years from Joel Myerson of the University of South Carolina.

I am again pleased to be able to acknowledge the expert help given me by several skilled research assistants: Iris Malveau worked on my calendar of Fuller letters; Edith Millikan transcribed letters to Fuller; Carolyn Kephart read manuscripts to me and translated the French passage from Adam Mickiewicz to Fuller; Charles Hackenberry not only read manuscripts but hunted down elusive quotations. Larry Carlson and Robert D. Habich helped with the annotations. H. Lewis Ulman worked on some of the most obscure of the annotations and checked complete drafts of the notes for this volume. Laura Pacciani assisted me with the English translations of the Italian letters, as did Chiara Briganti, who also reviewed them all and helped me revise them. As she has done for many years, Kay Hudspeth worked with me to make this a better edition.

This volume of Fuller letters has received financial assistance from the University of Washington Graduate School Research Fund, the Pennsylvania State University College of Liberal Arts Research Fund, and the Pennsylvania State University Institute for the Arts and Humanistic Studies. I am grateful for this support. The preparation of this volume was made possible in part by grants from the Program for Editions of the National Endowment for the Humanities, an independent federal agency.

R. N. H.

Editorial Method

This edition brings together for the first time all of the known extant letters written by Margaret Fuller. The texts are presented in their entirety in chronological order. Only conservative emendations, as outlined below under "Text," have been incorporated in the text; all others are recorded in textual notes. The text has been prepared from holographs whenever possible. When a holograph is lacking, the text is based on a manuscript copy of the lost holograph. When two manuscript copies of the same letter survive in the absence of a holograph, the more nearly complete version has been chosen. If both are of the same length, I have chosen the copy prepared by the Fuller family, because a spot comparison of other family copies with their surviving holographs shows them to be more nearly accurate than copies by other hands, if not exact. Only those letters with no manuscript authority have been taken from printed sources. Those letters dated by year only appear at the head of the year; those dated only by month, at the head of the month; undated letters come at the end of the edition, arranged alphabetically by recipient when known.

To establish the text, I first gathered microfilm or photocopies of all the manuscript letters and then made typed copies of these photoreproductions. I also typed all of the letters that now exist only in printed versions. I then corrected the typescript twice: first an assistant read aloud to me all of the photoreproductions and the printed versions of the letters; later, other assistants (working with me at different times) accompanied me to the libraries that hold the original manuscripts and read those manuscripts aloud to me as I again corrected the typescript. (Three letters were not read during this second check, for I was unable to visit two libraries.)

The final text was derived from the corrected typescript, and proof was read aloud.

Format

The letters are numbered chronologically and the recipients identified in uniform headings. All dates, locations, salutations, and signatures are regularized in the following manner: dates and locations are set flush against the right margin, salutations flush against the left margin; signatures are set in large and small capitals and indented from the right margin at the bottom of the letter; when two or more initials are used in a signature, they are regularized with a space between each pair.

Text

The text is presented as faithfully as possible with conservative emendations. Fuller's spelling, capitalization, and punctuation are retained, as are her occasional slips of the pen (e.g., *and and*). Punctuation of canceled words and interlined insertions follows Fuller's final intention with the original versions reported in the textual notes. Her end punctuation is often ambiguous, for her period resembles a comma. In all instances this mark is preserved as a period. Punctuation is supplied in brackets only when its absence leads to confusion. A paragraph is often indicated in the holographs only by a space at the end of the preceding line. In all such instances the following paragraph is silently indented. Fuller used the dash as an all-purpose mark of punctuation; her dashes are consistently retained. Abbreviations are not expanded save in those instances where ambiguities might otherwise result. When expanded, the additions are enclosed in square brackets. Cancellations are omitted from the text, and interlined additions are lowered; all such emendations are reported in the textual notes. Cross-hatching (Fuller occasionally turned the sheet and wrote at a right angle across her letter) and all symbols, notes, and marks added by later hands are emended and unreported. The German β is set as "ss"; "&" becomes "and." Unless otherwise noted, the matter canceled by a later hand in the collections at the Boston Public Library has been recovered. All the letters and fragments taken from Emerson's "Ossoli" journal (MH: bMS Am 1280 [111]) are in his hand.

Annotation and Index

The text of each letter is followed by a provenance note that indicates the source of the text, any surviving manuscript copies, and any previous publishing history; the name and address of the recipient as written by Fuller; the postmark; and the recipient's endorsement, if any. A brief biography of the recipient follows the provenance note to the first surviving letter to him or her, unless the recipient has already been identified. Then come textual notes listing editorial emendations, Fuller's cancellations, and her interlined insertions. Fuller's words here are set in roman type; editorial interpolations are set in italics.

The numbered annotations that follow the textual notes identify all people mentioned in the letter except those well known to readers (e.g., Dante, Shakespeare, Milton) and those previously identified, and all books, literary and historical allusions, and quotations that can be established. Brief biographies of well-known individuals who are not identified in the notes can be found in *Webster's Biographical Dictionary*. Citations to the Massachusetts vital records office take two forms. Citations to nineteenth-century records refer only to volume and page numbers. Thus "MVR 119:345" cites page 345 of volume 119 of the death record. Beginning in this century, the reference has a preceding date. Thus "MVR 1924 11:167" cites the death record for 1924, volume 11, page 167. Unless otherwise noted, all citations are to death records.

Publication data come from the *National Union Catalog* of the Library of Congress or, when necessary, from the *British Museum General Catalogue of Printed Books*. Occasional notes explain ambiguities in the text, summarize events in Fuller's life, or refer the reader to other letters. The surviving letters written to Fuller have provided explanatory material for many of the annotations. Unidentified items are silently passed over.

An appendix in the final volume lists chronologically the letters Fuller is known to have written but which have not survived.

Each volume of the letters has a separate index. A comprehensive index appears in the final volume.

Editorial Apparatus

Textual Devices

The following devices are used in the text:

[Square brackets] enclose editorial additions.
[*Italics*] indicate editorial comments.
[I] [II] [III] indicate sections of a letter recovered from various sources.
[   ] marks matter missing from the text.
Superscript[n] refers the reader to a textual note.
Superscript[1] refers the reader to an explanatory note.

The following devices are used in the textual notes:

⟨Angle brackets⟩ identify recovered cancellations.
⟨?⟩ identifies unrecovered cancellations.
↑ Opposed arrows ↓ indicate interlined insertions.
Italics indicate editorial comments.

Descriptive Symbols

AL	Autograph letter, unsigned
ALfr	Autograph letter fragment, unsigned
ALfrS	Autograph letter fragment, signed with name or initial(s)
ALS	Autograph letter, signed with name or initial(s)
EL	Edited letter, as previously published; holograph now lost
ELfr	Edited letter fragment, as previously published; holograph now lost
MsC	Manuscript copy of a Fuller letter in a hand other than Fuller's; unless otherwise indicated, the holograph has not been recovered
MsCfr	Manuscript copy of a fragment of a Fuller letter in a hand other than Fuller's; unless otherwise indicated, the holograph has not been recovered

MsL   Manuscript Fuller letter not in her hand
MsLS   Manuscript Fuller letter not in her hand but signed by her

Location Symbols

CSmH   The Huntington Library
MB   Boston Public Library, Department of Rare Books and Manuscripts
MCR-S   Radcliffe College, Schlesinger Library
MH   Harvard University, Houghton Library
MHarF   Fruitlands Museums, Harvard, Massachusetts
MHi   Massachusetts Historical Society
NBu   Buffalo and Erie County Library
NjHi   New Jersey Historical Society
NjP   Princeton University Library
NNC   Columbia University Library
NNPM   Pierpont Morgan Library
TxU   University of Texas, Humanities Research Center
ViU   University of Virginia Library
VtMiM   Middlebury College Library

Short Titles and Abbreviations

Acton, *Last Bourbons*: Harold Mario Mitchell Acton, *The Last Bourbons of Naples (1825–1861)* (New York: St. Martin's Press, 1962).

Annuario della nobiltà italiana: *Annuario della nobiltà italiana* (Pisa: Giornale Araldico, 1878 [1879]).

Baedecker: Karl Baedecker, *Italy from the Alps to Naples* (Leipzig: Baedecker, 1909).

Barr, *Mazzini*: Stringfellow Barr, *Mazzini: Portrait of an Exile* (New York: Henry Holt, 1935).

Berkeley: G. F.-H. Berkeley and J. Berkeley, *Italy in the Making: January 1st 1848 to November 16th 1848* (Cambridge: Cambridge University Press, 1940 [1968]).

Boase: Frederic Boase, *Modern English Biography*, 6 vols. (London: Frank Cass, 1892 [1965]).

Bullard, *Rotches*: John Morgan Bullard, *The Rotches* (New Bedford: Privately published, 1947).

Butler's Lives of the Saints: *Butler's Lives of the Saints*, ed. Herbert Thurston and Donald Attwater, 4 vols. (New York: P. J. Kennedy, 1956).

Byron, *Poetical Works*: George Gordon, Lord Byron, *The Poetical Works of Lord Byron* (London: Oxford University Press, 1904 [1960]).

Cambridge Modern History: *The Cambridge Modern History*, ed. A. W. Ward et al., 13 vols. (New York: Macmillan, 1902–11).

Chevigny: Bell Gale Chevigny, *The Woman and the Myth: Margaret Fuller's Life and Writings* (Old Westbury, N.Y.: Feminist Press, 1976).

Editorial Apparatus

Clough, *Correspondence*: *The Correspondence of Arthur Hugh Clough*, ed. Frederick L. Mulhauser, 2 vols. (Oxford: Clarendon Press, 1957).

DAB: *Dictionary of American Biography*, ed. Allen Johnson and Dumas Malone, 20 vols. (New York: Scribner's, 1928–36).

Dictionnaire de biographie française: *Dictionnaire de biographie française*, ed. J. Balteau et al., 15 vols. to date (Paris: Letouzey et Ane, 1933–).

Dizionario del risorgimento: *Dizionario del risorgimento nazionale*, ed. Michele Rosi, 4 vols. (Milan: Francesco Vallardi, 1930–37).

Dizionario enciclopedico: *Dizionario enciclopedico della letteratura italiana*, ed. Giuseppe Petronio (Bari: Laterza, 1966).

DNB: *Dictionary of National Biography*, ed. Leslie Stephen and Sidney Lee, 22 vols. (London: Oxford University Press, 1937–38).

Eaton: Charlotte Anne Eaton, *Rome in the Nineteenth Century*, 3 vols. (Edinburgh: A. Constable, 1820).

Enciclopedia italiana: *Enciclopedia italiana di scienze, lettere ed arti*, 36 vols. (Rome: Istituto della Enciclopedia Italiana, 1949).

Farini: Luigi Carlo Farini, *The Roman State from 1815 to 1850*, trans. W. E. Gladstone, 4 vols. (London: J. Murray, 1851–54).

Frothingham, *Memoir of William Henry Channing*: Octavius Brooks Frothingham, *Memoir of William Henry Channing* (Boston: Houghton Mifflin, 1886).

Goethe, *Gedenkausgabe*: Johann Wolfgang Goethe, *Gedenkausgabe der Werke, Briefe und Gespräche*, ed. Ernst Beutler, 24 vols. (Zurich: Artemis, 1948–54).

Goethe, *Italian Journey*: Johann Wolfgang von Goethe, *Italian Journey (1786–1788)*, trans. W. H. Auden and Elizabeth Mayer (New York: Pantheon, 1968).

Greenough, *Letters*: *Letters of Horatio Greenough, American Sculptor*, ed. Nathalia Wright (Madison: University of Wisconsin Press, 1972).

Groce: *The New-York Historical Society's Dictionary of Artists in America, 1564–1860*, ed. George C. Groce and David Wallace (New Haven: Yale University Press, 1957).

Higginson, *MFO*: Thomas Wentworth Higginson, *Margaret Fuller Ossoli* (Boston: Houghton Mifflin, 1884).

Howe, *Reminiscences*: Julia Ward Howe, *Reminiscences, 1819–1899* (Boston: Houghton Mifflin, 1899).

Hudson, *Browning*: *Browning to his American Friends*, ed. Gertrude Reese Hudson (New York: Barnes & Noble, 1965).

JMN: *The Journals and Miscellaneous Notebooks of Ralph Waldo Emerson*, ed. William H. Gilman et al., 16 vols. (Cambridge: Belknap Press of Harvard University Press, 1960–82).

King, *Italian Unity*: Bolton King, *A History of Italian Unity*, 2 vols. (London: J. Nisbet, 1899).

Mack Smith, *Making of Italy*: *The Making of Italy*, ed. Denis Mack Smith (New York: Walker, 1968).

Memoirs: *Memoirs of Margaret Fuller Ossoli*, ed. R. W. Emerson, W. H. Channing, and J. F. Clarke, 2 vols. (Boston: Phillips, Sampson, 1852).

Editorial Apparatus

Memoirs of Garibaldi: *The Memoirs of Garibaldi, edited by Alexandre Dumas*, trans. R. S. Garnett (New York: D. Appleton, 1931).

Miller: *Margaret Fuller: American Romantic*, ed. Perry Miller (Garden City, N.Y.: Doubleday, 1963).

Milne, *George William Curtis*: Gordon Milne, *George William Curtis and the Genteel Tradition* (Bloomington: Indiana University Press, 1956).

Mt. Auburn: Burial records, Mount Auburn Cemetery, Cambridge, Mass.

Murray: *A Handbook of Rome and the Campagna*, 16th ed. (London: J. Murray, 1899).

MVR: Massachusetts vital records, Boston.

National Cyclopaedia: *The National Cyclopaedia of American Biography*, 62 vols. to date (New York: James T. White, 1898–).

NAW: *Notable American Women, 1607–1950*, ed. Edmund T. James, 3 vols. (Cambridge: Belknap Press of Harvard University Press, 1971).

NEHGR: *New England Historical and Genealogical Register*.

NEHGS: New England Historic Genealogical Society, Boston.

Niecks, *Chopin*: Frederick Niecks, *Frederick Chopin as Man and Musician*, 2 vols. (London: Novello, Ewer, 1888).

OCGL: Henry Garland and Mary Garland, *The Oxford Companion to German Literature* (Oxford: Clarendon Press, 1976).

Phillips, *Reminiscences*: Mary Elizabeth Phillips, *Reminiscences of William Wetmore Story, the American Sculptor and Author* (Chicago: Rand McNally, 1897).

Rusk, *Letters of RWE*: *The Letters of Ralph Waldo Emerson*, ed. Ralph L. Rusk, 6 vols. (New York: Columbia University Press, 1939).

Scott, *Cranch*: Leonora Cranch Scott, *The Life and Letters of Christopher Pearse Cranch* (Boston: Houghton Mifflin, 1917).

Stock, *Consular Relations*: *Consular Relations between the United States and the Papal States*, ed. Leo Francis Stock (Washington, D.C.: American Catholic Historical Association, 1945).

Stock, *United States Ministers*: *United States Ministers to the Papal States*, ed. Leo Francis Stock (Washington, D.C.: Catholic University Press, 1933).

Sturgis of Yarmouth: *Edward Sturgis of Yarmouth, Massachusetts*, ed. Roger Faxton Sturgis (Boston: Privately published by Stanhope Press, 1914).

Van Doren: *The Lost Art: Letters of Seven Famous Women*, ed. Dorothy Van Doren (New York: Coward-McCann, 1929).

VR: vital records.

Wade: *The Writings of Margaret Fuller*, ed. Mason Wade (New York: Viking, 1941).

Weinstock, *Chopin*: Herbert Weinstock, *Chopin: The Man and His Music* (New York: Knopf, 1949).

WNC: Margaret Fuller Ossoli, *Woman in the Nineteenth Century, and Kindred Papers*, ed. Arthur B. Fuller (Boston: John P. Jewett, 1855).

Works: Manuscript copybooks, Fuller family papers, 3 vols., in Houghton Library, Harvard University.

THE LETTERS OF MARGARET FULLER

700. To Richard F. Fuller

Rome, 1st Jany 1848.

My dear Richard,

The clock striking eleven warns me that I must make haste, if I would wish you a happy new year which I do most fervently,—a year that may heal the wounds of the past and ripen seed for better joys.

It is long since I heard from you, and therefore I fear these are dark dull days for you always liked to speak from your bright expansive moods. I do not like to say much about it, because on former occasions I have wounded you by careless words. I could not help being glad your engagement ended as it did.[1] I felt as if you were saved from infinite ills; still I felt that "the sweet employment of your life was gone" and many fairest flowers of fancy blighted

You have talent, nobleness, a good person, good health, good position good education; I feel that, could you but be patient, six or seven years hence might see you at ease in your fortunes, with honors already gained and more in prospect, your true wife at your side, perhaps traversing these very beautiful lands where I am now; perhaps visiting my grave. I had such a vision of you the other evening as I lay tired and half asleep on the sofa.

But almost every one has his slave in the chariot which mars the whole, and I see that it is possible that the impetuosity which is associated with your energy may destroy all, that, seizing at the fruit before it is ripe, you may untimely strip your tree and leave yourself no harvest.

It was this trait that involved you with the Allens, that broke off un-

39

duly your intercourse with Anna Loring, and led to your late engagement, which could not have been love, but only the need of loving, else it would not have ended so.[2]

God knows I have not myself been wise in life. But I wish you might be wiser and happy. You are not yet four and twenty. Your fate is still undecided. I throw out these words, hoping they may be of use if not, let nothing in them make you feel less affectionately towards me.

I am not well at all this last[n] fortnight. The first two months of my stay in Rome were the best time I have had abroad, though less marked by events and sight of living celebrities than any other. But I thought and drank in the spirit of Rome.[n] I passed all my days in the open air; my nights were tranquil; my appetite and strength returned. But now 16 days of rain, unhappily preceded by three or four of writing have quite destroyed me for the present My health will never be good for any thing to sustain me in any work of value. I must content myself with doing very little and by and by comes Death to reorganize perhaps for a fuller freer life.

Write to me dear Richard, and write of yourself. Write also of Arthur; those repeated operations must shake his nervous system terribly.[3] His is a great and galling ill. I can sympathize with it. And poor Lloydie I hope much he is not unhappy; that his feelings are constantly consulted.[4] It is a sacred duty. It is one I can truly say I never neglected for any other object. Adieu, dear brother. My love and prayers are with you ever, Amen

MARGARET.

ALS (MH:fMS Am 1086 [9:143]); MsCfr (MH fMS Am 1086 [Works, 2:843–47]). *Addressed:* To / Mr Richard F. Fuller / 6 State St. Boston / Massachusetts / U.S.A. *Postmark:* Boston Mass. Feb 19. *Endorsed:* F.S.M. / S. Margaret Fuller / 1 & 12 Jan. 1848.

Margaret's brother Richard Frederick graduated from Harvard in 1844, studied law in Greenfield with George Davis, and attended Harvard Law School before becoming a partner with his uncle Henry Holton Fuller.

this last] this l⟨ef⟩ast
spirit of Rome.] spirit ↑ of Rome ↓ .

1. In 1847 Richard had been engaged to Anna De Rose of Canton, Massachusetts.
2. Richard had previously been in love with Mary Allen of Greenfield, who died in 1845, and with Anna Loring, daughter of Ellis and Louisa Loring of Boston.
3. Arthur Buckminster Fuller, another of her brothers, never recovered from an eye injury he suffered in his childhood. In 1847 he graduated from the Divinity School at Cambridge.
4. The emotionally troubled Lloyd Fuller, youngest of Margaret's siblings, had been admitted to the insane asylum at Brattleboro, Vermont, in the autumn of 1847 (Margarett Crane Fuller to Margaret Fuller, 8 October 1847 [MH]).

701. To Frederic H. Hedge

Monday
10th Jany [1848]

Dear Henry

shall you be well enough to go to the opera tonight; it is still Attila
our box is no 12 first row, come and knock and it will be opened[1]

M.

ALS (MH:fMS Am 1086 [10:106]). *Addressed:* Mr Hedge / 163 Barberino.

Frederic Henry Hedge, once Fuller's close friend in Cambridge, was a Unitarian
minister and German scholar.

1. Giuseppi Verdi's *Attila* was first performed in Venice on 17 March 1846. From
the beginning, the audience saw it as a political protest against the Austrian occupation
of Venice: "cheering crowds, with torches and a brass band, accompanied the composer
to his lodging" (Eric Blom, ed., *Grove's Dictionary of Music and Musicians*, 5th ed. [New
York, 1954], 8:732); George Martin, *Verdi: His Music, Life and Times* [New York, 1963],
pp. 166–67). In her *Tribune* letter Fuller described the "great applause" that followed
politically charged lines (*New-York Daily Tribune*, 7 February 1848).

702. To Caroline Sturgis Tappan

[I] Rome
11th Jany 1848

My dear Caroline,

Your letter came today and did me good. I wept long over it and
now I can hardly write for tears, but these relieve me more than anything, and in these days I cannot have them much.

I have begun to feel very sad at having no letter from you; it was a
year since I had one; all that time I had no line from William Channing; the friendships I had paid for with so much heart's blood, so
many thoughts in the long past seemed to flee from me, and I lost
courage for the ties of the present.[1] Now comes your letter and gives
me the dear certainty that there is love, is realization, hope and faith
in your life. At present you have really cast your lot with another person, live in a house I suppose; sleep and wake in^n unison with humanity; an island flowers in the river of your life.

I cannot say anything about it from my present self. Yet permanent
love for the same object does not seem to me impossible, though once
I thought, I felt it and have ceased to feel. At any rate the union of
two natures for a time is so great.

41

The shells I got for you in Venice they[n] *are* the same Consuelo used to gather; that was one reason I sent them.[2] I wrote in a hurry a few lines for the person who unexpectedly offered; he must have lost them. The little necklace with the cross I meant for Greta.[3] I did not think of it for you, supposing it too little and besides, it did not match the chain and bracelet, being set with different beads. But if you like it; keep it. I can get her something she will like as well.

But these are fragile things. I should like to give you something that may last and will send Raphael's[n] Poesy I have two copies[n] one of which I keep at the head of my bed;[4] perhaps you will put yours in the same place. I will send, also, a little rosary to hang beside it; red I think. I suppose you like red still.

At the time you dreamt of me I was in Venice, very ill, very suffering, but I could not have hated anything. I was very weary of the good friends who were with me, because they never knew what I was feeling, and always brought forward what I wanted to leave behind.[5] I wanted to forget myself in Italy, and, while with them, it was impossible. Yet I was unreasonable enough to feel some bitterness at the indifference with which they left me, alone in a foreign land, and to see that they were seemingly impatient to be delayed two or three days by the state of my health. Yet As as[n] I felt bitterness it was not against them, but the destiny which placed me with them, instead of those who fancied they loved me; to be sure I had not put their love to the proof.

My life in Lombardy and Switzerland was a series of beautiful pictures dramatic episodes, not without some noble genuine life in my own soul. The time when I wrote to you from Como was a peaceful external existence. I floated on the lake with my graceful Polish countess, hearing her stories of heroic sorrow, and I walked in the delicious gardens of the villas with many another summer friend.[6] Red banners floated; children sang and shouted; the lakes of Venus and Diana glittered in the sweetest sunshine. The pretty girls of Bellaggio, with their coral necklaces, all brought flowers to "the American Countess" and "hoped she would be as happy as she deserved". Whether this cautious wish is fulfilled I know not, but certainly I left all this glitter of life behind at Como.

My days at Milan were not unmarked. I have known some happy hours; [II] but they all lead to sorrow, and not only the cups of wine but of milk seem drugged with poison for me. It does not seem to be my fault,—this destiny: I do not court these things, they come. I am a poor magnet with power to be wounded by the bodies I attract.

[III] Leaving Milan, I had a brilliant day in Parma. I had not known Correggio before; he deserves all his fame. I stood in the parlor of the Abbess, the person for whom all was done, and Paradise seemed opened by the nymph, upon her car of light, and the divine children peeping through the vines.[7] Sweet soul of love! I should weary of you, too; but it was glorious that day.

I had another good day, too, crossing the Apennines. The young crescent moon rose in orange twilight, just as I reached the highest peak. I was alone on foot; I heard no sound; I prayed.

At Florence, I was very ill. For three weeks, my life hung upon a thread. The effect of the Italian climate on my health is not favorable. I feel as if I had received a great injury. I am tired and woe-worn; often, in the bed, I wish I could weep my life away. However, they brought me gruel, I took it, and after a while rose up again. In the time of the vintage, I went alone to Sienna. This is a real untouched Italian place. This excursion, and the grapes, restored me at that time.

When I arrived in Rome, I was at first intoxicated to be here. The weather was beautiful, and many circumstances combined to place me in a kind of passive, childlike well-being. That is all over now, and, with this year, I enter upon a sphere of my destiny so difficult, that I, at present, see no way out, except through the gate of death. It is useless to write of it; you are at a distance and cannot help me;— whether accident or angel will, I have no intimation. I have no reason to hope I shall not reap what I have sown, and do not. Yet how I shall endure it I cannot guess; it is all a dark, sad enigma. The beautiful forms of art charm no more, and a love, in which there is all fondness, but no help, flatters in vain. I am all alone; nobody around me sees any of this. My numerous friendly acquaintances are troubled if they see me ill, and who so affectionate and kind as Mr. and Mrs. S.? [IV] but kindness did me good at the time. Write, too, your new address. I have to write still to that which I have known; indeed it will be very strange to me to call you by another name, but I suppose it will be necessary. Ever dear Carrie yours in love

MARGARET.

I have found just such another shell necklace for Greta, so keep that one in peace

Jany 12th

Reading your letter I see that I have not answered your questions about Rachel.[8] I sent to her house my letter of introduction with a note a[s]king when she would see me. After some time, not receiving any answer, I sent to know if she had it. The porter said it had been sent up to her with others, but had, probably, never been read, as she often recd a hundred letters a day, and very often threw them by unopened! If I had then spoken French as well or known as much of foreign manners as now, I should have gone at once to see her, but then I felt timid; she looked so proud and broken-hearted, and I heard she was always surrounded by men. Since I have been in Italy I understood she has had two or three children by Count Walinski himself a natural child of Napoleon.[9] She used to come into Italy for their births. Last summer he married a little girl here, daughter of Prince Poniatowski, a natural son of the King of Poland by the daughter of a coach-maker, there were three children, the King legitimated them by will and left them great riches.[10]

The French papers said that at the annunciation of this marriage and Count Walinski's subsequent departure for Brazil, Rachel rushed into the country, leaving every thing in her house to be publicly sold, without excepting her album, or the gifts of numerous friends and lovers. It was said even her ring[s] and bracelets were sold.[11]

I do not know whether she loved Count W. really, or was tortured to be treated so. It was said she herself thought of marrying a Count Bertrand, a worthless young man. I have heard no more of this; we hear little of other countries in Italy.

The Prince Poniatowski, while I was in Florence, gave a splendid entertainment in the grand hall of the Palazzo Vecchio An opera was given composed by himself in which he and his brother took the principal parts; the music is nothing, but they sang beautifully and the orchestra was splendid. The court of Tuscany, that ugly stupid set were present, all the chief personages, also; the coachmaker's daughter now a full blown peony, in white satin, dress jewels, receiving compliments on acct of her sons, all was inane smile, and false applause. I thought of Rachel in all her native royalty discarded for such things as these. But the coachmaker's daughter will triumph where such a being fails. [   ]

Yesterday I saw Beatrice Cinci's prison and the place where she was tortured so long and never blinded.[12] There is, undoubtedly foundation for the story of a curse laid on Eve.

I: ALfr, collection of G. W. Haight; II: MsCfr (MH: bMS Am 1280 [111, pp. 51, 213–14]; III: ELfr, from *Memoirs*, 2:232–33; IV: ALfrS, collection of G. W. Haight. Published in part in *Memoirs*: 1:226, 2:231–33; *JMN* 11:468, 493; and Chevigny, pp. 440–42.

Caroline Sturgis, one of Fuller's closest friends, married William Aspinwall Tappan (1819–1905) in 1847 (MVR 1905 87:49). In later years she wrote children's books.

wake in] wake ↑ in ↓
Venice they] Venice ⟨?⟩ they
send Raphael's] send ⟨a head of⟩ Raphael's
two copies] two ↑ copies ↓
Yet As as] ↑ Yet ↓ As ⟨far⟩ as

1. William Henry Channing, a close friend, was a Unitarian minister devoted to Fourierite socialism. A nephew of Dr. William Ellery Channing, William Henry had had pulpits in Cincinnati and New York City.

2. Fuller refers to George Sand's novel *Consuelo*.

3. Margaret Fuller Channing (Greta to the family) was the eldest child of Margaret's sister, Ellen, and her husband, William Ellery Channing, another of Dr. Channing's nephews.

4. Shortly after his move to Rome in 1508, Raphael designed four medallions for the vault of the Segnatura: *Theology, Justice, Philosophy*, and *Poetry*. The latter depicts Poetry, who is crowned with laurel, holding a lyre (Giovanni Becatti, "Raphael and Antiquity," in *The Complete Work of Raphael* [Novara, 1969], pp. 508, 518–19).

5. Fuller had gone to Europe with Marcus and Rebecca Spring, friends from New York who also loaned her money for the trip. In the spring of 1847 they returned to the United States, but Fuller decided to go back to Rome.

6. She had met a Princess Radziwill.

7. Sometime around 1518 Correggio was commissioned by Giovanna da Piacenza (d. 1524), abbess of the convent of San Paolo, a Benedictine nunnery in Parma, to paint a series of frescoes in the convent. After her death the room was closed to visitors, and the frescoes were completely forgotten until 1794, when they were fully described for the first time (Selwyn Brinton, *Correggio* [London, 1907], pp. 34–35, 61; Cecil Gould, *The Paintings of Correggio* [Ithaca, 1976], pp. 51–52).

8. During her Paris visit Fuller had often seen performances by Rachel, the foremost actress of her day.

9. Alexandre Walewski (1810–68), illegitimate son of Napoleon I and Countess Marie Walewska, had been Rachel's lover from 1843 to 1846. A soldier and journalist, Walewski became a diplomat serving first as French minister to Tuscany (1849) and later to the courts of Naples, Spain, and England.

10. In 1846 Walewski married Anne-Alexanderine-Catherine de Ricci of Florence (Joanna Richardson, *Rachel* [London, 1956], p. 77).

11. The story told by later biographers differs from the one Fuller heard. Apparently while still attached to Walewski, Rachel became the mistress of Emile de Giradin, the illegitimate son of Comte Alexandre de Giradin (ibid. p. 75).

12. Probably Corte Savella, where Beatrice Cenci was taken from the Castel San Angelo in 1599 and subsequently tortured (Corrado Ricci, *Beatrice Cenci*, trans. Morris Bishop and Henry L. Stuart [New York, 1925], 2:92).

703. To Ellen Fuller Channing

Rome,
12th Jany, 1848

My dear Ellen,

I have had the pleasure to receive one letter from you since my return to Rome; you speak of having written two, but only one had reached me, this last was very good, do not talk of these letters being dull; they are just what I want to get, a faithful picture of your life and of the children. I assure the sight of many and rich things is from from spoiling the taste for what is familar and simple, rather it teaches to prize them and know that, after all, there is nothing better. The other night I dreamed of[n] riding in a chaise in the narrow lanes among the fields and hills of New England, it seemed as if it would be great happiness to be there again, but I suppose it would not. I can never be free from care for one thing, another is my bodily state never will or can be good. I suffered continually in N. E. I suffer in Italy; there more in the head here in the digestive organs, but always it is suffering somewhere. God grant that the grave may prove a door to some real peace.

To dear Greta I will write when I have a chance to send her cross. The little shell necklace I sent to Carrie with some ornaments of the same kind for herself.[1] The note that accompanied them seems to have been lost: they arrived just before her marriage and she seems so well pleased with them all, I should not like to take it away now. I am afraid I cannot get another of the same kind for Greta if I do not return to Venice, but will find her something equally pretty in place of it. Dear child! I think her circumstances happy in the country and with a mother she loves so much and who will take care that she is not forced or injured in any way.

The other little one I do not realize as she was such a wee bit when I saw her, but am glad she looks[n] so brightly and graciously out into the world; it is likely to make the world smile in its turn. Does Carrie take in her the interest of a namesake?

Where is E. Hoar?[2] She does not write to me now. Mr E's absence must make a terrible blank for her, yet I know she is glad to have him go to England.[3]

I never saw Ellery's book; we see nothing here that is not Italian; hardly a newspaper; but I hear it is very much liked.[4]

I was very happy the first two months of my stay here, seeing all the great things at[n] my leisure, but now after a month of continuous rain, Rome is no more Rome. The atmosphere is dreadful, far worse than that of Paris; it is impossible to walk in the thick mud. The air presses with such a weight as to destroy the appetite and every thing I do eat hurts me. The rains and other great objects, always solemn, be-c[om]e terribly gloomy steeped in continu[ou]s black rain and cloud, and my apartment in a street of high houses is dark all day. And this seems likely to continue, perhaps all this month and all February. If I could use the time for work I should not care, but this state of things makes me so unwell I can do very little.

There are many Americans here, among them William Story and his wife I like very much and take pleasure in seeing their children.[5] W. S. is going now to devote himself to Art; he can do it without care or pain, having a respectable income on which his family can live the while. I am glad to know one bright spot amid the troubled lives" here, for Rome is the place to see the struggles of artists I suffer for them and mourn that I have no means to relieve.

About engravings I cannot get them for you here cheap; Rome is only advantageous, because here you can make a choice. Titian's" Assumption of the Madonna, one of those I should like most, if I had money, is four dollars and a half.[6] But I do not see how you can send me a *little* sum, and I cannot buy them for you without, being in great fear myself lest I come to" the end of my funds alone here in a strange land. Very fine ones can be got in Paris, and perhaps, when Richard makes me a remittance next summer, you can add what you have to spend, and I will do what I can to please you. It is a great privation that I cannot buy for my friends any of the things I know would please them, but it must be borne. Ever, dear Ellen, your affecy

MARGARET.

I found yesterday a man who can get me one of those shell necklaces for Greta, so there is no harm done.

ALS (MH:fMS Am 1086 [9:113]). *Addressed:* To / Mrs Ellen Channing / Concord near Boston / Massachusetts / U.S.A. *Postmark:* Boston 10 Feb. *Endorsed:* 12 Jany 1848.

dreamed of] dreamed⟨I will⟩ of
she looks] she ⟨s⟩ looks
things at] things ⟨here⟩ at
troubled lives] troubled li⟨f⟩ves
choice. Titian's] choice. ⟨the⟩ ↑ Titian's ↓
come to] come ↑ to ↓

1. Caroline Sturgis Channing, second child of Ellen and Ellery Channing.
2. Elizabeth Sherman Hoar of Concord, another close friend of Fuller, had been engaged to Charles Emerson at his death in 1836.
3. Emerson's European trip lasted from October 1847 to July 1848 (Rusk, *Letters of RWE*, 3:419, 4:101).
4. Probably Channing's *Conversations in Rome: Between an Artist, a Catholic, and a Critic* (Boston, 1847). His *Poems: Second Series*, also published in 1847, gained little attention.
5. William Wetmore Story, son of Justice Joseph Story of Cambridge, had been Fuller's acquaintance during their youth. Although they had then been cool toward one another, they became close friends in Italy. Story had left a brilliant law career to become a sculptor. He and his wife, Emelyn Eldridge Story, had at this time two children, Edith Marion (1844–1917) and Joseph (1847–53) (Hudson, *Browning*, p. 363).
6. Titian's *Assumption and Coronation of the Virgin*, a twenty-three-foot-high altarpiece, was completed at Santa Maria Gloriosa dei Frari in Venice in 1518 (David Rosand, *Titian* [New York, 1978], p. 84).

704. To Richard F. Fuller

12th Jany [1848]

Again the letters arrive and none to me from any of my family. I have recd letters from my family only once and very soon after my arrival in Rome. You ought to remember that these long silences must always make me sad and uneasy. I am contented, if I hear once in six weeks, but a very long silence especially feeling as I do, that Mother's health is very frail must always disturb me.

I am anxious to know whether you have seen Mr Spring; how the affair of my debt to him has been arranged, and precisely what sum I may count upon it as remainder from Uncle A's bequest.[1] I am anxious to know about this by steamer of *1st March at latest*, and direct that letter to care of^n *Greene and Co Paris*.[2] It is possible I may go to Paris early in March, at any rate they will always have my address.

I do not expect to need to draw for that money whatever it is,^n till July or August, as Mr Greeley has asked me to draw on him in advance and already owes me some money.[3] But it is needful in order to form my plans that I should know what I have to depend on. And it would be much better if I could know earlier. Never forget how lonely my position is now and how desolate and suffering it might be made by a little neglect to write of these affairs.[4] Much depends on you Your sister

M.

ALS (MH:fMS Am 1086 [9:254]); MsC (MH:fMS Am 1086 [Works, 2:877–79]).

to care of] to ↑ care of ↓
money whatever it is,] money ↑ whatever it is, ↓

1. Abraham Williams Fuller, executor of her father's estate, left Margaret slightly more than $200 from his own extensive estate when he died in 1847.

2. Samuel Welles (1778–1841) of Natick, Massachusetts, graduated from Harvard in 1796 and moved to Paris, where he became a successful banker. In 1816 he married Adeline Fowle (Albert Welles, *History of the Welles Family in England and Normandy* [New York, 1876], p. 117).

3. Horace Greeley was paying Fuller $10 for each of her travel letters. On 29 September1847 he urged her to "draw when you need money, and write just when you feel like writing" (MH).

4. In his reply on 20 February (MH), Richard said that he and the family wrote seldom because they were afraid she would have to pay postage on the letters. He reported that as a gift to her he had paid Marcus Spring $200 on her draft and that the balance would be paid with her portion of the proceeds from the sale of some land. Finally, Richard said that the family was prepared to give her $500: "It is due to you as the bright ornament of our family, it is due for your cares and attentions in many years past."

48

705. To Costanza Arconati Visconti

Rome, 14 January 1848

What black and foolish calumnies are these on Mazzini![1] It is as much for his interest as his honor to let things take their course, at present. To expect anything else, is to suppose him base. And on what act of his life dares any one found such an insinuation? I do not wonder that you were annoyed at his manner of addressing the Pope; but to me it seems that he speaks as he should,—near God and beyond the tomb; not from power to power, but from soul to soul, without regard to temporal dignities.[2] It must be admitted that the etiquette, Most Holy Father, &c., jars with this.[3]

ELfr, from *Memoirs*, 2:233. Published in Chevigny, p. 442.

Costanza Trotti Arconati Visconti was a Milanese noblewoman who had been exiled with her husband for their political activities. She was Fuller's closest Italian friend.

1. In her letter of 12 January (MH), Arconati Visconti reported that attacks on the Jesuits in Genoa on 4 January had been "excited by the emissaries & the letters of Mazzini—I hope that this is not true, for I believe Mazzini to be an honest man, & that the 4th January it was intended to assassinate the Jesuits & burn them in their houses." During the revolutions of 1848–49 the Jesuits were expelled from almost all the Italian states.

2. On 8 September 1848 Mazzini wrote in an open letter to the pope: "Be a believer; abhor to be King, Politician, Statesman. Make no compromise with error; do not contaminate yourself with diplomacy, make no compact with fear, with expediency, with the false doctrines of a *legality*, which is merely a falsehood invented when faith failed" (*New-York Daily Tribune*, 19 February 1848). Such language caused Arconati Visconti to say in her letter that she did "not like his manner of addressing the Pope, it is presumptuous. Mazzini has the air of treating as from power to power, which is a language offensive not only from my point of view, but from Mazzini's own."

3. In her reply of 24 January (MH), Arconati Visconti said: "I have not believed the calumny which accused Mazzini, since you have made me love him, I am no longer unjust to him. It is his partisans, the lowest of his party who do him harm."

706. To Richard F. Fuller

Rome
8th Feby 1848

My dear Richard,

I wrote a letter[n] last steamer complaining of your silence, but two or three days ago one from you[n] was brought me dated 30th Novr, which was detained in England till Maquay and Pakenham could send on the postage, a process which occupies more than a month. This

Costanza Arconati Visconti. By permission of the Museo del Risorgimento, Milan.

must be owing to some negligence on my part. I thought when I asked my friends to write by care of M and P. I said *but always by French steamer* However that line is stopped now While I remain in Europe I think I shall have all my letters sent to care of *Greene and Co, Paris*. I will have that one steady address, for a good deal of expense is better than to bear the pain of the loss and delay of letters.

I dare-say your mood has changed since that letter was written so I will answer briefly to its thoughts. It is not reasonable to expect the world should pay us in money for what *we are* but for what we can do *for it*. Society pays in money for the practical talent exerted for its benefit, to the thinker, as such, only the tribute of materials for thought.

I have no doubt, if you persevered in your present path, that you would have rank, future, and the means to benefit others. Do not give these up lightly or rashly; they are not to be despised in this difficult world. Do not throw them aside till you are *very* sure of the main stress of your wants and tendencies. We cannot have every thing; we cannot have even many things; the choice is only between a better and worser.

With regard to our sometime living together in a very quiet and simple way; it would present to me a most desirable prospect. The world has inflicted on me extreme suffering has not given me in return much means to aid others, or even a freedom from the pettiest care. I should like to live with you, where Nature was beautiful, and only occasionally to see cities or men at large. But I have no idea you will eventually be content without marrying, nor am I so selfish as to wish it, wish you to do what is best for yourself. My love will always accompany you; my society, when possible, will be yours in the best sense. I wish God would give me more peace and health; then it would be worth more, but my birth-star was not a kindly one.

I am surprized you never heard of my seeing George Sand.[1] I wrote a full acct of it to E. Hoar, who wished it particularly, and supposed she would show it to all my *near* friends. I know Ellen has seen the letter; ask her" to show it you. I liked and loved Me Sand, but should not care particy to know her more, now I have the true picture of her. She is a woman, who, except by her lovers, may be as well known through her books as any other way.

I have lately seen a good deal of a very celebrated woman, the Princess Belgiojoso.[2] She passed some weeks here and is now gone to Naples. She is a woman of gallantry which Me Sand is not, though she also" has had several lovers, no doubt. The" public life of the Princess" has been truly energetic and beneficient, of her on that side I shall give some account in the Tribune.[3] Adieu, my dear Richard, ever most affecy yrs

M.

Address the care of[n] Greene and Co, Paris

ALS (MH:fMS Am 1086 [9:146]); MsC (MH:fMS Am 1086 [Works, 2:849–55]). *Addressed:* Mr R. F. Fuller / 6 State St. Boston / Massachusetts / U.S.A. *Postmark:* New York 18 Mar. *Endorsed:* F. S. M. / S. M. Fuller / 8 Feb. 1848.

a letter] a ↑letter↓
one from you] one ↑from you↓
ask her] ask ⟨th⟩ her
she also] she ↑also↓
doubt. The] doubt. ⟨?⟩ The
life of the Princess] life ↑of the Princess↓
Address the care of] Address ↑the care of↓

1. Fuller described her visit to Sand in a journal (MH) later published in *Memoirs*, 2:194–99.
2. Cristina Trivulzio di Belgioioso (sometimes spelled Belgiojoso) (1808–71) was an Italian nationalist who had lived in Paris from 1830 to 1848. A woman of many accomplishments, the princess was a scholar, political activist, feminist, and hostess of a brilliant salon. It was she who recruited Fuller's help in a hospital during the seige of Rome in 1849 (Beth Archer Brombert, *Cristina: Portrait of a Princess* [New York, 1977]).
3. It was not, however, until 1849 that Fuller wrote a short biographical sketch of the princess (*New-York Daily Tribune*, 23 June 1849).

707. To Margaret Fuller Channing

Rome
9th Feby 1848

My dear little Greta,

Your mamma says you want me to write you a little letter and I am going to do so only I shall expect you to answer it.

The other day came here an old gentleman with white hair, and his name is Dr Henry Gardiner; when he is at home he lives in Boston.[1] I gave him a little box in which was for your Mamma a great shell, and in it was made a pretty carriage [wi]th people riding in it, and pretty little creatures flew beside it strewing flowers. In the same box was the little cross for you, made of coral and gold, and a little heart made of Roman stone for Caroline.

There was also for you a little shoe, not made to wear; for it is too little for you and too big for Anna Barker, but made to hold sugar-plums, and in it are sugar-plums such as they make here in Rome.

You will do with these whatever you like and your mamma thinks best. I would have sent more but Dr Gardiner has a great many things to put in his trunk and a great way to carry i[t] He expects to get home in June when the roses are in blossom and I hope uncle Richard will bring the box safe to your house.

We have roses here all the winter, violets and other flowers, but they do not smell sweet. Still I know a little girl here who loves them very much; her name is Edith Story. When she is sick her mother gives her flowers to play with.

A great many children run about here ragged and dirty, calling to ev[ery] body "Give me a cent" [I] always feel s[or]ry to see them, but I do not give them cen[ts,] only roasted chestnuts to eat. For here people have fires in the streets and roast chestnuts at them all winter.

We have here in the house three little dogs. They are very pretty; quite black, with sparkling eyes, and do many funny things, but I do not like them, for they eat up my pens, and bark at every body that comes to see me. Still if you were here, it would make you laugh to see their ways.

Goodbye, I hear you are a good little girl and take kind care of your little sister. I love you, and hope you will love, even if you should not see her for a great while your affectionate

AUNT MARGARET.

ALS (MH:fMS Am 1086 [9:144]). *Addressed:* Greta. / brown cottage / Concord.

1. Henry Gardiner (1779–1858) graduated from Harvard in 1798, became a physician, and then served in the Massachusetts legislature. In 1810 he married Clarissa Holbrook (1784–1860) of Milton (Harvard archives; Milton VR).

708. To Jane Stirling

Rome
514 Corso,
8th March 1848

My dear Miss Stirling

That I have not written as you wished impute to my very bad health during the winter, you are often present to my thoughts. The same cause has prevented my cultivating the acquaintance to whom you introduced me and who promised to be very agreeable. Let me on my side present Mr Hedge, one of the most cultivated and refined minds of my country and a friend of Emerson's no less than mine.

What great and stirring times are these of Paris.[1] I should like much to receive a few lines from you about what you have known of them. Had I but been in Paris this 14th Feby as I was last year; it was on that day I went with you to hear Chopin and afterwards, the dear kind Chevalier.[2] Time permits today no word more except, dear Miss Stirling, in hope of sometime meeting again yours affly

S. M. FULLER.

ALS (NBu). *Addressed:* To / Miss Stirling / *12 bis* Rue Neuve de Berry / Paris.

Johanna Wilhelmina Stirling (1804–59), daughter of John Stirling of Kippendavie and Kippenross, Scotland, was a student of Chopin who had been living in Paris for several years (Niecks, *Chopin*, 2:290–92; Weinstock, *Chopin*, p. xv).

1. On 22 February 1848 a demonstration against the government broke out in Paris. The following day Louis-Philippe dismissed the ministry of François-Guillaume Guizot in an unsuccessful attempt to forestall a revolution. Following severe rioting, the king abdicated on 24 February, a republic was proclaimed, and a provisional government was established (*Cambridge Modern History*, 11:97–103).

2. Sigismund von Neukomm, the Austrian musician, whom they heard in Paris.

709. To Frederic H. Hedge

Wednesday eveg,
8th March, 1848.

My dear Henry,

The note to the princess may be left to her address at the post office.[1] I do not know where she is in Naples, if still there; if gone, she has" probably left orders to forward her letters.

The other will introduce you to a lady very agreeable and good, and of distinguished family and social position. Miss Stirling is Scotch, but usual[ly] lives in Paris with her sister, Mrs Erskine.[2] If these affairs do not drive her away, you will find her and had best present the letter early. If I know when Mr Emerson is there, I want him to see her too.[3]

I would like to know your address in Paris, perhaps I might forward letters for you to take home. I have some faint hope you will return to Rome, but if not, think of me ever as ever your friend

MARGARET.

If I never get back and in my sick moping moods I fancy I shall not; it seems so[n] far off; you must write a good verse to put on my tomb-stone.

I have recd a Tribune which contains a short notice of yr book, speaking favorably of its prospects and "with high consideration", of you[4]

ALS (MH:fMS Am 1086 [10:105]). *Addressed:* Mr Hedge / 55 via del Barberino. *Endorsed:* Margaret Fuller.

she has] she ⟨?⟩ has
not; it seems so] not; ⟨I⟩ it seems ⟨t⟩ so

1. Cristina Trivulzio di Belgioioso.
2. Katherine Stirling, Jane's elder sister, married her cousin James Erskine in 1811. He died not long after. In April 1848 the women persuaded Chopin to tour England and Scotland, where they stayed until November 1848. In 1849 they clumsily tried to give him an anonymous gift of 25,000 francs, which he refused (Niecks, *Chopin,* 2:290–92; Weinstock, *Chopin,* pp., 143–44; *Selected Correspondence of Fryderyk Chopin,* ed. and trans. Arthur Hedley [London, 1962], pp. 343–44, 356).
3. Emerson arrived in Paris on 6 May and stayed until 2 June. As Fuller here surmises, Stirling was in London, where Emerson met Chopin and heard him play at her home (Rusk, *Letters of RWE,* 4:72, 79, 84).
4. The brief notice described Hedge as "a scholar of rich and various culture," but it said almost nothing about Hedge's *Prose Writers of Germany* (Philadelphia, 1848) (*New-York Daily Tribune,* 31 December 1847).

710. To Ralph Waldo Emerson

Rome, 14 March 1848

Mickiewicz is with me here, and will remain some time; it was he I wanted to see, more than any other person, in going back to Paris, and I have him much better here.[1] France itself I should like to see, but remain undecided, on account of my health, which has suffered so much, this winter, that I must make it the first object in moving for the summer. One physician thinks it will of itself revive, when once the rains have passed, which have now lasted from 16th December to this day. At present, I am not able to leave the fire, or exert myself at all.

ELfr, from *Memoirs,* 2:233–34.
1. Adam Mickiewicz, the Polish poet and nationalist, had deeply moved Fuller when they met in Paris.

711. To Richard F. Fuller

Rome,
17th March, 1848.

My very dear Richard,

Today I receive your letter of 6th Feby. I had already answered that of 31st Jany, but not sent my letter to the post, and now I will condense its substance into this.

Your view of your relation with Henry seems to me just and corresponds with what I have known of him.[1] I do not think it can be for your interest to remain there. Yet do not for my sake break quite yet. I am anxious you should for a few months remain in Boston, and secure of your own subsistence. I should feel very desolate here, if I had not you to write to, able to do what is needful for me there. I will not be a restraint upon you long, but should like to feel sure you will be in Boston up to December of this year.

As to your going to the West, my instinct is not in favor of your doing so. From what I know of the west and of you it[n] does not seem to me your true sphere. Yet I may be wrong, and if *you* were *entirely sure* it were best for you, I could have nothing to say against it.

With regard to my living with you on a farm, it is a project that presents great charms to my imagination. Amid the corrupt splendors of the old world, I begin to pine for the pure air of my native land. Near sight of potentates and powers, the achievements of talent and great events only makes the very private simple sphere seem more attractive. I should be more likely to be content with such a life as you propose than ever before. I should like very much to live with you. And I agree that it is most undesirable for me to remain in a field, where the excitements of the hour use up my strength and prevent my doing any thing of permanent value, where I am ill paid, and where I *could* live but a very little longer, for my strength is almost spent. I would give almost any thing else for freedom from care and the most simple, congenial life. Or if not wholly congenial, yet at least unconstrained.

But could we *have* such freedom? I do not know enough about these farming affairs to judge *why*, but, of the many in our country who try these experiments, almost all fail.[n] It seems to me that devotion to the interests of a farm, and much physical force in the members of a family are necessary to a tolerable economic result. In the last of these no persons, accustomed to an intellectual life, are rich. As to money, apart from the world, if I could earn enough to provide for my own personal expenses, and a stout servant for us both, it would be all I could expect. As to personal exertion[n] I could order the accounts, give an air of comfort to the house, but as to *work*, that could not be I was never educated to it, and my natural delicacy is greatly increased now. A little exercise, a few arrangements are all to which I am equal.[n] (I keep writing words wrong speaking and hearing constantly Italian I much forget my English.)

Thus it stands with me. Should I live, should I return to my native country and free, and you were satisfied on these points I think *I* should like the plan.

But there are reasons why I cannot answer positively till the autumn of this year. There are circumstances and influences now at work in my life, not likely to find their issue till[n] then. If you still wish it, I think [I] shall [b]e able to answer by October of this year. Meanwhile you can keep the subject before you and write to me from time to time what you think.[2]

I feel afraid you may sometime love in a quarter that will make you regret having made choice of this narrow path when it is too late to change. Try fully to weigh this chance also.

I remember once when we lived in the Brattle house I was with Eugene in the garden and he said, "Our family[n] star has taken an unfavorable turn; father had always luck in aid of his efforts till now; now his fortunes begin to decline and we shall never be lucky any more."[3] I thought of this the other day after after reading Arthur's letter and yours. We are never wholly sunk by storms, but no favorable wind ever helps our voyages to surprizing good results. Eugene, I do hope, has found, after all his tribulation, the humble content he craves, but a little ill health, or unfavorable crisis in affairs could give him great trouble. Wm gets along, but seems likely never to do more.[4] Ellen has wed herself to difficulties from which only the death of her husband could free her.[5] Arthur, I had thought would have outward prosperity, but his calamity hangs on him like a cloud. Fortune does not yet favor you. I doubt your life like mine will be a battle. May you have greater physical energy to sustain it. My courage has at last given way, beneath a three months headach[n] and the deep disappointment of my plans for the employment of my [winter at Rome I][n] have earned no money I have done nothing. My plans are at a stand. I am tired of life and feel unable to face the future. But this last four or five days I am free from headach and cough; the physician assures me I shall be better so soon as the rains cease, which they seem resolved never to. Rain we have had from 16th Dec till now this 17th March. But when I *do* feel better, I will write again; no doubt things will look differently. I have learnt an immense deal, if ever I could have the force to make use of it. Meanwhile my dear brother, living or dying your affec sister and friend

M.

When you write to Mother say I am anxious to hear from her particularly and shall write soon. When does she return to N. England?

ALS (MH:fMS Am 1086 [9:147]); MsC (MH:fMS Am 1086 [Works, 2:855–65]). *Addressed:* To / Mr Richard F. Fuller / 6 State St. Boston Mass / U.S.A. *Postmark:* New York 25 April. *Endorsed:* F. S. M. / S. Margaret Fuller / 17th & 27th Mar '48.

you it] you ⟨as⟩ it
all fail.] all f⟨?⟩ail.
to personal exertion] to ⟨the house,⟩ ↑ personal exertion ↓
am equal.] am ⟨un⟩ equal.
issue till] issue ↑ till ↓
"Our family] "Our ↑ family ↓
months headach] months ⟨exhaustion⟩ ↑ headach ↓
Rome I] *Added from the copy.*

1. Richard, who was sometimes morose and self-pitying, often quarreled with his equally difficult uncle Henry Holton Fuller. In his reply of 2 May (MH), Richard said that he was then boarding in Canton and that he had plans to leave the partnership before January 1849.

2. This attitude toward the family future pleased Richard, who said in reply: "I have more practical wisdom than those persons who have failed; and if I *do* feel that it can be undertaken, we shall be likely to succeed."

3. Exactly what event Eugene meant is not clear, but it may have been his father's failure to obtain a foreign service appointment despite his support of John Quincy Adams in the presidential election of 1824.

4. Eugene was a newspaperman in New Orleans; their brother William Henry was a struggling businessman in Cincinnati.

5. Ellery Channing was both improvident and temperamental. Fuller was bitter about his decision in 1846 to go to Europe despite the approaching birth of his second child. Ellen and Ellery separated for a time from 1853 to 1855.

712.   To William H. Channing

Rome, 29 March 1848

I have been engrossed, stunned almost, by the public events that have succeeded one another with such rapidity and grandeur.[1] It is a time such as I always dreamed of, and for long secretly hoped to see. I rejoice to be in Europe at this time, and shall return possessed of a great history. Perhaps I shall be called to act. At present, I know not where to go, what to do. War is everywhere. I cannot leave Rome, and the men of Rome are marching out every day into Lombardy.[2] The citadel of Milan is in the hands of my friends, Guerriere, &c., but there may be need to spill much blood yet in Italy.[3] France and Germany are not in such a state that I can go there now. A glorious flame burns higher and higher in the heart of the nations.

ELfr, from *Memoirs*, 2:235. Published in Van Doren, p. 293, and Chevigny. p. 448.

1. Revolution broke out in Europe on 22 February, when the French demonstrated against the reign of Louis-Philippe. A French republic was proclaimed on 24 February. An uprising in Vienna on 12 March caused Prince Klemens Wenzel von Metternich to resign the next day. On 17 March Austria granted Hungary a separate ministry, and on 18 March an insurrection began in Berlin. By the day Fuller wrote this letter, all the German states had been forced to grant reforms or liberal concessions in the wake of popular agitation (*Cambridge Modern History*, 11:143–58).

2. The Austrian occupation of Lombardy and Venetia had its headquarters in Milan, where Field Marshal Joseph Wenzel Radetzky commanded a large and powerful army. On 1 January the Milanese began an antismoking campaign to diminish the Austrian tax revenues. In retaliation, Radetzky's troops provoked the public into an outbreak of disturbances. On 18 March 1848 an open rebellion began the famous "five days of Milan." After fierce street fighting Radetzky was forced to withdraw on 22 March and leave the city in the hands of a provisional government. On 24 March Charles Albert, king of Piedmont-Sardinia, declared war on Austria and began to pursue Radetzky, who was withdrawing toward Verona. On 24 and 25 March two columns of Roman troops, one of 7,000 regulars and one of 9,000 recruits, left Rome to join the Piedmontese forces (Berkeley, pp. 17–19, 79–100, 153–55).

3. Anselmo Guerrieri Gonzaga, whom Fuller met in 1847, was a member of the Milanese provisional government.

713. To Jane Tuckerman King

Rome April 1848

The Gods themselves walk on earth, here in the Italian Spring. Day after day of sunny weather lights up the flowery glades and Arcadian woods. The fountains, hateful during the endless rains, charm again. At Castle Fusano[1] I found heaths in full flower" I felt cheered." Such beauty is irresistible. But ah dearest, the" drama of my" fate is very deep, and the ship plunges deeper as it rises higher. You would be amazed, I believe, could" you know how different is my present phase of life, from that in which you knew me; but you" would love me no less; for it is still the same planet that shews such different climes.

You know me, because you never in your life wounded me, in the slightest way; you are always dear, and our intercourse always noble.

I touched your mental life at a point of light. I am not in so high a state of soul at present, as when you knew me: I am enlarging the circle of my experiences. I deepen the sources, but do not soar. But I always understand, and am always true.

I am very happy here; tranquil, and alone in Rome. I love Rome more every hour; but I do not like to write details, or really to let any one know any thing about it. I pretend to, perhaps, but in reality, I do not betray the secrets of my love.

Whatever may be the future developments of my life, *you* will always love me, and prize my friendship. Much has changed since we met; my character is not in what may be called the heroic phase, now. I have done, and may still do, things that may invoke censure; but in the foundation of character, in my aims, I am always the same:—and I believe you will always have confidence that I act as I ought and must,—and will always value my sympathy.

MsCfr (MH:fMS Am 1086 [Works, 1:111]); MsCfr (MB: Ms. Am. 1450 [168–69]). Published in part in *At Home and Abroad*, pp. 426–27.

Jane Tuckerman, once Fuller's pupil, was separated from her husband, John King.

full flower] *The second copy adds:* as large as one of our pear-trees.

I felt cheered.] *This sentence not in the second copy.*

dearest, the] *The second copy reads:* dear Jane! the

of my] *Here another copyist began.*

amazed, I believe, could] *The second copy reads:* amazed, could

but you] *The second copy reads:* but I think you

1. Castle Fusano is a seventeenth-century villa situated two miles south of Ostia, near Italy's west coast.

714. To Henry Colman

Rome
7th April, 48.

Dear Mr Coleman,

I write by private hand a few lines, uncertain whether you are still in Paris, yet "doubting" you will not leave it in these stirring times. I write to coax from you your narrative of these same times.[1] If you are there do write me your version of the past and present; we hear so very little and it seems to me the French journals are afraid to publish the full truth, lest it should do mischief abroad, while matters are in this transition state.

These are great times, my dear Mr Coleman. No piping times, but good loud swell of the trumpet, as for the drum in these quarters its rub a dub is even a little too constant. But I do assure you the men, women and children of Italy show a noble spirit and one that should lead to a solid peace, a real growth.

I have but a moment to write tonight, by Mr Hillard of Boston.[2] I had thought to come to Paris this spring. I am nailed here by want of money, if by no other reason. All I have is with Greene and Co and they will not take their paper here or any Paris paper. I suppose it is all nonsense and they suppose too that Greene and Co are perfectly firm, but they say we must wait. Please write me about this. And can you send me the address of Miss Fitten which I have lost. And could you get for me the pamphlet that contained the beautiful letters of the poor duchess de Praslin. I want them for the second part of Woman in the 19th century and fear they will slip out of print before I get to Paris.[3] Pardon, trouble I would take as much for you. I have been often interrupted and can at this moment say no more except ever with best wishes yours

S. M. FULLER.

Please address me here care Maquay Pakenham and Smythe, Rome

ALS (ViU). *Addressed:* Mr Henry Coleman / Care Greene & Co / Paris. *Endorsed:* S. M. Fuller.

Henry Colman (1785–1849) graduated from Dartmouth in 1805. At times a teacher, a minister, and a farmer, he was in Europe from 1843 to 1848 to study agricultural conditions. In 1807 he married Mary Harris (1782–1864) of Charlestown *(DAB;* MVR 176:57).

1. In his reply of 25 April (MH), Colman said that poor health had made it necessary to leave Paris for London. He described the revolution at length, calling Louis Blanc "a mischievous fool" and Lamartine "truly patriotic and disinterested."

2. George Stillman Hillard, Charles Sumner's law partner, was an old acquaintance of Fuller. He wrote of his Italian visit in *Six Months in Italy* (Boston, 1853).

3. Altarice-Rosalba Sebastiani (1807–47) married Charles-Laure-Hughes-Théobald (1805–47), duc de Choiseul, duc de Praslin, in 1824. On 17 August 1847 the duchess was killed in her Paris hotel. The duke was arrested and tried for her murder but died in prison, victim of either state murder or suicide *(Nouvelle biographie générale,* ed. Jean Chretin Ferdinand Hoefer [Paris, 1852–66]. Editions of *Extraits de lettres de madame la duchesse de Praslin* were published in 1847 in Paris and in Leipzig.

715. To Ann Waln Rotch

Rome
22d April, 1848

My dear Mrs Rotch,

It is long since I heard from you, but I hope you are well enough to take pleasure in receiving you[r] country people, when they are capable" of imparting any pleasure. This, which I could not say of all, I venture to of the lady who brings this, like your self one of the American [   ], like yourself full of vivacity and kind dispositions. If othe[r] wise you find her wanting in faculties that you possess, or any way wanting your counsel I doubt not you will render it with your accustomed generosity.

It is long since I heard directly from my dear Mrs Farrar, but my sister informs me Mr F. though still as suffering is much more cheerful;[1] how I rejoice in any alleviation of her troubles. I had an excellent le[tte]r from Maria, but it was old, having been sent to Rome New York, and waited there a long time before it could escape to Rome, Italy.

I write no more, this being Easter Sunday which closes a week whose gorgeous shows are fatiguing beyond any thing I ever experienced The *misereres* tire too miserably; the *benedicti* leave me unblest. The bearer, Mrs Ames, will have enough to tell of Rome, if you incline to hear; her husband has seen much of the Pope, who has sat to him with apparent satisfaction.[2] With much respect and affection, dear Mrs Rotch, yours

S. M. FULLER.

ALS (VtMiM).

Ann Waln Morgan married Francis Rotch of New Bedford in 1819. Fuller was fond of their daughter, Maria.

are capable] are capa⟨p⟩ble

1. Francis Rotch's sister Elizabeth married John Farrar, professor of mathematics at Harvard, who had been ill for several years. The author of a widely read book of advice to young women, Eliza Farrar was an old friend of Fuller.

2. Joseph Alexander Ames (1816–72) was a self-taught painter who, as Fuller says, painted the pontiff's portrait. He married Sarah Fisher Clampitt (1817–1901), who was a sculptor (*DAB*; Groce).

716.   To Mr. Page

174 Corso
Monday
[ca. May 1848]

Dear Sir,

Dr Masi, editor of the *Contemporaneo*, is desirous to make exchanges with some leading newspapers of the U.S. I know any of them would be much interested to receive his paper as the organ of the new movement in the Papal States. I recommended the Natl Intelligencer, the N. Y. Tribune, and the N. Y Evening Post as those which would be best for him to receive for his own purposes.[1] I shall write to these papers about the exchange and I told him of your being here and that you would know the best way to send and I presumed how send with some of your things the first nos for him. He will call at yr lodging, but as you will probably be out, I wish you with Mrs P. would come and take a cup of tea here with us after the fireworks. He will be here then and we can arrange it without detaining you long and have a pleasant little farewell meeting too.

If you can see Mr Duyckinck in course of your rambles please ask him and his friend Mr Butler[?] to come in also.[2] The two respected Drs we are always glad to see.

In too much haste yours

S M. FULLER

ALS (MCR-S).

1. Luigi Masi (b. 1814), born in Petrignano, was a doctor, journalist, poet, politician, and soldier. In 1847 he was the private secretary to Carlo Bonaparte, Prince Canino, and one of the founders of the newspaper *Il Contemporaneo*. In the defense of Rome in 1849 he served as a colonel under Garibaldi. The *Contemporaneo* was established early in 1847 as a voice of moderate reform, but it became increasingly radical and hostile toward the pope (G. F.-H. Berkeley and J. Berkeley, *Italy in the Making, June 1846 to 1 January 1848* [Cambridge, 1936 (1968)], pp. 103–4, 108). The *National Intelligencer* was published by Joseph Gales, Jr., and William W. Seaton in Washington, D.C.; the *New-York Daily Tribune* was Horace Greeley's paper, for which Fuller still wrote, and the *New York Evening Post* was edited by William Cullen Bryant (Mary Wescott and Allene Ramage, *A Checklist of United States Newspapers* [Durham, N.C., 1933], pp. 61, 414).

2. George Long Duyckinck of New York was then living in Europe. Later in 1848 he joined his brother, Evert, in editing the *Literary World* in New York.

717. To Ralph Waldo Emerson

[ca. May 1848]

[   ] Mickiewicz is here in Italy, as is Mazzini; you will not see either of the persons who have been most to me in Europe. Perhaps you would not have found common ground with them [b]ut I should like to have ha[d] you se[e] these personalities

Hicks will give you a piece of the porphyry pavement of the Pantheon, I have had made into a *presse-papier* for you. It would have been prettier bigger, but was the only piece I could have and g[ot] by bribe as they were mending the pavement. I shall not carry away for myself one stone from Rome, one grain of its dust, other than what [I] have assimilated.

No letters. [   ] the twenty m[   ] from Elizh [   ] she misses y[   ] had a sad t[   ] since you cannot alter, I am glad you are set apart from it for a time. I hear your little boy is a very fine child. I never took much interest in him, not liking to think of another in Waldo's place, but I am very glad for you.[1] Children, with all their faults, seem to me the best thing we have. [   ] had friendship [   ]y it seems [   ] ye, ever your

MARGARET.

I am going into the country [   ] still [   ] Care Maquay Pakenham and [   ] Ro[   ]

I shall often send for my [   ] Dont fail to write once [   ] leaving Europe.

ALfrS (MH: bMS Am 1280 [2380]). *Addressed:* R. W. Emerson / Paris / Inquire at the / American Legatio[n] / Mr Hicks.

Dated by the reference to her departure from Rome.

1. Her references are to Emerson's sons: Waldo, whose death in 1842 Fuller always mourned, and Edward Waldo, who was born in 1844.

718. To Elizabeth De Windt Cranch

Rome 14th May 48

My dear Lizzie,

I recd your note some three weeks since and was rejoiced to find all had gone so well with you. But Fortune favors the brave. I had half thought to salute you this week in person, being extremely tempted to accompany the Storys but on the whole could not make the expedition fit all inward and outward commands of the present hour.

Our Dr. Severin left Rome this day for Germany. It is not certain, but seems to me hardly probably he will come to you. He seemed pleased by your message and I doubt not would be much so by a picture from Pearse, but he does not easily commit himself by a direct reply.

I have had divers letters since you went away, but no important news of any of our friends. W. Russell mentioned seeing your sister

Louisa, that she was gradually regaining her strength.[1] W. Channing has finished his life of his uncle; it is published this month.[2] You know, I suppose that we have had great trouble at Rome, and how Pio has disappointed the enthusiasm he roused.[3] It is a sad affair. Italy was so happy in loving him and the world in seeing one man high placed, who became his place and seemed called to it by God. But it is all over. He is the modern Lot's wife and now no more a living soul, but cold pillar of the Past.[4]

For the rest Mrs Story will tell you all. Though you were so independent, it pleases me that you will have two female friends near when you are ill. I shall be anxious to know how you get through and if it is a girl that comes to help on the 19th century.[5] Remember me affecttely to Pearse and three kisses to Georgie that pretty boy from your tired and sleepy friend[6]

MARGARET F.

The spring here is glorious but *you* have the orange groves, if at Sorrento not to be mistaken for Pumpkins.

MsC (MB: Ms. Am. 1450 [60]). Published in Scott, *Cranch*, p. 142).

Elizabeth De Windt, a great-granddaughter of John and Abigail Adams, married the poet-painter Christopher Pearse Cranch.

1. Louisa De Windt Whittemore married Clarence Chatham Cook (1828–1900) in 1853 (*DAB*).

2. William Henry Channing, *Memoir of William Ellery Channing* (Boston, 1848). The *Christian Register* for 20 May reported that the book, published on 15 May, had already sold 1,000 copies.

3. The revolution in Milan and the war being waged by Charles Albert against Austria posed an insoluble dilemma for the pope, whose liberal reforms had in large measure brought about the confrontation. As an Italian prince, Pius was obliged to support the war for liberation, even though a victory would ensure Piedmontese hegemony, but as head of the Roman Catholic church, the pope could not wage war on a Catholic nation unless directly attacked. His response, one that outraged the republicans, was to issue an allocution on 29 April in which he disavowed the war and explicitly rejected the idea that he become the head of a republic: "We do urgently warn and exhort the said Italian people to abstain with all diligence from the like counsels, deceitful and ruinous to Italy herself, and to abide in close attachment to their respective sovereigns, of whose good will they have already had experience, so as never to let themselves be torn away from the obedience they owe them." In one stroke Pius IX removed himself as an Italian political leader (Mack Smith, *Making of Italy*, p. 152). The allocution caused immediate unrest in Rome, not only among the republicans but among parents who feared that as a result of the pope's action, their sons fighting under his flag would be shot as bandits by the Austrians. By 10 A.M. the Corso (where Fuller lived) was full of people and by late afternoon the civic guard occupied the city gates. Rome did not grow calm until 2 May (Berkeley, pp. 181–87).

4. Gen. 19:26.

5. A reference to Fuller's *Woman in the Nineteenth Century*, which she published in 1845. Leonora Cranch was born on 4 June 1848 (Scott, *Cranch*, p. 145).

6. George William Cranch, born in 1847.

719. To Thomas Hicks

dated at Rome, May 17. 1848.
You would say to those I leave behind that I was willing to die. I have suffered in life far more than I enjoyed, and I think quite out of proportion with the use my living here is of to others.

I have wished to be natural and true, but the world was not in harmony with me— nothing came right for me. I think the spirit that governs the Universe must have in reserve for me a sphere where I can develope more freely, and be happier— On Earth circumstances do not promise this before my forces shall be too much lavished to make a better path truly avail me—

MsCfr (MB: Ms. Am. 1450 [82]).

Thomas Hicks, whom Fuller first met in 1847, was an American painter living in Rome.

The copyist made a note on the letter: This letter was given to Mr Hicks as containing her last wishes in the event of her death.

720. To Ralph Waldo Emerson

Rome, 19 May 1848
I should like to return with you, but I have much to do and learn in Europe yet. I am deeply interested in this public drama, and wish to see it *played out*. Methinks I have *my part* therein, either as actor or historian.[1]

I cannot marvel at your readiness to close the book of European society.[2] The shifting scenes entertain poorly. The flux of thought and feeling leaves some fertilizing soil; but for me, few indeed are the persons I should wish to see again; nor do I care to push the inquiry further. The simplest and most retired life would now please me, only I would not like to be confined to it, in case I grew weary, and now and then craved variety, for exhilaration. I want some scenes of natural beauty, and, imperfect as love is, I want human beings to love, as I suffocate without. For intellectual stimulus, books would mainly supply it, when wanted.

Why did you not try to be in Paris at the opening of the Assembly? There were elements worth scanning.[3]

ELfr, from *Memoirs*, 2:239. Published in Chevigny, p. 453.

1. In response to Fuller's letter of 14 March, Emerson wrote on 25 April: "It made & makes me much uneasiness the bad account your letter gives of your health & wealth at Rome. I grieve to think of you alone there with so much debility & pain. You are imprudent to stay there any longer. Can you not safely take the first steamer to Marseilles, come to Paris, & go home with me" (Rusk, *Letters of RWE*, 4:61).

2. Emerson said: "Some excellent samples of the best varieties of private society I have studied with much curiosity and though the book is large & voluminous I am not now eager to go on with it. Indeed my interest already flags" (Rusk, *Letters of RWE*, 4:62).

3. On 26 February, shortly after its creation, the provisional French government had promised elections, which were held on 23 April. Voting under a plan of direct and universal suffrage, the French elected a constituent assembly that included royalists, republicans, and socialists. The assembly first met on 4 May 1848. By early summer the conservative republicans gained control of the body and grew increasingly hostile to the republicans in Italy. Louis Blanc described the situation forcefully: "The elections transferred political power from Paris to the Provinces, in other words from that part of France which was the most enlightened, to that part that was the least so. . . . The privileged classes were about to subdue the working classes by means of the peasants —the people by means of the people" (*Cambridge Modern History*, 11:103–8; Louis Blanc, *1848: Historical Revelations* [New York, 1971], pp. 382, 384).

721. To Richard F. Fuller

Rome
20th May, 1848.

My dear brother,

I have been hoping to receive a letter from you, before leaving Rome, but if it does not come today, I shall not hear, perhaps for a fortnight. Tomorrow I go into the mountains, and, in those remote country towns, shall be able to get my letters only at irregular intervals. I shall employ a friend to get them from the banker here and send them to me when he can.

My health is much revived by the spring, here as gloriously beautiful as the winter was dreary. We know nothing of spring in our country; here the soft and brilliant weather is unbroken, except now and then by a copious shower which keeps every thing fresh. The trees, the flowers, the bird-songs are in perfection. I have enjoyed greatly my walks in the Villas here whose grounds are of three or four miles in extent, and like free nature in the wood glades and still[n] paths, while they have an added charm in the music of their many fountains and the soft gleam here and there of sarcophagus or pillar. I have also been a few days at Albano, and explored its beautiful environs alone to much greater advantage than I could last year in the carriage

67

with my friends.¹ I have been to Frascati and Ostia with an English family who had a good carriage and were kindly intelligent people, who could not disturb the Roman landscape.²

Now I am going into the country, where I can live very cheaply, even keeping a servant of my own, without which I should not venture alone into the unknown and wilder regions. I do not travel this summer, though I have recd several good invitations for several reasons, a sufficient one is the agitated state of Europe. I hope the pure air of the mountains will strengthen me and that I shall be able to write, but we can only know by trying. I have been so disappointed in my Roman winter, I dare not plan and hop[e] decisively again. I have suffered much with Rome, and her enervating breath still paralyzes my body, but in soul I know and love her profoundly and do hope, my dear Richard, you will see her sometime. The expression "City of the Soul" does indeed designate her and her alone.

I earnestly hope you have vindicated your rights so far as to take lodgings in the country and come to the Office from them. This to you is indispensable. For the rest, let us wait till autumn. I sometimes am seized with a fit of longing for my native air and your faces, so that I think I *must* leave all and come home this autumn. But this is not my prevalent feeling. I shall certainly want no money before Septr, perhaps not so soon. Dr Gardner of Boston brings a little box for Ellen, Mr Hillard something for Mother. By Mr Page of Boston I wrote Mother a long letter; it will probably arrive soon after this. Write often as I hope to do to" you from my mountain solitude and let us believe that if there is a God, he must yet give us what we want and need.

Ever your friend and loving sister

MARGARET.

Write of Arthur what his position is.

ALS (MH: fMS Am 1086 [9:148]); MsC (MH: fMS Am 1086 [Works, 2:865–71]); MsCfr (MH: bMS Am 1280H [112d]). Published in part in *Memoirs*, 2:239–40. *Addressed:* To / Mr Richard F. Fuller / 6 State St. / Boston, Mass / U.S.A. *Postmark:* Boston Mass. Jun 14. *Endorsed:* F. S. M. / S. Margaret Fuller / 20. May 1848.

and still] and ⟨f⟩ still
to do to] to ↑ do to ↓

1. Albano lies on the Campagna, southeast of Rome. A popular summer resort known for beautiful surroundings, it was once a villa of the emperor Domitian. Between it and Frascati lies Castel Gandolfo, the pope's summer residence (Murray, p. 408).

2. Frascati sits at the lower part of the Tuscan hills, southeast of Rome. Like Albano, it was and is a popular resort town. The main tourist attraction is the Villa Aldo-

brandini, which dates from the sixteenth century (Murray, p. 402). Ostia, 15 miles from Rome almost at the mouth of the Tiber, is noted for extensive ruins of ancient and medieval Roman buildings (Murray, p. 442).

722.   To Costanza Arconati Visconti

[I] Rome 27 May 1848

This is my last day at Rome. I have been passing several days at Subiaco and Tivoli, and return again to the country to-morrow.[1] These scenes of natural beauty have filled my heart, and increased, if possible, my desire that the people who have this rich inheritance may no longer be deprived of its benefits by bad institutions.

The people of Subiaco are poor, though very industrious, and cultivating every inch of ground, with even English care and neatness;— so ignorant and uncultivated, while so finely and strongly made by Nature. May God grant now, to this people, what they need!

An illumination took place last night, in honor of the "Illustrious Gioberti."[2] He is received here with great triumph, his carriage followed with shouts of "*Viva Gioberti, morte ai Jesuiti!*" which must be pain to the many Jesuits, who, it is said, still linger here in disguise. His triumphs are shared by Mamiani and Orioli, self-trumpeted celebrities, self-constituted rulers of the Roman state,— men of straw, to my mind, whom the fire already kindled will burn into a handful of ashes.[3]

I sit in my obscure corner, and watch the progress of events. It is the position that pleases me best, and, I believe, the most favorable one. Everything confirms me in my radicalism; and, without any desire to hasten matters, indeed with surprise to see them rush so like a torrent, I seem to see them all tending to realize my own hopes.

[II] My health and spirits now much restored, I am beginning to set down some of my impressions. I am going into the mountains, hoping there to find pure, strengthening air, and tranquillity for so many days as to allow me to do something.

I: MsCfr (MH: MS Am 1280H [112d]); II: ELfr, from *Memoirs*, 2:240–41. Published in Chevigny, p. 454.

1. The ancient town of Tivoli (Tibur) antedates Rome. Its attractions include a temple of Vesta, the Villa d'Este, and a set of falls on the river Anio. Subiaco is noted for its scenery and for the monastery of Santa Scolastica (Murray, pp. 376–77, 386–87).

2. Vincenzo Gioberti was a philosopher-priest whose writing had encouraged Pius

to embark on his reforms and whose attack on the Jesuits was well received in the revolutionary days of 1848. Gioberti went to Rome supposedly to pay his respects to the pope, but he was widely suspected of working for the interests of Charles Albert. Gioberti was made a citizen of Rome and, as Fuller says, feted by the people, but both the republicans and the conservatives deeply distrusted his motives (Farini, 2:208). Fuller despised Gioberti because his goal of Italian confederation was a major challenge to Mazzini's ideal of Italian unity.

3. Terenzio Mamiani (1799–1885), conte della Rovere, a philosopher and teacher, had been exiled for his revolutionary activities in 1831. Pius had readmitted him in 1847 and then asked Mamiani to lead the government on 2 May. He resigned on 19 July, unable to resolve the impasse that Rome faced when Austria invaded Ferrara. Mamiani unsuccessfully sought to divorce the clerical and temporal offices of the papacy (Berkeley, 3:333–49). Francesco Orioli (1785–1856) was an archaelogical scholar, writer, and politician who had returned from exile in 1846 (*Dizionario enciclopedico*; Berkeley, 2:76, 104).

723. To Mary Rotch

Tivoli[n]
29th[n] May 1848.

Dear Aunt Mary

Just before leaving Rome I had the luck to get your letter of March 29th. It made me laugh much to see the desperate measures you were obliged to take in copying *my marks* for the address. In future address *Greene and Co, Paris*. I trust I have written this plainly.

The history of the notes that tarried so long is this. A gentleman offered to take every thing any thing straight to America for me. My postage bill is so great that I am sometimes tempted[n] to make use of private opportunities, though I find I always have cause to regret it. I spent ten days in preparing a parcel to go[n] by this person, who had promised to take it from Civita Vecchia I paid its passage there by Diligance, and supposed it gone when lo! comes a letter from the Gent. *regretting I had not sent it to Leghorn instead* as it was not convenient for him to call at C. V. as he had promised! Not being in a form to go by regular post, I was obliged to write to our Consul to take the parcel to pieces and send me back part of the notes and letters and the rest to America as he could. It was a most vexatious and expensive affair at the time, but to know that the letters lingered four months on the road adds gall to bitterness.

While I am thinking of money I will add one thing more. Dear Aunt Mary, I am rather sore at being continually[n] congratulated about my uncle's legacy. My friends are under some mistake, I fancy. My uncle died as he had lived, hard-hearted against me. For eleven years that I had struggled amid so many difficulties and ill health, he, far from aiding, wished to see me fall, because I acted against his opinion in giving my family advantages he thought, with his narrow views, useless, and defended my mother against his rude tyranny. When I came to Europe he, a little ashamed perhaps, said he "had thought of making me a present, but was short of cash just then." In his will he left me no legacy. *After the legacies were paid*, I came in with 62 other heirs for my share of what was left, less than a thousand dollars, of which I owed at that time near four hundred. Even this was certainly a blessing, because, but for its receipt, I must have returned last Autumn, deeply dissatisfied. But it makes me sad to think how easy it would have been for my uncle by a legacy of a few thousands to put[n] an end to the embarrassments and cares of which I have, perhaps, had my share, and without injury to others, for some to whom their legal fraction went were not in need. As it is I believe if his ghost knows any of my plans have been aided at all though him, it sighs at the thought.

It seems cruel that such people should jog on undisturbed through life and such as Andrew Robeson who was disposed to make a kindly liberal use of his money be deprived of it, but the summing up of these accounts lies elsewhere.[1] I hope that sweet-faced Mrs Tucker does not suffer in these changes.[2]

I was very glad to get some exact news of your health. I cannot help being very anxious about it sometimes. You and my mother are the only two of my home possessions that seem to me held by a frail tenure, and when I plan to stay away, I feel always desirous to know that you are both as well as when I left. So write now and then, once in four or five months at least, only not such a letter as to hurt or fatigue yourself.

You must always love me whatever I do. [I] depend on that. And this thought puts m[e] in [m]ind to ask whether you are not aware that I am as great an Associationist as W. Channing himself, that is to say as firm a believer that the next form society will take in remedy of the dreadful ills that now consume[n] it will be voluntary association in small communities.[3] The present forms are become unwieldly. But what I think on this subject I hope to have force and time to explain in print. Not in the Tribune; you have, probably, seen my last letter to that Journal.[4] I am now hoping, in the silence and retirement of the country to write more at length on the subjects that have engaged my attention for some time back. But who knows? The disturbances of the times, or an unfavorable state of health may mar my purpose as has often happened before.

You will have seen my account of the measures by which the Pope has lost all substantial influence in Italy and Europe.[5] There is something fatal in a priestly environment: he remained a layman to so late an age one might have hoped he would not get stupified by the incense of the church, but remember how things looked beneath the open heavens. But the influence of the crafty priests that surrounded him was unhappily too much for his strength. However God has blessed his good intent and a work is begun which his failure cannot check.

I hear often from Waldo; he sees much, learns much always but loves not Europe. There is no danger of the idle intimations of other minds altering his course more than of the moving a star. He knows himself and his vocation.

Goodbye, dear Aunt Mary, if I live, you will always hear from me now and then. Give my love to Maria Rotch Tell her there is not a Jesuit in Italy that would venture to give so plausible a version of Catholicism as Coolidge Shaw: he is quite sincere, but not to be trusted as a thinker.[6] Love to Mary.[7] Best wishes ever for the continuance of peace and the increase of joy to both from

MARGARET.

ALS (MH: fMS Am 1086 [9:145]); MsC (MH: fMS Am 1086 [Works, 1:63–71]); MsCfr (MH: bMS Am 1280 [111, p. 200]). Published in part in *JMN*, 11:490. *Addressed:* Miss Mary Rotch / New Bedford, Mass / U.S.A. *Postmark:* Boston 12 Jul.

Mary Rotch, a member of a wealthy and powerful New Bedford Quaker family, had a long friendship with both Fuller and Emerson.

Tivoli] ⟨Rieti⟩ Tivoli
29th] ⟨3⟩ 29th
sometimes tempted] sometimes ⟨a⟩ tempted
parcel to go] parcel ↑ to go ↓
being continually] being ↑ continually ↓
to put] to ⟨b⟩ put
now consume] now ⟨perva⟩ ↑ consume ↓

1. Andrew Robeson (1787–1862) was a wealthy New Bedford businessman. He married Anna Rodman (1787–1848), Mary Rotch's niece (Bullard, *Rotches*, pp. 493–94).
2. Martha Robeson (1820–52), daughter of Andrew and Anna Rodman Robeson, married Alanson Tucker of New Bedford in 1841 (Bullard, *Rotches*, p. 494).
3. That is, Fuller and Channing were attracted to the writings of Charles Fourier, the French socialist.
4. Because of her pregnancy, Fuller suspended her letters to the *Tribune* until early in 1849.
5. Fuller wrote of the pope: "The loss of Pius IX is for the moment a great one. His name had real moral weight, was a trumpet appeal to sentiment. It is not the same with any man that is left" (*New-York Daily Tribune*, 15 June 1848).
6. Joseph Coolidge Shaw, Frank Shaw's brother, was a Roman Catholic priest who was studying theology in Rome.
7. Mary Gifford, Mary Rotch's companion.

724. To Costanza Arconati Visconti

[I] 22 June 1848

I write such a great number of letters, having not less than a hundred correspondents, that it seems, every day as if I had just written to each. There is no one, surely, this side of the salt sea, with whom I wish more to keep up the interchange of thought than with you.

I believe, if you could know my heart as God knows it, and see the causes that regulate my conduct, you would always love me. But already, in absence, I have lost, for the present, some of those who were dear to me, by failure of letters, or false report. After sorrowing much about a falsehood told me of a dearest friend, I found his letter at Torlonia's, which had been there ten months, and, duly received, would have made all right.[1] There is something fatal in my destiny about correspondence. [II] The loss of two successive letters from the man on earth I have most loved, broke our relation at the time it might have become permanent.

[III] But I will say no more of this; only the loss of that letter to you, at such an unfortunate time,— just when I most wished to seem the loving and grateful friend I was,— made me fear it might be my destiny to lose you too. But if any cross event shall do me this ill turn on earth, we shall meet again in that clear state of intelligence which men call heaven.

I see by the journals that you have not lost Montanelli. That noble mind is still spared to Italy.[2] The Pope's heart is incapable of treason; but he has fallen short of the office fate assigned him.[3]

I am no bigoted Republican, yet I think that form of government will eventually pervade the civilized world.[4] Italy may not be ripe for it yet, but I doubt if she finds peace earlier; and this hasty annexation of Lombardy to the crown of Sardinia seems, to me, as well as I can judge, an act unworthy and unwise.[5] Base, indeed, the monarch, if it was needed, and weak no less than base; for he was already too far engaged in the Italian cause to retire with honor or wisdom.

I am here, in a lonely mountain home, writing the narrative of my European experience. To this I devote great part of the day. Three or four hours I pass in the open air, on donkey or on foot. When I have exhausted this spot, perhaps I shall try another. Apply as I may, it will take three months, at least, to finish my book.[6] It grows upon me.

I: ELfr, from *Memoirs*, 2:242; II: MsCfr (MH: bMS Am 1280 [111, p. 13]); III: ELfr, from *Memoirs*, 2:242–43. Published in part in *JMN*, 11:460–61.

1. Giovanni Torlonia (1754–1829) established a bank in Rome in 1814. In 1848 his son, Prince Alessandro Torlonia (1800–1886), was the object of public resentment for his conduct of the bank (*Enciclopedia italiana*; *New-York Daily Tribune*, 13 March 1848).

2. Giuseppe Montanelli (1813–62) was a Florentine writer and teacher. In May he had commanded a battalion of volunteers at the battle of Curtatone, where he was wounded. In June an unfounded rumor of his death caused widespread concern in Florence (*Dizionario enciclopedico*: Berkeley, pp. 300–301).

3. In her letter of 3 June (MH), Arconati Visconti said that the republicans "are ungrateful to Pius IX because they need him no longer, for the rest, he has spoken in his address as he has always spoken when they have left him free to do so. Only they interpreted his words to suit themselves. His reign is over, but he is neither a traitor, nor an apostate."

4. Fuller echoes her friend, who had written in her letter: "I must tell you at once, that if I am opposed to an Italian republic, it is not from any aristocratic prejudice, far from me be such meanness. I am convinced that the republic would cause still greater disunion, and irremediable, between the different elements which in Italy are so hardly held together. . . . We shall be again precipitated into the abyss, by the hand of those who pretend to be our liberators."

5. Mazzini was in Milan, where he opposed the provisional government, which was sympathetic to Charles Albert. They wanted an alliance with Piedmont, while Mazzini worked for a republic that was federated, not fused with the kindgom of Piedmont-Sardinia. The political debate paralyzed the Milanese, leaving the war completely to Charles Albert. Late in May a plebiscite in Milan resulted in an overwhelming vote for fusion. Piedmont and Milan signed an agreement on 13 June; when they were joined by Parma (on 16 June), Modena (on the 21st), and Venice (on 4 July), the kingdom of Northern Italy was established. On 9 August, however, when the Salasco treaty ended the war with Austria's complete triumph, the new kingdom ceased to exist (Berkeley, pp. 324–28). Fuller's suspicion was based on her contempt for Charles Albert.

6. Fuller's manuscript history of the Italian revolutions was lost in the wreck of the *Elizabeth* in 1850.

725. To Emelyn Story

22nd June 1848

My dear Emelyn,

I dont send to Rome very often for my letters, so your first and Lizzie Cranch's, and your second of the 15th June came near together; How enchanting the description both give. I should have been most happy to see thus Naples and Sorrento, and I should have loved your society, my friends.

But as far as regards my book, I believe I chose for the best; for it advances rapidly now. I write on it all day except when engaged in open air. I see no one but Italian Contadines, and study nothing that can distract me. Even thus I think it will take three months to write out what has passed in my head and before my eyes for two years. It is true that as I write, it don't seem worth making such a fuss about, but one must persist to get anything done in this dissipated world. It is a thousand pities, I could not do it in Winter, but I could not and there is an end. *É il mie destine*, as say the Italians. Had I time I would describe in my turn some of the beautiful things I have seen, but my man starts for Rome in an hour, and if I do not send now, I may not have a good chance for 10 days. I shall write again and also the Cranches. I am rejoiced all is well and a little girl; just what they wished. But why Leonora? Not Burger's Leonora? Not Miss Barrett's? Give them my love.[1]

How grieved I am, dear Emelyn, to hear of the sad news! Poor Mary! There was always something melancholy in her eyes; and it *is* sad to go away and leave little children; nothing, nothing can make good the place of a mother. Since William must suffer this; at least it is good to be in that still beautiful place; grief becomes hallowed so and clustered with thoughts as they cannot amid the press of glassy eyes in a city![2]

I saw Dr. Loring several times and he told me many trifles of friends at home.[3] He was very happy in his travelling but much disappointed not to see you. He had for you Lowell's poems.[4] He goes back in Septr.

A letter from U. S. mentions Cary as living this summer at Staten Island, and very happy. I hear no news of importance from home. From my family no letter for two months.

This day last year I was at Arezzo in Vasari's house, still full of his paintings, where I saw the procession; before it boys strewed the street with golden blossoms of the broom, it seemed to walk on light.[5] Neither year do I see this greatest show of Rome, but I was sated with the shows of Rome. I enjoy exceedingly the mountain views and silence; the pure air has much restored my strength already. I am entirely another from what I was in Rome, and should be much better worth your seeing. I am much pleased with your affectionate wish to see me, my dear Emelyn, and that all your party sympathize; dont let it die, and if I do not come this summer, perhaps I may join you in some plan for the Autumn. If anything should occur to change my plans for the summer, I know how to come to you, if you stay at Naples. But write again by and by to say what you are like to do and of all that concerns you.

Send the letters to Hooker, surely, he can also send you your valise.[6] A kiss to dear Edie and Josey the comforter. Please remember me affectionately to William and Uncle Tom.[7] My best wishes to Katy. Ever Yours

M. F.

MsC (MB: Ms. Am. 1450 [147]).

1. Leonora Cranch was named for Leonora d'Este, the princess to whom Tasso dedicated his poems. On the evening she was born, Vesuvius was erupting (Scott, *Cranch*, p. 145). Gottfried August Bürger (1747–94) published a popular ballad, *Lenore*, in 1774; it was translated by Walter Scott (*OCGL*).

2. Mary Oliver Story (1817–48), William Wetmore Story's sister, married George Ticknor Curtis in 1844. They had two children, Joseph Story Curtis (b. 23 July 1845) and George William Curtis, Jr. (1847–88) (CVR; Harvard archives; Perley Derby, "Elisha Story of Boston and Some of His Descendants," *Essex Institute Historical Collections* 51 [1915]; 49).

3. Probably George Bailey Loring (1817–91), surgeon of the Marine Hospital at Chelsea, Massachusetts. He graduated from Harvard in 1838 and from its medical school in 1842. Both he and Emerson were visiting Europe at this time (Charles Henry Pope and Katharine P. Loring, *Loring Genealogy* [Cambridge, 1917], p. 193; *DAB*).

4. James Russell Lowell, *Poems: Second Series* (Boston, 1848), had been published in late December 1847 (Luther Livingston, *A Bibliography of the First Editions . . . of James Russell Lowell* [New York, 1914], p. 25).

5. Giorgio Vasari (1511–74) bought a house in his native Arezzo in 1540. It survives intact with his frescoes on the walls and ceiling (T. S. R. Boase, *Giorgio Vasari: The Man and the Book* [Washington, D.C., 1979], p. 168).

6. James Clinton Hooker (1818–94), who was born in Vermont, became associated with the banking firm of Maquay, Packenham in Rome. In 1856 he married Elizabeth Temple Winthrop (Edward Hooker, *The Descendants of Rev. Thomas Hooker* [Rochester, 1909], p. 202).

7. Thomas Wetmore (1794–1860), William Story's uncle, was traveling with the Storys. Wetmore graduated from Harvard in 1814 and became a lawyer (Hudson, *Browning*, p. 363).

726.   To Charles King Newcomb

22d June 48

My dear Charles,

It was a very pleasing surprize this morng to see your hand writing. You speak of you and your Mother having written, but I have never recd any letter from either, nor any answer to the questions I have asked our mutual friends about you.[1] I remember just about the time you wrote 15th May, I sent a message to your Mother in a letter written to America and thought at the same time I wish I could know about Charles now.

You ask if I never feel home-sickness. I have at times fits of deep longing to see persons and objects in America. At times my ear^n and eye grow weary of the sound of a foreign tongue, and the features of a foreign race. But then my affections and thoughts have become greatly interested in some things here, and I know if I once go to the U. S. I can never come back.

Then you know, dear Charles, *I* have no "home," no peaceful roof to which I can return and repose in the love of my kindred from the friction of care and the world. My Mother has love enough and would gladly prepare me such an one, but I know she has not money. Returning to the U. S. seems return to a life of fatigue, to which I feel quite unequal, while I leave behind many objects in whose greatness and beauty I am able for a time to forget these things. Thus I prize the present moment and get what I can from it. I may be obliged to return ere long, for nothing in outward life favors my plans, nor do any letters bring any but bad news.

At present my outward environment is very beautiful. I am in the midst of a theatre of mountains, some of them crowned with snow, all of very noble shapes. Along[n] three sides run bridle paths, fringed with olive and almond groves and vineyards; here and there gleams a church or shrine. Through the valley glides a little stream, along its banks here and there little farm houses; vegetation is most luxuriant in this valley. This town is on a slope of one of the hills, it is a little place, much ruined, having been once a baronial residence, the houses of these barons are gone to decay; there are churches now unused, with faded frescoes over the arched portals, and the open belfry and stone wheel-window that are so beautiful. Out of town sweet little paths lead away through the fields to Convents, one of Passionists, another of Capuchins, both seem better than the monks found near great cities; it looks very peaceful to see their drape[d] forms pacing up the hills, and they have a healthy red in the cheek, unlike the vicious sallowness of monks of Rome. They get some life from their gardens and birds, I suppose. In the churches still open are pictures, not by great masters, but sweetly domestic, which please me much. There is one of the Virgin offering the nipple to the child Jesus; his little hand is on her breast, but he only plays and turns away; others of Santa Anna teaching the Virgin, a sweet girl of ten years old,[n] with long curling auburn hair to read, the Virgin leans on her mother's lap; her hair curls on the book. There is another of the Marriage of the Virgin, a beautiful young man, one of three suitors, and like her as if her cousin, looks sadly on while she gives her hand to Joseph. There is often sweet music in these churches, they are dresst with fresh flowers, and the mountain breeze sweeps through them so freely, they do not smell too strong of incense.

Here I live with a lively Italian woman who makes me broth of turnips and gets my clothes washed in the stream. I shall stay here sometime, if the beautiful solitude continue to please. The country people say "Povera, sola, soletta," poor one, alone, all alone![n] the saints keep her," as I pass. They think me some stricken deer to stay so apart from the herd. But the cities are only 3 days off, if I wish to go, full of wars and the rumors of wars and all sorts of excitements,[2] which have proved beyond my strength to share for the present. Good bye, dear Charles. I have written little, you know it is but little one can write in a letter. Address always Greene and Co. they will forward the letter. My love to your Mother and sisters.[3] I was pleased you mentioned Cary.[4] I wish she would write

Ever yours

MARGARET.

ALS (MB: Ms. Am. 1450 [124]). Published in part in *Memoirs*, 2:294–95. *Addressed:* Charles King Newcomb / Providence, Rhode Island / U.S.A. *Postmark:* New York 3 Aug. *Endorsed:* Recd Aug 7th.

Charles King Newcomb had lived at Brook Farm. A contributor to the *Dial*, he never fulfilled the literary promise that Fuller thought he had.

my ear] my ⟨eye⟩ ear
shapes. Along] shapes. ⟨a⟩ Along
years old,] years ⟨a⟩ old,
soletta," poor one, alone, all alone!] soletta," ↑ poor one, alone, all alone! ↓

1. Newcomb's mother was Rhoda Mardenbrough Newcomb, with whom Fuller had a sometimes stormy friendship.
2. Matt. 24:6 and Mark 13:7.
3. The Newcomb daughters living at home at this time were Elizabeth and Charlotte.
4. In his letter of 15 May (MH), Newcomb said he had visited the Tappans on Staten Island and that Caroline still wore Fuller's emerald ring.

727. To Giovanni Angelo Ossoli

Martedi 27th [juigno] 48

Mio Caro,

Anche oggi non viene niente, adesso due settimane che non ricevo i giornali, da te viene nulla righa in risposta a mie due ultime. Non[n] so niente delle cose chi m'interessan; mi sento tutta sola, imprigionata, troppo infelice

Credo bene che non è tuo defetto; — che tu hai scritto o inviato, ma non mi fa di bene, come per qualche ragione non ricevo.

Non mancate venire il Sabato; io morro[n] esser lasciato cosi Fa un gran calore qui; non piove, e io non prendo piu piacer sortire. Come mia testa era molto sturbata, ho fatta cavare sangue. Son debole e soffro nel petto, altro non sto male.

Un parte delle truppe, de questi bimbini chi son ritornati da Lombardia sta nel Castello, uno dei loro Ufficiali in questa locanda, sovente[n] molti di loro vengon qui pel pranzo, fan grande romore.

Addio, non ho coraggio dire niente più. Il giorno che tu vieni, si non hai già mie lettere dalla Banca invia questa e cercale. Dio ti benedica mio amico,

Tuesday 27th [June] 48

My dear,

Also today I received nothing, now for two weeks I have not received any papers, nor have I heard from you in reply to my last two letters. I know nothing about the things that I am interested in; I feel lonely, imprisoned, too unhappy.

I am sure it is not your fault;—certainly you have written and sent them, but I am sorry since for some reason I do not receive anything.

Do not fail to come on Saturday; I will die if left so It is very hot here; it does not rain and I do not like to go out anymore. As I suffered from a terrible headache, I had a bloodletting. I am weak and suffer in my chest, the rest is not bad.

A part of the troops of these infants who have come back from Lombardia are living in the castle, one of their officers is often in this inn, many of them come here for lunch, they make a lot of noise.

Good bye, I have no more spirit to tell you more. The day that you come, if you have not yet gotten my letters from the bank, send this one and look for them. God bless you, my friend.

AL (MH: fMS Am 1086 [9:181]); MsC in English (MH: fMS Am 1086 [Works, 2:97−99]). *Addressed:* Il Nobil Uomo / Sige mse Gio. Angiolo Ossoli. / Roma. *Postmark:* Rieti.

Non] ⟨In⟩ Non
io morro] io morr⟨?⟩o
locanda, sovente] locanda, ↑ sovente ↓

728. To Giovanni Angelo Ossoli

Aquila
Giugno 29, Giovedi. [1848]

Ieri, mio caro, ricevevo dalla posta molti giornali, Epoca al 23 questo mese, e quelli dieci di Milano. Era un Epoca del 10, qui aveva dentro una tua lettrina, suppongo in tutt, venti giornali Eran marcati *Citta Ducale*, io non so si son stati la tutto questo tempo o altra parte Non avevo l'idea cercarli" alla Posta, avendo ricevuto tutte i altri del libraio.

È stato crudele per me non ricevere quando stavo sicuro che tu hai inviato, ma adesso e passato; fido vederti la domenica o lunedi; allora combinerem in altra maniera.

Adesso fa una settimana che non ricevo tue nove, ma son risoluta non sturbarmi più, fidando vederti subito. Quanto desidero vederti una volta più al mio lato, e impossibile dire.

Non piove; fa un calore terribile, mi dispiace per te che" tua visita, tuo viaggio sarebbero si faticosi. Ma alfine bisogna parlare" un poco; sara molto piacer in tutto evento.

Le donne voglion molto per te cercare si stan alla Posta di Roma lettere" per *Giuditta o Maria*" *Bonanni*. Giuditta, poverina, spera ricever denaro che qualche persona a promesso chi sta indebitato a lei, a avuta sogno che questo denaro stava in posta.

Io voglio, si tu hai commodo, per ti cercarmi da *Soave*, Piazza di Spagna, una bottiglia di suo *ottima* acqua di Cologne prezzo 5 paoli.

Addio, tutto caro, ti riceve[r]o con grandissimo piacer. Si solamente era possibile venire più vicino a ti, perche questo sito altro che per buon aria e" sicurezza non mi piace niente

Addio—

Aquila
June 29, Thursday [1848]

Yesterday, my dear, I received many newspapers in the mail, Epoca up to the 23 of this month, and those ten from Milan. It was an Epoca of the 10, which contained a dear letter of yours, I suppose twenty newspapers altogether They were postmarked *Citta Ducale*, I don't know if they have been there all this time or somewhere else I had no idea to look for them at the postoffice, since I had received all the others from the bookstore.

It has been cruel for me not to receive anything when I was sure that you had sent, but now it is over; I trust I will see you on Sunday or Monday; then we will arrange things in a different manner.

Now it is a week since I received your news, but I am determined not to worry anymore, trusting to see you soon. How much I wish to see you once again at my side, it is impossible to say.

It doesn't rain; it is terribly hot, I am sorry that your visit, your journey should be so fatiguing. But we need finally to talk a little; in any case it will give us much pleasure.

The women want very much for you to find out whether at the postoffice in Rome there are any letters for *Giuditta or Maria Bonanni.* Giuditta, poor thing, hopes to receive some money that a person owes her and has promised to return, and she had a dream that this money was at the postoffice.

If it is not inconvenient to you, I want you to get me at Soave's, Piazza di Spagna, a bottle of their excellent Cologne price 5 paoli.

Goodbye, my dear, I will receive you with the greatest pleasure. If only it was possible to come closer to you for I don't like this place at all except for the good air and its safety

Goodbye

AL (MH: fMS Am 1086 [9:208]); MsC in English (MH: fMS Am 1086 [Works, 2:99–103]). Published in part in *Memoirs*, 2:295. *Addressed:* Il Nobil Uomo / Sigr Mse Gio. Angiolo Ossoli / Roma. *Postmark:* Rieti.

l'idea cercarli] l'idea c⟨?⟩ercarli
te che] te ⟨?⟩ che
bisogna parlare] bisogna ⟨?⟩ parlare
Roma lettere] Roma ↑ lettere ↓
Giuditta o Maria] Giuditta ⟨e⟩ o Maria
aria e] aria ⟨i⟩ e

729.   To Richard F. Fuller

1 July 1848

Italy is as beautiful as even I hoped, and I should wish to stay here several years, if I had a moderate fixed income. One wants but little money here, and can have with it many of the noblest enjoyments. I should have been very glad if fate would allow me a few years of congenial life, at the end of not a few of struggle and suffering. But I do not hope it; my fate will be the same to the close,—beautiful gifts shown, and then withdrawn, or offered on conditions that make acceptance impossible.

ELfr, from *Memoirs*, 2:241–42.

730. To Richard F. Fuller

Mountains of Central Italy
3d July, 1848

My dear Richard,

It pains me to be always troubling you about money, and I have waited till the last moment, hoping it would not be necessary. But now in the trouble I am, it seems as if I could rely on no friend, unless yourself.

I wrote to you before leaving Rome that I should need no more money from you before the autumn. This was on the strength of a letter from Mr Greeley, assuring me that he had made the necessary arrangements for me to receive a remittance through Baring and Brothers.[1] His letter was dated 8th April.[n] No letter of exchange coming from them, I wrote to them to ask for it, and the heat becoming excessive, I ventured to go away, without having received their answer, desiring it should be forwarded to me.

It arrived some three weeks since, and imagine my pain, on being assured date *26th May*, that they had recd no funds for me, but adding that *when they did* they would forward a credit instantly. I wrote to Mr Greeley, to inquire a[n]d show what a state I was left in. Then I waited hoping the credit[n] would yet arrive.

Now *3d July*, it has not, and I dare no longer trust to him alone. I have money for four or five weeks, but, if no more come by the end of that time, shall be obliged to run into debt he[re] and cannot leave here till it comes.[2]

I do not expect to wish to go away before Septr, (only if I did wish[n] in case of difficulties through the war, I could not) By that time I can hear from you. And I wish you to send me money. I will not say *how much*, as I write before you expected, *but what you conveniently can*, by a credi[t t]hrough *Baring and Brothers* directing them to send it to me, *S. M. Fuller, care Maquay, Pakenham and Co* Rome, but writing to me yourself that it is forwarded, and send yr letter[n] to care *Greene and Co, Paris*.

I am writing a book and, if my health were not so uncertain, should say it will be finished by Septr.

If my affairs do not go better I shall return home next Spring. I will not stay here to trouble my friends too much. It is true I had plans I should have liked to carry out, but that is not my destiny.

Dear Richard, I hope if we do meet again, there may be some good hours, I want very much to hear from you. It troubles me much to think of what you may be having to endure in that ungenial connexion which has kept its promise so ill. But another summer it will not be so.

4th July "Independence"! "I'm independent" as Arthur shouted and waved his flag when Eugene cruelly stopped him and made him come in to learn his lesson!

It is so now with these poor Italians whose hopes have been so boiling and who have just received such cruel blows in consequence of the treachery of the King of Naples.[3]

Yet they feel very resolute, and if there be a God who takes a paternal interest in human affairs, something might be hoped from him it would seem.

I send to Rome this week for my letters warmly hoping one from you. My next shall contain something written from our *real* life. Has dear Mother returned yet? Ever yours

M.

ALS (MH:fMS Am 1086 [9:149]); MsCfr (MH: fMS Am 1086 [Works, 2:817–23]). *Addressed:* Mr R. F. Fuller / 6 State St. Boston, Mass / U.S.A. *Postmark:* Boston Mass Aug 14. *Endorsed:* Miss Margaret Fuller / 3 & 4. July 1848.

His letter was dated 8th April.] ↑ His letter was dated 8th April. ↓
the credit] the ⟨exchange⟩ ↑ credit ↓
(only if I did wish] (only ↑ if I did wish ↓
forwarded, and send yr letter] forwarded, ↑ and send yr letter ↓

1. In a letter of 4 April (MH), Greeley promised Fuller $600: "$100 from the office" and $500 as a personal loan. He glumly described his finances as "this chief misery of life." He told Fuller that he had "been hard at work to raise the money for you to go by the steamship from Boston to-morrow. I have just accomplished it, but it has nearly broken my back. I regularly spend all the money I can get and as fast as I can get it; but about once in two years I get behind a long way, through endorsements, etc. and have to resort to some extraordinary course to extricate myself." He went on to say that he had sold a part interest in the *Tribune* "and devoted the proceeds to buying off most of my embarrassments, reserving $3,000 for Mrs. Greeley, having promised her so much to buy a house and piece of ground with."

2. The combined difficulties of foreign exchange, poor mail service, and Greeley's habits created confusion and hard feelings. He wrote her on 27 June (MH) to reimburse her for her postage and to pay extra for some of her letters that had been unusually lengthy: "I want the account so adjusted that you shall be entirely satisfied. What we pay you by agreement ($10 per letter) is just twice what we pay for any other European Correspondence, but we are very well aware that the quality justifies this." Then on 29 July he heatedly wrote her: "It seems to me a clear case of infatuation that you, after requesting me to send you money to one especial place, should send for it and write about it to almost every body else, but not at all to the very place where you told me to send it, and where I accordingly *did* send it at the time I said I would, and whence I had assurance of its receipt months ago" (MH). He went on to explain that he had sent the $600 by way of Baring Brothers in London to Greene & Co. in Paris. Fuller apparently wanted the money sent to Maquay, Packenham. Greeley probably came close to the truth when he said, "I have to imagine a medley of bad luck and hallucination to account for this imbroglio."

3. Ferdinand II (1810–59), the Bourbon monarch of the Kingdom of the Two Sicilies was the most repressive of the Italian heads of state. Under pressure, the king had granted a constitution on 29 January. One provision called for a parliament to sit on 15 May. As the day approached, Ferdinand and the opposition leaders struggled over an oath to the new constitution. Violence erupted between the army and the people; the army brutally attacked the barricades and then pillaged Naples. Then, on 18 May, Ferdinand recalled his troops from the War against Austria. Luigi Farini, who was much more conservative than Fuller, termed the recall "the greatest, and perhaps the only effective cause of our misfortunes, and of the Austrian victory, in so far as the human mind can judge." In her *Tribune* dispatch, Fuller called it "the first great calamity of the war" (Berkeley, pp. 271–86; King, *Italian Unity*, 1:239–40; Farini, 2:179; *New-York Daily Tribune*, 19 January 1849).

731. To Giovanni Angelo Ossoli

Sabato, 8 luglio, [1848]

tua lettrina, caro, è venuta questa mattina. Mi consola, come sempre, ricevere tue nuove. Ma non stai "tristissimo" non divieni si magro. Bisogna sperare che il destino s'annoiera di perseguitare alfine.

Tu sai bene si mai è possibile per me aprire per te qualche [*illegible*], lo faro. Adesso tutto pare oscuro, ma il sole può venire ancora.

Tua visita, benchè troppa corta, mi ha fatta di bene, sto più tranquilla, altro che soffrendo sovente negli denti. La levatrice dice che bisogna aver pazienza e aspettar adesso soffrire[n] questo, che e cosa commune a questo tempo. Sentire queste donne, bisogna credere che questa condizione è davvero un martirio.

M'incresceva che non potevi stare qui il giovedi. Era la festa di questa cattiva regina che diceva 15 Maggio "questo è il più bello giorno di mia vita"—Le truppe facevan grande mostro; le bande suonavan a vicenda; la sera era bellissima musica per due ore.

I soldati han detto giù che aspettan partire subito.

Il povero malatto moriva e era sepolto giovedi. Il prete e Giuditta stavan con lui una grande part[e] della notte. Diceva sovente "sempre, sempre aspetto miei amici, ma nessuno viene mai." A voluto sempre prendere il mano di Giuditta, ella ha fatta suo possibile per lui e era, soppongo, la sola persona che piangeva sua morte; questa donna a b[u]on cuore, e, si[n] p[   ] felice nelle circostan[ze] di sua vita, sarebbe stata eccellente. Addio, tutto caro, ti bacio bene. Spero ricever altre righe da ti il Martedi;—il Giovedi io anche scrivero una altra volta.

Addio, con affetto grande, tua

Saturday, 8 July, [1848]

Your dear letter arrived this morning, my dear. As always, it is a comfort for me to receive your news. But do not be "very sad," do not become so thin. We must hope that destiny will get tired of persecuting us.

You know very well that if it would be possible for me to open for you some [*illegible*], I would do it. Now everything seems dark, but the sunshine can come again.

Your visit, although much too short, did me good. I am more relaxed, but suffer often in my teeth. The midwife says that we must have patience and suffer this, as it is not unusual at this time. According to these women, one must think that this condition is really a martyrdom.

I am sorry that you could not be here Thursday. It was the feast of this bad Queen, who said of May 15th "this is the best day of my life"— The troops made a great show; the bands played in turn; in the evening there was very beautiful music for two hours.

The soldiers said that they are expecting to leave soon.

The poor sick man died and was buried on Thursday. The priest and Giuditta remained with him for most of the night. He often said "I always, always wait for my friends but nobody comes." He always wanted to take Giuditta's hand, she did her possible for him, and was, I suppose, the only person who cried for his death; this woman has a good heart and if [   ] happy in the circumstances of her life, she would have been excellent.

Good bye, my dear, I kiss you, I hope to receive other lines from you on Tuesday; I will write to you another time on Thursday.

Good bye, with great affection, your

AL (MH: fMS Am 1086 [9:198]); MsC in English (MH: fMS Am 1086 [Works, 1:107–11]). *Addressed:* Il Nobi[   ]mo / Sige Mse Gio. Angiolo Ossoli / Roma. *Postmark:* Rieti.

adesso soffrire] adesso soffri⟨e⟩re
e, si] e, ↑si↓

732. To Ralph Waldo Emerson

[I] Rieti, [Tivoli] 11 July 1848

Once I had resolution to face my difficulties myself, and try to give only what was pleasant to others; but now that my courage has fairly given way, and the fatigue of life is beyond my strength, I do not prize myself, or expect others to prize me.

Some years ago, I thought you very unjust, because you did not lend full faith to my spiritual experiences; but I see you were quite right. I thought I had tasted of the true elixir, and that the want of daily bread, on the pangs of imprisonment, would never make me a complaining beggar. A widow, I expected still to have the cruse full for others.[1] Those were glorious hours, and angels certainly visited me; but there must have been too much earth,—too much taint of weakness and folly, so that baptism did not suffice. I know now those same things, but at present they are words, not living spells.

[II] I hear at this moment the clock of the church del Purgatorio telling noon in this mountain solitude. Snow yet lingers on these mountain tops, after 40 days of hottest sunshine last night broken by a few clouds prefatory to a thunderstorm this morning. It has been so hot that even the peasant in the field, says *non posso piu resistere,* and slumbers in the shade rather than sun. I love to see their patriarchial ways of guarding the sheep, and tilling the fields. They are a simple race, remote from the corruptions of foreign travel, they do not ask for money, but smile upon and bless me as I pass for the Italians love me; they say, I am so *simpatica*. I never see any English or Americans, and now think wholly in Italian Only the surgeon who bled me the other day was proud to speak a little French, which he had learnt at Tunis! The ignorance of this people is amazing. I am to them a divine visitant, and instructive Ceres telling them wonderful tales of foreign customs and even legends of their own saints They are people whom I could love and live with. Bread and grapes among them would suffice me, but I have no way of earning these from their rich soil.

I: ELfr, from *Memoirs*, 2:243–44; II: MsCfr (MH: bMS Am 1280 [111, pp. 37–39]). Published in part in *JMN*, 11:465–66.

1. Elijah and the widow of Zarephath, I Kings 17:10–16.

733. To Giovanni Angelo Ossoli

Aquila
13 luglio 48

Martedi, caro, ho ricevuta tua lettera, colle altre dalla Banca, anche tutti i Giornali per la Posta.

Ma perche non scrivi un poco di te, non mi dici niente, e questo mi fa paura che stai molto triste e sturbato Eran lettere di mia famiglia; questi stan bene, ma mi han fatti piangere molto, pregan[do m]io ritorno. Non era lettera col denaro e adesso sarebbe bene per te [   ] era io posso avere i 200 franchi, sul lettera di *Greene & Co. Parigi.* Si non posso, si non ricevo l'a[l]tro cambio, fra pochi giorni, scriverò a qualche amico.

S'arrivan più soldati, anche si dice troppo son venuti in Citta Ducale. Sto incerta si non saro pregata fuggire da qui, e venire in Rieti. Dimando tutti i giorni ma sento niente di certo.

Queste lettere fami il piacer[e] rimettere alla posta e pagare al frontiera. Anche ritirale mie lettere dalla banca e inviate subito, spero ancora ricevere il cambio," eglin dicen ch'era inviato.

Si vedi l'Ungherese domandi si *Michele Kovacy*[?] sta ancora in Roma o e partito perla patria, la povera Giuditta soffre che non riceve lettere da lui. È stato qui molta pioggia, adesso la campagna e rinfrescata e bella. Io non sto male, altro che i denti ancora mi tormentan. Quanto voglio abbracciarti, mio caro e buono. Prego sovente per ti adesso che non posso altro e son sempre tua affezionata

Aquila
13 July 48

On Tuesday, my dear, I received through the post your letter, with the others from the bank, and also all the newspapers.

But why do you not write something about yourself, you do not tell me anything, and I am afraid you are very sad and worried. There were letters from my family; they are well, but they made me cry very much begging for my return. There was no letter with the money and now it would be good for you [   ] I can have the 200 francs, on the letter of *Greene & Co. Paris.* If I cannot, if I do not receive the other exchange, in a few days, I will write to some friend.

More soldiers are coming, also it is said that troops have arrived in Citta Ducale. I do not know if I will be asked to flee from here and come to Rieti. I ask every day but so far I hear nothing certain.

Please mail at the post these letters and pay at the frontier. Also collect my letters from the bank and send them at once, I still hope to receive the exchange, they say that it was already sent.

If you see the Hungarian, ask if *Michele Kovacy*[?] still lives in Rome or if he has left for his own country. The poor Giuditta suffers because she does not receive letters from him. There was a lot of rain here, now the country is refreshed and beautiful. I am not so bad, only that the teeth still torment me. How much I want to embrace you, my dear and good. I often pray for you, now that I cannot do more, and am always your affectionate

AL (MH: fMS Am 1086 [9:178]); MsC in English (MH: fMS Am 1086 [Works, 2:103–5]). English copy published in part in *Memoirs*, 2:295. *Addressed:* Il Nobil Uomo / Sige Mse Gio. Angiolo Ossoli / Roma. *Postmark:* Rieti.

il cambio,] il cam⟨?⟩bio,

734. To Giovanni Angelo Ossoli

Sabato 15 luglio,[1848]

Questa mattina, caro, ricevo 4 Epoce, dentro uno tua lettrina del 13 dove dici non aver nuove di me. Io ho scritta come ho promessa il[n] 8, una settimana fa, e mandata la lettera pel libraio, queste mancanze mi disgustan assai.

Arrivan sempre qui più soldati, ieri han apportati sei persone dalli paesi e imprigionati nel Castello. La guardia qui a loro commando a deposto armi. Cosi terminan loro vanti.

Adesso fa bel tempo, fresco, e io sto meglio questi due giorni passati. Ho trovato[n] altre strade passeggiare, mi pare adesso che conosco bene Aquila. Ho letto ancora una storia della città che m'ha interressata molto;[n] quanto mi piacerebbe dirti, mostrarti queste cose.

Aspetto sentire da te il martedi, ma scrivi più di te, non mi dici niente questo mi sturba.

Addio, prega sempre per ti tua

io ho scritto ancora il[n] 13 Giovedi, col dui lettere[n] dentro tua per Milano e Ingilterra

Saturday 15 July, [1848]

This morning, my dear, I received 4 Epochs, with enclosed your letter of the 13th in which you say that you have no news from me. As I promised I wrote to you on the 8th, a week ago, and I sent the letter by the bookseller, these failures displease me very much.

Still more soldiers are arriving here, yesterday they captured six people from the nearby villages and imprisoned them in the castle. The guard surrendered at their command. So they will give up their boasts.

Now it is good weather, cool, and I am better these last two days. I have found other routes to go out for a walk, I think that now I know Aquila very well. I have read another story about the city that has interested me very much; how much I would like to tell you about these things and show them to you.

I wait to hear from you on Tuesday, but write more about yourself, you do not say anything and this worries me.

Good bye, always praying for you your

I wrote to you also on Thursday the 13th, with two letters enclosed in yours for Milan and England

ALfr (MH: fMS Am 1086 [9:198]); MsC in English (MH: fMS Am 1086 [Works, 2:111–13]). *Addressed:* Il Nobil Uomo / Sigr Mse Gio. Angiolo Ossoli / Roma. *Postmark:* Rieti.

promessa il] promessa ↑ il ↓
Ho trovato] Ho tr⟨?⟩ovato
interressata molto;] interressata mo⟨?⟩lto;
ancora il] ancora ↑ il ↓
dui lettere] dui lett⟨r⟩ere

735. To Giovanni Angelo Ossoli

Martedi 18. [luglio 1848]

Ricevo questa mattina, amore, tua lettera, ma m'incresce che non scrivi niente da te. Io non scrivo più, si tu fai cosi: voglio tue nuove.

Altro ho scritto tre volte la settimana passata; non è difetto mio, si tu non sai di me, ma de questo" maledetto posta che pare voler tormentare.

Ho i giornali, ma non ancora la medicina, ma ti ringrazio tanto.

Questa lettera dentro fate vostro servo prendere pel Sigr Hooker, impiegato del[la] banca si sta la, cercare risposta, si e sortit[o] ritornare cercare due, tre ore dopo." Ho pensata ch'era di bisogno" scrivere alfine sul affare di denaro.

Quando ricevo sua risposta scriverò che penso di tuo ritorno rivedermi ancora una volta. Ma adesso non son capace, son stata molto malatta la notte. Non stai sturbato per questo, io penso che è passato, ma son oggi troppo indebolita scrivere più che è di bisogno. T'abbraccio con sempre stessa affezione—" tua

Tuesday 18. [July 1848]

I have received this morning your letter, my love, but I am sorry that you do not write anything about yourself. I will not write anymore if you do so: I want your news.

Next, I wrote you three times last week; it is not my fault if you have no news from me, but that of this cursed post that seems to want to torment me.

I have the newspapers, but not yet the medicine, but I thank you very much.

This letter I am enclosing please have your servant take to Mr. Hooker, the bank employee[;] if he is there, try to get an answer, if he is not, send back for him two or three hours later. I have thought that it was necessary now to write about the matter of the money.

When I receive his answer I will write what I think about your return to see me once again. But now I cannot, I have been very ill during the night. Do not be worried about this, I think it is all past, but today I am too weak to write more than is necessary. I embrace you always with the same affection— your

AL (MH: fMS Am 1086 [9:212]); MsC in English (MH: fMS Am 1086 [Works, 2: 113–15]). *Addressed:* Il Nobil [   ]mo / Sigr Mse / Gio. Angiolo Ossoli / Roma. *Postmark:* Rieti.

de questo] de quest⟨a⟩o
si e sortit[o] ritornare cercare due, tre ore dopo.] si ⟨non⟩ ↑ e sortit[o]↓ ritornare ↑ cercare due, tre ore dopo ↓ .
di bisogno] di bi⟨o⟩sogno
stessa affezione—] stessa affe⟨c⟩zione—

736. To James C. Hooker

[I] Rocca Saro
18th July, 1848

My dear Mr Hooker,

I have no excuse for troubling you with my affairs, other than that I am a *"distressed female"* and you are a *"Chevalier,"* but I believe it is one to which you will not be deaf.

You know that I took money from the Bank, on the strength of a remittance which Mr Greeley, in a letter dated *8th April* last said he had made for me to the *Barings* and that, on leaving Rome, I wrote to them, asking a credit.

In their answer *26th May* they say they have not yet recd the funds, but will let me know so soon as they do. I have no letter from them and begin to feel much troubled.

On the reception of theirs I wrote to Mr Greeley and if he is at home, shall receive the explanation and the money in the course of August.

I recd also through you a letter from my brother in which he says he had collected money for me, but *hearing from Mr G. that I had already this remittance*, he delays sending till he hears from me.

I wrote, forwarding the letter through you, for him to send at once. But as he is on a journey I fear that money may not arrive before Septr.

Meanwhile I unfortunately spent a large portion of what I took in Rome, on engravings &c ordered by friends in the U. S. which I sent by Mr Hicks fearing I should have no oppory later, and I shall be moniless very soon now. Under these circumstances can I have another hundred dollars from the bank on my word merely? It does not seem the thing to ask of *a bank*, but, in my distance from Rome and all my friends, I am at a loss what to do.

If I can thus be accomodated I shall send an order to you in Rome, so soon as a person goes on whose fidelity I can rely.

If not agreeable to Mr Maquay to do this, will you inclose this letter to Mr Mozier and see if he will make some arrangement by which I can take this money from you[1] As he is a resident in Italy[n] I suppose it may not be inconvenient to him, and he always shows me great friendliness.

Whoever lends it, I feel as sure as the distance from the U. S. and the [II] occasional failure of letters permits of being able to repay it when I return to Rome in Septr or early in Octr.

I should write to Mr Mozier, but have been for a few days so ill, in consequence of over fatigue, I believe, that writing just now is painful. As soon as I recover I shall do so. Generally the pure country air and tranquil life has done me much good, but I continue locally weak, with cough &c at times.

By acting for me at this moment, so as to free me[n] from care, you will do me favor, of[n] which I hope I may in some way be able to show my sense.

I have another kindness to ask. In one of those letters, a friend expresses great desire for a rosary and cross blessed by the Pope. Can you buy me a pretty rosary[n] with one of the little silver crosses, such as Mrs Story has, and get it blessed when there is a presentation. I may not have a chance in the brief stay I expect to make in Rome this autumn, and I will then settle with you for this as well as the big favor.

I was very sorry not to see Mrs [*illegible*] one of my favorite acquaintance. She expresses a lively sense of obligation to you in Rome. I should have liked to go about with her much, as to others, I wish to see no one, as I work away all the time my strength permits at a book, and when so engaged it is best to be only with the birds, drink milk and go to bed early.

Is *Mr Martin* in Rome?[2] Have you ever heard if *Mr Hicks* arrived safe in Paris? Any items of[   ]would be thankfully received

I: ALfr (MH: fMS Am 1086 [9:151]); II: ALfr (MH: fMS Am 1086 [Box A]). *Addressed:* Mr Hooker / 20 Piazza di Spagna / Rome. *Endorsed:* Miss Fuller / 17. July—

resident in Italy] resident ⟨here⟩ ↑in Italy↓
free me] free ↑me↓
favor, of] favor, ↑of↓
pretty rosary] pretty ⟨one⟩ ↑rosary↓

1. As Fuller says here and elsewhere, she received frequent help from Joseph Mozier, an American artist living in Italy. He and his wife had, for example, nursed her back to health when she fell ill on her trip from Milan to Rome in 1847. According to Nathaniel Hawthorne, however, Mozier spoke with contempt of her and Ossoli in later years.

2. Hooker was at this time secretary of the American legation in Rome. On 1 April, Jacob Martin of North Carolina, secretary of the American legation in Paris, was appointed chargé d'affaires to the Papal States. He died, however, on 16 August (Stock, *United States Ministers*, pp. 1, 15).

737. To Giovanni Angelo Ossoli

Sabato 22d luglio [1848]
Aquila.

Caro mio

questa mattina ho tua lettrina del 20 e i giornali.

Martedi avevo tua altra con quella per Giuditta &—

Si, davvero questi son giorni terribili per Roma, io non posso pensare come le cose torneran.

La debolezza deplorabile del Papa a fatta più di male a Italia che il tradimento del Re di Napoli.

Penso un poco venire da Rieti. Decidero martedi prossima, si ricevo, come spero per te una risposta dal banchiere. Ma le cose stan si ritardate; io non so che aspettare. La lettera pel banchiere ti ho inviata martedi passata, dopo sua risposta dicedero anche che fare pel denaro.

Non sto bene, mi duole adesso molto la testa ma questa settimana non più[n] i denti e va bene perchè la medicina provista per tua affezione non arriva.[1]

ho fatta conoscenca per accidente cogli Marchesi de Torres, due fratelli, e signori principali qui.[2] Non era molto prudenti per qualchi ragioni ma come la cosa e fatta, si voglio partire domanderò consiglio di loro.

Scrivero più martedi spero molto che posso decidere allora e che tu recev[e]rai per tempo mia lettera[n] Sempre tua

Saturday, 22d July [1848]
Aquila

My dear,

I have this morning your dear letter of the 20th and the newspapers.

Tuesday I had your other with the one for Giuditta &c— Yes, indeed these are terrible days for Rome, I cannot think how these things will turn out.

The deplorable weakness of the Pope has caused more troubles to Italy than the King of Naples' betrayal.

I am thinking about coming to Rieti. I will make up my mind this coming Tuesday, if I receive, as I hope, an answer by you from the banker. But these things are going on very slowly; I do not know what to expect. I sent you last Tuesday the letter for the banker, after receiving his answer, I will also decide what to do about the money.

I am not well, now my head is hurting me but not my teeth this week and this is good because the medicine by your affection has not arrived[1]

I met by accident the Marchesi de Torres, two brothers, and outstanding personalities here.[2] It was not too prudent for various reasons but since it has happened, if I want to leave I will ask advice of them. Tuesday I will write again[;] I very much hope that I can decide then and that you will receive my letter in time. Always your

AL (MH: fMS⸱Am 1086 [9:199]); MsC in English (MH: fMS Am 1086 [Works, 2: 105–7]). *Addressed:* Il Nobil Uomo / Sige Mse Gio. Angiolo Ossoli / Roma. *Postmark:* Rieti.

settimana non più] settimana ⟨ancora⟩ ↑ non più ↓
mia lettera] mia lett⟨ra⟩era

1. In his response of 27 July (MH), Ossoli said that he sent the medicine by post on 15 July.

2. Probably Ferdinando de Torres (1790–1861) and his younger brother Bartolomeo, sons of Giovanni and Elisabetta de Torres. Ferdinando was a poet who wrote several books (Giuseppe Rivera, *Memorie biografiche degli scrittori aquilani* [Aquila, 1898], pp. 186–87).

738. To Giovanni Angelo Ossoli

il giovedi
27th luglio 48

È mio disegno, caro, venire in Rieti il sabato.

Subito che son arrivata, ti scrivero, inviarò anche un ordine sul mio banchiere, chi mi ha scritto, che posso avere da lui denaro pel mio bisogno. Tu prendrai questo, e spero che puoi venire da me *sabato 5, agosto* stare due tre giorni

Io andrò a la locanda *Renzi* in Rieti, ma cercerò da la[n] appartamento

Ho ricevuta lettere e giornali martedi passato, questa mattina no, cosi, non posso sapere le nuove ultime da Roma avanti di partire, ma suppongo son tutte cattive

Quando ricevi questa, scrivimi subito e invii i giornali alla casa de *Trinchi, Rieti*; l'avvertirò io.

Non scrivo più; perche non sto male, ma anche mi stanca adesso scrivere. Quando ti vedo, posso dire tutto e son sempre la tua

Fatemi il piacer impostare questa inchiusa per Ingilterra e paga alla portiera

Thursday
27th July 48

It is my intention, my dear, to come to Rieti on Saturday.

As soon as I arrive there, I will write you and I will also send an order to my banker, who wrote me that I could have money for my needs from him. Take this, and I hope you can come to me on *Saturday August 5th* and stay here two or three days.

I will go to the *Renzi's* inn in Rieti, but from there I will look for an apartment.

Last Tuesday I received the letters and newspapers, this morning nothing, so that I cannot know the latest news from Rome before leaving, but I suppose they are all bad.

94

As soon as you receive this, write me at once and send the newspapers to *Trinchi's house in Rieti*, I will inform them.

I write no more; because I am not bad, but now writing tires me. When I see you, I can tell you all and remain always your

Please mail the enclosed letter to England and pay to the porter

AL (MH: fMS Am 1086 [9:179]); MsC in English (MH: fMS Am 1086 [Works, 2:115–17]).

cercerò da la] cercerò ↑da la↓

739. To Giovanni Angelo Ossoli

Rieti
30 luglio 48

Son arrivata, caro, meno sofferente dal viaggio che ho aspettata. Son venuta da Campana, la locanda da Renzi era disfatta. Adesso cerco appartamento. Mi piace che son partita da Acquila, era troppo annojata la e troppo lontano da te.

Adesso spero vederti, domenica prossima, si puoi partire da Roma sabato la sera. Prendi questo denaro dal banchiere ti raccomando grande cura; perche ne'[qu]esto mancava non so dove poteva trovare altro in questo momento.

Ho scritto per 105 scudi, perche ha detto lui che sarebbe d'obbligo domandare molto commissione e voleva avere almeno 100.

Come questo è per me cosa molto importante, rispondi subito quando ricevi questa alla casa di Trinchi. Anche m'invii i giornali.

Il banchiere ti dara mie lettere si son tali, prendi tu del denaro pel tuo viaggio. Fammi il piacer demandare si il medico e ritornato ancora, non cerchi vederlo, ma solamente che io posso saper dove sta.

Non dico più, amore, perche mi stanca troppo scrivere, aspettando, volendo tanto vederti Addio,

Ho scritto al banchiere [ch]e ti scrivo prendere questo denaro, perche [   ]ce uno mio amico chè sui mezzo inviar da me. co[   ] là questa volta in persona. Si lui domandi a di me, dici che tu invii in Monte Rotondo e che la io invio prender le. Si non domanda, tu non dici niente Egli parla Italiana.

E megliio per lui inviar il denaro in *oro*. Quando venite domandi qui dove sto o da Trinchi.

95

Rieti
30 July 48

I am arrived, my dear, suffering less from the trip than I expected. I have come to Campana, the Renzi's inn was destroyed. Now I am looking for an apartment. I am glad I left Aquila, I was too bored there and too far from you.

Now I hope to see you next Sunday, if you can leave Rome on Saturday night. Take this money from the banker[;] I recommend you take the best care of it because if this fails I do not know where to find more at this moment.

I have written for 105 scudi, because he said that there would be a heavy commission and I wanted to have at least 100.

As for me this is a very important thing, answer me as soon as you receive this to Trinchi's house. Send me also the newspapers.

The banker will give you my letters[;] if so, take the money for your trip. Please ask if the doctor has already come back, do not look for him, I only want to know where he is.

I write no more, my love, because writing tires me too much, while waiting, wanting so much to see you, good bye.

I have written to the banker that I wrote to you to take this money, because [   ] a friend of mine that [   ] through him to send to me in person this time. If he asks for me, tell him that you will send to Monte Rotondo and that I will send someone over there to take them. If he does not ask for me, do not say anything. He speaks Italian. It is better for him to send the money in *gold*. When you come ask here or at the Trinchi's where I live.

AL (MH: fMS Am 1086 [9:180]); MsC in English (MH: fMS Am 1086 [Works, 2: 117–19]). *Addressed:* Il Nobil Uomo / Sige Mse Gio. Angiolo Ossoli / Roma. *Postmark:* Rieti.

740.   To James C. Hooker

Rocca di Saro[n]
30th July, 1848.

Dear Mr Hooker,

I have written to a friend in Rome, Marquis Ossoli, to take the money for me, as he has a friend in the place where I think to go next. I have ordered 105$ that I might be sure to have what I need with such commission as you please. Thank you much. I do not believe you can have any cause to regret accommodating me; if I live, I shall be at Rome in Octr, and can hardly fail to receive money from my family by that time, if this tiresome remittance from Mr G. never arrives. I am much pleased to hear of your new arrangements which must be to you so agreeable and will not fail to speak as you wish to the Tribune and in other quarters where it may be useful to you.

What new had happened to Mr Mozier? I thought he had taken his new house not meaning to go home for several years. I hope nothing ill has happened.

The country continues most beautiful and they have been threshing the grain in a patriarchal manner very pretty to see. But the heat is now excessive What times in Rome![1] If it were not too far, I would go there a few days, to see for myself, but the heat is too great. I would like to sleep till it rains. Truly yours

S. M. FULLER.

ALS (MH: fMS Am 1086 [9:150]). *Addressed:* Mr Hooker / 20 Piazza di Spagna / Roma. *Endorsed:* 1848 / S M Fuller Rocca di Suli / Recd Ju 30th / Ansd.

di Saro] di ⟨?⟩ Saro

1. On 14 July the Austrians crossed the Po, the river that separates Lombardy from the Papal States, and forced Ferrara to resupply the troops under the command of Prince Franz Lichtenstein. This invasion prompted a vigorous debate in Rome, where the republicans and the radical popular clubs used the event to try to force the pope to declare war on Austria. Pius, however, confined himself to a formal protest to the European powers. The debate in the Chamber on 19 July was unusually tumultuous (Farini, 2:294–300; Berkeley, pp. 346–49).

741.   To Giovanni Angelo Ossoli

Rieti

2 agosto 48

Mio caro,

Ricevo questa mattina la tua, scritta ieri, cosi mi trovo davvero più vicino da te e spero sicuro rivederte domenica la mattina

Quanto m'ha fatta allegra la tua notizia di una vittoria, ma mi sorprende che l'Epoca[n] del 31 luglio non parla del bulletino. Aspetto ansiamente un altro giornale.[1]

Ho trovata un apartamento che mi conviene si bene, è sopra la fiume, e un veduta che ti piacera molto anche, pare fresca e più ariosa[n] che a Aquila, e senza questa romore terribile; si sente solamente il fiume, qui posso trovare piacere davvero stare con te, vieni la domenica e stai lungo come e possibile.

Sento cura di sapere, si tu recevi mia lettera scritta la domenica 30 luglio, contiene ordine sul banchiere pel denaro, di che adesso sto in bisogno, e per mie lettere &c per star sicura ho fatto ordine *per te in persona prendere questo denaro.* Addio, caro, non manca la domenica, tu arriverai di bon ora, e io vedo passare la dilligenza sul ponte.[n] Sto in casa di un certo Fassetti, strada Vendana, questo uomo e cancelliere del vescovo, ma si altro non mi trovi, domandi del albergo Campana, e vieni vieni[n] presto alla tua affa

Rieti

2 August 48

My dear,

This morning I received the letter you wrote yesterday, so now I feel really closer to you and hope to see you surely on Sunday morning.

How glad I was in hearing from you the news of a victory, but I am surprised that the Epoca of July 31 does not mention the bulletin. I am anxiously waiting for another newspaper.[1]

I have found an apartment that fits well, it is along the river, and has a view that you will surely like[;] it seems cool and more airy than in Aquila, and there is not that terrible noise; you can only hear the river, here I can really enjoy being with you[;] come on Sunday and stay as long as you can.

I am anxious to know if you received the letter I wrote you on Sunday July 30[;] it contains an order to the banker for the money I need now, and for my letters &c to be on the safe side I made out an order so that *you personally can take this money.* Good bye my dear, do not miss next Sunday, you will arrive early and I will see the stagecoach passing across the bridge. I live in the house of a certain Fassetti, Vedana street, this man is the bishop's chancellor, but if you do not find me there, ask for hotel Campana, and come come soon to your affectionate

AL (MH: fMS Am 1086 [9:182]); MsC in English (MH: fMS Am 1086 [Works, 2: 119–21]). *Addressed:* Il Nobil Uomo / Sige Mse Gio. Angiolo Ossoli / Roma. *Postmark:* Rieti.

l'Epoca] ↑ l' ↓ Epo⟨?⟩ca
più ariosa] più ⟨arioso⟩ ariosa

dilligenza sul ponte.] dilligenza. ↑ sul ponte ↓
vieni vieni] vieni vien⟨a⟩i

1. On 1 August Ossoli wrote that "a bulletin of war was published here on Sunday, 30th, with the victory of Charles Albert, which will be given more in detail in the journals— It has given great pleasure throughout Rome." (Ossoli's letters are in MH; they have been translated for this edition.) The battle was probably rear-guard action at Cremona as the Piedmontese retreated toward Milan (King, *Italian Unity*, 1:258).

742.   To Giovanni Angelo Ossoli

Rieti
domenica 13 Agosto 48.

Mio caro,

Pare miracolo come tutte cose van contrarie a noi. Che la Bologna [h]a resistita va bene, ma che questo farebbe probabile per te partire precise a questo momento![1]

Ma fai che è bene per tuo onore. Io non credo molto che il Papa decidera inviare la Civica, ma si questo si fa e si c'è di bisogno per tuo onore, parti e io cercerò sostenermi.[2]

Non trovo niente di alterazione in mio stato, avanti di ricever tua lettera pensava scriverti^n che non credeva^n sarebbe di bisogno per ti venire avanti il Sabato. Adesso lascio al tuo giudizio quando venire si davvero tu puoi venire mai più. In tutto evento spero sentire qualche cosa martedi la mattina e io allora scrivero un altra volta. Tua visita m'ha fatta di bene son stata dopo più tranquilla. E almeno noi abbiam avuti alcune ore di pace insieme, si adesso è tutto terminato.

Addio, amore, t'abbraccio sempre e prego per tuo bene.

Un addio affettuosissimo

Rieti
Sunday 13 August 48

My dear,

It seems very strange how everything is going against us. The fact that Bologna has resisted is good, but that this would make it likely for you to leave at this very moment![1]

But do what is right for your honor. I do not really think that the pope will decide to send the Civic Guard, but if it happens, and if it is necessary for your honor, leave and I will try to be strong.[2]

There is no change in my health, before receiving your letter I intended to write you that I did not think it was necessary for you to come here before Saturday. But now I leave to your judgment when to come if really you can ever come again. In any case I hope to hear something on Tuesday morning and then I will write you once again. Your visit did me good and afterward I was calmer. And at least we have had some peaceful hours together, if now everything is over.

Goodbye my love, I always embrace you and pray for your well-being.

A very warm goodbye

AL (MH: fMS Am 1086 [9:183]); MsC in English (MH: fMS Am 1086 [Works, 2:121–23]). English copy published in part in *Memoirs*, 2:296–97. *Addressed:* Al Sige Mse / Gio. Angiolo Ossoli / Roma. *Postmark:* Rieti.

lettera pensava scriverti] lettera ↑ pensava scriverti ↓
non credeva] non credev⟨o⟩a

1. On 6 August Radetzky had reentered Milan, effectively ending the war with Piedmont. Two days later a detachment of his army invaded the Papal States and attacked Bologna. The city, however, defeated the Austrians and remained defiant. On 11 August news of the battle reached Rome. The next day, Odoardo Fabbri, Mamiani's successor, announced a call for volunteers. Neither the government in Rome nor Fuller in Rieti could know that the Austrians had already withdrawn and that the crisis was over (Berkeley, pp. 377, 389; Farini, 2:323–24.)

2. Ossoli answered the next day (MH) and described the pope's reception of the civic guard, which had been called to Monte Cavallo: "It was supposed that the Pope would speak favorably and would animate them still more to the support of his state." The pontiff, however, said only, "At the present moment I have nothing to say to you except that I renew the apostolic benediction." Ossoli said that the crowd "retired coldly and sad, with anger, cheated of their expected encouragement."

743. To [?]

[ca. 15 August 1848]
But one loses sight of all this dabbling and pretension when seated at the feet of dead Rome,— Rome so grand and beautiful upon her bier. Art is dead here; the few sparkles that sometimes break through the embers cannot make a flame; but the relics of the past are great enough; over-great, we should do nothing but sit and weep and worship.

It is useless to try and write of these things, volumes would hardly begin to tell my thoughts; I do not know whether of any worth or not, but the Italian sun has wakened a luxuriant growth that covers my mind; this green may be all of weeds; I hardly care,— weeds are beautiful in Italy.

In Rome, one has all the free feeling of the country; the city is so interwoven with vineyards and gardens, such delightful walks in the villas;— such ceaseless music of the fountains,— and from every high point the Campagna and Tiber seem so near. Full of enchantments has been my summer, passed wholly among Italians, in places where no foreigner goes, amid the snowy peaks, in the exquisite valleys of the Abruzzi. I have seen a thousand landscapes, any one of which might employ the thoughts of the painter for years. Not without reason the people dream that at the death of a saint columns of light are seen to hover on these mountains. They take, at sunset, the same rose-hue as the Alps. The torrents are magnificent. I knew some noblemen, with baronial castles nestled in the hills and slopes, rich in the artistic treasures of centuries. They liked me, and shewed me of the hidden beauties of Roman remains. Oh how much I might write, if I had only force!

MsCfr (MH: fMS Am 1086 [Works, 1:337–39]); MsCfr (MH: fMS Am 1086 [9: 237]). Published in part in *At Home and Abroad*, p. 426.
Dated by Fuller's reference to the Abruzzi Mountains.

744. To Giovanni Angelo Ossoli

Rieti
15 agosto 48
Per nostro conto, amore, sarò molto grata si tu non stai d'obbligo partire, ma ah! come è indegno il Papa! Pare adesso uomo senza cuore: è questo traditore di Carlo Umberto: Saran maladetti per tutti i secoli avvenire.[1]

In mio condizione non e ancora cambio importante; ho fatto cavare sangue; il medico mi piace; penso che è una persona in che posso fidare per curarmi bene si viene da difficolta. Lui dice che è impossibile fissare un giorno per mi ma pensa fra poco. Io apparecchio tutto quanto e possibile.

Adesso spero molto rivederti[n] domenica la mattina, m'incresce per ti viaggiare in quello[n] carrettino, ma tu avrai il tempo riposare dopo. Si e possibile tu starai ancora la settimana. Si vivo si sto bene, spero in pochi giorni dopo l'evento essere capace governare miei affari, ma allora starei molto più tranquilla averti al mio lato.

Ma ancora ridico che ho detta in mia ultima tu farai che è meglio

per te, si un dovere previene da venire qui, io cercherò curarmi; voglio tuo bene in questi giorni[è] importante, più che tutt'altro. La luna e stata si bella queste ultime sere, m'ha indollorata non avere tua compagnia Ma speriamo un poco ancora,
    sempre tua con molta affezione

Rieti
15 August 48

For our sake, my love, I will be very grateful if you are not obliged to leave, but ah! how contemptible is the pope! He seems now a man who has no heart: and this betrayer of Charles Albert: they will be cursed for all ages to come.[1]

There is not yet any important change in my condition; I was bled; I like the doctor; I think he is a person whom I can trust to take care of me if something goes wrong. He says that it is impossible to settle a day for me But he thinks soon. I will arrange as much as possible.

Now I really hope to see you on Sunday morning, I am sorry that you have to travel in that little coach, but then you will have time to rest afterward. If it is possible please stay here for a week. If I live and if I am well, I hope a few days after the event to be able to manage my affairs, but then I would be much calmer having you at my side.

But I repeat what I told you in my last letter[;] do what is better for you, if a duty hinders your coming here I will try to take care of myself; in these important days I want your good above all. The moon was very beautiful these last nights, it grieved me not to have your company. But let us hope a little more.
    Always with all my affection

AL (MH: fMS Am 1086 [9:184]); MsC in English (MH: fMS Am 1086 [Works, 2:123–27]). English copy published in part in *Memoirs*, 2:297. *Addressed:* al Signe Mse / Gio. Angiolo Ossoli / Roma. *Postmark:* Rieti.

    molto rivederti] molto rive⟨?⟩derti
    in quello] in ⟨questo⟩ ↑ quello ↓

    1. After the Piedmontese defeat at Custoza, Charles Albert returned to Milan to prevent a republican revolution. Once there, he decided to abandon the city to the Austrians, and then barely escaped alive from an enraged Milanese mob. He fled on 5 August; Radetzky reentered on the 6th, and on 9 August the Salasco armistice brought the war to an end. When the Piedmontese withdrew behind the Tincio River, Austria once more occupied all of Lombardy (Mack Smith, *Making of Italy*, p. 155; Berkeley, pp. 376–81). In her *Tribune* essay, Fuller heaped scorn on the monarch called Re Tentenna (King Wobble): "The Austrians would again have suffered repulse from [the Milanese], but for the baseness of this man, on whom they had been cajoled into relying: a baseness that deserves the pillory. . . . He made use of his power only to betray Milan; he

took from the citizens all means of defence, and then gave them up to the spoiler; he promised to defend them 'to the last drop of his blood,' and sold them the next minute; even the paltry terms he made he has not seen maintained. Had the people slain him in their rage, he well deserved it at their hands; and all his conduct since had confirmed that sudden verdict of passion" (*New-York Daily Tribune*, 19 January 1849).

745. To Richard F. Fuller

Mountains of Southern
Italy, 16th August 48

My dear brother,

In a letter recd from you about the middle of June, you say you are going to Lennox to make a visit, and after that and previous to going into Ohio you shall write to me. But I suppose you did not. This is the only letter I have from any member of my family for near four months. Indirectly I heard that Arthur was ordained at Manchester in April and that Mother had returned from the West.[1]

I wrote to Mother and to E. Hoar by a Mr Page who left Rome early in May. By Dr Gardner of Boston who expected to be there in June, I sent Ellen her Cameo and the coral cross for Greta. By Mr Hillard a mosaic to Mother. I want to know if these things have come safe.

In an evil hour, wishing to save you pressure I trusted for the expenses of the summer to a remittance from Mr Greeley, which up to this hour has never arrived. I begin to believe I shall never receive it, as in a letter dated the 27th June, he says he supposes I have it long since. He does not say how it came. Meanwhile not only my mind has been harassed, but much of the benefit of my summer has been forfeited by this failure. I have been unable to procure reference books which would have been most precious to me, and of which I can never again make use to this same advantage. I have been prevented from making the most interesting excursions among others the want of a few dollars prevented my seeing the birth-place of Ovid and Lake Facino.[2]

Now I do not know what will become of me, if I do not, in the course of Septr receive the money either from you or Mr G. I shall not have the means to leave Italy, nor even to return to Rome, if indeed I could still have food and lodging here. It makes me heart-sick to think how long I have waited and of the uncertainty of correspondence at this distance.

Sometimes it seems to me I have no friend, or some one would divine how I am placed and find the means to relieve me. Yet I know I *have* friends better than the average of human nature supplies. As to Mr Greeley he shows no disposition to further my plans. Liberality on the part of the Tribune would have made my path easy. And I feel that if any one in America had been interested to enable me here to live and learn on my own way, I could have made, at least, a rich intellectual compensation. But people rarely think one like me worth serving or saving. Still I must not be ungrateful having to thank 1st the Springs 2d the Mannings who volunteered a loan, 3d Mrs Farrar who has now offered to lend me a hundred dollars and 4th and most you, who, amid your own difficulties, have never forgotten me.[3] And I feel sure that if you have recd my last letter I shall be relieved before the end of Septr. Hoping it may be so I try to keep my mind tranquil and make as much use as possible of the present moment.

I have changed place since I wrote last and am now in a spot less rich in historic association, yet of the ancient Umbrian dominion and enchanting in its natural beauty. The house is upon a rapid river. I occupy its upper apartment, containing a chamber for my servant a little room for eating, and mine, a large brick paved room of the simplest finish and furniture but with a *loggia* upon the river with its whispering willows. This *loggia* a wooden terrace is long enough for an evening walk, and these glorious moonlight nights, I pass many hours there, uninterrupted by a sound except the rush of the stream and occasionally a soft bell from a convent of Cappucins high among the mountains. A rich vineyard is opposite my window, and there the contadini work a little sing and play more. I see too an ancient villa with its cypress plantations and a distant cleft among the mountains leads on the eye and fancy. I never in my life had a room I liked as I do this. I can open the whole apartment and let the breeze draw through. Below my servant washes the clothes on a" large stone in the running water which leaves them white as snow. For the apartment I pay nine dollars a month. Figs, grapes, peaches the most delicious I can have enough for the day for five or six cents. The best salad enough for two persons for one cent a day. Here I make the nearest approach to economical living I have been able to in Italy. My servant is from Rome. I could not live without her; the country people are too dirty, and she cooks sews and irons for me" but it is rather a bore to have her she does not like so much solitude and wonders I do not "go mad writing"

Goodbye, my dear Richard, much shall I have to say, if ever we meet again, but three sheets of paper (and I pay eighty cents to get *one* to you) come to an end in a moment. Hoping to hear much from you and with love to dearest Mother your sister

M.

I do not say anything of public affairs, but all goes wrong. My dearest friends are losing all, and the Demon with his cohort of traitors, prepares to rule anew these heavenly fields and mountains. But I do not quite despair yet. France may aid.[4] If not Italy [w]ill be too hot or too cold[n] to hold me.

ALS (MH: fMS Am 1086 [9:152]). *Addressed:* Mr Richard F. Fuller / 6 State St. Boston / Massachusetts / U.S.A. *Postmark:* New York 14 Sep.

on a] on ↑ a ↓

dirty, and she cooks sews and irons for me] dirty, ↑ and she cooks sews and irons for me ↓

hot or too cold] hot ↑ or too cold ↓

1. Arthur Fuller was ordained at Manchester, New Hampshire, on 29 March 1848. He served there until 1853 (*General Catalogue of the Divinity School of Harvard University, 1901* [Cambridge, 1901], p. 46). Mrs. Fuller had visited Eugene in New Orleans.

2. Ovid was born in Sulmona, 50 miles southeast of Aquila, in the Abruzzi Mountains. Lake Fucino lies due west of Sulmona on the road to Avezzano.

3. Richard Henry and Mary Weeks Manning were Fuller's friends in New York.

4. On 7 August the Piedmontese ambassador at Paris asked the French for 60,000 foreign troops to help fight the Austrians, but France was unwilling to be drawn into combat (Farini, 2:352).

746. To Giovanni Angelo Ossoli

Rieti
17th Agosto. 48

Non ricevo, caro, niente oggi da Roma, si dice perche era festa 14. Ma non aspetto per domani scrivere, perchè voglio stare sicuro per te ricever l'inchiusa lettera per tempo, inviare[n] alla Banca il sabato. Questa lettera il[n] banchiere inviera in America.

Sto molto la stessa; Il[n] medico dice che e impossibile fissare per me un giorno, ma che pare che manco poco. Non scrivo piu a questo momento perche mi stanca troppo, altro che voglio [se]mpre sempre sentire nuove da te e rivederti. Ha piovuto qui e la campagna e molto rinfrescata sarà più piacevole per te si puoi venire. Sempre, amore tua—

Rieti
17 August. 48

Today, my dear, I receive nothing from Rome, they say that it is because the 14th was a holiday. But I will not wait for tomorrow to write, because I want to be sure that you will receive the enclosed letter on time to send to the bank on Saturday. The banker will send this letter to America.

I feel the same. The doctor says that it is impossible to fix a day for me, but it seems we are close. I write no more now because it tires me too much, but I want always always to hear news from you and see you again. It rained here and the country is much refreshed[;] it will be more pleasant for you if you can come. Always, love your—

AL (MH: fMS Am 1086 [9:203]); MsC in English (MH: fMS Am 1086 [Works, 2:127]). *Addressed:* al Sige Mse Gio. Angiolo Ossoli / Roma. *Postmark:* Rieti.

lettera per tempo, inviare] lettera ⟨quando inviato⟩ ↑ per tempo, inviare ↓
Questa lettera il] ⟨Sto⟩ Questo lettera ↑ il ↓
stessa; Il] stessa; ↑ Il ↓

747. To Giovanni Angelo Ossoli

Rieti
18 agosto [1848]

Sento, amore, una simpatia profonda pegli tuoi tormenti, ma non son capace ti dare un consiglio perfettamente savio. Solamente mi pare un cattivissimo momento entrare nell'armata altra che per causa del dovere, del onore. Il Papa, si freddo, suo ministro indeciso, niente sarà ben fatto ni con successo. Come si spera questo intervento della Francia e Inghilterra e anche incerta si, la^n guerra continua. Si non, tu lasci Roma e il impiego col zio per niente.[1]

Si e possibile aspettare^n due o tre settimane lo stato pubblico e anche il mio saran decisi, e tu puoi star piu tranquillo per un decisione.

Altro non mi pare che devo dire ma lasciar a tuo giudizio che fare. Solamente si parti, vieni qui primo, bisogna che noi^n ci revidiamo ancora una volta

M'incresce tanto che non posso dirti qualche cosa certa di me, ma sto ancora stessa aspettando. Ho passata una cattivissima notte, mia testa e, questa mattina, molto sturbata; molto sangue e^n uscita pel naso, è difficile per me scrivere.

Non domandi permesso del zio, si è si difficile; noi cerceremo ordinare le cose senza questo.
Si tu non vieni aspetto la domenica" una lettera da ti, anche si son alcuni dalla Banca e anche i ultimi di quelli giornali di Milano.

Rieti

18 August [1848]

My love, I feel a deep sympathy with your pains, but I am not able to give you perfectly wise advise. Only I think it is a very bad moment to enter the army other than for the reason of duty, of honor. The pope so cold, his minister irresolute, nothing will be well done nor successfully. As one hopes for the intervention of France and England, it is also uncertain if the war continues. If not, you leave Rome and the employment with your uncle for nothing.[1]

If it is possible to wait two or three weeks the public situation and mine also will be decided, and you can make a decision with more tranquillity.

I think I have nothing else to add but leave what to do to your judgment. Only if you leave, come here first, we must see each other again.

I am very sorry that I cannot tell you something certain about me, but I am still waiting myself. I had a terrible night, this morning my head is very bad; I had a nosebleed, and it is difficult for me to write.

Do not ask permission of your uncle, if it is so difficult; we will try to arrange things without it.

If you do not come I will wait for a letter from you on Sunday, also if there are some from the bank and the more recent newspapers from Milan.

ALfr (MH: fMS Am [1086 [9:200]); MsC in English (MH: fMS Am 1086 [Works, 2:127–31]). English copy published in part in *Memoirs*, 2:297–98; English copy published entire in Higginson, *MFO*, pp. 250–51.
si la] si ⟨si⟩ la
possibile aspettare] possibile ⟨possibile⟩ aspettare
che noi] che ⟨ci⟩ noi
sangue e] sangue ↑ e ↓
aspetto la domenica] aspetto ↑ la domenica ↓

1. Though unwilling to send troops, France and England offered to mediate between Piedmont and Austria after the battle of Custoza. The victorious Austrians refused to negotiate (*Cambridge Modern History*, 11:92). In Venice, Daniele Manin, angry at the armistice of Salasco, repudiated the act of fusion with Piedmont, but his attempts to lure the European powers into the war were as unsuccessful as those of Charles Albert (King, *Italian Unity*, 1:261–62; Berkeley, p. 385).

748. To Giovanni Angelo Ossoli

la domenica
20th Agosto [1848]

Mio caro,

ti aspettavo un poco questa mattina, e aveva tuo caffè tutto pronto ma credo tu hai ragione aspettare. Si trovi[n] niente al contrario, vieni il sabato sera[n] prossimo.

Miei notti divengon più e più sturbati, e questa mattina stavo d'obbligo fare un altro sanguigno, dopo mi trovo sollevata ma debole e non capace dire altro che son sempre tua affeza

Inchiudo un altra ordine pel banchiere, si tu vieni il sabato Scrivo lo adesso non essendo sicura che posso scrivere molti giorni più. T'abbraccio.

Sunday
20th August [1848]

My dear,

I was waiting for you this morning, and I had your coffee ready but I think you are right to wait. If nothing prevents you, come this Saturday evening.

My nights become more and more disturbed, and this morning I had to have another blood letting, afterwards I feel better but weak and I am not able to say more than I am always your affectionate

I enclose another order for the banker, if you come on Saturday. I write it now because I am not sure I can write in the next few days. I embrace you.

AL (MH: fMS Am 1086 [9:204]); MsC in English (MH: fMS Am 1086 [Works, 2:131–33]). English copy published entire in Higginson, MFO, pp. 251–52. *Addressed:* Sigr Mse / Gio. Angiolo Ossoli / Roma. *Postmark:* Rieti.

Si trovi] Si ⟨viene⟩ ↑ trovi ↓
il sabato sera] il sabato ↑ sera ↓

749. To Giovanni Angelo Ossoli

Rieti,
22 agosto 48

Sto un poco meglio, caro, ma si posso passare cosi il giorno meno soffrente, al contrario m'annoja che questo pare dire bisogna aspettare ancora.

Aspettare!! che noja sempre. Ma— si stava sicura fare bene, vorrei molto passare questa prova avanti tuo arrivo, ma quando penso che è possibile per me morire sola senza che poteva toccare una cara mano, voglio piu aspettare. Cosi spero tua presenza la domenica mattina

Io vedo pel giornale che il Papa fa sospendere la partenza della truppa, lui agisce come io pensavo, e mi piace molto" adesso per ti non entrare ancora. Fra poco questi affari staran più certi; tu puoi prender ere qualche risoluzione più a vantaggio che adesso.

Cerca si puoi sentire alcuni dettagli di Milano Non sarebbe possibile nel caffè degli Belle Arti? m'incresce molto pel destino dei cari amici, come deven soffrire adesso.

Penso anche tanto di [te], spero che sei [me]no tormentato, si noi stavam insiemi sarebbe un consolo ma" Adesso tutto va male, ma non e possibile che va cosi sempre, sempre. Addio, amore. Mi dispiace che bisogna passare tanti giorni avanti tua venuta, tanti tanti. Mi piace che ho adesso il piccolo ritratto, lo riguardo sovente. Dio ti conserva.

Rieti

22 August 48

I am some better, my dear, but if I can get through the day with less pain, on the contrary I am very bored that this means that we must still wait.

To wait!! What a bore. But— if I were sure to do well, I would rather pass this ordeal before your coming, but when I think that it is possible for me to die alone without touching a dear hand, I prefer to wait. So I hope for your presence on Sunday morning

I see from the newspaper that the pope suspends the departure of the troop, he is acting as I thought, and now I am very happy for you not to go in yet. Soon these affairs will be more certain; you can take some decisions more to your advantage than now.

See if you can hear some news from Milan, could it not be possible in the Caffe delle Belle Arti? I am very sorry for the fate of the dear friends, how they must be suffering now.

I think often of you, I hope you are less worried, if we could be together it would be a consolation, but now everything is going badly, but it is not possible that it will always be this way, always always good bye love. It makes me unhappy that it is necessary to wait so many days before you come, so many so many. I am happy that now I have your little portrait, often I look at it. God keep you.

AL (MH: fMS Am 1086 [9:184]); MsC in English (MH: fMS Am 1086 [Works, 2:133–35]). English copy published in part in *Memoirs*, 2:297. English copy published entire in Higginson, *MFO*, pp. 252–53; Wade, p. 579; and Chevigny, p. 455. *Addressed:* Il Sige Mse / Gio. Angiolo Ossoli / Roma. *Postmark:* Rieti.

piace molto] piace ⟨?⟩ molto
consolo ma] consolo ⟨Ma⟩ ma

750.   To Giovanni Angelo Ossoli

Rieti
25 agosto. [1848]

Mio amore,

ricevo questa mattina tua lettrina di mercoledi tu non dici si vieni il sabato sera o non, ma io lo spero sicuro, non poteva in nul evento aspettare più, si non era d'obbligo per tuoi affari.

Per mi viene ancora niente; non so che pensare.

C'è vicino un bellissimo sito dove noi possiamo andare[n] insieme si sto capace ancora sentire quando vieni.[n]

T'aspettero domenica la mattina e avro pronta tua caffe anche un altra volta; altro non più adesso, perche scrivere[n] e davvero difficile per tua affea,—

non ti sturba cercare di Milano io vedo è impossibile saper a questo momento

Rieti
25 August. [1848]

My love,

this morning I receive your dear letter of Wednesday[;] you do not say if you will come Saturday evening or not, but I certainly hope you will, in any event I could not wait longer, if it were not necessary because of your affairs.

For me still nothing comes, I do not know what to think.

Near here there is a beautiful place where we can go together if I am able to go out when you come.

I will wait for you on Sunday morning and again I will have your coffee ready; but no more now, because writing is truly difficult for your affectionate—

do not bother to find out about Milan I see it is impossible to know at this time

AL (MH: fMS Am 1086 [9:201]); MsC in English (MH: fMS Am 1086 [Works, 2:135–37]). English copy published in part in *Memoirs*, 2:296; English copy published entire in Higginson, *MFO*, p. 253. *Addressed:* Sige Mse / Gio. Angiolo Ossoli / Roma. *Postmark:* Rieti.

possiamo andare] possiamo ↑ andare ↓
sentire quando vieni.] sentire ⟨ancora⟩. ↑ quando vieni ↓
perche scrivere] ⟨?⟩ perche ⟨la⟩ scrivere

751. To Giovanni Angelo Ossoli

Rieti 7 Settembre 1848

Cmo Consorte

Io sto bene molto meglio che io sperava. Il Bambino anche va bene ma piange molto ancora, e spero che sarè più tranquillo quando tu vieni. Per altro voglio che per me sii tranquillo, e ti darò spesso mie nuove scrivendoti di nuovo ben presto. La mia lettera che hai per Parigi potrai affrancarla alla Posta.

Tutti di questa famiglia dove io mi trovo ti salutano. Dandoti un abbraccio, ed un bagio in questo caro Pupo che ho nelle braccia sono Tua Affma

MARGHERITA

Rieti
September 7 1848

Dearest Husband

I feel much better than I hoped. The child is doing well too but he still cries a lot, and I hope he will be calmer when you come. As for the rest I want you to be reassured, and I will often give you my news writing again very soon. The letter of mine you have for Paris you can stamp at the postoffice.

All the people in the family where I am staying send their regards. Embracing you and kissing you in this dear baby I have in my arms I am Your Affectionate

MARGARET

MsLS (MH: fMS Am 1086 [9:185]); MsC in English (MH: fMS Am 1086 [Works, 2: 137]). English copy published entire in Higginson, *MFO*, p. 254.

752. To Giovanni Angelo Ossoli

Sabato
[9 settembre 1848]

Mio bene,

Scrivo nel letto alcune parole solamente. Ricevo tuo questa mattina, e spero altro per domani. Son stata male col febbre di latte ma oggi meglio e spero tutti i giorni stare più forte. C'e di bisogno; son d'obbligo oggi inviare Giuditta in Roma; lei non può fare niente adesso. Io prendo una che ha anche latte si mio non basta.

Il bambino e molto bello, tutti dicon cosi io prendo molto piacere riguardarlo. Lui ti da un bacio come anche tua

M.

Saturday
[9 September 1848]

My love,

I write only a few words in bed. I receive[d] yours this morning, and I hope for another one to-morrow. I have been sick with nursing fever but today I am better and I hope I will grow stronger every day. There is need for it; I must send Giuditta to Rome today; she cannot do anything now. I [will] take one who can also breastfeed since my milk is not sufficient.

The child is very beautiful, everybody says so[;] I enjoy very much looking at him. He sends you a kiss as does also your

M.

ALS (MH: fMS Am 1086 [9:210]); MsC in English (MH: fMS Am 1086 [Works, 2:137–39]). English copy published entire in Higginson, *MFO*, p. 254. *Addressed:* All'Illmo Sig Sig. Pne Clmo / Il Sig. March. Giovanni Angelo Ossoli / Roma. *Postmark:* Rieti.

753. To Giovanni Angelo Ossoli

Rieti 10 Settembre 1848

Cmo Consorte

Ho ricevuto le due crme lettere che mi hai dirette. Quando ti scrissi avanti jeri io aveva la febbre solita ad aversi per causa del latte: ma addesso stò meglio, e molto più tranquilla che ho fatta partire Giuditta. Ho detto ad essa che non bisogna che venga a ricercarti in Roma, poichè non voglio aver più che fare con Lei. Adesso son contenta di altra donna trovatami dal Sig. Giovanni che serve a me, ed al nostro Bambino, ripromettendo essa di essere molto buona. Con Lei il Bambino riposa molto bene, e mostra molto buona salute. La lettera che mi hai acclusa è della mia amica che viaggiava con me quando la prima volta mi conoscesti; essa pure si aspetta di partorire in questo corrente mese, e se questa sarà bambina gli darà il mio nome di Margherita. Sii tranquillo per me, perchè la casa dove mi trovo è molto buona per me, ed io avrò consiglio e ajuto.

Martedì ti scriverò di nuovo, ed intanto godendo di rivederti nel caro Bambino che ho sempre a me vicino, e per te baciandolo, sono Tua Affma

MARGHERITA

Rieti 10 September 1848

Dear husband,

I have received the two kind letters that you sent me. When I wrote to you, the day before yesterday, I had the fever that one usually has because of nursing: but now I am better and I am also calmer because I sent Giuditta away. I told her that she is not to look for you in Rome, as I want to have nothing to do with her. Now I am satisfied with the other woman Mr. Giovanni found who serves me, and our baby, and I expect that she is very good. With her the child sleeps quietly and is in perfect health. The letter you enclosed is from the friend of mine who travelled with me when you met me the first time; she is expecting her confinement this month, and if it will be a girl, she will give her my name of Margaret. Do not be worried for me, because the house where I live is very good for me, and I can have advice and help.

Tuesday I will write you again, in the meantime I am delighted to see you in the baby who I have always close to me and, kissing him for you, I am your affectionate

MARGARET

MsL (MH: fMS Am 1086 [9:186]); MsC in English (MH: fMS Am 1086 [Works, 2:139–41]). *Addressed:* All'Immo Sig Sig Pne Clmo / Il Sig. Marchese Giovanni Angelo Ossoli. *Postmark:* Rieti.

754.   To Giovanni Angelo Ossoli

Rieti
Mercoledi 13 [settembre 1848]

Mio caro,

promettevo scrivere ieri, ma non stava capace, era mio primo giorno di riposo, e potevo sentire quanto son stata agitata, faticata. Oggi principio star meglio ma posso scrivere solamente poche parole. Il bambino sta bene; è molto caro. Mi piace anche mia nova serva, chi è[n] anche sua balia, perchè ancora egli ricusa prendere latte di me. La famiglia e molto buona per me eglino ti salutan.

M'incresce non vederti[n] per tanto tempo, ma in compenso spero allora esser piu forte, il bambino più bello e che noi possiam prender più di piacer insieme.

Sempre tua

M.

Rieti
Wednesday 13 [September 1848]

My dear,

I promised to write to you yesterday, but I was not able, it was my first day to rest, and therefore I was able to realize how tired I actually was. Today I am beginning to feel better but I can write only a few words. The child is well; he is very dear. I also like my new maid, who is also his wetnurse, because he still refuses to take my milk. The family is very good to me[;] they greet you.

I am sorry that I will not see you for a long time, but at that time I hope to be stronger, the baby more beautiful and that we can have more pleasure together.

Always yours

M.

ALS (MH: fMS Am 1086 [9:201]); MsC in English (MH: fMS Am 1086 [Works, 2:141–43]). *Addressed:* Sigr Mse Gio. Angiolo Ossoli / Roma. *Postmark:* Rieti.
serva, chi è] serva, ↑ chi è ↓
non vederti] non ve⟨?⟩derti

755. To Giovanni Angelo Ossoli

venerdi
15 Settembre [1848]

Mio amore

io ricevo questa mattina tue care lettrine e i giornali Le nuove da Milano mi sembran troppo buone essere vere, ma aspetto con ansia sentire di più.

Quando non ricevi nuove di me non stai presto sturbato, sapete che bisogna per mi ancora essere molto debole, non sempre son capace di scrivere o di alzare e Sr Giovanni non sta sempre qui scrivere per mi. È miracolo che sto bene come mi trovo; mie circostanze son state si difficile. Adesso che mi trovavo si contenta con mia balia suo bambino diviene" ammalato, si lei e forzata lasciarmi la guerra ricommincia, spero" di no; ma si bisogna soffrire questo anche posso sperare solamente un consiglio di Dio. Quando lei sta qui io non ho troppo di riposo come sto d'obbligo tenere mio bambino a mio lato le notte e come" lui ricusa mio petto io non posso tranquillizzarlo quand[o] piange. Ma spero campare come l'ho fatto altre volte" di mia vita nelle circonstanze difficillissime. Addio Amore, ti benedico" e sto sempre tua

M.

Si viene il tutore, mio medico seguiter [   ] resto, fa solament[e] che riceve mia lettera, si cura ancora per mi, rispondera, si non bisogna che cerco consiglio altra parte si puoi trovi si e sposato questa state" mi sembra probabile che si.

Friday
15 September [1848]

My love

this morning I receive your dear letters and the newspapers The news from Milan seems to me too good to be true, but I wait with anxiety to hear more.

When you do not receive news from me, do not be immediately worried, you know that I must still be very weak[;] I am not always able to write or get up and Mr. Giovanni is not always here to write for me. It is a miracle that I feel comfortable where I am; the circumstances have been so difficult for me. Now that I was so satisfied of my new nurse, her baby has become ill, if she is forced to leave me, the difficulties start again, I hope not; but if we have to suffer for this too, I can hope only for advice from God. When she is here I do not

115

have much rest because I have to keep my child at my side during the night and since he refuses my breast I cannot soothe him when he cries. But I hope I will survive as I did other times in very difficult circumstances of my life. Good bye my love, I bless you and I am always your

M.

If the guardian will come, my doctor will go [   ] let him only receive my letter, if he cares about me, he will answer, if not I will need to ask advice of somebody else[;] if you can, find out if he got married this summer I think it is possible.

ALS (MH: fMS Am 1086 [9:202]); MsC in English (MH: fMS Am 1086 [Works, 2:143–45]). English copy published in part in Higginson, *MFO*, pp. 255–56. *Addressed:* Sigre Mse Gio. Angiolo Ossoli / *Roma. Postmark:* Rieti.

bambino diviene] bambino divi(n)ene
ricommincia, spero] ri(m)commincia, (ma) spero
e come] e ↑ come ↓
altre volte] altre volte(e)
ti benedico] ti benedi(o)co
sposato questo state] sposato ↑ questo state ↓

756.   To Giovanni Angelo Ossoli

domenica
17th Settembre [1848]

Mio amore,

questa mattina non ricevo altro da te che il giornale di venerdi.

Soppongo adesso avrò aspettare a Martedi tue nuove come non viene posta domani.

Il bambino della balia sta meglio, e io sento sollevata. Bisogna avere coraggio, ma[n] è grande cura stare sola e ignorante con un bambino in questi primi giorni di sua vita. Quando lui avra un mese io sentirò[n] più di riposo; allora lui stara piu forte pegli cambii che avra sostenere. Adesso egli sta bene; commincia dormire bene e molto bello[n] per sua età e tutti dintorno senza sapere che nome io pensava dargli l'han chiamato *Angiolino* perche e si grazioso. Ha tua[n] bocca, mano, piede;[n] mi pare che suoi occhi saran turchini. Peraltro e tutto birbone; capisce bene, è molto ostinato avere sua volontà.

116

Avrò molto a dire quando tu vieni, e anche allora noi avrem molto combinare, perchè sara troppo freddo in questo appartamento per mi stare qui tard[i] nel autunno. Le quaranta giorni terminan 15th Ottobre, e" io voglio lasciare presto dopo come e possibile; i 20 o 25 si posso. Addio, amore, sempre la tua

M.

Sunday
17 September [1848]

My love,

this morning I receive nothing from you but the Friday newspaper.

Now I suppose I have to wait till Tuesday for your news since tomorrow the mail does not come.

The wetnurse's baby is better and I feel relieved. We must have courage but it is a great anxiety to be alone and so ignorant with a baby in these first days of his life. When he will be one month old I will have more rest; then he will be stronger for the changes which he will have to bear. Now he is well; he is begining to sleep well and is very beautiful for his age and everybody, without knowing what name I intended to give him, called him Angiolino because he is so nice. He has your mouth, hands, feet; I think his eyes will be turquoise. He is very naughty; understands well, is very obstinate to have his will.

I will have a lot of things to tell you when you come and also at that time we will have much to decide because it will be too cold in this apartment for me to stay here late in the fall. The forty days will finish the 15th of October, and I want to leave as soon as possible thereafter, on the 20th or 25th if I can. Good bye, love, always your

M.

ALS (MH: fMS Am 1086 [9:204]); MsC in English (MH: fMS Am 1086 [Works, 2:145–47]). Published in part in *Memoirs*, 2:298; English copy published entire in Higginson, *MFO*, pp. 256–57, and Wade, p. 580. *Addressed:* Sigre Mse Gio. Angiolo Ossoli / Roma. *Postmark:* Rieti.

coraggio, ma] coraggio, ↑ ma ↓
io sentirò] io sentir⟨a⟩ò
molto bello] molto ⟨gr⟩ bello
Ha tua] ⟨1⟩ Ha tua
mano, piede;] mano, pie⟨e⟩de;
Ottobre, e] Ottobre, ↑ e ↓

757. To Giovanni Angelo Ossoli

Rieti

Martedi 19th [settembre 1848]

Mio caro,

Oggi ricevo le lettere dalla Banca e il foglio di Sabato. Credo che le lettere eran ritardate alla posta di Roma.

M'incresce che tu stai poco bene, io credo che e da questa freddezza, qui anche e stato terribile; oggi va meglio. Mi ho spiegata male, non pensavo di cambiar casa qui in Rieti, ma che devo andare via da Rieti[n] le 20th o 25 *Ottobre*, si possibile, perche temo che piu tarde queste camere saran troppo fredde per mi e pel[n] bambino. Altro mi piacerebbe stare con lui lungo come è possibile; è si caro, si piace tanto dormire in mio seno; e conosco bene che nessuna altra può curarlo bene come io.

Queste due[n] giorni le cose van meglio; io ho avuta più di riposo ma ancora sto molto[n] debole. Alzare un poco, lavarmi, mangiare, e scrivere[n] questa lettera e tutto che posso fare, anche mi stanca troppo. La settimana prossima spero stare più forte; intanto scusate tutte mancanze di tua affezionata

M.

Il bambino si piace come tu col grande calore. Quando tu vieni io ti abbracciero come lui e ti faro di bene.

Rieti

Tuesday 19th [September 1848]

My dear,

Today I receive the letters from the bank and the paper of Saturday. I think that the letters were delayed at the Rome postoffice.

I am sorry that you are not well, I think that it is caused by this cold weather, it was also terrible here; today is better. I explained myself badly, I did not think to change house here in Rieti, but that I must leave Rieti the 20th or 25th of *October*, if possible, because I am afraid that later these rooms will be too cold for me and the child. Besides I would like to be with him as long as possible; he is so dear, it makes him so happy to sleep on my breast; and I know very well that no one else can take care of him as well as I.

These two days things are going better; I have had more rest but I am still very weak. To get up briefly, to wash myself, to eat, and to write this letter is all I am able to do, even if it makes me very tired.

Next week I hope to be stronger; meanwhile forgive me for not being able to do more. Your affectionate

M.

The baby likes the warm weather as you do. When you come I will embrace you as I embrace him and I will do you well.

ALS (MH:fMS Am 1086 [9:195]); MsC in English (MH:fMS Am 1086 [Works, 2:147–49]). *Addressed:* Sigre Mse / Gio. Angiolo Ossoli / Roma. *Postmark:* Rieti.

via da Rieti] via ↑ da Rieti ↓
e pel] e ⟨il⟩ pel
Queste due] Queste d⟨?⟩ue
sto molto] st⟨a⟩o molto
e scrivere] e s⟨?⟩crivere

758.   To Giovanni Angelo Ossoli

giovedi 21st [settembre 1848]

Mi pare, caro, si il dottore pensa ancora di me, scrivera quando ha ricevuto la mia lettera; io aspettero un poco vedere che fa.

Il bambino di questo mia balia adesso sta bene, e nostro anche ieri e oggi. Questa balia sarebbe bene contenta andare in Roma, stare col un suo fratello e tenere[n] nostro bambino, speranda dopo lavoro come sarta Lei è una persona che mi piace bene, ma son alcuni incommodi nel disegno.[n] Domandi[n] tutto che puoi delle balie, loro prezzi &c; io aspettero si non posso sentire dal dottore, e quando tu vieni[n] noi parleremo di tutto.

Io ho sofferto molto con una gonfiatura sopra la spalla che mi faceva guassi impossibile reggere mio braccio. Oggi sta un poco meglio, ma anche mi stanca molto scrivere, cosi t'abbracciando come fa anche il caro bellino la tua

M.

Thursday 21st [September 1848]

I think, my dear, that if the doctor still cares for me, he will write as soon as he receives my letter; I will wait for a while and see what he will do.

The baby of my nurse is well now as is our baby, yesterday and to-day. This nurse would be very happy to go to Rome, to live with a brother of hers and keep our child, hoping afterwards to find work as a dressmaker. She is a person whom I like very much, but there are some problems in the plan. Ask as much as you can about nurses, the prices &c; I will wait, if I do not hear anything from the doctor, and when you come we will talk of everything.

I suffered very much for a swelling on my shoulder which made it almost impossible to hold my arm. Today it is some better but it tires me very much to write, therefore I embrace you as does also our baby[;] your

M.

ALS (MH:fMS Am 1086 [9:205]); MsC in English (MH:fMS Am 1086 [Works, 2:151−53]). *Addressed:* Sigre Mse / Gio. Angiolo Ossoli / Roma. *Postmark:* Rieti.
  e tenere] e ⟨d⟩ tenere
incommodi nel disegno.] ⟨e⟩incommodi. ↑ nel disegno ↓
  Domandi] ⟨In d⟩ Domandi
tu vieni] tu vi⟨?⟩eni

759. To Giovanni Angelo Ossoli

Rieti
sabato 23 settembre [1848]

Mio caro,
  ricevo questa mattina il giornale e tua lettrina.

Io sento la verità di che tu dici che bisogna per prendere una balia la grandissima cautela; io aspettero per tutto consultare con ti. Pensi solamente si il bambino sta fuori di Roma, tu non puoi vederlo sovente. Altro, l'aria della campagna sarebbe meglio, senza dubbio, per sua salute[1]

È si caro; mi pare qualche volte, per tutte le difficolta e le disgrazie, che si vive, si sta bene può divenire un tal tesoro per noi tutti due, e un compenso per tutto. Io voglio molto per ti rivederlo; ma bisogna per ti avere pazienza sentirlo strillare sovente; è un ostinato. Anche per tua venuta io spero che mia spalla può essere guerita ancora e io forte assai sortire un poco con ti.

Adesso fa[n] bel tempo e io sorto sulla loggia. Ser Giovanni e buono per me, ma sue sorelle son de[te]stabi[li] mescolando in tutto, e si avare, si interressate,[n] si vogliono risparmian mi[n] mi denaro, vogliono riprenderlo per loro. Ma anche cerco io tenere la pace con loro; si trovan cattivi gent[i] [   ] tutta parte, e questi,[n] si interressati e volgare, almeno non sono perfide come la Giuditta. Addio, amore, abbracceandoti[n] son la tua

M.

Dimmi si stai meglio in salute co[   ] spero di si, perche e più caldo.

Rieti
Saturday, 23 September [1848]

My dear,

I receive this morning the newspaper and your dear letter.

I feel the truth in what you say that we must be very cautious in hiring a nurse; I will wait about everything to take counsel with you. Only think that if the baby is out of Rome, you can not see him very often. Furthermore, without doubt the air of the country would be better for his health[1]

He is so dear; sometimes I think that for all the misfortunes and difficulties, if he lives, if he is well, he can become a great treasure for the two of us, and a compensation for everything. I want you very much to see him; but you must be very patient when you hear him scream often; he is obstinate. Also, when you come I hope my shoulder will be well and that I can be strong enough to go out with you for a while.

The weather is beautiful now and I go out on the loggia. Mr. Giovanni is good to me, but his sisters are detestable, meddling in everything and so stingy and self-centered; they want me to save money, so that they can have it for themselves. Anyway I try to keep the peace with them; one can find bad people [   ] everywhere and these, if greedy and vulgar, at least are not as perfidious as Giuditta. Goodbye my love, embracing you I am your

M.

Tell me if you feel better [   ] I hope yes because it is warmer.

ALS (MH:fMS Am 1086 [9:205]); MsC in English (MH:fMS Am 1086 [Works, 2:149–51]). Published in part in *Memoirs*, 2:298; English copy published entire in Higginson, *MFO*, p. 257. *Addressed:* Sigre Mse / Gio. Angiolo Ossoli / Roma. *Postmark:* Rieti.

Adesso fa] Adesso ⟨ce⟩ fa
si interressate,] si interress⟨?⟩ate,
risparmian mi] risparmian⟨o⟩ ↑ mi ↓
parte, e questi,] part⟨i⟩e, e ques⟨?⟩ti,
amore, abbracceandoti] amore, abbr⟨i⟩acceandoti

1. Ossoli had said in his previous letter (MH) that "this matter ought to be treated with the greatest imaginable caution, since my thought would be, to keep the baby out of Rome, for the sake of greater secrecy, if we can find a good nurse who will take care of him like a mother."

760. To Giovanni Angelo Ossoli

Rieti
Martedi 26, Settembre [1848]

M'incresce tanto, amore, sentire che non stai bene ancora; è allora qualche cosa seria che hai. Se non stai bene, non vieni qui la notte nel maledetto carrettino, aspetta[n] per la diligenza; è vero che ho bisogno vederti presto e lungo come possibile ma aspettero piutosto che esporre tua salute.

Ma il giovedi scrivi[n] precise quando posso aspettarti; voglio stare pronta. Invio qui giù un ordine sulla banca pelle mie lettere; tu puoi inviarlo il giorno che vieni. Anche cerchi a la[n] grande posta, e *poste restante* si non c'è niente per mi, e dimando una volta ancora a la posta del Dottore dove è andato e quando ritorna in Roma. E m'apporti questa volta mia Cologne e miei guanti.

Scusa tutto l'incommodo.

Adesso noi commenciamo stare davvero bene, mio bambino e io. Lui dorme tutta la notte, e mia spalla, l'ultima[n] notte, non m'ha tormentata; cosi io anche ho dormita.[n] Lui è sempre si grazioso come è possibile per mi mai, mai lasciarlo? Sveglio la notte, lo riguardo, e penso ah, è impossibile lasciarlo. Addio, amore, si senti come io tu sei impaziente venire; allora noi possiamo parlare e avere ancora alcuni felici momenti di più La tua

M.

Rieti
Tuesday 26, September [1848]

I am very sorry, my love, to know that you are not well yet; it is then something serious that you have. If you are not well do not come here in the night by that cursed small cart but wait for the stagecoach; it is true that I need to see you soon and as long as possible but I will wait rather than to expose your health.

But on Thursday write exactly when I can expect for you; I want to be ready. Enclosed here I send another order on the bank for my letters; you can send it the day you come. Also look at the main post office and the *Posta Restante* if there is something for me and ask once again at the post office about the doctor; where he is gone and when he will come back to Rome. And this time bring me my cologne and my gloves.

Excuse all the inconveniences.

Now we are beginning to be really well, my baby and myself. He sleeps all night long, and my shoulder did not hurt me last night, so that I could have some sleep too. He is always so nice, how would it ever be possible for me to leave him? I wake up in the night, look at him, and I think ah, it is impossible to leave him. Goodbye my love, if you feel like me, you are very impatient to come; then we can talk and have more happy moments together Your

M.

ALS (MH:fMS Am 1086 [9:206]); MsC in English (MH:fMS Am 1086 [Works, 2:153–55]). English copy published in part in Higginson, *MFO*, p. 258. *Addressed:* Sige Mse / Gio. Angiolo Ossoli / Roma. *Postmark:* Rieti.

carrettino, aspetta] carrettino, ⟨i⟩ aspetta
giovedi scrivi] giovedi scriv⟨o⟩i
cerchi a la] cerc⟨i⟩hi a ↑ la ↓
l'ultima] l'u⟨?⟩ltima
ho dormita.] h⟨a⟩o dormita.

761. To Giovanni Angelo Ossoli

Giovedi
[28 settembre 1848]

Mi faceva ridere molto, amore, questa apparizione del Nicodemo sotto suo terzo nome.[1] Davvero noi abbiamo conosciuto[n] un bel nido dei volpi. Io ho veduto più cattivi genti questo anno passato che in tutta mia vita primo, e temo non aver terminata ancora.

Penso da tua lettera che arrivi la domenica la mattina; quanto voglio vederti! Il bambino non cresce molto, ma è sempre si grazioso; a davvero maniere delicate come una ballerina

Per altro, posso dire tanto meglio che scrivere che aspettando tua visita non dice piu adesso la tua sempre

M.

sto molto meglio adesso.

Thursday
[28 September 1848]
This appearance of Nicodemo's under his third name made me laugh a lot, my dear.[1] We have indeed met quite a den of foxes. I have seen more mean people this past year than in all my life before and I am afraid I am not finished yet.

I suppose from your letter that you will arrive on Sunday morning; how much I want to see you! The child doesn't grow much, but he is still so pretty; he indeed has gestures as delicate as a ballerina's

As for the rest I can tell you so much better than in writing so that while waiting for your visit I will not say any more yours always

M.

I am much better now.

ALS (MH:fMS Am 1086 [9:209]); MsC in English (MH:fMS Am 1086 [Works, 2:161]). English copy published in part in Higginson, *MFO*, p. 259. *Addressed:* Sigre Mse Gio. Angiolo Ossoli / Roma. *Postmark:* Rieti.

This letter answers Ossoli's of 26 September.
abbiamo conosciuto] abbiamo c(?)onosciuto

1. In his letter (MH), Ossoli described a meeting with Giuditta's brother, Nicomedi, a fellow member of the civic guard, who was in Rome under an assumed name.

762. To Giovanni Angelo Ossoli

Rieti
7 oct 1848,
Mio caro,

Ricevo questa mattina il giornale e tua lettrina. Mi piace che almeno tu hai avuto una notte tranquilla pel viaggio; ieri ricomminciava piovere qui. Tutto che ho detto al ser Giovanni era che sarebbe piacevole avere qualche amico per compare. Io non son molto competente dare consiglio in questo affare del battesimo, che non capisco bene, ma il compare che mi piacerebbe aver pel bambino è mio amico il Polacco Lui conosce del esistenza del bambino è Catolico[n] divoto, è un uomo distinto chi poteva essere un ajuto per lui nella sua vita futura, e voglio per lui avere qualche amico in caso d'accidente a noi Potete pensare di questo si non avete amico di fidanza che volete per compare, chi poteva interessarsi pel bambino si eravate d'obbligo lasciarlo.[1]

Bisogna pensare che vostro nipote conoscera questo affare alfine per via di Catalani. Ma io non conosco tuoi parenti ne si è possibile per te fidare in uno di loro.

Pel Polacco, come non conosco dove sta adesso, non poteva ricevere certificato da lui bisognerebbe lasciare il ufizio di compare" vuoto per lui, ma son sicuro lo prenderebbe, e noi possiamo dire che noi aspettiamo suo assenso. M'incresce che non posso spiegarmi meglio per scrittura, in Italiano è troppo" difficile per me.

Il caro bambino sembrava cercarti la notte dopo tua partenza. Avanti mattina svegliava, cercava, ricusava suo latte piangeva molto e sembrava cercare qualche cosa che non poteva trovare. Alfine son alzata io, e lo presa negli braccie, parlava molto con lui, e alfine si consolava. Sta bene oggi, fa bel tempo; io penso sortire con lui.

Addio, mio sempre caro. Dio ti protegga.

Rieti
7 Oct 1848,

My dear,

This morning I receive the newspaper and your dear letter. I am happy that at least you had a peaceful night for the trip; yesterday it began to rain again here. The only thing that I said to Mr. Giovanni was that it would be pleasing to have some friends for godfather. I am not very competent to give advice about baptism, which I do not understand well, but the godfather whom I would like to have for the baby is my friend the Pole. He knows about the existence of the baby[;] he is a devout Catholic, he is a distinguished man who could be a help to him in his future life, and I want him to have some friend in case something happens to us You can consider this if you do not have a faithful friend whom you want for godfather, who will look after the child if you must leave him.[1]

You must realize that your nephew will finally learn about this through Catalani. But I do not know your relatives nor if it is possible for you to trust one of them.

As far as the Pole, since I do not know where he is now, I cannot receive a certificate from him[;] we should leave the position of godfather open for him, but I am certain that he would accept it, and we can say that we are waiting for his acceptance. I am very sorry that I cannot make myself clearer in writing, it is too difficult for me in Italian.

The dear child seemed to look for you the night after you left. He woke up before sunrise, looked, refused his milk[;] cried very much

125

and seemed to look for something that he could not find. Finally I got up, and took him in my arms, spoke a great deal with him, and finally he was consoled. He is well today, the weather is good; I think I will go out with him.

Goodbye, my eternal love. God protect you.

AL (MH:fMS Am 1086 [9:188]); MsC in English (MH:fMS Am 1086 [Works, 2:155–59]). English copy published in part in Higginson, *MFO*, pp. 258–59. *Addressed:* Sigre Mse / Gio. Angiolo Ossoli / Roma. *Postmark:* Rieti.

è Catolico] è Catol⟨l⟩ico
lasciare il ufizio di compare] lasciare il ⟨funzione⟩ ↑ ufizio di compare ↓
è troppo] è ⟨?⟩ troppo

1. In his letter of 6 October (MH), Ossoli said guardedly:"Sigr. Giovanni said to me that being in Rome I could get a *procura* to baptize the baby from a godfather of my selection, whom we might have in Rome—as we had said that we should have a godfather in Rome. And this disturbed me a little, but I hope that you can help me with your advice, at least so far as to learn from S. Giovanni if it can be done in any other way—but be careful not to let him know that I have written, because he might understand too much of what our idea is."

763.   To Giovanni Angelo Ossoli

Rieti
8 ottobre 48

Mio Caro,

Io credo che ho scritta dopo le parole *Scudi Romane One hundred,* che è Inglese per *Cento*! mi ricordo l'aver scritta

L'infamia di Giuditta e che devo aspettare ma quando penso della possibilità di riveder la, appena voglio ritornare in Roma.

Mi sorpre[nd]e tutto che il dottore lascia Roma dove prendeva tanto denaro; bisogna che qual[che] cosa strana e accaduta in suoi affari. È grande fortuna per mi cosi che ho trovata balia e non ho bisogno di lui. Ma tutt'altro è meglio non rivederlo.

Ho ritornata la visita della Siga Rosati e lei a detta tanto buono di Chiara, dice anche che sua zia e eccelente e i fratelli tutti buoni. Il Mogliani dice stessa cosa, questo me consola un poco [d]el prospetto di lasciar mio bambino. Lo fo innestare la settimana prossima.

Gli ho data tuo bacio, ma non lo merita; è cattivo oggi e io molto stanca curarlo. Addio, amore, sempre la tua

M.

Rieti

8 October 48

My dear,

I think that after the words *Scudi Romane* I wrote *One hundred* which is the English for *Cento*! I remember that I have written it.

The infamy of Giuditta is that I must wait, but when I think of the possibility of seeing her again, then I immediately want to go back to Rome.

I am very surprised that the doctor leaves Rome where he earned so much money; something strange must have happened in his affairs. It was lucky for me that I found a nurse and I do not need him. But perhaps it is better not to see him again.

I returned the visit of Signora Rosati and she said so many good things of Chiara, she also said that her aunt is excellent and all the brothers are good. Mogliani says the same thing, this comforts me a little about the prospect of leaving my child. I will have him immunized next week.

I gave him your kiss, but he does not deserve it; he is bad today and I am very tired of taking care of him. Goodbye, love, always your

M.

ALS (MH:fMS Am 1086 [9:187]); MsC in English (MH:fMS Am 1086 [Works, 2:161–63]). *Addressed:* Sige Mse / Gio. Angiolo Ossoli / Roma. *Postmark:* Rieti.

764. To Giovanni Angelo Ossoli

Rieti

11 Ottobre 48.

ricevo, mio bene, tua lettera questa mattina. Parlero a Giovanni quando posso, adesso e sortito. La famiglia si dispiace più sempre con mi, perche prendo vino altra parte, avendo trovato che domandan di me sempre 2½ baiocchi la bottiglia, e 2 da tutti i altri compratori, senza vergogna per mie serve a che han pretiso[n] volere tanto risparmiare per mi. Ma Giovanni sarà tutto contento alfine si tu prendi per[n] lui un bel regalo, e questo voglio io e allora dire addio a questa casa.

Lunedi andai in legno col bambino a Citta Ducale. Fermai nel piazza lasciava passeggiare un poco Nana che m'aveva pregata nella maniera la più sfacciata per un posto e Chiara che in tutta sua vita non ha lasciata mai Rieti primo per un viaggio si lungo.

I soldati correvano e forzavan mi e il bambino salire a *l'intendente*! Non era Falcine più ma un vecchio signore chi loro gridavan molto per loro" sciocchezza. Mi faceva ridere che pensavan nostro bambino una persona si pericolosa.

Ieri andavo nel giardino [de]l vescovo [   ] mattina e prende va sedia con lui vedere la vendemmia. I contadini mi regalavan una grande canestra de ottime uve e uno mazzetta di malva. Mi pare che gli fa di bene stare fuori cosi.

Questa mattina e allegro e molto bello.

Quando ai preso il denaro *16, th* invia a me" 10 scudi nel modo che tu trovi il più convenevole. Sempre la tua

M.

Rieti
11 October 48.

This morning I receive your letter, my dear. I will speak to Giovanni as soon as I can, now he is out. The family is more displeased with me than ever because I buy the wine from another place, having found that they always charge me 2½ baiocchi per bottle, while they charge everybody else only 2, without feeling embarrassed with my servants with whom they pretend to want me to save a lot. But Giovanni will be very happy anyway if you take a good gift for him, and this is what I want and then to say goodbye to this house.

On Monday I went with the baby to Citta Ducale by coach. I stopped in the square to let Nana walk a little, who begged me in the most impudent way for a seat and Chiara who never in her whole life has left Rieti before, for so long a trip. The soldiers ran and obliged me and the child to go to the *intendente*! He was no longer Falcine, but an old man who shouted at them quite a bit for their foolishness. It made me laugh that they thought our child such a dangerous person.

Yesterday I went to the Bishop's garden [   ] morning and I sat with him to see the vintage. The peasants gave me a large basket of excellent grapes and a bunch of mallow. I think it is good for him to stay outside.

This morning he is cheerful and very pretty.

When you have taken the money, on the *16th*, send me 10 scudi in the way you think more convenient. Always your

M.

ALfr (MH:fMS Am 1086 [9:189]); MsC in English (MH:fMS Am 1086 [Works, 2:163–65]). *Addressed:* Sigre Mse / Gio. Angiolo Ossoli / Roma. *Postmark:* Rieti.

han pretiso] han pret⟨?⟩iso
prendi per] prendi p⟨iu⟩er
per loro] per l⟨?⟩oro
invia a me] invia ↑ a me ↓

765.   To Giovanni Angelo Ossoli

Rieti
venerdi 13 [ottobre 1848]

Mio Caro,

E qualche cambio nella posta, io ricevo lettere e fogli solamente 4 volte la settimana; credo è stesso con ti in Roma. Bisognerà per ti trovare un *compare*. Giovanni dice senza *procura legale* di qualche persona il battesimo non sarebbe legale; e si non si fa quando noi stiamo qui, il parroco &c faran grande difficolta dopo nostra partenza e probabile scriveran in Roma. È troppo tarde cercar procura dal Polacco, altro non so io dove sta adesso. Mi dispiace molte, ma bisogna per ti parlare a qualche amico.

Il bambino sta oggi davvero troppo bello e buono. Io poteva morire per lui. T'invia un bacio; almeno a sorriso quando lo domandato.

La condotta di Chiara mi piace bene, si bisogna lasciarlo, almeno spero che lui può stare bene con lei

Scrivi, amore si tu stai bene e senza dolori nel petto" a tua

M.

Il Ser Giovanni para sempre volere servirci pare tutt'altro da sue disgustose sorelle.

Rieti
Friday 13 [October 1848]

My dear,

There is some change in the postal service, I am receiving letters and newspapers only 4 times a week; I believe this is the same for you in Rome. You have to find a *godfather*. Giovanni says that without the *legal agency* of some person the baptism will not be legal; and if it is not done while we are here the priest &c will make a great deal of trouble for us after our departure and probably they will write in Rome. It is too late to try to get the proxy from the Pole, besides I do not know where he is now. I am very sorry, but it is necessary for you to speak to some friend.

The child is indeed too good and beautiful today. I could die for him. He sends you a kiss; at least he smiled when I ask for it.

Chiara's conduct pleases me very much, if it is necessary to leave him, at least I hope that he will be safe with her

Write, my love if you are well and without pain in your chest to your

M.

Mr. Giovanni always appears to want to help us[;] he seems to be very different from his disgusting sisters.

ALS (MH:fMS Am 1086 [9:195]); MsC in English (MH:fMS Am 1086 [Works, 2:167−69]). *Addressed:* Sige Mse / Gio. Angiolo Ossoli / Roma. *Postmark:* Rieti.
   bene e senza dolori nel petto] bene ↑ e senza dolori nel petto ↓

766.   To Giovanni Angelo Ossoli

Rieti
15 Ottobre, 48

Mio amore,
   una della lettere che tu hai inviata, mi fa conoscere la morte della vecchi Siga mia amica di che ti ho parlata sì sovente.[1] Ho pianto tanto, mi ho fatta malatta, ma non potevo altro; non era nel Mondo persona piu buona, nè più affettuosa per me. Ho perduta una ottima amica
   Le altre lettere sono importanti, ti dirò quando vieni.
   Pensa sempre in cercando casa per mi non compromettermi stare in Roma, mi pare sovente non posso stare lungo" senza rivedere il bambino, è sì caro e la vita mi pare sì incerta; non so come lasciar miei cari. Prendi l'appartamento per poco di tempo, bisogna che starò in Roma almeno un mese scrivere e anche stare vicino di te, ma voglio stare libera ritornar qui, si sento troppo ansiosa per lui, troppo soffrente.
   O Amore come e difficile la vita! Ma tu, tu" sei buono, si mi era solamente possibile farti felice!
   Il bachiere mi ha dato ricevute in sua lettera. Anche vuole ricevere subito l'inchiuso; vedi tu che l'ha subito; e mia firma per cambio in Parigi dice piu presto l'invio il meglio può fare per mi.
   Non pensi un momento di Giovanni come compare Sarebbe, mi

pare, fidare troppo in lui; io non lo credo degno. E meglio per ti
fidare in qualche tuo eguale, chi come gentil'uomo guardera tuo
segreto. Più un altra volta da tua

M.

Ho qualche cosa curiosa dirti di Giovanni quando vieni. Ieri il bambino pareva soffrire e era cattivo ma oggi sta bene e sì bello! Scrivi subito che tu hai ricevuto queste

Rieti
15 October, 48

My love,

one of the letters that you sent let me know about the death of the
elderly lady, my friend of whom I often spoke to you.[1] I cried so
much that I became ill, but I could not help it; no one in the world
was better and more affectionate to me than she was to me. I have lost
a very good friend

The other letters are important, I will tell you when you come.

Always remember in looking for a house for me not to commit me
to living in Rome; often I think that I could not stay for a long time
without seeing the baby again, he is so dear and life seems so uncertain; I do not know how to leave my dear ones. Take the apartment
for a short time; I need to stay in Rome for at least one month to
write and to be close to you, but I want to be free to come back here if
I am too anxious and grieved about him.

Oh dear, how hard life is! But you are so good, if it were only possible for me to make you happy! In his letter the banker sent me the
receipts. He also wants to receive the enclosed at once; take care that
he has it at once; about my signature for the exchange in Paris, he
says that the quicker I send it the better it will be for me.

Do not think for a moment about Giovanni as godfather. It would
be, I think, to trust too much in him; I do not think he is worth it. It is
better for you to trust in someone your equal who as a gentleman will
protect your secret. More another time from your

M.

I have something curious to tell you about Giovanni when you come.
Yesterday the child seemed to suffer and was bad, but today he is well
and so beautiful! Write to me as soon as you receive these

ALS (MH:fMS Am 1086 [9:189]); MsC in English (MH:fMS Am 1086 [Works, 2:169–71]). English copy published in part in Higginson, *MFO*, p. 260, and entire in Chevigny, p. 456.

stare lungo] stare ↑ lungo ↓
tu, tu] tu⟨a⟩, tu
1. Mary Rotch died on 4 September (Bullard, *Rotches*, p. 96).

767. To Giovanni Angelo Ossoli

Rieti
18 Ottobre, 48.

Mio Caro,

15 Scudi per mese mi pare troppo, altro son sicuro non volere l'appartamento per 6 mesi. Possibile per 4, ma non voglio legarmi avanti vederlo Sapete che si pago 15 scudi, si lontano da tutte le trattorie, si non posso ordinare bene mie spese di servizio, spenderò ancora piu che l'inverno passato e bisogna spendere molto meno.

Si voglion, e tu pensi bene" prendero questo appartamento per 2 settimane, provarlo si poco di tempo non puo prevenire d'affittarlo.Si no, e tu non trovi niente che me conviene precise, io verro in Roma in Albergo Cesari, e noi cercheremo insieme. Io conosco che è molto difficile trovare buono appartamento per una persona sola, ma questo inverno quando son pochi forestieri deve essere più facile e avevo sperata non spendere piu que 8 o 10 scudi pigione.

Per altro mi riferisco a tuo giudizio. Tu sai che me bisogna adesso per la creatura che è si caro per tutti dui e per altre ragioni stare molta economa

Ma anche per mia salute non posso soffrire una casa sporca nè molto umida. Altro si e *solo* è vero che costa molto meno per poco. Tu puoi agire a tuo giudizio conoscendo tutte le circostanze. Ma ho avuto una esperienza si triste che mi piacerebbe molto più provare o almeno vedere la casa e genti della casa avanti di m'impiegar

Tu sai anche che per ragione della cattiva Giuditta o altr[   ] e possibile che puo divenire molto dispiacevole per mi stare questo inverno, in Roma" noi non possiam conoscere ancora.

Io potevo stare contenta con *una* camera sola in casa particola[re] per primo mese, si vol[ev]an mi dare colazione nella camera, e capivan che penso cambiare, non potevo stare cosi tutto linverno.

Puoi prendere l'appartamento del Barberini per *una* settimana, si voglion loro, si puoi per prezzo ragionevole e si pensi che è meglio che per mi andare al albergo.

La diligenza *non* m'apportata il denaro ieri sera, bisogna aspettare Giovedi! –

Il caro bambino sta bene, è si bello, ma mi dispiace tanto che il Mogliani non viene fare l'innesto come ha promesso temo che è come l'altri Rietini; i cattivissimi genti che ho veduto mai, io.

Addio, amore! bisogna stare buono uno per l'altro noi dui. Mi dispiace molto che tu hai tutto questa noia per l'appartamento ma davvero bisogna stare prudente adesso, per nostro caro, e per noi. Sempre con benedizione la tua

M.

Rieti
18 October, 48.

My Dear,

15 Scudi per month appears to me too much, further I am sure that I do not want the apartment for 6 months. Perhaps for 4, but I do not want to bind myself before seeing it You know that if I pay 15 scudi, so far from all the inns, if I cannot arrange well my housekeeping expenses, I will spend more than the past winter, and we must spend much less.

If they let me, and you think it well I will take that apartment for 2 weeks; trying it for such a short time could not prevent them from renting it to others. If not, and you do not find something that exactly fits me, I will go in Rome to the Cesari Hotel, and we will look together. I know that it is very difficult to find a good apartment for just one person, but this winter, when there will be few foreigners, it must be easier, and I had hoped to spend no more than 8 or 10 scudi for rent.

Anyway I refer to your own judgment. You know that now I must be very economical, for the child so beloved to us and for other reasons

But also for my health I cannot endure a dirty house nor a very humid one. Further *only* if it is true that it costs much less for a short period. You can proceed by your own judgment since you know the circumstances. But I had such a sad experience that I would like very much to try or at least to see the house and the people before committing myself

You also know that because of the wicked Giuditta or for other [   ] it is possible that it could become very unpleasant for me to be in Rome this winter[;] we cannot know yet.

I could be contented with only *one* room in a private house, if they wanted to bring me breakfast into the bedroom, and if they understood that I am thinking of changing, I could not stay in such a way for the whole winter.

You can take the Barberini apartment for *one* week, if they let you, if you can get a reasonable price and if you think that it is better than for me to go to the hotel.

The stagecoach *did not* bring me the money yesterday evening, we have to wait for Thursday!—

The dear child is well and so pretty, but I am so sorry that Mogliani does not come to give the immunization as he promised[;] I am afraid that he is like the other people of Rieti; the worst people whom I have ever seen.

Goodbye, love! we have to stay well for each other. I am very sorry that you have all this trouble with the apartment but really we must be careful now for our dear child and for ourselves. Always a blessing your

M.

ALS (MH:fMS Am 1086 [9:190]); MsC in English (MH:fMS Am 1086 [Works, 2:171–77]). *Addressed:* Sige Mse / Gio. Angiolo Ossoli / Roma. *Postmark:* Rieti.
voglion, e tu pensi bene] voglion, ↑ e tu pensi bene ↓
inverno, in Roma] inverno, ↑ in Roma ↓

768. To Giovanni Angelo Ossoli

Rieti

20 ottobre [1848]

Mio amore,

ho ricevuto i dieci scudi era mio difetto che non gli avevo primo, aspettavo per loro avvertirmi, loro per mi inviar alla Uffizio.[n]

amore, non prendi[n] appartamento per mi ancora,[n] io non so ancora si posso venire 1st nov! questo Mogliano e detestabile, senza fede come gli altri, io non posso dire quanto soffro, basta che non voglio lasciar Rieti senza fare l'innesto del bambino quando morion tanti[n] d'intorno col vajuolo e[n] che lui non ha fatto niente, che soppongo staro d'obbligo chiamare un altro, chi sa quanto di tempo staro d'obbligo trattenere per questo, basta— non dormo la notte, e piango il giorno; sono si disgustata, ma tu non puoi ajutarmi sei troppo distante, io scrivero quando conosco si posso venire o no, possibile posso scrivere la domenica che farò; intanto vedi tu[n] l'apartament, e quando vengo, noi possiam veder[   ] i ottimi presto e posso eleggere io.

Domandate a 75 *via Sistina* e 79 via 4 Fontane, anche si senti qualche cosa in via Gregoriana. Scusa incommodo, amore si noi possiamo fare [b]ene in questo affare sara meglio per tutti dui. Si tu puoi vendere l'oro che hai[n] a vantaggio piu beni che posso usare qui in[n] Roma fai cose al tua discrezione.[n]

Il bambino e più bello tutti i giorni, vale la pena, ma è molta pena per mi poverina, sola qui, abusata per tutti. Spero [   ]iere piu allegra la Domenica[n] io sono sempre la tua

M.

Rieti
20 October [1848]

My love,

I have received the 10 scudi[;] it was my fault that I did not have them before, I waited for them to notify me, and they for me to send to the office.

my love, do not take an apartment for me yet, I still do not know if I can come on the 1st November! this Mogliani is detestable, untrustworthy like the others, I cannot tell you how much I am suffering, it is enough that I do not want to leave Rieti without having the baby innoculated since all around here are dying of small pox and he has done nothing which I suppose obligates me to call another, who knows how long I will have to stay here for this, enough— I do not sleep at night and I cry all day; I am so disgusted, but you cannot help me, you are too far away, I will write when I know whether or not I can come, possibly I can write on Sunday which I will do; in the meantime you look at the apartment and when I come, we can see [   ] the best quickly and I can choose.

Inquire at 75 *via Sistina* and 79 via 4 Fontane, also if you hear anything in via Gregoriana. Excuse the trouble, my love if we can do well in this business it would be better for both of us. If you can[,] sell in Rome the gold that you have at a good price plus the goods that I am using here[;] use your own judgment.

The baby is more beautiful every day, he is worth all the suffering, but it is a lot of suffering for poor me, alone here, abused by everybody. I hope to [   ] be happier on Sunday I am always your

M.

135

ALS (MH:fMS Am 1086 [9:191]); MsC in English (MH:fMS Am 1086 [Works, 2:177–79]). English copy published in part in *Memoirs*, 2:298. *Addressed:* Sige Mse / Gio. Angiolo Ossoli / Roma. *Postmark:* Rieti.

alla Uffizio.] alla ⟨O⟩ Uffizio.
non prendi] non prend⟨o⟩i
me ancora,] me, ↑ ancora ↓
morion tanti] m⟨?⟩orion tant⟨t⟩i
vajuolo e] vajuolo ↑ e ↓
vedi tu] vedi ↑ tu ↓
l'oro che hai] l'oro ↑ che hai ↓
qui in] qui ⟨?⟩ in
fai cose al tua discrezione.] fai ↑ cose al tua discrezione ↓ .
la Domenica] la ⟨d⟩ Domenica

769. To Giovanni Angelo Ossoli

mercoledi 25—[ottobre 1848]

Mio amore,

Questo odio dentro Ebrei e Romani deve produrre effetti molto cattivi qualche giorno, si non adesso—[1]Per la fuga del re di Napoli temo credere, non è probabile.[2]

Il Mogliani prega per ti, si puoi, domandare *alla Spezieria di San Pantaleo ossia del Sigr L'Angeli*[n] *vicino dalla piazza Pasquina Professor Francesco Bacci.* Dice che a questo *Prof. Bacci* a scritto diverse lettere per la *materia* e non riceve risposta; voule per questo *Bacci* inviar la materia a lui, Mogliani, per la posta di[n] *venerdi,* o darla a ti. Si tu la[n] hai, bisogna inviar la in una lettera, marcato fuori che cosa è, come si mette in una penna. Io penso che tu recevra questo troppo tarde[n] per Venerdi, ma spero non per domenica Non bisogna dire chi sei o altro che tu lo pregi dal Mogliano di Rieti non tardare, ma inviare subito. Temo sara di noia per te, ma fa lo per amore di nostro caro.[3]

Io voglio per ti venire qui, si non scrivo al contrario, Sabato[n] *4 novembre.* Trattendendo questa [se]ttimana più a[ltro] [s]pero, questa buona conseguenza che come il 4, Sabata, e festa del Morte, tu puoi lasciar il zio e venire qui pel Diligenza del giorno. Noi cosi avrem 3 giorni col nostro bambino, e io ritornero con ti il Mercoledi dopo.

Io penso che andrò si l'innesto non si fa perche dopo, venendo il freddo, sarà poco di pericolo pel bambino, e per molti ragioni è si difficile per mi [res]tare qui più. Ma si [l']innesto[n] può far si, starò molto più tranquilla Sempre, amore, la tua

M.

Wednesday 25 [October 1848]

My love,

This hatred between Jews and Romans must produce very bad effects some day if not now—¹About the flight of the king of Naples, I fear, it is not probable.²

Mogliani asks you, if you can, to inquire *at the Spezieria of San Pantaleo that is of Mr. L'Angeli near Piazza Pasquina* of *Professor Francesco Bacci.* He says that he has written many letters to *Prof. Bacci* for the *material* and he has not received an answer. He wants this *Bacci* to send the material to him, Mogliani, in *Friday's* mail, or give it to you. If you have it, you must send it in a letter marked on the outside in pen as to what it is. I think that you will receive this too late for Friday, but I hope not for Sunday You do not have to say who you are or anything more than that you are asking him on behalf of Mogliani of Rieti not to delay. I fear it will be a nuisance for you, but do it for love of our dear.³

I want you to come here, if I do not write you to the contrary on Saturday *4 November.* If I stay this week and the next, I hope as a good consequence that since the 4th, Saturday, is All Soul's Day, you can leave your uncle and come here by the day coach. So we will have 3 days with our child, and I will return with you next Wednesday.

I think I will go if the immunization is not done because after, when the cold comes, it will not be very dangerous for the child, and for many reasons it is difficult for me to stay here longer. But if the immunization can be done, I will be much more content Always, love, your

M.

ALS (MH:fMS Am 1086 [9:199]); MsC in English (MH:fMS Am 1086 [Works, 2:179–83]). *Addressed:* Sige Mse / Gio. Angiolo Ossoli / Roma. *Postmark:* Rieti.

Sigr L'Angeli] *Sigr L'⟨a⟩Angeli*
posta di] posta ↑ di ↓
tu la] tu ↑ la ↓
troppo tarde] troppo ta(?)rde
contrario, Sabato] contrario, ↑ Sabato ↓
si [l']innesto] si[l'] ↑ innesto ↓

1. In his letter of the previous day (MH), Ossoli described in detail a bloody three-day battle between the civic guard and inhabitants of Rome's Jewish ghetto. On Sunday, 22 October, a group of Jews and guards fought; the next day the guards plundered and burned the ghetto. The fighting continued into Tuesday, 24 October, despite the attempts of the police to end it.

2. As Fuller surmises, the rumor was false, for Ferdinand did not abandon his throne. He was, however, even more hated at this time because of his brutal suppres-

sion of the Sicilians at Messina during the first week of September. Because of the bombardment of the city, Ferdinand became known as "King Bomba" (King, *Italian Unity*, 1:316).

3. Ossoli reported on 27 October that he had sent the serum by diligence (MH).

770.   To Giovanni Angelo Ossoli

venerdi 27— [ottobre 1848]

Mio amore,

m'incresce molto che tuo zio è il solo Italiano che non osserva feste, giusto per nostra noja. Sarà molto freddo il 4, per ti venire la[n] notte, anche suppongo piovera allora e tutti i giorni di tua visita qui e il giorno di nostro ritorno. Adesso son begli giorni.

Altro mi[n] piace stare una settimana più con mio bambino. Sta tutti i giorni più interessante. Altro sento il bisogno stare un pezzo con ti, e andare una volta più nel mondo da che son stata aparte adesso 5 mesi. Ma non voglio fissarmi in Roma cosi che non posso lasciare si son troppo infelice separata dal bambino o per altra ragione voglio. Sarebbe meglio prendere un peggiore appartamento o una camera sola che fare grande spese o m'obbligarmi per lungo tempo. Cosi è meglio non decidere avanti la mia venuta in Roma.

Per mia salute non va male, solamente non guadagno forza e son sovente rinfreddata alzando la notte col bambino. Starò bene quando ho viaggiato, passeggiato un poco. Pel innesto noi faremo nostro possibile e si non può farsi, io spererò che lui stara sicuro nel inverno, e io stesso cercerò materia la primavera senza fidando in nul Rietino.

Son due, tre begli passeggi che spero fare con ti si per miracolo noi abbiamo sole quando tu stai qui.

Quanto m'incresce non sentire che Milano si leva contro Radetzky a questo momento importante. Io teme fideran in questo maladetto cattivo Carl Alberto troppo lungo e che Italia sia perduta quando era ancora possibile per lei stare felice.

Inchiudo un ordine alla Banca pegle mei lettere, che voglio ancora una volta e t'abbracciando[n] con grande affezione come fa anche nostro caro tua

M.

FRIDAY 27th [October 1848]

My love,

I am really sorry that your uncle is the only Italian who does not observe the holidays, just for our aggravation. It will be very cold on

138

the 4th, for you to come at night, I suppose it will also rain then as well as for the whole time of your visit and on the day of your return. Now the days are beautiful.

On the one hand I am happy to spend another week with my baby. He becomes more interesting every day. On the other hand I feel the need to spend some time with you and to go once again into the world from which I have been apart now for 5 months. But I don't want to settle in Rome so as not to be able to leave if I am too unhappy away from the baby or for any other reason. It would be better to take a worse apartment or only a room rather than making great expenses or committing myself for a long time. So it is better not to decide before my coming to Rome.

My health is not bad, only I am not gaining any strength and I often have a cold from getting up at night with the baby. I will be well after having travelled, walked a bit. As for the immunization we will do our best and if it cannot be done I will hope that he will be safe during the winter and I myself will look for the material in the spring without relying anymore on this person from Rieti.

There are two or three walks which I would like to do with you if by a miracle we have some sun when you come here.

How much I regret not to hear that Milan revolts against Radetzky at this important moment. I am afraid that they will trust in this cursed and bad Charles Albert for too long and that Italy will be lost when it was still possible for her to be happy.

I enclose an order to the Bank for my letters, which I want once again, and embracing you with great affection as does also our dear one your

M.

ALS (MH: fMS Am 1086 [9:210]); MsC in English (MH: fMS Am 1086 [Works, 2:183–87]). *Addressed:* Sige Mse / Gio. Angiolo Ossoli / Roma. *Postmark:* Rieti.

venire la] venire ⟨il⟩ la
Altro mi] ⟨Ancora⟩ ↑ Altro ↓ mi
e t'abbracciando] e t'ab⟨r⟩bracciando

771. To Giovanni Angelo Ossoli

Sabato la sera 28. [ottobre 1848]

Mio Caro,

Io son meno stanca questa sera che e ordinario per me adesso, cosi comincierò mia lettera per domani.

Il Mogliani e venuto ieri sera, fa belle scuse me chi sa? Dice che aspetta la materia da Roma, da Milano, che aspetta domani, si non Mercoledi. Si non viene" avanti Mercoledi, io temo bisogna trattenere più, altro chi sa si verrà Mercoledi. Io comincio non fidar in nessuno, non credere niente

Piove fortissime tutti i giorni. Ma oggi io son stata più tranquilla, e il caro nostro e stato si buono, ho preso tanto" piacere stare con lui. Quando" sorride in suo sonno, quanto fa battere mio core! E in grassato molto e tutto bianco, commincia giuocare ballare. Tu avrai molto piacer rivederlo, t'invia molti baci. Inchina sua testa a mi quando domando il bacio.

Domenica la mattina

Ricevo tua lettrina; mi consola, t'amo molto più che nelli primi giorni, perchè vedo per pruova come tuo core e buono e puro. Quando ci rivediamo, ti diro tutte mie ragioni per essere sturbata, tu non sarai sorpreso, anche non oso stare" troppo tranquilla, perchè trovo si non seguito, non insisto non fo il spione sopra tutte queste persone, mi abaseran.

Il Mogliani non viene" oggi, ma io cercherò avere pazienza. Non oso più sortire col bambino, mi pensavo" sicuro prendendo lo nel giardino del Vescovo e un bambino e morto la del vajioulo la settimana passata, è tutto accidente che egli non lo prendeva. Cosi sto prigioniere qui e non so per quanto di tempo, ma almeno posso vederlo ancora. Il Mercoledi ti scriverò si posso partire come noi avevam convenuti o non.

Il Giovanni cerca *corrompere Chiara*, e lei sta arrabbiata e vuole molto andare a sua casa. Ma non mi lascierà avanti mia partenza Lei ha detta a Giovanni si parla più a lei verra da mi." Questo posso dire solamente a ti, lei ha grande paura per suo marito conoscerlo. Anche egli ha detto a lei che ha fatto tanto per noi e noi non abbiam datogli nient[e] stai sicuro che prendi per lu[i q]ualche cosa di valore. E tutt[   ] come le sorelle" solamente copre un poco meglio sua disposizione. Mi piace tanto che tu hai trovato compare e in tua famiglia; per tutti ragioni va meglio cosi. Per loro non fai niente si è cosi, io pensavo possibile potrai fare qualche" cosa per tuo vantaggio, si non, mi fa niente.

Altro non prendi l'incommodo pegli appartamenti di che ho parlato. Parlava di questi solamente pensando avere sentita che avevan padrone buone. Quanto voglio vederti, mio caro.

con tutta l'affezione tua

M.

Saturday evening 28th [October 1848]

My Dear,

I am less tired this evening than it is common for me now, so I will begin my letter for tomorrow.

Mogliani came last night, he puts forward nice excuses but who knows? He says that he expects the material from Rome, from Milan, that he expects it tomorrow, if not Wednesday. If it doesn't arrive before Wednesday, I am afraid that we will have to stay longer, on the other hand who knows if it will come Wednesday. I am beginning not to trust anybody, not to believe anything

It pours every day. But today I have been calmer, and our dear one has been so good, I had much pleasure being with him. When he smiles in his sleep, how he makes my heart beat fast! He has grown much fatter and all white, he starts to play [and] dance. You will have much pleasure in seeing him again, he sends you many kisses. He bends his head toward me when I ask for a kiss.

Sunday morning

I receive your dear letter; it consoles me, I love you much more than during the first days because I have proof of how good and pure your heart is. When we meet again, I will tell you all my reasons for being worried, you will not be surprised, besides I dare not relax too much, because I find that if I don't continue, don't insist on spying on all these people, they will take advantage of me.

Mogliani does not come today, but I will try to have patience. I dare not to go out with the baby any longer, I thought I was safe in taking him to the garden of the Bishop and [then] last week a child died there from small pox and it was mere chance that he didn't catch it. So I stay here like a prisoner and I don't know for how long, but at least I can still see him. On Wednesday I will write you whether I can leave as we had agreed upon or not.

Giovanni tries to *corrupt Chiara* and she is very angry and wants very much to go home. But she will not leave me before my departure She told Giovanni that if he talks to her again she will come to me. This I can tell only you, she has a great fear that her husband will find out. Also he told her that he has done so much for us and we have not given him anything[;] make sure you get him something valuable. He is exactly like his sisters only he covers up his disposition a little better. I am very happy that you found a godfather and that he is a relative of yours; for all reasons it is better this way.

For them don't do anything if it is like that, I thought that possibly you could do something to your advantage, if not, it doesn't matter to

141

me. Do not bother about the apartments I told you about. I mentioned them only thinking I had heard they had good landladies. How much I long to see you, my dear.

with all my affection your

M.

ALS (MH: fMS Am 1086 [9:211]); MsC in English (MH: fMS Am 1086 [Works, 2:191–97]). English copy published in part in Higginson, *MFO*, p. 261. *Addressed:* Sige Mse / Gio. Angiolo Ossoli / Roma. *Postmark:* Rieti.

non viene] non ↑ viene ↓
preso tanto] preso tant⟨a⟩o
lui. Quando] lui. Quan⟨t⟩do
oso stare] oso st⟨r⟩are
Il Mogliani non viene] Il Moglian⟨o⟩i non vi⟨n⟩ene
mi pensavo] mi pensav⟨a⟩o
casa. Ma non mi lascierà avanti mia partenza Lei ha detta a Giovanni si parla più a lei verra da mi.] casa. ↑ Ma non mi lascierà avanti mia partenza Lei ha detta a Giovanni si parla più a lei verra da mi. ↓
le sorrelle] le s⟨a⟩orrelle
fare qualche] fare qua⟨c⟩lche

772. To Giovanni Angelo Ossoli

domenica 29, Oct 48

Mio amore,

la materia veniva l'innesto e fatto, quanto ti ringrazio come fa anche nostro caro con mille sorrisi oggi. È si bono e bello oggi. Ma ha preso una cattiva fantasia alzare due tre ore avanti il giorno, in questo[n] modo mi ha stancato terribile iere e oggi, insiste alzar e vedere il lume.

Adesso spero tanto che niente può prevenire nostro rincontro, questa[n] altra Domenica, assicurarti di bon ora col postino si bisogna per ti venirecon lui, ma m'incresce molto per ti stare fuori la notte adesso che fa si freddo.

Io aparecchio[n] bauli e tutto avanti, che io sia libera stare sempre conti.

Fai a tua discrezione per la[n] procura o altro.

Non so perche non hai ricevuto mia lettera di venerdi, era impostata di buon ora, era inchiusoun ordine sul banca pelle mie lettere spero ricevere queste colle tue nuove il mercoledi, adesso e si tarde che non ho tempo dire[n] altro che con tanto amore la tua

M.

142

voglio per ti comprare in Roma e apportare qui una canestra di paglia" come questa che tiene miei libri, si tu ricordi. Ho bisogno lasciar" dentro la roba del Bambino per Chiara" e niente si trova qui. Questo costova 5 paoli."

Sunday 29, Oct 48

My love,

the material arrived and the immunization is done, I thank you so much as does also our dear one today with a thousand smiles. He is so good and beautiful today. But he has taken the bad fancy to wake up two or three hours before sunrise, in this way yesterday and today he has tired me terribly, he insists to get up and see the light.

Now I really hope that nothing can prevent our reunion the Sunday after the next, check well in advance with the mailman if you must come with him, but I am very sorry that you will be out at night now that it is so cold.

I will prepare the trunks and all beforehand, so as to be free to be always with you.

Act at your own judgment about the proxy or anything else.

I don't know why you haven't received my letter from Friday, it was mailed early, there was enclosed an order to the bank for my letters[;] I hope to receive them with your news on Wednesday, now it is so late that I have no time to add anything more than with much love your

M.

I want you to buy in Rome and bring here a straw basket like the one that keeps my books, if you remember. I need to leave in it the child's things for Chiara and here I can find nothing. This one cost 5 paoli.

ALS (MH: fMS Am 1086 [9:207]); MsC in English (MH: fMS Am 1086 [Works, 2: 187–89]). *Addressed*: Sige Mse / Gio. Angiolo Ossoli / Roma. *Postmark*: Rieti.
in questo] in que⟨?⟩sto
rincontro, questa] rincontro, qu⟨s⟩esta
Io aparecchio] Io apar⟨c⟩ecchio
per la] per ↑ la ↓
tempo dire] tempo ⟨ajutar⟩ dire
canestra di paglia] canestra ↑ di paglia ↓
bisogno lasciar] bisogno lasc⟨a⟩iar
Bambino per Chiara] Bambino ↑ per Chiara ↓
5 paoli.] 5 pa⟨?⟩oli.

773. To Giovanni Angelo Ossoli

Rieti

1st Novr [1848]

Mio caro,

ricevo tua lettrina e i fogli. Spero davvero che tu puoi venire il giorno di Sabato, si pioverebbe forte la notte, come piove si sovente adesso, sarebbe terribile a questa stagione. I giorni adesso sono belli, ma bisogna aspettare nostre disgrazie ordinarie di piove, piove sempre. Ma piove" o non si il bambino sta bene io partirò con ti. Io commincio soffrire molto nella testa, sturbata la notte, come son, il bambino e adesso pesante, e Chiara ritornando due volte il giorno a casa, io ho sovente portarlo nelle braccie quando pare" ingiuriar me. Altro suo bambino sta male e lei incresce lasciarlo, anche" la notte strilla molto. Io spero non farà cosi quando tu stai qui. Altro non dirò più oggi, sperando subito che posso dirti tutto, e soffrente nella mia testa. Questo e mia ultima lettera, come non posso impostare domani. Tu non hai scritto che hai presto per Giovanni, si non trovi facile regalo" conveniente non prendi niente d'incommodo, noi gli daremo denaro, per lui sara la stessa, non ha la minima delicatezza. Addio, mio ben, sperando fra poco t'abbracciar la tua

M.

Credo ho scritto per ti apportare cosa, canestra di paglia" come mia in che tengo i libri" per la roba del bambino. Egli ti saluta. La mattina e si bel e allegro, la sera un poco cattivo.

Rieti

1st Novr [1848]

My dear,

I receive your dear letter and the papers. I really hope that you can come on Saturday, if it rains hard during the night, as it rains so often now, it would be terrible in this season. The days are beautiful now, but we must expect our usual troubles rain, always rain. But whether it rains or not, if the child is well I will leave with you. I am beginning to suffer very much in my head, disturbed in the night, as I am, the child is very heavy now, and since Chiara returns home twice a day, I have to carry him very often in my arms when he seems angry with me. Her baby is also ill and she does not want to leave him, he also cries much during the night. I hope that he will not do so when you are here. I will say nothing more today, I hope to tell you everything very soon, and I am suffering from a headache. This is my last letter, since I cannot mail another tomorrow. You have not written what you bought for Giovanni, if you do not easily find a suitable gift, do not buy anything you are not comfortable with, we will give him money, for him it will be the same, he has no delicacy. Goodbye my love, I hope to embrace you very soon your

M.

I think I wrote to you to bring something, a straw basket like the one I have in which I keep the books for the baby's things. He says hello to you. In the morning he is beautiful and cheerful, in the evening a bit bad.

ALS (MH: fMS Am 1086 [9:191]); MsC in English (MH: fMS Am 1086 [Works, 2:189–91]). *Addressed*: Sige Mse / Gio. Angiolo Ossoli / Roma. *Postmark*: Rieti.

Ma piove] ⟨?⟩ Ma piove
quando pare] quando p⟨?⟩are
lasciarlo, anche] lasciarlo, ↑ anche ↓
facile regalo] facile ⟨cose⟩ ↑ regalo ↓
canestra di paglia] canestra ↑ di paglia ↓
mia in che tengo i libri] mia ↑ in che tengo i libri ↓

774. To Margarett C. Fuller

Rome, 16 November 1848

Of other circumstances which complicate my position I cannot write. Were you here, I would confide in you fully, and have more than once, in the silence of the night, recited to you those most strange and romantic chapters in the story of my sad life. At one time when I thought I might die, I empowered a person, who has given me, as far as possible to him, the aid and sympathy of a brother, to communicate them to you, on his return to the United States.[1] But now I think we shall meet again, and I am sure you will always love your daughter, and will know gladly that in all events she has tried to aid and striven never to injure her fellows. In earlier days, I dreamed of doing and being much, but now am content with the Magdalen to rest my plea hereon, "*She has loved much.*"[2]

You, loved mother, keep me informed, as you have, of important facts, *especially* the *worst*. The thought of you, the knowledge of your angelic nature, is always one of my greatest supports. Happy those who have such a mother! Myriad instances of selfishness and corruption of heart cannot destroy the confidence in human nature.

145

I am again in Rome, situated for the first time entirely to my mind. I have but one room, but large; and everything about the bed so gracefully and adroitly disposed that it makes a beautiful parlor, and of course I pay much less. I have the sun all day, and an excellent chimney. It is very high and has pure air, and the most beautiful view all around imaginable. Add, that I am with the dearest, delightful old couple one can imagine, quick, prompt, and kind, sensible and contented. Having no children, they like to regard me and the Prussian sculptor, my neighbor, as such; yet are too delicate and too busy ever to intrude. In the attic, dwells a priest, who insists on making my fire when Antonia is away. To be sure, he pays himself for his trouble, by asking a great many questions. The stories below are occupied by a frightful Russian princess with moustaches, and a footman who ties her bonnet for her; and a fat English lady, with a fine carriage, who gives all her money to the church, and has made for the house a terrace of flowers that would delight you. Antonia has her flowers in a humble balcony, her birds, and an immense black cat; always addressed by both husband and wife as "Amoretto," (little love!)

The house looks out on the Piazza Barberini, and I see both that palace and the Pope's. The scene to-day has been one of terrible interest. The poor, weak Pope has fallen more and more under the dominion of the cardinals, till at last all truth was hidden from his eyes. He had suffered the minister, Rossi, to go on, tightening the reins, and, because the people preserved a sullen silence, he thought they would bear it.[3] Yesterday, the Chamber of Deputies, illegally prorogued, was opened anew. Rossi, after two or three most unpopular measures, had the imprudence to call the troops of the line to defend him, instead of the National Guard. On the 14th, the Pope had invested him with the privileges of a Roman citizen: (he had renounced his country when an exile, and returned to it as ambassador of Louis Philippe.) This position he enjoyed but one day. Yesterday, as he descended from his carriage, to enter the Chamber, the crowd howled and hissed; then pushed him, and, as he turned his head in consequence, a sure hand stabbed him in the back. He said no word, but died almost instantly in the arms of a cardinal. The act was undoubtedly the result of the combination of many, from the dexterity with which it was accomplished, and the silence which ensued. Those who had not abetted beforehand seemed entirely to approve when done.[4] The troops of the line, on whom he had relied, remained at their posts, and looked coolly on. In the evening, they walked the streets with the people, singing, "Happy the hand which rids the world of a tyrant!" Had Rossi lived to enter the Chamber, he would have seen the most terrible and imposing mark of denunciation known in the history of nations,—the whole house, without a single exception, seated on the benches of opposition. The news of his death was received by the deputies with the same cold silence as by the people. For me, I never thought to have heard of a violent death with satisfaction, but this act affected me as one of terrible justice.

To-day, all the troops and the people united and went to the Quirinal to demand a change of measures. They found the Swiss Guard drawn out, and the Pope dared not show himself. They attempted to force the door of his palace, to enter his presence, and the guard fired. I saw a man borne by wounded. The drum beat to call out the National Guard. The carriage of Prince Barberini has returned with its frightened inmates and liveried retinue, and they have suddenly barred up the court-yard gate.[5] Antonia, seeing it, observes, "Thank Heaven, we are poor, we have nothing to fear!" This is the echo of a sentiment which will soon be universal in Europe.

Never feel any apprehensions for my safety from such causes. There are those who will protect me, if necessary, and, besides, I am on the conquering side. These events have, to me, the deepest interest. These days are what I always longed for,—were I only free from private care! But, when the best and noblest want bread to give to the cause of liberty, I can just not demand *that* of them; their blood they would give me.

You cannot conceive the enchantment of this place. So much I suffered here last January and February, I thought myself a little weaned; but returning, my heart swelled even to tears with the cry of the poet:—

"O, Rome, *my* country, city of the soul!"[6]

Those have not lived who have not seen Rome. Warned, however, by the last winter, I dared not rent my lodgings for the year. I hope I am acclimated. I have been through what is called the grape-cure, much more charming, certainly, than the water-cure. At present I am very well; but alas! because I have gone to bed early, and done very little. I do not know if I can maintain any labor. As to my life, I think that it is not the will of Heaven it should terminate very soon. I have had another strange escape. I had taken passage in the diligence to come to Rome; two rivers were to be passed,—the Turano and the Tiber,—but passed by good bridges, and a road excellent when not broken unexpectedly by torrents from the mountains. The diligence sets out between three and four in the morning, long before light. The director sent me word that the Marchioness Crispoldi had taken for herself and family a coach extraordinary, which would start two hours later, and that I could have a place in that, if I liked; so I accepted. The weather had been beautiful, but, on the eve of the day fixed for my departure, the wind rose, and the rain fell in torrents. I observed that the river which passed my window was much swollen, and rushed with great violence. In the night, I heard its voice still stronger, and felt glad I had not to set out in the dark. I rose with twilight, and was expecting my carriage, and wondering at its delay, when I heard, that the great diligence, several miles below, had been seized by a torrent; the horses were up to their necks in water, before any one dreamed of the danger. The postilion called on all the saints, and threw himself into the water. The door of the diligence could not be opened, and the passengers forced themselves, one after another, into the cold water,—dark too. Had I been there I had fared ill; a pair of strong men were ill after it, though all escaped with life.

For several days, there was no going to Rome; but, at last, we set forth in two great diligences, with all the horses of the route. For many miles, the mountains and ravines were covered with snow; I seemed to have returned to my own country and climate. Few miles passed, before the conductor injured his leg under the wheel, and I had the pain of seeing him suffer all the way, while "Blood of Jesus," "Souls of Purgatory," was the mildest beginning of an answer to the jeers of the postilions upon his paleness. We stopped at a miserable osteria, in whose cellar we found a magnificent remain of Cyclopean architecture,—as indeed in Italy one is paid at every step, for discomfort or danger, by some precious subject of thought. We proceeded very slowly, and reached just at night a solitary little inn, which marks the site of the ancient home of the Sabine virgins, snatched away to become the mothers of Rome. We were there saluted with the news that the Tiber, also, had overflowed its banks, and it was very doubtful if we could pass. But what else to do? There were no accommodations in the house for thirty people, or even for three, and to sleep in the carriages in that wet air of the marshes, was a more certain danger than to attempt the passage. So we set forth; the moon, almost at the full, smiling sadly on the ancient grandeurs, then half draped in mist, then drawing over her face a thin white veil. As we approached the Tiber, the towers and domes of Rome could be seen, like a cloud lying low on the horizon. The road and the meadows, alike under water, lay between us and it, one sheet of silver. The horses entered; they behaved nobly; we proceeded, every moment uncertain if the water would not become deep; but the scene was beautiful, and I en-

joyed it highly. I have never yet felt afraid when really in the presence
of danger, though sometimes in its apprehension.

At last we entered the gate; the diligence stopping to be examined,
I walked to the gate of Villa Ludovisi, and saw its rich shrubberies of
myrtle, and its statues so pale and eloquent in the moonlight.

Is it not cruel that I cannot earn six hundred dollars a year, living
here? I could live on that well, now I know Italy. Where I have been,
this summer, a great basket of grapes sells for one cent!— delicious
salad, enough for three or four persons, one cent,— a pair of chickens, fifteen cents. Foreigners cannot live so, but I could, now that I
speak the language fluently, and know the price of everything. Everybody loves and wants, to serve me, and I cannot earn this pitiful sum
to learn and do what I want.

Of course, I wish to see America again; but in my own time, when I
am ready, and not to weep over hopes destroyed and projects unfulfilled.

My dear friend, Madame Arconati, has shown me generous love;—
a *contadina*, whom I have known this summer, hardly less. Every
Sunday, she came in her holiday dress,— beautiful corset of red silk
richly embroidered, rich petticoat, nice shoes and stockings, and
handsome coral necklace, on one arm an immense basket of grapes,
in the other a pair of live chickens, to be eaten by me for her sake,
("*per amore mio*,") and wanted no present, no reward; it was, as she
said, "for the honor and pleasure of her acquaintance." The old father of the family never met me but he took off his hat, and said,
"Madame, it is to me a *consolation* to see you." Are there not sweet
flowers of affection in life, glorious moments, great thoughts?— why
must they be so dearly paid for?

Many Americans have shown me great and thoughtful kindness,
and none more so than W. S——and his wife. They are now in Florence, but may return. I do not know whether I shall stay here or not;
shall be guided much by the state of my health.

All is quieted now in Rome. Late at night the Pope had to yield, but
not till the door of his palace was half burnt, and his confessor killed.
This man, Parma, provoked his fate by firing on the people from a
window. It seems the Pope never gave order to fire; his guard acted
from a sudden impulse of their own.[7] The new ministry chosen are
little inclined to accept.[8] It is almost impossible for any one to act, unless the Pope is stripped of his temporal power, and the hour for that
is not yet quite ripe; though they talk more and more of proclaiming
the Republic, and even of calling my friend Mazzini.

If I came home at this moment, I should feel as if forced to leave my own house, my own people, and the hour which I had always longed for. If I do come in this way, all I can promise is to plague other people as little as possible. My own plans and desires will be postponed to another world.

Do not feel anxious about me.[9] Some higher power leads me through strange, dark, thorny paths, broken at times by glades opening down into prospects of sunny beauty, into which I am not permitted to enter. If God disposes for us, it is not for nothing. This I can say, my heart is in some respects better, it is kinder and more humble. Also, my mental acquisitions have certainly been great, however inadequate to my desires.

ELfr, from *Memoirs*, 2:245–52. Published in part in *At Home and Abroad*, pp. 427–30, and in Chevigny, pp. 459–63.

1. Thomas Hicks.

2. Luke 7:47: "Wherefore I say unto thee, Her sins, which are many, are forgiven; for she loved much: but to whom little is forgiven, the same loveth little."

3. Pellegrino Rossi (1787–1848), a native of Carrara, began his career as a lawyer and professor. Exiled to France in 1815 for his support of Murat, he attracted the notice of François Guizot, the French premier, who made Rossi the French ambassador to Rome in 1845. A nationalist but a moderate who hated republicanism, Rossi had been a friend and adviser to Pius, who appointed him to succeed Eduardo Fabbri as his minister on 16 September. Rossi made significant internal improvements in the Papal States, but he bitterly opposed a plan that Montanelli drew up in Florence to assemble a constituent assembly from all of Italy, and he broke with Piedmont. His haughty demeanor and his scathing talents as a speaker intensified the opposition to his policies (King, *Italian Unity*, 1:277; Farini, 2:340; Berkeley, 395–409).

4. The days before 15 November, when the Chamber was to meet, were full of intrigue and warnings that Rossi's life was in danger. Already willing to show force, he called troops to Rome to supplant the civic guard, which he did not trust. A menacing crowd met him as he appeared at the palace on 15 November. As Rossi ascended the steps to the chamber he was stabbed. He fell to the ground and soon died. The assassination was probably planned by Pietro Sterbini, who deeply hated Rossi; the fatal blow was "certainly delivered by Luigi Brunetti, eldest son of Ciceruacchio" (Angelo Brunetti, the head of the most radical of the Roman "clubs") (King, *Italian Unity*, 1:280; Berkeley, pp. 416–32).

5. Francesco-Maria Barberini-Colona (1772–1853) (*Annuario della nobiltà italiana*, p. 89).

6. From Byron's *Childe Harold's Pilgrimage*, canto IV, stanza 78:

Oh Rome! my country! city of the soul!
The orphans of the heart must turn to thee,
Lone mother of dead empires! and control
In their shut breasts their petty misery.

(Byron, *Poetical Works*, p. 237.)

7. The day following Rossi's murder a crowd gathered to demand a constituent assembly for Italy. The event became a general upheaval when the crowd marched on the Quirinal Palace. Pius, however, refused to come to terms with their demands, so the enraged mob fired on the palace, killing Monsignor Palma. Under duress, the pope agreed to form a cabinet, and the crowd was satisfied (Farini, 2: 414–21; Berkeley, p.

455). In her *Tribune* dispatch, Fuller all but called the pontiff a coward: "I would lay my life that he could have shown himself without the slightest danger; nay, that the habitual respect for his presence would have prevailed, and hushed all tumult. He did not think so, and, to still it once more degraded himself and injured his people, by making promises he did not mean to keep" (*New-York Daily Tribune*, 26 January 1849).

8. Antonio Rosmini, whom the pope named president of the new ministry, refused the office. Pius then turned to Monsignior Carlo Emmanuele Muzzarelli, whom the republicans favored. Other members of the ministry were Pietro Sterbini, Mamiani, Giuseppe Galletti, and Giuseppe Lunati. Farini says that Galletti and Sturbini held actual power in the ministry (Farini, 2:421–23).

9. In her letter of 3 October (MH), Mrs. Fuller had urged her daughter to come home and given a bleak account of the family's finances.

775. To Richard F. Fuller

Rome 17th Novr 1848

My always dear Richard

I wrote you a long letter, but have destroyed it, the Socratic demon advising me that it was not best to send it at this time. Some from you certainly have been lost, and I suppose from the tone of the only one I have recd for some months that events have occurred in your life that I do not know

This one letter contained the second of exchange on Brown Shipley[n] and Co, the first I never recd. The last from you previous was dated 13th May. I thank you much. Since circumstances stand so ill with us, I will try to trouble you as little as possible. I will not write more now my mind lies dubious,[n] I cannot see how to act yet and writing would not help me.

I fear you have acted rashly to take an office in Boston, without an opening [a]lready made for business that can hardly go, why not try a country town of N. England? I did not want you to go to the West, but, if alone, I fear you will have to wait long for practice in B. and lead a life less congenial to you than that of a country town.

Have patience and strive for a cheerful view. Your destiny *may* be steadily unpropitious, but in the greater number of instances a man can conquer such a destiny, if he wastes none of his strength. Do not regret that you could not carry out the plans you had for a life with[n] me. I am no longer equal to my part, and yours would not have sufficed to make you happy. I hope you will have a better career than that and connections more fitted to fill the heart. Domestic life with wife and children a man needs to sweeten this bitter life.

The letter to Mother you can read and it will tell you as much of

151

me as it avails to know for the present, before long I write again. Now I am anxious to close for the post; this letter I have been unable to write before since the reception of yours. Now if I do not close you will have to wait a week or fortnight longer and I think you might become anxious about Your sister and friend

MARGARET.

Name your new address when you write.

ALS (MH: fMS Am 1086 [9:154]); MsC (MH: fMS Am 1086 [*Works*, 2:871–77]). *Addressed:* Richard F Fuller / Boston / Mass. U.S.A. *Postmark:* New York 2 Jan. *Endorsed:* F.S.M. / Margaret / Nov. 48.

Brown Shipley] Brown Shi⟨l⟩pley
lies dubious,] lies d⟨u⟩ubious,
for a life with] for ↑a life with↓

776. To Marcus Spring

Rome, 23 November 1848

Mazzini has stood alone in Italy, on a sunny height, far above the stature of other men. He has fought a great fight against folly, compromise, and treason; steadfast in his convictions, and of almost miraculous energy to sustain them, is he. He has foes; and at this moment, while he heads the insurrection in the Valtellina, the Roman people murmur his name, and long to call him here.[1]

How often rings in my ear the consolatory word of Körner, after many struggles, many undeceptions, "Though the million suffer shipwreck, yet noble hearts survive!"

I grieve to say, the good-natured Pio has shown himself utterly derelict, alike without resolution to abide by the good or the ill. He is now abandoned and despised by both parties. The people do not trust his word, for they know he shrinks from the danger, and shuts the door to pray quietly in his closet, whilst he knows the cardinals are misusing his name to violate his pledges. The cardinals, chased from Rome, talk of electing an anti-Pope; because, when there was danger, he has always yielded to the people, and they say he has overstepped his prerogative, and broken his papal oath. No one abuses him, for it is felt that in a more private station he would have acted a kindly part; but he has failed of so high a vocation, and balked so noble a hope, that no one respects him either. Who would have believed, a year ago, that the people would assail his palace? I was on Monte Cavallo yesterday, and saw the broken windows, the burnt doors, the walls marked by shot, just beneath the loggia, on which we have seen him giving the benediction. But this would never have happened, if his guard had not fired first on the people. It is true it was without his order, but, under a different man, the Swiss would never have dared to incur such a responsibility.

Our old acquaintance, Sterbini, has risen to the ministry.[2] He has a certain influence, from his consistency and independence, but has little talent.

Of me you wish to know; but there is little I can tell you at this distance. I have had happy hours, learned much, suffered much, and outward things have not gone fortunately with me. I have had glorious hopes, but they are overclouded now, and the future looks darker than ever, indeed, quite impossible to my steps. I have no hope, unless that God will show me some way I do not know of now; but I do not wish to trouble you with more of this.

ELfr, from *Memoirs*, 2:252−54.

1. After the Piedmontese withdrew from Milan, Mazzini joined Garibaldi's mountain guerrillas until August, when he went into exile at Lugano, Switzerland. As he had done in the past, he immediately began to work for a popular uprising against the Austrians, but he had as little success as he had had in previous years. Mazzini planned a revolt for 29 October in the Valtelline area of northern Lombardy. His agents were to capture three steamers on Lake Como to use as mobile fortresses and then lead a popular demonstration. The Austrians moved first, however, so when Mazzini invaded Lombardy, the citizens refused to follow him. He proclaimed a republic, but the attempt failed completely after three days (Barr, *Mazzini*, pp. 194−96).

2. Pietro Sterbini (1795−1863) studied medicine in Rome but became instead a writer and political agitator for Mazzini's Young Italy. After a period of exile, Sterbini returned to Rome in 1846, worked with Masi on the *Contemporaneo*, and became one of the leading radical agitators. He joined the government as minister of commerce and public works following Rossi's assassination (*Dizionario enciclopedico*).

777. To [?]

Rome, [23 November] 1848

It is a time such as I always dreamed of; and that fire burns in the hearts of men around me which can keep me warm. Have I something to do here? or am I only to cheer on the warriors, and after write the history of their deeds? The first is all I have done yet, but many have blessed me for my sympathy, and blest me by the action it impelled.

My private fortunes are dark and tangled; my strength to govern them (perhaps that I am enervated by this climate) much diminished. I have thrown myself on God, and perhaps he will make my temporal state very tragical. I am more of a child than ever, and hate suffering more than ever, but suppose I shall live with it, if it must come.

I did not get your letter, about having the rosary blessed for ——, before I left Rome, and now, I suppose, she would not wish it, as none can now attach any value to the blessing of Pius IX. Those who loved him can no longer defend him. It has become obvious, that those first acts of his in the papacy were merely the result of a kindly, good-natured temperament; that he had not thought to understand their bearing, nor force to abide by it. He seems quite destitute of moral courage. He is not resolute either on the wrong or right side. First, he abandoned the liberal party; then, yielding to the will of the people, and uniting, in appearance, with a liberal ministry, he let the cardinals betray it, and defeat the hopes of Italy. He cried peace, peace![1] but had not a word of blame for the sanguinary acts of the King of Naples, a word of sympathy for the victims of Lombardy. Seizing the moment of dejection in the nation, he put in this retrograde ministry; sanctioned their acts, daily more impudent; let them neutralize the constitution he himself had given; and when the people slew his minister, and assaulted him in his own palace, he yielded anew; he dared not die, or even run the slight risk,— for only by accident could he have perished. His person as a Pope is still respected, though his character as a man is despised. All the people compare him with Pius VII. saying to the French, "Slay me if you will; I *cannot* yield," and feel the difference.[2]

I was on Monte Cavallo yesterday. The common people were staring at the broken windows and burnt door of the palace where they have so often gone to receive a blessing, the children playing, "*Sedia Papale. Morte ai Cardinali, e morte al Papa!*"

The men of straw are going down in Italy everywhere; the real men rising into power. Montanelli, Guerazzi, Mazzini, are real men; their influence is of character.[3] Had we only been born a little later! Mazzini has returned from his seventeen years' exile, "to see what he foresaw."[4] He has a mind far in advance of his times, and yet Mazzini sees not all.

ELfr, from *Memoirs*, 2:236–38.

Dated by the reference to her visit to Monte Cavallo and the damaged palace. The Memoirs *editors misdated the letter as 30 April 1848.*

1. Jer. 6:14: "They have healed also the hurt of the daughter of my people slightly, saying, Peace, peace; when there is no peace."

2. Barnabò Chiaramonti (1742–1823) became Pope Pius VII in 1800. In 1809, after the pope refused to join a confederation of French allies, Napoleon incorporated the Papal States into the empire and arrested the pope, who refused thereafter to perform any office as head of the church (*The Popes: A Concise Biographical History*, ed. Eric John [New York, 1964], pp. 406–8).

3. In 1849, Giuseppe Montanelli, Dominico Guerrazzi, and Giuseppe Mazzoni became triumvirs of the Florentine republic (Berkeley, p. 291).

4. Mazzini arrived in Milan on 7 April (Berkeley, p. 324). Fuller quotes Wordsworth, "Character of the Happy Warrior":

> Whose powers shed round him in the common strife,
> Or Mild concerns of ordinary life,
> A constant influence, a peculiar grace;
> But who, if he be called upon to face
> Some awful moment to which Heaven has joined
> Great issues, good or bad for human kind,
> Is happy as a Lover; and attired
> With sudden brightness, like a Man inspired;
> And, through the heat of conflict, keeps the law
> In calmness made, and sees what he foresaw.

(*The Poetical Works of William Wordsworth*, ed. Ernest de Selincourt and Helen Darbishire, 5 vols. [Oxford, 1940–49], 4:87.)

778.   To William H. Channing

Rome 23d November, 1848.

I do not write you of myself because there is too much to tell. There are things I long for you to know but in the right way, all the scene grouped and colored as I could give it if we passed two or three days together. Let me say *when* we shall pass two or three days together. Is that too much for me to count on in life? Suffice for now to say that my heart is full, my mind lively, engaged. I have these two terrible drawbacks, frequent failure of health and want of money but the first I should not mind, if it were not for the latter. Ah! my dear William, what a vast good would money be to me now, and I cannot get it. This is too hard, so many people have it to whom it is of no use, and to me it would give happiness, days and months of real life. I may complain to you, as you have none to give me; it is some relief to mourn.

MsCfr (MB: Ms. Am. 1450 [102]).

779. To Charles King Newcomb

Rome 24th Novr
1848.

My dear Charles,

I recd your second letter with much gladness; none that come seem so domestic as yours. I love you very much, my dear Charles, how harmonious has our intercourse been an intercourse of ten years now and nothing to wound me in the retrospect.

I would fain hope we may visit together these solemn beautiful haunts also, and ever it seems to me that we may.

I am deeply touched by the faithful forgiving friendship of your mother[n] and it seems to me if she came here now, she would not demand of me what is uncongenial to me, and that I could contribute to her happiness without being false to myself. I feel much for her sorrows. I should like to show that, if I am not sand, I am not flint either. —

Rome! oh my mother! how sadly tender I return into thy arms. I should like, Charles, to tell you a little of what she has done for me, but somehow I cannot. I have suffered too much I am almost like a disembodied spirit. I can express on earth very little of my thought.

You ask me of the climate and this also has much engaged my attention. I have watched every day and night the skies and the earth. I know all their expressions.

The winter I like much less than ours The rain falls in torrents, almost without intermission for three months and when by chance there is a day without rain, it is not one of cheer, no animating breeze drives quickly away the clouds They lie low and threaten while the earth reeks with cold pestiferous mist.[n]

The spring is glorious, about the end of Feby the beds of[n] narcissus are in full bloom and, after, the heavens seem to stoop daily nearer till at last the earth seems drunk with light and her every pulse makes music.

The summer again I do not like so well as ours. The first weeks of June indeed are very beautiful there is still the magnificent luxuriance of vegetation as in spring, the vineyards are in the fullest spendor of their drapery and all dotted with young grapes. The earth is carpeted with fields of grain, tenderest green, embroidered with the brilliant red of the poppy the brilliant blue of the cornflower. Every old wall and ruin is festooned with roses. But afterwards the heat is too great and steady. It never rains, the fields are polluted with dust, also brown and dry. One longs for the showers and thunderous emancipations of our country. True! *we* have too much rain in the summer, but also[n] such splendid variety of cloud change; in Italy one tires of the forever cloudless sky. There was only rain twice for four months where I was, and then only a few minutes at a time.

The autumn is like ours in the air; the same lovely happy, weather generally, the same wild storms now and then. I lived on the bank of a river which became in those a wild torrent, and lit up almost constantly by flashes of lightning. The sound of its rush was very sublime. I see it yet as it swept away in its dark green stream the little barks of lighted straw the children let down from the bridge. Opposite my window was a vineyard, where white and purple clusters were my food near three months. It is pretty to see the vintage, the asses and waggons loaded with this wealth of amber and rubies, the nut brown maids and naked boys singing in the trees on which the vines are trained.[n] as they cut the grapes, the women in their red corsets and white head cloths receiving them below while their babies crow amid the grass where they have laid them. Good bye, dear Charles, the paper is full. Your friend ever

MARGARET.

ALS (MB: Ms. Am. 1450 [125]); MsCfr (MH: bMS Am 1280 [111, pp. 33–34, 87]). Published in part in *JMN*, 11:465, 474. *Addressed:* Charles K. Newcomb / Providence / R.I. *Endorsed:* Rd Jan'y 3.

your mother] *These words have been canceled by a later hand but are here recovered.*
mist.] mist. ⟨The⟩
beds of] beds ⟨of⟩ of
but also] but ↑also↓
trees on which the vines are trained.] trees ↑on which the vines are trained.↓

780.   To Emelyn Story

Rome,
28th Novr 1848.

Here I am again, my dear Emelyn. I passed the road and meadows overflowed because the Tiber was swollen by recent rain; Rome was all reeking with the same cold mist that made me suffer so much last winter, and yet— how beautiful and dear it seemed to be here again, to hear the voices of the many fountains, to see in that pale struggling moonlight[n] the obelisks and ruins more eloquent than ever!

O Rome, *my* country bad as the winter damp is, and lazy as the climate makes me, I would rather live here than any where else in the world.

The scarlet abomination, as our Puritan ancestors deemed it, has had a good dip in the stream of progress, since you were here and the red certainly looks spotted and *streaky*. I am living in a Rome without Pope or Cardinals.[1] Some old persons weep the desecration. But Rome in general takes it very coolly, though ignorant where the "immortal", now, alas! immortally contemptible, Pio is gone, and to what measures he may suffer himself to be led against her."

But the" Romans had grown weary of being duped and so sure that they had nothing to hope from him, that the universal feeling seems to be "Let go" at any rate.

My fear is that Rome cannot hold together in her present form against innovation and that we are enjoying the last hours of her old solemn greatness. Will you not return then to see her once more! Florence, full of beautiful things as it is, is, to my mind, just nothing compared with Rome, and, in its intellectual atmosphere, no Italy at all.

Write to me of what and whom" you find. I want to know if Wm takes as much pleasure in Powers and his works as he expected and how he is.[2] I heard he was not well. And the children how fare they? and are they very happy? I hope yes, and that Edith enjoys being in the city of flowers, only I suppose there are few now." In June, when I was there first, the flowers are enchanting! And Uncle Tom? is he happy? and does he not want to take a palazzo and a villa here, instead of his nice house in Boston?

"Crodie" has a most sweet place; it is fine that any one can have such apartments, such a garden, and such a view for only 240 dollars a year only I wish" you had them instead of her, especially as I am not far off. in" Piazza Barberini I suppose you could take them for the year they are to be absent, if you wished, studio and all.

I am almost alone in Rome, there is hardly a person I know here, I have screwed my expenses down to the lowest possible peg; at least it seems so now, but I dont know;— that art seems to be capable of gai[   ] indefinite perfection in Italy. Meanwhile I have a room I like very [m]uch and two nice old people to take [ca]re of me, as clean and "smart" and less cunning than the Marchesa. My rooms in her house are still free if you know any single gentle man coming on from Florence that want such, indeed now is accomodation for two single gentlemen, if *not* rolled into one, as she has made a pretty bedroom of her little parlor, and the whole may be had very cheap as indeed may rooms of any description in this present Rome; should the Assembly for the Constituente be held here, they may be filled up, but the Murray guide book mob fight shy, which makes it quite delightful for me to be here now.

Do you see much of the Greenoughs?[3] Mrs G. is a woman of the world, and does not interest me, but is sweet tempered and kindly. Greenough, in the right mood, I think a delightful companion; he has a vein of delicate wit, and is a poet when he speaks of birds and animals; he can describe their looks and motions with almost Shakspearean power. Are the Brownings still in Florence and have you made their acquaintance?[4] if not, should you like to do so through a note from me. Goodbye, dear Emelyn, again write quick and tell me if you hear anything of Amern friends, especially Caroline, Jane and the Lorings.[5] I know nothing; people in U. S. are fast forgetting me. Affecy

What is become of the Blacks?[6]

Crodie says Mrs Ames is really a mother, pray write if you know any thing about *that*.

ALS (NNC). *Addressed:* William Story Esq / for Mrs Story / Care Maquay Pakenham & Co / Florence. *Postmark:* Roma 28 Nov 48. Firenze 30 Nov 1848. *Endorsed:* Margaret Fuller. / 28 Nov 1848.

struggling moonlight] struggling mo(?)onlight
against her.] against ⟨them⟩ ↑ her ↓ .
But the] But ⟨they⟩ the
and whom] and who ↑ m ↓
few now.] few now ⟨now⟩.
view for only 240 dollars a year only I wish] view ↑ for only 240 dollars a year ↓ only ↑ I wish ↓
off. in] off. ↑ in ↓

1. On the evening of 24 November the pope, dressed as an ordinary priest, slipped out of a secret exit from the Vatican and left Rome for Gaeta, just over the border in the kingdom of Naples, where he remained until after the fall of the Roman republic. Gaeta thus became the center of intrigue for France, Austria, and Spain, all of whom wanted to neutralize Neapolitan influence over the pontiff (King, *Italian Unity*, 1:282–84; Berkeley, p. 460).

2. The American sculptor Hiram Powers (1805–73) had been living in Florence since 1837.

3. Horatio Greenough (1805–52) graduated from Harvard in 1825, then studied sculpture in Italy, where he spent most of his later life (*DAB*). In 1837 Greenough married Louisa Ingersoll Gore (1813–91), daughter of John Gore of Boston (Greenough, *Letters*, p. 219).

4. Robert and Elizabeth Barrett Browning were living in Florence.

5. Ellis and Louisa Loring of Boston.

6. Charles Christopher Black (1809–79) was in later life the curator of the South Kensington Museum in London and was for a time on the staff of the Victoria and Albert Museum (Nathaniel Hawthorne, *The French and Italian Notebooks*, ed. Thomas Woodson [Columbus, 1980], p. 847; Hudson, *Browning*, p. 269).

781. To Richard F. Fuller

Rome
7th Decr 1848

My very dear Richard,

I write now principally to enclose this letter. It is to me of great importance that it should go straight and safe to Caroline. Her address you will find from Jane or one of her sisters, envelope and send it to her.

When you have found her right address dont fail to copy it exactly into the next letter you write to me. I have reasons for not wishing to send mine to the care of her father.[1]

I received last week a joint letter from Mother and Arthur. Give to them much love and [say] that I shall answer early in Jany. I [do] not now, because only two weeks since I dispatched to your care a long let[ter] for Mother. Say that I am uncommonly well that the rains hold off more than last year and I hope to pass a better winter.

The weather is still glorious; how much should I like to pass a week of it in walking about Rome with you How happy you would be, as I always am, when not sick or tormented with care. Surrounded every where by this sublime unobtrusive society. These great souls, great natures, great men. Have patience, have obstinate perseverance; we may yet be here together you may come as U.S. ambassador and I will be your cicerone. Should my hair then be white (dont be anxious, it is still brown and the admiration of the Italians) my soul will still be young, and richer than ever.

That would be very different, I assure you from being together in *Canton*!

Were it possible to make one's experience available for another I would pray you to waste no moment's strength in sorrow that you could help. I have wasted a great deal of my strength prematurely. Since, I have found that this life, if full of unexpected conflicts and strange agonies, also never ceases to open up new founts of joy and new great occasions for those who are fitted to use them.

Precious indeed to me now would be all that strength so prodigally lavished. Foolish indeed was the fancy that because one lovely garden perished in the storm, rich nature could not create another. Such is the meaning of the solemn word, "Man is punished until he ceases to strive."

I am again reading Nieb[uh]r this winter and if I get time shall read [   ] also.[2] Ever yours

M.

ALS (MH: fMS Am 1086 [9:155]). *Addressed:* Mr / Richard F. Fuller / State St. Boston / Massachusetts / U.S.A. *Postmark:* Boston Mass Jan 12.

1. Apparently this letter told Tappan of Fuller's child. Caroline's father was William Sturgis, a Boston merchant.

2. Barthold Georg Niebuhr (1776–1831), a German historian and statesman, had been Prussian ambassador to Rome from 1816 to 1823. He published *Römische Geschichte* in Berlin in 1811–12 and expanded it in 1828. English translations were published in London, Philadelphia, and Cambridge, Massachusetts.

782. To William Wetmore Story

[I] 9 December 1848

As to Florence itself, I do not like it, with the exception of the galleries and churches, and Michel Angelo's marbles. I do not like it, for the reason you *do,* because it seems like home. It seems a kind of Boston to me,— the same good and the same ill; I have had enough of both. But I have so many dear friends in Boston, that I must always wish to go there sometimes; and there are so many precious objects of study in Florence, that a stay of several months could not fail to be full of interest. Still, the spring must be the time to be in Florence; there are so many charming spots to visit in the environs, much nearer than those you go to in Rome, within scope of an afternoon's drive. I saw them only when parched with sun and covered with dust. In the spring they must be very beautiful. [   ]

[II] I have thus far passed this past month of fine weather most delightfully in revisiting my haunts of the autumn before. Then, too, I was uncommonly well and strong; it was the golden period of my Roman life. The experience what long confinement may be expected after, from the winter rains, has decided me *never* to make my hay when the sun shines: *i.e.,* to give no fine day to books and pens.

The places of interest I am nearest now are villas Albani and Ludovisi, and Santa Agnese, St. Lorenzo, and the vineyards near Porta Maggiore.[1] I have passed one day in a visit to Torre dei Schiavi and the neighborhood, and another on Monte Mario, both Rome and the Campagna-day golden in the mellowest lustre of the Italian sun.[2] [   ] But to you I may tell, that I always go with Ossoli, the most congenial companion I ever had for jaunts of this kind. We go out in the morning, carrying the roast chestnuts from Rome; the bread and wine are found in some lonely little osteria; and so we dine; and reach Rome again, just in time to see it, from a little distance, gilded by the sunset.

161

Basilica of Santa Maria Maggiore, Rome. From *Raccolta delle principali vedute di Roma* (Rome, n.d.), courtesy of The Pennsylvania State University Libraries.

This moon having been so clear, and the air so warm, we have visited, on successive evenings, all the places we fancied: Monte Cavallo, now so lonely and abandoned,— no lights there but moon and stars, — Trinità e' Monti, Santa Maria Maggiore, and the Forum.[3] So now, if the rain must come, or I be driven from Rome, I have all the images fair and fresh in my mind.

About public events, why remain ignorant? Take a daily paper in the house. The Italian press has recovered from the effervescence of childish spirits;— you can now approximate to the truth from its reports. There are many good papers now in Italy. Whatever represents the Montanelli ministry is best for you. That gives the lead now. I see good articles copied from the "Alba."

I: ELfr, from *Memoirs*, 2:254, II: ELfr, from *Memoirs*, 2:256−57.

The second fragment is joined to the first because the time seems clearly to be late 1848, and it would be only to the Storys that Fuller would mention Ossoli, for they knew him as her friend.

1. The Villa Albani dates from 1760 and contains a collection of antiquities; the Villa Ludovisi, no longer standing, occupied the site of the ancient gardens of Sallust on the Via Veneto. Santa Agnese borders the Piazza Navona, once the Circus of Domitian; San Lorenzo fuori le Mura was founded by Constantine; the Porta Maggiore was once part of the Aqua Claudia and then converted into one of the city's gates by the emperor Aurelian (Baedecker, pp. 310, 215, 235, 224, 225).

2. Monte Mario is on the Campagna outside the Porta del Popolo, near which Fuller lived (Baedecker, p. 310).

3. The church of Santissima Trinità de' Monti is on the Piazza della Trinità. Santa Maria Maggiore, the largest church in Rome, dates from the fifth century (Baedecker, pp. 213, 222).

783. To Giovanni Angelo Ossoli

[22] Dec. [1848]
Rieti
venerdi la mattina

Mio amore,

Faceva bene il viaggio, e arrivavo qui alle 4 1/2— Trovo nostro caro poco cambiato, molto meno che aspettavo. Che mi sorprende e che pare grasso assai, pare stare tutto bene, ma non è molto più grande che quando lo lasciavo.[n] A stesse maniere, è molto grazioso, ma peraltro fa meglio che con me, dorme si bene la notte, piange di rado e allora non forte.

Si diverte in questa famiglia vedendo tante persone e tutte giuocan con lui e sembran[n] volergli bene. La casa è terribile, vento entrando per tutte i lati, ma lui [n]on sembra rinfreddato [sic]uro che sara più forte per stando esposto cosi negli[n] -primi mesi. Ha avuto il vajuolo terribile, sua testa sue corpo è stato coperto colle macchie, è tutto per grazia di cielo che ha passato si bene, il medico Mogliani non venieva mai visitarlo; sua famiglia dice che io son avara, io soppongo pensava non valeva la pena salvare nostro bambino. Suo viso non è offeso. Non ho cambiato ancora casa e non so si lo farò; parlan in quella casa di ricevere dieci scudi il mese per una camera, questi Rietini [son] tutti simili, si[n] posso senza prejudizio a mia salute staro qui.

Non ho ricevuto niente da ti questa mattina, e la famiglia qui non ha ricevuto la lettera che veniva impostata il Sabato avanti il Mercoledi. Cosi si manci mai lettera d[i] me, pensi e difetto della posta, io scriverò tutti i giorni di posta

Il bambino ti saluta con molti baci. Sembrava riconoscermi,[n] quando lo prendevo riposava si lungo sua cara testa sulla mia spalla La notte prendevo tanto piacere domire con lui il giorno non va si bene c'è fame, freddo. Addio, mio caro, scrivero alcune righe la Domenica, tutti i dettagli ti diro quand[o] vengo, sempre la tua

M.

[22] Dec. [1848]
Rieti
friday morning

My love,

I had a nice journey, and I arrived here at 4 1/2 — I find our dear one little changed, much less than I expected. What surprises me is that he looks very plump, he seems to be well, but he is not much bigger than when I left him. He has the same gestures, he is very gracious, but for the rest he does better than with me, he sleeps well at night, cries rarely and then not loudly.

He enjoys himself in this family[,] seeing so many people and they all play with him and seem to love him. The house is terrible, the wind comes in from all sides, but he doesn't seem to have a cold[;] surely he will be stronger for having being so exposed in his first few months. He had small pox very badly, his head and body were all covered with spots, it is only thanks to heaven that it all went away so well, doctor Mogliani never came to see him; his family say that I am stingy, I suppose he thought it wasn't worth saving our child. His face is not injured. I have not moved yet and I don't know if I will; in that house they talk of charging 2 1/2 scudi per week[;] if I can without prejudicing my health I will stay here.

I haven't received anything from you this morning, and the family here has not received the letter that was mailed the Saturday before Wednesday. So if you ever fail to receive a letter from me, think of a problem with the mail, I will write every day that the mail functions.

The baby greets you with many kisses. He seemed to recognize me, when I picked him up he rested his dear head on my shoulder for so long At night I had so much pleasure in sleeping with him[;] during the day it doesn't go so well[;] there is hunger, cold. Goodbye, my dear, I will write a few words on Sunday, I will give you all the details when I come, always your

M

ALS (MH: fMS Am 1086 [9:207]); MsC in English (MH: fMS Am 1086 [Works, 2:197–201]). English copy published entire in Higginson, *MFO*, pp. 261–62. *Addressed:* Sigre Mse / Gio. Angiolo Ossoli / Roma. *Postmark:* Rieti.

Dated by the fact that Fuller left Rome late in the week of 17–23 December for Rieti (Ossoli to Fuller, 21 December 1848, MH).

lo lasciavo.] lo⟨?⟩lasciavo.
e sembran] e sem⟨p⟩bran
cosi negli] cosi negl⟨o⟩i
simili, si] simili, ⟨ha parlato di 2 1/2 scudi la settimana⟩ si
Sembrava riconoscermi] Sembrava ri⟨?⟩conoscermi

784. To Giovanni Angelo Ossoli

Rieti
domenica 24 Dic [1848]

Mio amore,

ricevo questa mattina tre fogli[n] colle tue care lettrine. Mi contenta sapere che fa freddo a Roma anche, perche qui e davvero terribile. Avrei sofferta molto sul viaggio, si son stato nel cabriolet, era buona fortuna per noi non trovare quella posta, io ritornero anche dentro. M'aspettate sicuro il venerdi, si il bambino sta bene come adesso, io vengo sicuro, e avvertite Antonia che può avere buon foco pronto per mi. Non venite fuori dalla porta nè state sulla guardia sarebbe

165

troppo difficile per ti, ma venite dopo pranzo perche avro mille cose dirti di nostro caro.

Lui sta molto bene, questo mi consola per tutto, a certo modi graziosi è davvero carino. Lui ho dato tutti tuoi baci. A Niccola ho[n] fatta cercare altra casa[n] che noi possiam star bene quando veniammo, degli condizioni ti dirò quando vengo. Aspetto una altra lettrina da ti mercoledi più tardi non scrivi, ni invii fogli sempre la tua

M.

Cura bene tua salute io son molto rinfreddata, gia.

Rieti
Sunday 24 Dec. [1848]

My love,

This morning I receive three papers with your dear letters. I am happy to know that it is cold in Rome too, because it is really terrible here. I would have suffered very much on the trip if I had been in the open carriage, it was good luck for us not to find that seat[;] I will also return by the closed one. You can expect me for sure on Friday, if the child is well as he is now, I will definitely come and you tell Antonia that she can have a good fire ready for me. Do not come outside of the gate nor watch for me[;] it would be too difficult for you, but come after dinner because I will have a thousand things to tell you about our dear child.

He is very well, this comforts me for everything, and of course he has charming habits[;] he is really dear. I have given him all your kisses. I have asked Niccola to look for another house where we can be comfortable when we come, I will tell you about the conditions when I come. I look forward to another letter from you on Wednesday[;] do not write after that, nor send papers always your

M.

Take care of your health I already have a very bad cold.

ALS (MH: fMS Am 1086 [9:192]); MsC in English (MH: fMS Am 1086 [Works, 2:201–3]). *Addressed:* Sigr Mse / Gio. Angiolo Ossoli / Roma. *Postmark:* Rieti.

tre fogli] tre fo⟨l⟩gli
A Niccola ho] ⟨Gli⟩ ↑ A Niccola ↓ ho
altra casa] altra ↑ casa ↓

785.   To Giovanni Angelo Ossoli

Rieti
27 Decr [1848]

Mio caro,

ricevo questa mattina uno foglio da ti; soppongo non c'è piu, come Lunedi[n] era Natale.

Io vengo Venerdi. Mi rincresce lasciar nostro caro. Ma non potevo, si volevo, stare più in questa casa, son forte rinfreddata, mi duole la testa. Pare che lui sta bene e diviene tutti i giorni piu interressante. Si diverte molto col somarello. Non ha ancora capegli. Ma io avrò mille cose dirti di lui quando vengo. Venerdi la sera ci revediam, spero e son sempre la tua

M.

Il bambino faceva bene la vigilia del Natale. Sembrava tutto eccitato pelle campanelle, non voleva dormire nè lasciar dormire gli altri.

Rieti
27 Decr [1848]

My dear,

I receive a newspaper from you this morning; I suppose there are no more, since Monday was Christmas.

I come on Friday. I am very sorry to leave our dear child. But even if I wanted to, I could not stay longer in this house, I have a terrible cold and my head hurts me. It seems that he is well and every day he becomes more interesting. He plays often with the little donkey. He still does not have any hair. But I will have many things to tell you about him when I come. Friday evening we will see each other again, I hope and I am always your

M.

The child was good on Christmas Eve. He seemed very excited by the bells, he did not want to sleep, nor let the others sleep.

ALS (MH: fMS Am 1086 [9:192]); MsC in English (MH: fMS Am 1086 [Works, 2:203–5]). *Addressed:* Sigre Mse / Gio Angiolo Ossoli / Roma. *Postmark:* Rieti.

come Lunedi] come <?>Lunedi

786. To Jane Tuckerman King

Rome, January 1849.

The artists' life is not what you fancy; poor, sordid, unsocially so-cial, saving baiocchis and planning orders; the path does not open straight and clear for him in this our day. It is much harder for him not to be servile in mind and mean in conduct, than for others. Surely some escape but I say it is hard.

My poor Italian brothers, they bleed! I do not love them much,— the women not at all; they are too low for me; it will be centuries be-fore they emerge from a merely animal life.

The men too, though their sentiment is real, are in thought too much the fanfaron. Except Mazzini, dearest, reverend friend, my first Italian friend, still infinitely my most prized,— a great and solid man.

MsCfr (MH: fMS Am 1086 [Works, 1:111–13]); MsCfr (MB: Ms. Am. 1450 [169]).

787. To Emelyn Story

Rome January 7. 1849.

My dear Emelyn,

Mr Wetmore sent me your letter on Wednesday and made me a short visit the next day. He was in a hurry, saying he was seeking for rooms, and I was not able to talk thoroughly with him about your coming. I have deferred writing, in hopes of his return, but he does not come. I hope I may interpret his absence into his finding many agreeable occupations and companions, so that he will write that he wants you to come.

I cannot promise to give quite disinterested advice, for I should like to have you here; this past week, when the fineness of the weather and my consequent good health have enabled me to enter into the humors of the time, and amuse myself at the Fair of St Eustachio, the little theatres &c.[1] I have regretted much that you were not here, as I like to be with you at such times.

About coming, both as regards yourselves and the children, Rome is tranquil, and likely to remain so. Indeed there can be no doubt that a secret and wily foe will try every means to excite disturbance both during the Elections and the sittings of the Constitutional Assembly, but the people are on their guard, and have given such earnest of their intelligence and good sense, that I think there is little probability of any disturbance, and at present I see *no* chance of disturbance that could annoy a foreigner.[2] But should any such unexpectedly occur, it is always easy to leave here and go to Leghorn or Genoa. It would be better to take rooms only by the month, and I presume you can with perfect ease, and at half the usual expense, suit yourselves with pleasant rooms. As to the weather, it has been perfectly delightful with the exception of that cold "spell," which we had as well as you. It might spitefully begin to rain as soon as you arrive, but even in case of this malice of Fate, the suffering would not be long, as the Roman winter yields in the end of February or beginning of March. As to the journey, the children could not suffer. You go by railroad to Leghorn; you pass but one night in the steamer, you will take a vettura, or the interior of a diligence for yourselves, so that you can wrap them up warm, and arrive in Rome by night. Here you know they have always the Pincian, and I believe no playground like it in Florence.

As to the inducements, Rome is always Rome; and if I may judge by experience, the privilege of passing days here, must at each return be more deeply felt, more duly prized; three or four months here cannot fail to be precious, especially if you are not sure you shall sometime make Rome your home; and the spring is always the most beautiful season.

I have made no step towards acquaintance; as my circumstances now restrict me to one room, the reception of others than friends would not be convenient.

My own society is composed of two persons; Ossoli, with whom I go out when I need a companion, and who finds for me the news of every day, and sees to my little affairs, and Dr Maestri, one of my most valuable Milanese friends, and now one of the leading members of the republican party.[3] He is much engaged, but when now and then he gives me an hour, it is full of interesting informations, I do not know whether Macpherson is here or not; poor fellow! his loss was that his apartment was stripped by robbers early in the Winter.[4] I should like to see him, but have thought we should meet by chance, and being much occupied, have made very little effort.

I sit still in my corner, supposing Fate will, as usual, send me a little group of companions, sooner or later. Should it send you, I should be very glad. I am less at leisure than last Winter, but better worth seeing, when I have time. I should pass some evenings with you; we should go out together sometimes, and there would be a good deal interesting to say. Had I more to offer I would urge you to come more;

but there is only myself; I have now no pleasant circle as sometimes in my life has been the case and you would leave the Brownings just as you had made their acquaintance. Reading over my letter, I begin to be afraid you will not come, and with all my pretence of disinterestedness, I shall be much disappointed if you do not come. Who knows where we shall meet again otherwise? for my coming to Florence is not now probable. I love Rome, and it has now become the centre of the Italian movement; and thus for me peculiarly interesting just now. I wish the Brownings would come too. Why do they not? How can people stay in Florence always when they might be in Rome? Adieu dear Emelyn; my love to William and the children; if you answer the letter in person, it will gladden me,— only I do not want you to come and then regret it afterwards, so I have stated both sides as impartially as I could, being Affectionately your friend

S. M. F.

MsC (MH: fMS Am 1086 [Works, 1:237–43]; MsC (MH: fMS Am 1086 9:224]).
The second copy has the following changes:
on Wednesday] on Tuesday
return, but he does not come.] return that he does not come
may interpret] may interpret his absence
occupations and companions,] companions and occupations
like to] like much to
much you] much that you
been perfectly] been most
restrict me to one room, the reception] restricting me to one room reception
made very little effort.] made no efforts.
you had] you have
just now.] just now. Do come.
wish the Brownings] wish they

1. In her *Tribune* dispatch, Fuller described the fair held in the quarter of St. Eustachio, which was "turned into one toy-shop; the stalls are set out in the street and brightly lighted up. These are full of cheap toys,—prices varying from half a cent to twenty cents. . . . Among the toys are great quantities of whistles, tin trumpets, and little tamborines; of these every man, woman and child has bought one and is using it to make a noise" (*New-York Daily Tribune*, 31 March 1849).

2. Rome was an uneasy city without the pope, whose departure created a vacuum that had not yet been filled. On 20 December the provisional junta announced its intention to form a constituent assembly, dissolved the rump parliament, and formed a ministry under Muzzarelli. Then, on 29 December, the junta published a proclamation that fixed the election date for 21 January 1849. It called for the creation of a national assembly, direct universal suffrage, and a secret ballot, and named 5 February as the date for the assembly to convene (King, *Italian Unity*, 1:289–91; Farini, 3:86–87, 119–21).

3. Pietro Maestri (1816–71) was a Milanese doctor and statistician. A veteran of the "five days" revolution, he later was a leader in the committee of public defense that opposed the Austrians after the battle of Custoza (*Enciclopedia italiana*).

4. Robert Macpherson (d. 1873), a grandnephew of the poet James Macpherson, was a painter who turned to photography in Rome. In 1849 he married Gerardine Bate (1830?–78), Anna Jameson's niece (Boase).

788. To Sarah Ann Clarke

Rome, 18th Jany
'49

My dear Sarah,

I receive your letter of Decr You will see that I in part had answered it before receiving. In my last I had told you in general about expenses here and expressed the warm hope that you would come while I can be of use to you. It would give me great satisfaction to arrange every thing for you, as I believe I could to advantage and be no trivial compensation for all the annoyances I have had while" acquiring this kind of skill. Then, though there are not so very many I wish to see here, you are one, and one to whom it would give me greatest delight to open the way to these magnificent enjoyments, and instructions worthy of, as the expression of the noblest spirits.

Should the state of affairs favor [   ] give you all the detailed infor[mation][   ] and by [   ] by the danger of a fu[rther inter]vention, should the Italians be left to settle the[ir] own affairs, you can come well enough. But the Russian presses onward, the Austrian seems likely to conquer Hungary and be at leisure to pursue his murderous work here.[1] France is not to be d[e]pende[d o]n and the Pope is now become decidedly a traitor, willing to make use of any means to recover his temporal power. He may call the aid of the foreign armies.[2] We shall know by April or May," in good time for you, probably. You do not *need* a gentleman but it would be so pleasant and good to have James come I hope he will.[3] If you want to come direct to Italy at little expense, you would come by sail-ship to Genoa, or Leghorn as [   ] and [   ] sparing, and James could [   ] England if [   ] leaving you here.

About your Mother, there is always a small Amern society at Florence and even a larger circle both at Florence and Rome in peaceful times.[4] The Amern society here last winter was large and pleasant. She would no doubt unearth many subjects unknown to me, as I seek little either Amern or English society, preferring foreign, while I am here both for my pleasure and my profit. *Good* English society is not accessible to Americans, except from partic[ula]r introductions. I mean you will not naturally meet any of the desirable persons except at public places. Bad English society abounds on the continent and the good stands yet more firmly entrenched against it than at home" The way Mrs Farrar recommended is the usual and the only agreeable way for most persons, but you might, if you found the living in lodgings [lonely] for your mother, live at an Amern [boardinghouse like] Mrs Clarke's here in Rome, and there is an English[n] too in Florence.

As to language, French is of very little use in Italy. You had better begin at once to practice writing and speaking Italian. Do not spend your time in reading Italian authors into English, but translate short stories or dialogues from English[n] into Italian under correction of a master, learn the phrase book by heart, and see that you have all the rules clear in your head. Even thus prepared it will probably be long before you speak with ease if you are always using English with your Mother. After leaving the Springs I always lived with Italians yet it is only after six months total abstinence from English that I speak fluently and to do so is for many reasons of great importance.

I believe I have now answered as far as is worth while at this moment, so soon as I find that public affairs [permit] your coming if you will, I sh[al]l write in detail. Meanwhile study and prepare all you can; the moments here are so precious, every precaution should be used to turn them to the best advantage.

About our loved Ellen, I am quite clear that her departure is an excellent thing.[5] She suffered too much, she was too ill-placed Probably all those hours she lay weeping on the nursery bed, or stifled the sweet song of her soul, the sparkles of her wit and fancy, in presence of the dull man to whom she had so unhappily bound herself, spirits in some other sphere were pining for want of just such a presence or sympathy as hers. We may hope she will now rejoin them and live more freely unoppressed by unfit ties. Yet for me, I should have loved so dearly to see her again, and I wish I could have seen her dead, have kissed her face and her hands. I wish you would write me of the last days, if you saw her often and how she died, and how her face looked under the last impress. Also, if any of her children is at all like her.[6] The poems ought to be printed if not published, an edition for her friends, if this is not done, I am very anxious to have them all copied into a book for me. I think no one would oppose this, as she loved to sh[ow] me whatever she wrote and left it in my hands as long as I pleased. Jane, now unlawfully called King, would I know copy them for me, if she has time. Thank much for those you did send. The *horizon line* she had shown me but I had not kept a copy[7]

Were you but here today, dear Sarah, A day so c[   ] the gods walking on the earth, just that "in hopes of light" that modern painters speak of. How you [   ] love Italy. I do hope we shall meet here and am ever yours

MARGARET.

ALS (MH: bMS Am 1569 [1349]). *Addressed:* Sarah Clarke.

Sarah Ann Clarke was a Boston artist whom Fuller had known for many years. The two toured the Midwest together in 1843.

had while] had ⟨in⟩ ↑ while ↓

by April or May,] by ↑ April or ↓ May,

continent and the good stands yet more firmly entrenched against it than at home] continent ↑ and the good stands yet more firmly entrenched against it than at home ↓

is an English] is ⟨one⟩ ↑ an English ↓

dialogues from English] dialogues ↑ from English ↓

1. The Austrians defeated the Hungarians at Schwechat on 30 October 1848. By 4 January they had abandoned Pest, the capital, and appeared to be routed. Fuller's reference to Russia is unclear (*Cambridge Modern History,* 11:202–3).

2. Her analysis was accurate: France under Louis Napoleon betrayed the Roman republic; Austria and Naples, despite their distrust of each other and of the French, worked for the restoration of the papacy. Fuller refers specifically to the monitory that Pius issued on 1 January 1849, in which he condemned the election for a constituent assembly and forbade Catholics under penalty of excommunication to take "any part in any meetings which may audaciously be held for the nomination of persons to be sent to the Assembly we have condemned." In publishing a translation of the monitory in the *Tribune,* Fuller said that "it is probably the last document of the kind the world will see" (Farini, 3:132–34; *New-York Daily Tribune,* 31 March 1849).

3. James Freeman Clarke, Sarah's brother, was a Unitarian minister whom Fuller had known since her youth. In her letter of 15 December 1848 (MH), Sarah reported that James "says that when he was in College he was studying metaphysics and that you suggested that the brain would not be too dry at forty for that use— This checked his enthusiasm, and now as he nears forty he fears it may become too dry to enjoy Italy unless he goes immediately." Fuller's jest was in a letter to James Clarke: "Time enough at six-and-twenty to form yourself into a metaphysical philosopher. The brain does not easily get too dry for *that*" (*The Letters of Margaret Fuller,* ed. Robert N. Hudspeth [Ithaca, 1983], 1:179).

4. Rebecca Hull Clarke.

5. Ellen Sturgis Hooper, wife of Robert Hooper, a Boston physician, and sister of Caroline Sturgis Tappan, had died on 3 November 1848. Hooper was a poet whose work Fuller published in the *Dial.* In her letter, Sarah Clarke said of Hooper: "I am glad for her, but to me it is like blotting the evening star out of the sky."

6. The Hooper children were Ellen Sturgis (1838–86), Edward William (1839–1901), and Marian (1843–85). Marian, known as Clover, married Henry Adams in 1872 (*The Letters of Mrs. Henry Adams, 1865–1883,* ed. Ward Thoron [Boston, 1936], p. xiii).

7. The Houghton Library now owns a copy of her privately printed poems.

789. To James F. Clarke

Rome
19th Jany 1849.

Spirits that have once been sincerely united and tended together a sacred flame, never become entirely stranger to one another's life.

When the attention of one is turned upon the other, a responsive thrill is felt. It is thus that while for several years, though James is always my loved friend, though I rejoice always that his hopes have found a haven and feel unvarying confidence in his work and aim, I had not been occupied by thought of him, nor he by the thought of me, when lo! these last three or four months I have thought of him repeatedly, have seemed to have interviews, have put the thoughts into words "I hope he will come here" and now[n] he writes that he thinks of coming.

Fail not to act out that thought, O my friend. It is just what you need to give your life a fresh impulse. The sight of all the monuments of the great past will renew your poetic life. You will escape from the routine of which the best [pr]ofessional career[n] has [   ] return new nerved to the tug of daily cares and expected work.

I find thee very inconsistent O Jamie, to write me of Brownson Alcott and other rusty fusty intel. and spiritual-ities, and to tell me that the best the soul can do in some of your diggings is to put on the filthy popish rags which will scarce hold together on the worst of priests here, then ask me to come back.[1] What come back for? Here is a great past and a *living* present. Here men live for something else beside money and systems, the voice of noble sentiment is understood, nor are they catiff in action. 'Tis a sphere much more natural to me than what the old puritans or the modern bankers have made. I would not have[n] been born in this age other than an American for America is the land of promise but I was somewhat tired of so much promise [   ] the sight of [   ] of wax to my flickering taper. Come and see them too, and in Roman fraternity in old Greek community of thought as in our other days we will live yet some few more together.

I shall show Powers the lines though he probably will not understand them. As he spoke of Anna Ward after making that noble bust, which shows the possibilities of her character "Yes"! says[n] he "she was a handsome girl then. I hear she has lost her good looks:— however she is a *good worthy*[n] *person* still"!!

I wear your ring "Feed my lambs" and feed all I can catch, with the same straw I get myself. Generally they run at last into the wolf's mouth. Looking at *it* (the ring)[n] and remembering some verses you wrote me once I think to send you the inclosed invocation addressed to me by an illustrious person of Europe, the first time he saw me.[2] Show it to Sarah alone, then burn, as he did not wish me to give it to any o[   ] but I thought read [   ] Beethoven interlude of astronomy as studied from Boston common.

174

Give my love to Anna your wife, a fair strong nature of which I like to think. Kiss for me your children I hope to make their acquaintance yet. You must miss dear Ellen Hooper *too* much. Happy we, however, who had the[n] benefit of some of that perfume much was wasted on the desert wind

Dear James,

MARGARET.

I have written jestingly, let not that deceive you, dear James, as to my feeling of the character of the paper I inclose. I look upon it with great reverence as one of the very few addresses to me to which I could respond. What he says of my having sinned in the old world, still finding my sustaining point there and trying to make it known to the new is so[n] deeply true, also of my being purely idealist [   ]

ALfrS (MHi).
and now] and <?> ↑ now ↓
[pr]ofessional career] [pr]ofessional <?> ↑ career ↓
not have] not <be> have
"Yes"! says] "<?> Yes"!s<?> ays
good worthy] *good* <?> *worthy*
(the ring)] ↑ (the ring) ↓
had the] had <?> the
is so] is ↑ so ↓

1. Orestes Brownson was a minister and writer whose religious seeking took him from Universalism through Unitarianism to the Roman Catholic church. He had edited his own journal in Boston. Bronson Alcott was at this time living in Concord.

2. After their meeting in France, Adam Mickiewicz sent the following character analysis to Fuller:

Feby 1847

Parvenue au sentiment de son droit inné de prendre acte de son existence, aspirant au droit de constater cette existence, de la manifester en soupirs, en paroles, en essais d'action, *appellée* à maintenir ses droits en actes.

Esprit qui a connu le vieux monde, qui a peché dans le vieux monde et qui cherche a faire connoitre ce vieux monde dans son monde nouveau.

Son *point d'appui* est dans le vieux monde; sa *sphere d'action* est dans le nouveau monde; sa *paix* est dans le monde d'avenir.

Elle est appellée à sentir, à parler, à agir dans ces trois mondes.

La seule des femmes initiée purement au monde antique, la seule a qui il a ete donné de toucher à ce qu'il y a de decisif dans le monde actuel et de presentir le monde d'avenir.

Votre esprit est lié a l'histoire de la Pologne, de la France, et commence à se lier a l'histoire de l'Amerique.

Vous appartenez a la seconde generation des esprits

Votre mission est de concourir à la deliverance de la femme Polonaise, Francaise et Americaine.

Vous avez aquire le droit de connoitre et de maintenir les droits et les obligations, les esperances et les exigences de la virginité.

Pour vous le premier pas de votre deliverance et de la deliverance de votre sexe (d'une certaine classe) est de savoir s'il vous est permis de rester vierge.

Tu dois apporter au nouveau monde le fruit muni par des siecles, les fruits excitans. Tu dois manifester ton esprit par ton regard, par ton geste, par ton action. Arrachez, ma Marguerite, arrachez au mal les hommes qui cherchent un regard encourageant, un geste qui pousse, un coup de main qui confirme, et qui ne trouvent rien de semblable dans le monde actuel. Arrachez ces hommes aux regards, aux gestes de celles qui ont reussi a contrefaire tous les actes de l'esprit, parce qu'elles sentaient le besoin de l'esprit. Donnez de votre esprit et à ceux qui sent prepares to recevoir, donnez le tout avec ton frere.—

Arrived at the perception of her innate right to take action in her existence, aspiring to the right of establishing that existence, of manifesting it in sighs, in words, in attempts at action, *summoned* to maintain her rights by actions.

A spirit who has known the old world, who has sinned in the old world and who seeks to make known that old world in the new.

Her *base* is in the old world; her *sphere of action* is in the new world; her *peace* is in the world to come.

She is called upon to feel, to speak, to move within these three worlds.

The only one among women genuinely initiated into the antique world, the only one to whom it has been given to touch that which is decisive in today's world and to comprehend in advance the world to come.

Your spirit is bound to the history of Poland, of France, and begins to bind itself to the history of America.

You belong to the second generation of minds.

Your mission is to contribute to the deliverance of the Polish, French, and American woman.

You have acquired the right to know and maintain the rights and obligations, the hopes and exigencies of virginity.

For you, the first step in your deliverance and in the deliverance of your sex (of a certain class) is to know if it is permitted to you to remain virgin.

Thou must bear to the new world the fruit furnished by the ages, the animating fruit. Thou must manifest thy spirit by thy regard, thy gesture, thy action. Rescue, my Margaret, rescue from evil the men who seek a look of encouragement, a forceful deed, a confirming sudden surprise. Rescue these men from the looks, the deeds of those who have succeeded in counterfeiting all the actions of the mind, because they lack the mind. Give of your intellect and, to those who feel prepared to receive, give all with your brother. [MH: bMS Am 1569.7 (473)]

790. To Margarett C. Fuller

Rome
19th Jany 1849.

Dearest Mother,

A letter from Mrs Farrar lets me know that you were well early in December; it is always great satisfaction to me to know this much.

I received your second dear letter and have delayed answering what you said about Aunt Mary thinking I should certainly hear at last and be able to write to you that she *had* left me something.[1] I suppose now it must be that she did not, but omission seems to me strange I had no claim and had formed no expectations, but she was so particularly tender and thoughtful of me, as to my health and material wants, that it seems to me strange she should not have left me at least a small legacy. I should have been very glad of money, but apart from that[n] I am even[n] pained that she should forget me. I cannot understand it; she wrote to me constantly even after it had become very distressing for her to write, her last letter was in May in that she expresses great hope of seeing me again. There was nothing to change her sentiments toward me, nor was she one to change towards a person she had loved without great and solid reason. I cannot understand it.

I had hoped that something might occur to prevent my needing the aid of dear Eugene, but as it is, if still convenient to him I accept it. Write to him, dear Mother, to say so, but ask h[im] if he sends the money to use every precaution that the letter[n] may not be lost. Strange things happen. I lose many letters. Greene and Co. never notified me of the reception of the money from Mr Greeley thus occasioning all that pain and difficulty. Several letters from Richard, perhaps from others, have been lost, one containing the first of exchange on Brown, Shipley and Co. It now appears that some one made use of that bill, forging my signature Thus I never received it all summer, and now the second of exchange is protested. I can have the money having sold it, but the affair is unpleasant to me.[   ]

I think I will consult the banker here as to what Eugene had better do to preclude, if possible, all mistakes or delay and inclose in a slip of paper which you can send him immedy It will be a long affair at any rate, as it will be a month before you get this letter and then a month before he gets yours, and then two months before I have the answer. Who knows, but I may have to use the money to come home. I shall, if possible, stay here another year, coming back in the summer of 1850, but it must depend somewhat on the position of public affairs and they look just now very threatening But do not feel anxious about me. During this winter, the most beautiful ever known, continual sunshine as the last was continual rain, I have become stronger and now feel equal to take care of myself and conflict with difficulties, if they come. God grant this may last, at any rate I am now enjoying and using the time and feel much encouraged. [   ]

What helps encourage me is a letter I have received from Mrs Farrar stating that my "best and most loving friends have united to assure me for my life and theirs three hundred a year." The reception of this to begin on my return to the U S. I do not know why they put this condition and I wish they had not; the money would have been so precious in case of my wishing to remain a while longer, but on the reception of so great a boon I have no right to remonstrate. I feel unspeakably grateful for an act which will on my return, if I wish, after the efforts needed to pay a debt, enable me to live in the retirement and tranquillity of the country. Return had seemed so dreadful to me, I felt as if I should have[n] so much to contend with, so much to undertake and to live always in the crowd as only there could sufficient employment be found. Now I feel at least as if there was a possibility of repose in the future, the sum is small, but when I needed repose I would absolutely limit my other[n] wants to it, when I wanted a small addition I could earn it by the pen, or by giving occasional lessons, it will not be always excitement, always care. We shall, I trust, have some peaceful days together. It seems the movers in this work were Mrs Farrar and Elizabeth Hoar, bless them both, my dear Mother. We must ever feel that Mrs F. has been practically one of my two or three best friends, and through what a length of years has she been faithful and generous to me. I feel now that I never did what I ought for her. I hope I shall be able in some future day to contribute a little to her happiness As to Elizh she is one of the saints; her peace, her home are above.

I have left no room to write about any thing but these affairs. With love to Aunt Abba, cousin Ellen[2] and Lloyd yr ever affece

M.

You had better not show this letter to any one. I dont like to have any one think I dwell at all on Aunt Mary not leaving me any thing. I do most truly feel that her love while living was the most precious gift and then I thought of none other. As to the other fact of this arrangement made for me by friends[n] please communicate *to A. and R. alone, and request them not to speak of it.* When you see Mrs F or E. say what you please, *to them* but who the others are engaged in this act of affection I do not yet know, and for reasons I have not room to give, nothing had best be said about it on our side. Beside who ever hears of it will think as they did about the fabulous legacy of Uncle A that I can never want any aid or employment more, but am rich and great already.

ALS (MH: fMS Am 1086 [9:151]). *Addressed:* Mrs Margaret Fuller.

but apart from that] but ↑ apart from that ↓
am even] am ↑ even ↓
that the letter] that ⟨it⟩ ↑ the letter ↓
should have] should ↑ have ↓

my other] my ↑ other ↓
fact of this arrangement made for me by friends] fact ↑ of this arrangement made for me by friends ↓
    1. Mary Rotch divided her large estate between her long-time companion, Mary Gifford, and her lawyer, Thomas Dawes Eliot. Gifford got $60,000 in cash and Rotch's home in New Bedford; Eliot received the remainder (Bullard, *Rotches*, p. 96). Thomas Dawes Eliot (1808–70) was admitted to the bar in 1829, served in the state legislature, and was later one of the founders of the Republican party. In 1834 he married Frances Brock (*National Cyclopaedia*).
    2. Abigail Crane, Margaret's maiden aunt, lived in Canton. Ellen Crane Hill was the daughter of Simeon and Elizabeth Crane of Canton. .

791. To Richard F. Fuller

Rome.
19th Jany 1849.

My dear Richard,

    With my window open looking out upon towards[n] St Peter's and the glorious Italian sun pouring in, I was just thinking of you. I was just thinking how I wished you were here that we might walk forth and talk together under the influence of these magnificent objects. I was thinking of the proclamation of the Constitutional Assembly here a measure carried by courageous youth in the face of age sustained[n] by the prejudices of many ages. The ignorance of the people and all the wealth of the country. Yet courageous youth faces not only these, but the most threatening aspect of foreign powers, and dares a future of blood and exile to achieve priveleges which are our (American)[n] common birthright. I thought of the great interests which may in our country be sustained, without obstacle[n] by every able man, interests of humanity, interests of God.

    I thought of the new prospects as to wealth opened to our country men by this acquisition of New Mexico and California the vast prospects of our country every way, so that it is in self a vast blessing to be born in America, and I thought how impossible it is that one like Richard, of so strong and generous nature shall, if he can but patiently persevere, be defrauded of a rich, manifold, powerful life.[1] Perhaps I should have written much of hopes, but Mr Hooker, my banker entered and obliges me to abandon the future for the annoyance of the present.

    I wrote you that no doubt several letters from you were lost among them one containing the first of exchange on Brown Shipley and Co.

179

Now it seems some one, intercepting that letter, has forged my signature and taken the money. They B. S. and Co[n] have protested the second of exchange saying they had paid the first.

I am no longer responsible having sold the bill to the bankers here and paid commission still it will be very unpleasant for me, if they have difficulty about it. When you write let me know if your letter was not sent as usual through *Greene and Co* I cannot doubt *it was* as all your letters are, but answer to this, and tell if you know any circumstance elucidating this affair.

I was disturbed enough before to lose letters containing, I suppose, some important part of your mental history. Just so with dear Eugene the letters were lost in which he spoke of his acquaintance with[n] and growing love for Eliza.[2] My apparent silence made him silent, the precious habit of intimacy was broken. Some peculiar aspect of my star indicates misfortune from the loss of letters. What I have had to endure at different periods[n] from this cause would if written down[n] make a romance. Now when I am to be separated from a friend I begin at once to fear to lose him quite from such a cause.

To have another summer all poisoned by cares and embarrassments as last was would be dreadful. I had reduced my expenses to the lowest possible amount and done without every thing hoping at least thus to feel free and not think about money. Now I do not feel pleasantly because, if the bank is called on to give me much money and does not receive it they will be annoyed So, dear R. tax your memory to know whether you ever sent letters without posting them yourself, or through any channel other than Greene and Co, and answer by next steamer after receiving this.

I will wait and not close up this leaf till the last moment, perhaps there will be something important to say.

Thursday eveg 25th Jany. This has been a most beautiful day and I have been a long walk out of town. How much I should like to walk sometimes with you again!

I went to the Church of St. Lorenzo, one of the most ancient in Rome, rich in early mosiacs also with spoils from the temples, marbles, ancient sarcophagi with fine basso relievos, magnificent columns. There is a little of every thing but the medley is harmonized by the action of time and the sensation induced is that of homely repose. It has the public cemetery and there lie the bones of many poor; the rich and noble lie in lead coffins in the church vaults of Rome Rome.[n]

But St Lorenzo loved the poor[3] When his tormentors insisted to know where he had hid his riches "There" he said pointing to[n] the crowd of wretches who hovered near his fiery bed, compelled to see the tyrants of the earth hew down the tree that had nourished and sheltered them

Amid the crowd of inexpressive epitaphs one touched me erected by a[n] son to his father. He was, says the son,[n] an angel of prosperity, seeking our good in distant countries with unremitting toil and pain. We owe him all. For his death it is my only consolation "that in life I never left his side."

Returning I passed the Pretorian Camp, the Campus Scelesadus[?], where Vestals that had broken their vows were buried alive in the city whose founder was born from a similar event, such are the usual, the frightful inconsistencies of mankind.

From my windows I see the Barberini Palace. In its chambers are the portrait of the Cenci, and the Galatea so beautifully described by Goethe.[4] In the garden are the remains of the [*illegible*] of Servius Tullius.

Yesterday as I went forth I saw the house where Keats lived in Rome where he died. I saw the Casino of Raphael. Returning I passed the Villa where Goethe lived when in Rome; afterwards the houses of Claude and Poussin.[5]

Ah, what human companionship here, how everything speaks!

I live myself in the apartment described in Andersen's "Improvisatore" which get you and read as scene of the childhood of Antonio.[6] I have the room, I suppose, indicated as being occupied by the Danish Sculptor. Read also Goethe's Year in Rome and Romish Elegies, Brownings "Bells and Pomegranates" at least those whose scene is laid in Italy and a book of late production (I mean within these past two or [three] years)[7] We shall talk to better advantage on my return if you know these books.

The inclosed letters, being written on very thin paper I want you to inclose seal and send to their respective addresses. I have prepared the packet in this way to save postage, even so I pay two or three dollars, so grudge not thy trouble

The note to Mrs Ames I wish you would take yourself and make her acquaintance. Miss Peabody will tell you where she lives.[8] She was with m[e] much in Rome, could tell you much abou[t] me, and I think you will like her. She may seem to you frivolous at first as she says every thing good or bad without distinction that comes into her head, but she has a beautiful character, entirely simple and generous.

[Te]ll me with whom you associate now. I [kn]ow nothing, having lost those letters. Tell all you can. I always fear to seem flimsy in speaking of your feelings. You say none can thread my mind and destiny that is true, even if with you and knowing as much as one can of another I could still only hope to offer good suggestions, and now I have not seen you so long your character is doubtless developed on other sides, presents new features *I* am no longer young, yet still so often new and surprizing to myself, you are at a more growing age.

28th As usual I have to send of the packet before receiving my letters, The mails are now so arranged that I can never answer to the latest intelligence But Mrs Crawford has a letter giving account of the suicide of Emerson.[9] When he was here though in such florid youth, it struck me he would not live long there were in his face signs of his fate

Adieu dear R. dont die you, prays your sister and friend

MARGARET

ALS (MH: fMS Am 1086 [9:156]); MsC (MH: fMS Am 1086 [Works, 2:587–601]). Published in part in *At Home and Abroad*, pp. 430–32. *Addressed:* Mr / Richard F. Fuller / Boston / Mass / U.S.A. *Postmark:* New York 24 Feb.

upon towards] upon ↑ towards ↓
age sustained] age ⟨armed⟩ ↑ sustained ↓
our (American)] our ↑ (American) ↓
sustained, without obstacle] sustained, ⟨unimpeded⟩ ↑ without obstacle ↓
They B. S. and Co] They ↑ B. S. and Co ↓
acquaintance with] acquaintance ↑ with ↓
endure at different periods] endure ↑ at different periods ↓
would if written down] would ↑ if written down ↓
in the church vaults of Rome Rome.] in ↑ the church⟨es⟩ ↑ vaults ↓ of Rome ↓ Rome.
pointing to] pointing ↑ to ↓
by a] by ⟨his⟩ a
the son,] the s⟨u⟩on,

1. The Treaty of Guadalupe Hidalgo ended the Mexican war and compelled Mexico to cede the land that is now California and New Mexico to the United States. The treaty was ratified on 10 March and took effect on 4 July 1848 (Richard B. Morris, ed., *Encyclopedia of American History* [New York, 1953], pp. 207–8).

2. Eliza Rotta, whom Eugene Fuller married in 1845.

3. Saint Lawrence of Rome (d. 258) was one of the deacons of Pope Sixtus II. After the pope was put to death by the emperor Valerian, Lawrence was commanded by the Roman prefect to give over the church's wealth. Lawrence then assembled a crowd of beggars and said, "I pray you come with me and view / The wondrous riches of our God / Displayed for you in sacred shrines." For his defiance Lawrence was slowly roasted alive on a gridiron (*Butler's Lives of the Saints*, 3:297–98; *Poems of Prudentius*, ed. Sister M. Clement Eagan [Washington, D.C., 1962], p. 112).

4. Fuller has an uncharacteristic lapse of memory. Goethe visited the Barberini Palace, but it was Leonardo da Vinci's work, not the Cenci, that he describes. Moreover, it is Raphael's *La Fornarina* that hangs there, not *The Triumph of Galatea*, which is in the Villa Farnesina (Goethe, *Italian Journey*, p. 360; Jean-Pierre Cuzin, *Raphael: His Life and Works*, trans. Sarah Brown [Secaucus, N.J., 1985], pp. 134, 233).

5. Keats had lived at 26 Piazza di Spagna and Goethe at 18 via del Corso (Murray,

Piazza di Spagna, Rome. From *Raccolta delle principali vedute di Roma* (Rome, n.d.), courtesy of The Pennsylvania State University Libraries.

Piazza del Popolo, Rome. From *Raccolta delle principali vedute di Roma* (Rome, n.d.), courtesy of The Pennsylvania State University Libraries.

p. 15). The Casino di Raffaello, next to the Villa Borghese, has paintings and medallions by the painter (Eaton, pp. 96–97). Claude Lorrain lived on via Margutta, near the Piazza di Spagna.

6. Hans Christian Andersen (1805–75), whose *Improvisatore; or Life in Italy* had been translated by Mary Howitt in 1845. It is Federigo, a young painter rather than a sculptor, who lived in the room described by Antonio, the narrator.

7. Goethe's *Italienische Reise* was published in 1816–17; the *Römische Elegien*, a cycle of twenty poems, was written from 1788 to 1790 and published by Schiller in *Die Horen* in 1795 (*OCGL*). Fuller had reviewed Browning's *Bells and Pomegranates* for the *New-York Daily Tribune*.

8. Elizabeth Palmer Peabody, a writer, publisher, and bookseller who was active in many intellectual and reform movements.

9. Louisa Ward married Thomas Crawford (1813–57) in 1844. After his death she married Luther Terry, a painter (*Correspondence of Governor Samuel Ward, May 1775–March 1776*, ed. Bernhard Knollenberg [Providence, 1952], p. 223). George Samuel Emerson (1825–48), depressed by his religious emotions, shot himself on 19 December. The son of George Barrell and Olivia Buckminster Emerson, he graduated from Harvard in 1845 (Harvard archives).

792. To Arthur B. Fuller

Rome
20th Jany 1849

My dear Arthur,

Your letter and Mothers of Octr gave me the first account of your illness.[1] Some letters were lost during the summer, I do not know how. It did seem very hard to have that illness[n] upon you just after your settlement, but it is to be hoped we shall sometime know a good reason for all that seems so strange. I trust you are now becoming fortified in your health, and, if this can only be, feel as if with you things would go well in this difficult world. Often I hear how much esteemed and beloved you are. Your letters seem as if your chief youthful fault a spice of presumption (which perhaps was useful in its day to buoy you up) was corrected. I trust you are on the threshhold of an honorable and sometimes happy career, from many pains, many dark hours let none of the progeny of Eve hope to escape.

It is very kind in you to have our poor Lloydie there, but why was he obliged to leave Brattleborough this I do not understand. Fain would I hope that some path may open to occupy his strong body and good will, can it be that our country, so rich in occasions, will offer none.

I often think of your great trouble I have never again been to Paris, and if I go, it will be on the way home. Mr. Brisbane, who was here the other day, is anxious for you to go, but you have not, like him, a rich father to pay your expenses and the journey and a couple of months in Paris, if you went nowhere else (and you would not be content to come so to Europe) would cost some hundreds.[2] I trust with perseverance to distinguish yourself, your people may send you by and by or some business may offer to pay the expenses. We live in a time, and you in a country, full of changes and opportunities for those who have patience to await and capacity to use them.

Meantime I hope to find you in your home and make you a good visit there. Your invitation is sweet in its tone and rouses a vision of summer woods, and N England Sunday morng bells. I would go to hear you preach, a thing I am likely to do for very few in future. It seems to me from your letter and Mothers that she is at last truly in her sphere, while living with one of her children. Watch over her carefully and dont let her do too much; her spirit is only all too willing, but the flesh is weak and her life so precious to us all.

Death begins to play its part in my absence. Uncle Abraham, Eugene's sweet baby, Miss Rotch, one of my kindest and noblest friends, and now Mrs Ellen Hooper to me very dear I do not for herself regret her departure she was married to a man, not ill intentioned, but so inferior to her, and she had such an anxious delicate sense of what was due to him, that she could never have any free harmonious life in this world. But for me it is sad that I shall no more see her face, so beautiful and be gladdened by her mind so full of genius and exquisitely refined. I have seen no woman in Europe more distinguished by nature than she. Nature was bountiful, but Destiny most unkind.

Remember me with love to Ellen when you write. I feel sad that she is to have another child by a man who ran away and left her to sustain alone her last time of trial but since it is so, I hope she will, this time, have a son; that will please Dr. C.[3] She seems to love you very much I hope you see her sometimes. Her courage in sustaining the consequences of her mistaken choice is truly admirable. Farewell, dear Arthur take good care of yourself and our beloved Mother. Ever affecy yr sister

M.

Was a packet recd from me last summer including letters for you, Eugene and Lloyd?

ALS (MH: fMS Am 1086 [9:153]); MsCfr (MH: fMS Am 1086 [Works, 1:663–67]). Published in part in *WNC*, p. 374. *Addressed:* Arthur.

hard to have that illness] hard ↑ to have that illness ↓

1. Mrs. Fuller's letter of 3 October 1848 (MH) described a lingering cold and lung trouble that Arthur had suffered.

2. Whom Fuller met is not clear. Albert Brisbane had been in Rome, but he and his family left for Naples on 10 December 1848 (*Gazzetta di Roma*, 12 December 1848).

3. Walter Channing (1849–1921), third child and first son of Ellen and Ellery, was born on 14 April and named for Ellery's father, Dr. Walter Channing, a Boston physician. The younger Channing graduated from Harvard medical school and became a psychologist (*National Cyclopaedia*).

793. To Ralph Waldo Emerson

Rome 21st Jany 49[n]

A year and no letter from Elizh, six months and no letter from Waldo.

I waited knowing E. first had to write to Waldo and then to welcome him back. I waited knowing he had to get back and divide the crumbs of the foreign banquet among dear five hundred friends. Now I want 2 letters, one from Elizh good household bread with a bunch of violets beside the plate. One from Waldo. He may put sentences into it from the Lectures, if he likes, but he must not begin[n] half way down the page and scrawl the lines desperately wide apart. Begin at top of the page and think of M. how much she loves you and how many times will read the letter and a good one will come.

I am leading a[n] lonely life here in Rome which seems my Rome this winter. The sun shines every day. I feel well and my spirits have risen again to concert pitch. What the demons tried me so hard for last year I don't yet see, perhaps the morale will come lagging on yet. Meanwhile, I try to forget all but the present, a present superficial enough but that I do not decline.[1] One don't want deep calling unto deep always, the shallows with their gold and silver fishes may take their turn.[2]

I have nothing particular to tell you which drops from my pen at once. As to persons, I have made acquaintance this past year mostly with thieves and prostitutes, and must say my faith in t[he] hopes of Lazarus are shaken.[3] I did think bad people were more hopeful than good, but think now the [ch]ances are about equal. Write dear Waldo write and so will I your

MARGARET.

ALS, collection of Nelson C. White. *Addressed*: R.W. Emerson/Concord/Mass.

49] *Under the date Fuller wrote:* day of universal and direct suffrage for a constitutional assembly in the old rotten hive of Papal droneism.

not begin] not ⟨g⟩ begin

leading a] leading ⟨th⟩ a

1. Balloting for the assembly was extended by three days. It was an orderly process, accompanied by some show: "Every evening the ballot-boxes were carried in procession, with blazing torches and military music" (Farini, 3:178). The deputies were chosen mostly from the landed or professional classes (King, *Italian Unity*, 1:292).

2. Ps. 42:7. "Deep calleth unto deep at the noise of thy waterspouts: all thy waves and thy billows are gone over me." Emerson had used the passage in "Nature": "Deep calls unto deep. But in actual life, the marriage is not celebrated" (*The Collected Works of Ralph Waldo Emerson*, ed. Robert E. Spiller and Alfred R. Ferguson [Cambridge, 1971], 1:43).

3. Lazarus the beggar, Luke 16:19–25.

794. To Emelyn Story

Rome
27th Jany 1849

My dear Emelyn

I was quite disappointed by the reading of your letter. Though I wrote you as well as I could both pros and cons, I had hoped very much you would come. And I still hope your doubts will end so. Now I shall write with that view because if I should have a chance to talk with you about your further plans and projects writing is superfluous.

Mr. Wetmore says he shall persist in asking you to come, and I wish it might be so as to arrive by the 5th Feby.[n] They are making great preparations here for opening the Constitutional Assembly. Then, after that, begins the Carnival on the 10th.[1] It will not be brilliant, as masks in the day time are forbidden, still you might like to see it again.

I write in the expectation that all will remain tranquil, as there is every reason to expect it will unless the incredible treachery now surmised of the French President should be actuated[2] In any event, we do not think that you need [n] apprehend any annoyance.

I have been to look at Poussin's house for you and also the *Casa del Scimia*!! in Quattro Fontane. I prefer the monkey apartment, it is large, sunny, a beautiful saloon, two very large bedrooms two good size, 7 beds in all,[n] a good dining room, abundant linen and table service, a small kitchen. The entrance is fine. The back windows look on the Barberini gardens, and they have a garden of their own. The walks from[n] this part of Rome would be comparatively new to you; the air is the best. This apartment I think you can have for 40 a

month, perhaps for 30 or 35, while Poussin would not come down below 70, and *I* should, at any rate, like monkey house better. Then for
me; I like the name; it presents a refreshing contrast to the glories
and classicalities so eternal in eternal Rome. There is something so
original in the sign; it befits the house of *Barberini*.

I flatter myself that when this arrives William will have finished his
model (he is not firm of health enough to stay in a studio damp as
you describe) the fit of content with Florence gone off, for to my
mind 'tis only a paroxysm, and the trunks ready to be packed for
here. Come on at once, if you can. It would be only a night at the Hotel d'Angleterre if the lodgings were not taken. I would go with you
next morning and you would be sure of being content with them
which is more than any person the most desirous of studying the
tastes of another can feel in taking rooms for a friend.[n]

I have a letter from Mrs. Browning in which she expresses their
pleas[ure] in making your acquaintance. I am very glad for both.
Since I cannot see them now, I want some of their thoughts and,
think you,[n] not they be so candid as to lend me a copy of Bells and
Pomegranates. I want so much to read again the poems about Italy
and can't get them. I would easily find an oppory[n] to send them back.

I am not at all surprized at what you say of Keats. I always thought
with Byron "Strange that the mind, that very fiery particle, could let
itself be snuffed out by an article."[3] Anna Parsons, dwelling[n] in her
trance on a private letter of his (Keats's)[n] was much distressed at finding a degree of self-seeking unworthy of his genius.[4]

I would be glad for William to call with the inclosed letter on Madame Arconati. He will thus, if she is at home, see one who is considered by many the most distinguished woman in Italy and who would
be distinguished where there was a far greater number of worthy
competitors If she is not at home will he leave his card and address,
provided you still expect to stay some days in Florence. I have left her
free to call or not. At an earlier period she would not have failed so to
do on a friend of mine, but now cares and sorrows are accumulated
upon her and I ask her to do as she feels, but if she does not call, she
may send me something by you. Have you Murray's Hand Book of
Southern Italy, if so, bring.[5] I cannot find it in Rome. I trouble you
much, dear Emelyn, but you know I would gladly do as much for you.
Affecy yr friend

MARGARET.

M. Arconati speaks English well. A beautiful presence is fled. Ellen
Hooper! did you know her well?

When William calls on Madame A, he will send her in the letter first, with his card and then she will come into parlor having read it and knowing about him. She knew and liked Julia Howe when in Milan.[6] Remember that she is a Milanese.

If you come and take an apartment large enough I might pass two or three weeks with you in April, when I have done working and we could run about to see pikters. I think monkey house has no couch for me, however it would be very near this one, if I keep this room then We would talk of that when you come. If you think of the Grecian expedition, would not William naturally meet Mr Black here?

ALS (TxU). Published in part in Phillips, *Reminiscences*, pp. 92–94. *Addressed:* William W. Story Esq / for Mrs Story / Care Maquay Packenham & Co / Florence.

5th Feby.] 5th ↑ Feby ↓.
you need] you ⟨could⟩ ↑ need ↓
beds in all,] beds ↑ in all ↓
walks from] walks ⟨of⟩ ↑ from ↓
for a friend.] for ⟨them⟩ ↑ a friend ↓.
now, I want some of their thoughts and, think you,] now, ↑ I want some of their thoughts and, think you, ↓
easily find an oppory] easily ↑ find an oppory ↓
Parsons, dwelling] Parsons, ⟨once⟩ dwelling
his (Keats's)] his ↑ (Keats's) ↓

1. The Roman Carnival lasted from the second Saturday before Ash Wednesday to Shrove Tuesday. Normally the processions filled the corso with people, who pelted each other with comfits. In 1849, however, the tradition that allowed revelers to be masked was suspended because of the tense political situation (Eaton, pp. 231–41).

2. Louis Napoleon (1808–73), nephew of Napoleon I, had been elected president of the French republic on 10 December 1848. Despite his previous anticlerical bias, he worked for the restoration of the temporal power of the papacy. At the time Fuller wrote, the French had made moves in both Gaeta and Paris. Latour d'Auvergne joined with the Duc d'Harcourt at Gaeta to urge the pope to call on France before Austria, should armed force become necessary. They promised that if Austria moved toward Rome, the French would create a garrison in the Papal States. Paris was excited by news about military preparations taking place in France's southern seaports, signs of imminent movements toward Rome (Farini, 3:200–201; Ross William Collins, *Catholicism and the Second French Republic, 1848–1852* [New York, 1923], p. 200).

3. The lines are from *Don Juan*, canto 11, stanza 60:

> John Keats, who was kill'd off by one critique,
>   Just as he really promised something great,
> If not intelligible, without Greek
>   Contrived to talk about the Gods of late,
> Much as they might have been supposed to speak.
>   Poor fellow! His was an untoward fate;
> 'Tis strange the mind, that very fiery particle,
> Should let itself be snuff'd out by an article.

(Byron, *Poetical Works*, p. 795.) The tradition grew from the attack leveled against Keats by John Gibson Lockhart in "Cockney School of Poetry," *Blackwood's Edinburgh Magazine* 3 (1818): 519–24. Among other jibes, Lockhart said that "Mr. [Leigh] Hunt is a small poet, but he is a clever man. Mr. Keats is a still smaller poet, and he is only a boy of pretty abilities, which he has done every thing in his power to spoil" (p. 522).

4. Anna Quincy Thaxter Parsons was a Boston woman who held mesmeric trances during which she read the characters of authors by holding their manuscripts. Fuller and the Clarkes often spent such evenings with her in the 1840s.

5. Octavian Blewitt (1810–84), secretary of the Royal Literary Fund, published Murray's *Handbook for Travellers in Central Italy* in 1843 (*DNB*).

6. Julia Ward Howe was in Milan during her wedding trip in 1843. "We greatly enjoyed the beauty of the cathedral and the hospitality of our new friends," she said. "Among these were the Marchese Arconati and his wife, a lady of much distinction, and in after years a friend of Margaret Fuller's" (Howe, *Reminiscences*, p. 119). Fuller probably carried a letter of introduction from Howe to Arconati Visconti in 1847.

795. To Maria Rotch

Rome

3d Feby 1849

My dear Maria,

I hear you are engaged to be married and I am glad.[1] You are just at the right age, with mind and character developed, yet the feelings still fresh. All else is yours, love friends, fortune enough, good health, an excellent mind, an engaging person. If now you have also found a companion whom you can love, in whom you can trust, you have all of good that is given to mortals. What a smiling morning! We cannot expect the day to be throughout free from clouds, but may even the dark parts aid in the fair result of the who[le] picture!

You are capable of great good, dear Maria, of a progressive [an]d beneficent life. I believe you will have thought of this, no less than of happiness. In all the good you have and do I shall find my part and pride, believing the trust I felt in you and to[n] which you always corresponded was not without use to you in early days.

Should you feel like it I wish you might write and tell me somewhat of yourself at this important time. Put no price on your feelings, only if you *can* write it will be very pleasing to your friend

MARGARET FULLER.

My best regards to your parents and brother.[2] I hope they do not lose your society, or at least not throughout the year. Butternuts seems such a safe home. I am sorry now I never have been there.

ALS (MH: fMS Am 1086 [9:173]). *Addressed:* Maria Rotch.
and to] and ↑to↓

1. On 20 September 1849 Maria Rotch married Radcliff Hudson, the son of Henry and Maria Holly Hudson of Hartford (Bullard, *Rotches*, p. 443).
2. Her brother was Francis Morgan Rotch.

796. To Costanza Arconati Visconti

Rome, 5 February 1849

I am so delighted to get your letter, that I must answer on the instant. I try with all my force to march straight onwards,— to answer the claims of the day; to act out my feeling as seems right at the time, and not heed the consequences;— but in my affections I am tender and weak; where I have really loved, a barrier, a break, causes me great suffering. I read in your letter that I am still dear to you as you to me. I always felt, that if we had passed more time together,— if the intimacy, for which there was ground in the inner nature, had become consolidated,— no after differences of opinion or conduct could have destroyed, though they might interrupt its pleasure. But it was of few days' standing,— our interviews much interrupted. I felt as if I knew you much better than you could me, because I had occasion to see you amid your various and habitual relations. I was afraid you might change, or become indifferent; now I hope not.

True, I have written, shall write, about the affairs of Italy, what you will much dislike, if ever you see it. I have done, may do, many things that would be very unpleasing to you; yet there *is* a congeniality, I dare to say, pure, and strong, and good, at the bottom of the heart, far, far deeper than these differences, that would always, on a real meeting, keep us friends. For me, I could never have but one feeling towards you.

Now, for the first time, I enjoy a full communion with the spirit of Rome. Last winter, I had here many friends; now all are dispersed, and sometimes I long to exchange thoughts with a friendly circle; but generally I am better content to live thus:— the impression made by all the records of genius around is more unbroken; I begin to be very familiar with them. The sun shines always, when last winter it never shone. I feel strong; I can go everywhere on foot. I pass whole days abroad; sometimes I take a book, but seldom read it:— why should I, when every stone talks?

In spring, I shall go often out of town. I have read "La Rome Souterraine" of Didier, and it makes me wish to see Ardea and Nettuno.[1] Ostia is the only one of those desolate sites that I know yet. I study sometimes Niebuhr, and other books about Rome, but not to any great profit.[2]

In the circle of my friends, two have fallen.[3] One a person of great wisdom, strength, and calmness. She was ever to me a most tender friend, and one whose sympathy I highly valued. Like you by nature and education conservative, she was through thought liberal. With no exuberance or passionate impulsiveness herself, she knew how to allow for these in others. The other was a woman of my years, of the most precious gifts in heart and genius. She had also beauty and fortune. She died at last of weariness and intellectual inanition. She never, to any of us, her friends, hinted her sufferings. But they were obvious in her poems, which, with great dignity, expressed a resolute but most mournful resignation.

ELfr, from *Memoirs*, 2:257–59.

1. Charles Didier (1805–64), a Swiss writer, spent several years in Italy and published his *Rome souterraine* in 1833. He was a friend of Lamennais and one of George Sand's lovers (*Dictionnaire des lettres françaises: Le dix-neuvième siècle*, ed. Pierre Moreau [Paris, 1971]).

2. In her journal Fuller noted that she also read Mazzini's journal, *Ricordi di giovani d'Italia* (Leona Rostenberg, "Margaret Fuller's Roman Diary," *Journal of Modern History* 12 [1940]: 212).

3. Mary Rotch and Ellen Hooper.

797. To Richard F. Fuller

Rome
23d Feby 1849.

My dear Richard,

I wrote you some weeks since about Brown and Shipley's protesting the bill, but it was all a mistake, is cleared up now and I understand from the banker they pay the money.

I am sorry now I troubled you about it, but was afraid to wait, communications take up so much time. I shall be very glad when the steamers again begin to ply every week.

How long it is since I heard from you; it makes me feel very badly, as if you were having such dark days. Yet surely with youth and strength, unspotted honor and excellent abilities, you must make your way in social life. The life of the soul is incalculable.

It is something if one can get free foothold on the earth, so as not to be jostled out of hearing the music, if there should be any spirits in the air to make such.

For my part I have led rather too lonely a life of late. Before it seemed as if too many voices of men startled away the inspirations, but having now lived 8 months much alone, I don't know that any great good has come of it, and think to return and herd with others for a little. I have realized in these last days the thought of Goethe

> He who would in loneliness live
> ah he is soon alone,
> Each one loves, each one lives
> and leaves him to his pain.[1]

I went away and hid all the summer, not content with that I said on returning to Rome, I must be busy and receive people little; they have taken me at my word and hardly any one comes to see me: now, if I want some play and prattle, I shall have to run after them.

It is fair enough that we all, in turn, should be made to feel our need of one another.

Never was such a winter as this. Ten weeks, now, of unbroken sunshine and the mildest breezes. Of course its price is to be paid. The Spring, usually divine here with luxuriant foliage and multitudinous roses, will be all parched and dirty; there is fear too of want of food for the poor Roman State.

I pass my days in writing, walking, occasional visits to the galleries. I read little except the newspapers: these take up an hour or two of the day. I am ardently interested in these present struggles of the nations. I have my thoughts fixed daily on the bulletin of men and things. I expect to write the history, but because it is so much in my heart

If you were here, I rather think you would be impassive, like the two most esteemed Americans I see They do not believe in the sentimental nations. Hungarians, Poles, Italians are too demonstrative for them, too fiery, too impressible, they like better the loyal slow moving Germans, even the Russian with his dog's nose and gentlemanly servility please them better than my people. There is an antagonism of race betwixt them. Good bye. You probably will not hear from me again this good while. I shall write a number of letters for U. S. by Mrs Crawford who expects to arrive there early in May ever affecy

M.

ALS (MH: fMS Am 1086 [9:157]); MsC (MH: fMS Am 1086 [Works, 2:883–89]). Published in part in *Memoirs*, 2:259–60, and Miller, pp. 281–82. *Addressed:* Mr. Richard F. Fuller. / Boston / Mass. *Endorsed:* F.S.M. / Margaret / 23 Feb / 49.

1. From Goethe's *Wilhelm Meisters Lehrjahre*:

> Wer sich der Einsamkeit ergibt,
> Ach! der ist bald allein;
> Ein jeder lebt, ein jeder liebt,
> Und lässt ihn seiner Pein.

(Goethe, *Gedenkausgabe*, 7:147).

798. To Emelyn Story

[ca. early March 1849]

Do dear Emelyn, as you yourself think best. I think you may very well excuse yourself to Cropsey, having given her one evening, unless you think there will be metal more attractive than herself.[1] I go out of town Tuesday morng and Thursday shall be much engaged in making little preparations, so have only free today and tomorrow. And tomorrow you go to Grotto Ferrata, do you not?[2]

I will expect to hear from you in the course of the day[n] again of your decision. If you pass the eveg with me, will you come directly after dinner and make it a good long one. If you will lend me a tea pot you shall have your cup of tea.[n]

I too have several days been haunted by headach; yesterday it was very bad and to day has fled.

I send you "Piccinino" I believe the understanding is for you to return it to Mr. Perkins when you have read it[3] Affly

MARGARET

ALS (MH: fMS Am 1086 [9:174]). *Addressed:* Mrs. Story.

Dated by the fact that the Storys had arrived in Rome around 1 March and that the Cropseys, who left Rome in mid-March, were still there.
you in the course of the day] you ↑ in the course of the day ↓
tea.] tea. ⟨I⟩

1. Jasper Francis Cropsey (1823–1900), a landscape painter and architect, went to Europe in 1847 and remained there until 1849. In 1847 he married Maria Cooley (d. 1906), daughter of Isaac Cooley of Greenwood Lake, New Jersey. The Cropseys, friends of the Storys and Cranches, left Rome early in April to avoid the war (Groce; William S. Talbot, *Jasper F. Cropsey, 1823–1900* [New York, 1977], pp. 36, 61–66, 251).

2. Grotto Ferrata is a small town east of Rome, on the Campagna between Frascati and Marino. Its main attractions are the monastery of St. Basilio and a chapel with frescoes by Domenichino (Murray, pp. 421–22).

3. George Sand's novel *Il Piccinino*.

799. To Giuseppe Mazzini

Rome
3 March, 1849.

Dear Mazzini,

Though knowing you occupied by the most important affairs, I again feel impelled to write a few lines. What emboldens me is the persuasion that the best friends,— in point of perfect sympathy and intelligence the only friends,— of a man of ideas and of marked character, must be women. You have your mother; no doubt you have others, perhaps[n] many; of that I know nothing; only I like to offer[n] also my tribute of affection.[1]

When I think that only two years ago, you thought of coming into Italy with us in disguise, it seems very glorious, that you are about to enter Republican Rome as a Roman Citizen.[2] It seemed almost the most sublime and poetical fact of history.[n] Yet, even in the first thrill of joy, I felt, "He will think his work but beginning now"

When I read from your hand these words "il lungo esilio testè ricominciato, la vita non confortata fuorchè d'affetti lontani e contesi, e la speranza lungamente protratta e il desiderio che commincia a farmisi supremo di dormire finalmente in pace, dachè non ho potuto vivere in terra mia"[3]

When I read these words they made me weep bitterly and I thought of them always with a great pang at the heart. But it is not so, dear Mazzini. You do not return to sleep under the sod of Italy, but to see your thought springing up all over her soil. The gardeners seem to me, in point of instinctive wisdom or deep thought, mostly incompetent to the care of the garden, but an idea like this will be able to make use of any implements, it is to be hoped[n] will educate, the men by making them work. It is not this, I believe, which still keeps your heart so melancholy, for I seem to read the same melancholy in your answer to the Roman assembly. You speak of "few and late years," but some full ones still remain; a century is not needed, nor ought the same man, in the same form of thought, to work too long on an age. He would mould and bend it too much to himself, better

Giuseppi Mazzini. George Peabody Collection, The Johns Hopkins University.

for him to die and return incarnated to give the same truth aid on yet another side. Jesus of Nazareth died young; but had he not spoken and acted as much truth as the world could bear in his time? A frailty, a perpetual short-coming, motion in a curve line, seems the destiny of this earth. The excuse awaits us elsewhere; there must be one, for it is true, as said Goethe, that "Care is taken that the trees grow not up into heaven."⁴ Then, like you, appointed ministers, must not be the less earnest in their work, yet to the greatest, the day, the moment is all their kingdom. God takes care of the increase.

Farewell! For your sake I would wish at this moment to be an Italian and a man of action. But *though an American*, I am not even *a woman of action*; so the best I can do is to pray with the whole heart. Heaven bless dear Mazzini, cheer his heart and give him worthy helpers to carry out its holy purposes!

AL (MH: fMS Am 1086 [11:105]); MsC (MH: fMS Am 1086 [Works, 1:233–37]). Published in *WNC*, pp. 374–76; Wade, pp. 581–82; and Chevigny, pp. 469–70. *Addressed:* Al cittando / Rappresentante del / Popolo Romano / Firenzi.

others, perhaps] others, ⟨b⟩ perhaps
to offer] to ⟨?⟩ offer
poetical fact of history.] poetical ↑ fact of history. ↓
implements, it is to be hoped] implements, ↑ it is to be hoped ↓

1. On her arrival in Italy in 1947, Fuller spent three days visiting Maria Mazzini in Genoa.
2. On the evening of 8–9 February 1849 the assembly declared Rome to be a republic. Mazzini, who had been in Florence, working for a union of Tuscany and Rome, was made a citizen on the 12th and invited to Rome. He arrived on 5 March and visited the assembly the following day (Farini, 3:228, 297; Barr, pp. 200–201). Fuller quoted from his address to the assembly and added: "Mazzini is a man of genius, an elevated thinker, but the most powerful and first impression from his presence must always be of the religion of his soul, of his *virtue*, both in the modern and antique sense of that word" (*New-York Daily Tribune*, 16 May 1849).
3. "The long exile that has just recommenced, the life unconsoled unless by affections that are remote and contested, and the long-protracted hope and the desire that has become deep of sleeping in peace at last since I could not live in my land."
4. Goethe's motto for the third part of *Dichtung und Wahrheit*: "Es ist dafür gesorgt, dass die Bäume nicht in den Himmel wachsen" (Goethe, *Gedenkausgabe*, 10:491).

800. To Caroline Sturgis Tappan

[I] Rome. 8 March. 1849.

I sent you a sad cry from my lacerated affections. Now I have learned more fortitude, I feel very calm but sternly towards fate. This last plot against me has been too cruel and too cunningly wrought I shall never acquiesce; I submit because a useless resistance is degrading, but I demand an explanation. I see that it is probable I shall receive none while I live here, and I suppose I can bear the rest of the suspense, since I have comprehended all its difficulties in the first moments. Meanwhile I live day by day, tho' not on manna.

Could I but have remained in peace, cherishing the messenger dove, I should have asked no more. I should have felt overpaid for all the pains and bafflings of my previous sad broken difficult life.

How many nights I have passed entire in contriving every possible means by which, through resolution and energy on my part, I could avoid that one sacrifice. It was impossible. My love for others had turned against me, I had given to other sufferers what I now needed for myself so deeply, so terribly! I shall never again be perfectly, be religiously generous; I understand why others are not. I am worse than I was. But enough of this— it makes my head ache. I hope when you receive these words your head will be clear and your heart happy. I still like to know that others are happy— it consoles me. [II] [   ] The Abruzzi, where I passed last summer are glorious snow covered mountains with their pedestals garlanded, with the olive, the mulberry and the vine. The valleys are yellow with saffron flowers, the grain-fields all enamelled with corn-flowers and red poppies, the valleys are of intoxicating beauty; there is nothing like it in America. The old genius of Europe has mellowed all its marbles here. Earth is so full of it that one cannot have that feeling of holy virgin loveliness as in America. I cannot feel alive here, the spirits of dead men crowd me in the most apparently solitary places. I have no genius at all. I am all the time too full of sympathy. It would sometimes be so pleasant to be in America for a day. But I cannot want to go there yet, it will be more [*illegible*] for me there than ever, I think, and here I have been so beloved, both by ghosts and fleshly men.

Hicks is going home this summer, you must see him. He is the only American with whom I have been intimate; at first I was not intellectual enough for him; but we were always becoming intimate. Frank Heath is here, at least he says he is Frank Heath.[1] I can hardly believe it eight years seeming to have changed every atom of his original composition, and not by [*illegible*] only slow ripening sun has turned the white slender flower into a thick coated nut, but white within too, and of best flavor meseems. He seemed to be wonderfully struck by my having been a woman, always the first time of meeting, beginning "On account of your sex"— "As a woman" &c We made last night the tour of the Vatican by torch light. I go every [   ] works it round so; this is now the third Spring. It is odd how people meet at last, being an American party, there were the Storys with whom I am on a very cordial footing. William shows more and more talent; he is always the same, only more manly and boyish; quite handsome now that he had modelled several things that please him.[2] Charles Perkins about whom you know enough, Crawford and Louisa Ward his wife.[3] I had not seen so many persons together connected with the old phase. I walked rather sad and strange among them. I wish we could meet tonight, that I might tell you the thoughts suggested by various marbles. There was Sam's Amore Antico, I always make them throw the light on that.[4] How exactly he corresponded to that once, and now?—planet why hadst thou so many moons? I love him very dearly still; it seems as if sometime we might meet again, but no matter!

I wore a pin with the head of Raphael my Italian servant dreamed that she asked me whose portrait it was, and I replied, of my son who is dead!

I am gossipping, but I think of the tragic figures [*illegible*] puts me in mind of Rachel. You will find a good little notice of her in Ana [*illegible*] memoir of himself. The silliest book [*illegible*] but about her the notice was faithful. Also an attempt to paint her in Eugene Sue's *Martin the Valet de Chambre* which would interest you to read I think.[5] I read it, translated into Italian, when I was getting well.

I write now from no particular impulse indeed I cannot write really, but because Mrs Crawford will carry some letters, and these shreds and patches I send may not come amiss now in your more housewifely existence. Yet for tonight, good night. It is full moon and I go forth As you have never been in Rome moonlight nights, don't fancy yourself well enough off— This is the city of fountains and they talk a great deal nights. *None of the nymphs* are dead. [   ]

I: MsCfr (MB: Ms. Am. 1450 [151]); II: ALfr, collection of G. W. Haight; MsCfr (MB: Ms. Am. 1450 [106]). Published in part in *Memoirs*, 2:299–302.

1. John Francis Heath (1815–62) was born in Virginia, graduated from Harvard in 1840, and became a doctor after study in Göttengen and Heidelberg. During the Civil War, Heath was in charge of a Confederate hospital in North Carolina, where he died (*Harvard College University at Cambridge New England: Class of 1840* [London, 1895], p. 29).

2. William Story.

3. Charles Callahan Perkins (1823–86) was the son of a wealthy Boston family. After graduation from Harvard in 1843 he became an art critic and an advocate of art education in public schools. Perkins helped found the Boston Museum of Fine Arts (*DAB*).

4. Sam Ward.

5. Eugène Sue, *Martin, l'enfant trouvé; ou, Les Mémoires d'un valet de chambre* (Paris, 1846).

801. To Marcus Spring

[I] Rome, 9 March 1849

Last night, Mazzini came to see me. You will have heard how he was called to Italy, and received at Leghorn like a prince, as he is; unhappily, in fact, the only one, the only great Italian. It is expected, that, if the republic lasts, he will be President. He has been made a Roman citizen, and elected to the Assembly; the labels bearing, in giant letters, "*Giuseppe Mazzini, cittadino Romano,*" are yet up all over Rome. He entered by night, on foot, to avoid demonstrations, no doubt, and enjoy the quiet of his own thoughts, at so great a moment. The people went under his windows the next night, and called him out to speak; but I did not know about it. Last night, I heard a ring; then somebody speak my name; the voice struck upon me at once. He looks more divine than ever, after all his new, strange sufferings. He asked after all of you. He stayed two hours, and we talked, though rapidly, of everything. He hopes to come often, but the crisis is tremendous, and all will come on him; since, if any one can save Italy from her foes, inward and outward, it will be he. But he is very doubtful whether this be possible; the foes are too many, too strong, too subtle. Yet Heaven helps sometimes. I only grieve I cannot aid him; freely would I give my life to aid him, only bargaining for a quick death. I don't like slow torture. I fear that it is in reserve for him, to survive defeat. True, he can never be utterly defeated; but to see Italy bleeding, prostrate once more, will be very dreadful for him.

He has sent me tickets, twice, to hear him speak in the Assembly. It was a fine, commanding voice. But, when he finished, he looked very exhausted and melancholy. He looks as if the great battle he had fought had been too much for his strength, and that he was only sustained by the fire of the soul.

All this I write to you, because you said, when I was suffering at leaving Mazzini,— "You will meet him in heaven." This I believe will be, despite all my faults. [   ]

[II] What would I not give that my other two brothers, R.W.E. and W.H.C., could see him! All have in different ways the celestial fire, all have pure natures. They may have faults, but no base alloy. To me they form a triad. I know none other such.

I: ELfr, from *Memoirs*, 2:262–63; II: ELfr, from Octavius B. Frothingham, *Memoir of William Henry Channing* (Boston, 1886), p. 181. Published in part in Van Doren, pp. 294–96.

802.   To Margarett C. Fuller

Rome
9th March, 1849.

My dear Mother,

Again begin the long silences of my family. I beg of you to manage these thing differently. Where there are so many persons to write, if you will only make some arrangement among yourselves, I certainly could receive news once in^n a month, or six weeks. These long silences give me useless pain. Richard has entirely ceased to write. All the winter never one line from him.

I wrote to you about Aunt Mary's will. I no longer feel specially excluded as all her friends and relatives are also forgotten and a fortune of 150000 dollars divided between Mary Gifford and her lawyer. But it seems dreadful that a person who understood so well the wants of others should have neglected this great occasion of making many happy. To good of^n a little given to me would have been all but infinite. I presume others feel the same. It seems quite unlike her and to me is as unaccountable as sad.

Dark or bright, life goes on and men and woman are decoyed or hunted up the hill. My step has been lighter than last year; this winter of perpetual sunshine in glorious Rome, is of itself a great boon. I wish to thank for it. Enabled to take constant exercise, my health is much improved; that is an immense good. I feel almost strong now, able to stand up against ill.

My soul was yesterday refreshed by the sight of my noble friend, Mazzini, his twenty years of martyrdom have received their palm branch he enters Rome for the first time as a Roman citizen; he enters to defend Italy, if any man can, against her foes. Can any?— I feel no confidence: they are so many. His life has known one hour of pure joy, but I fear, I fear the entrance into Jerusalem may be followed by the sacrifice.

March 17th

Yesterday came a letter from Richard. He said of the family in general merely that all were well and, what I could not understand, that Ellen was living with you at Manchester.[1]

He also told me of his own marriage, and, if you can, I wish you would tell me something about this as I never even heard of the maiden. I hope it is something not painful and careful for you. But do not mention that I spoke of it at all and burn this letter.

And has not Arthur some attachment? I hear nothing of the kind from him this very long time.

I wait anxiously for one of your nice long fine-hand letters and *do not this time forget to tell me if the hand that writes so fine suffers still and how your general health is.*

Life goes on much the same as yet with me. The Storys are here for two months, more interesting and agreeable to me than any of the other American William S. thinks of you with affection. Their children are charming.

Should there be time before closing the packet, I write another leaf, if not ever affecy yr

M.

ALS (MH: fMS Am 1086 [9:158]). *Addressed:* Mrs. Margaret Fuller / Manchester, / New Hampshire. *Postmark:* Boston 8 May.

once in] once ↑ in ↓
good of] good ↑ of ↓

1. In his letter of 9 February (MH), Richard announced his marriage to Sarah Kollock Batchelder of Canton, whom he married on 10 January (*The Record of Births, Marriages, and Deaths . . . in the Town of Canton from 1797–1845*, ed. Frederic Endicott [Canton, Mass., 1896], p. 261). Ellen is either Ellen Fuller Channing or Ellen Crane Hill.

803. To Elizabeth De Windt Cranch

Rome.
9th March, 1849

Dear Lizzie,

I was very glad to have you write that you are going home. For, though I sympathize most deeply with any one who is fitted to prize Italy and has to leave her, and know how much I shall suffer myself, yet this is no time for an artist to be here. Nor is there any strong probability of tranquillity at present. Few people would come, Pearse would have but few and scanty orders, and with those two young children, and your constitution so delicate you might have too trying a time and become old! That is the poison of care, one might bear the strongest dose, just for the time, but it makes youth grey-haired. I hope you will find many friends, new and old, who will carry about Georgie and Nora in their arms, and prize the genius of Pearse and that some few years hence you will return under happier circumstances to Venice, to Florence, to Rome.

O Rome, seat of the gods! I do regret you have not been here this winter of perpetual sunshine.

The Cropseys will be disappointed at not finding you, they go from here the 18th and Mr C. had expected to enjoy sketching excursions with Pearse in the neighborhood of Florence. I met him this morning and could not well understand what he said about the money, but I believe it was that he had remitted it to Florence. If you send it me by Hooker, write me a line at the same time; he is little interested to give information to one so slender in purse as I am.

Also I hope when you are well refreshed at home, you will write me a joint letter telling me of yourselves and all other persons and things you think will interest me. It will be a great boon; write fine and much, and tell me of my friend Carrie anything you may know. I hear little from herself I hope she will have a dear child.[1] It grieves me that I could never see Nora; every one says she is so lovely. Give her and George both a kiss for me. If you *do* write me a line now, let me know how it has gone with Mrs. Browning. I am very glad you had such pleasure in their acquaintance; a little of the salt of the earth is more than ever needed in this hot climate. It is a shame I cannot have the "Bells" &c. It is *here* I want to read the Italian things again; half memories of them keep tormenting me.

Pearse's Colonna poem was incorporated into one of my letters with mention of the picture, and, no doubt, printed, though I never recd the number of the Tribune which contained it.[2] The poem from Naples I never sent. That needs the clear type and margins of a magazine, or perhaps he will publish a vol on his return. Now you are going, I wish you would send me Emerson's poems, else, I may see them no more for a long time, unless you have made pencil marks, or for some other reason are anxious to keep that particular copy.

The Storys have been here a week, after a doleful detention at Leghorn, and a very sick night on the steamer. They have a tolerably pleasant apartment and enjoy themselves as usual. The first day they were seeking the apartment, Sunday, we had luncheon at Mr. Crawford's and afterwards went to St. Peter's where the only time this winter was *not* fine music. The second day, I passed with them, and in the afternoon we walked about Villa Borghese. Wednesday evening we saw the Vatican by torchlight; it is now my third enjoyment of this always greater delight. Since, I have not seen them. My friend Mazzini is now here; his proper great occasion has come to him at last, whether he can triumph over the million difficulties with which it is beset I know not, but he will do all that may become a man. Goodbye, and may your homeward course be every way prosperous. We shall meet again probably in a year or two, meanwhile I pray you keep your hearts ever open for your friend—

MARGARET F.

Hicks wished me to say he hopes to paint your picture in N. York without regard to price. He also will return this summer.

Remember me to your sister Louisa, write how you find about her. I trust she let lightly go of Barrett's cold love.

MsC (MB: Ms. Am. 1450 [61]). Published in part in Scott, *Cranch*, pp. 168–70.

1. Ellen Sturgis Tappan (1849–1924) was born on 11 February (*Sturgis of Yarmouth*, pp. 43, 65).

2. It was published in the *Tribune* on 4 May 1848.

804.   To William Henry Channing

Rome, March 10th 1849

Father of light, conduct my feet
    Through life's dark, dangerous road;
Let each advancing step still bring
    Me nearer to my God.

These clumsy lines from some hymn, I learned in childhood are always recurring. Ah! how very sad it is, that all these precious first feelings that were meant to kindle steady fire on the altar of my life were wasted.

I am not what I should be on this earth. I could not be.

My nature has need of profound and steadfast sentiment, without this it could have no steadfast greatness, no creative power.

I have been since we parted the object of great love from the noble and the humble. I have felt it towards both; Yet a kind of chastened libertine I rove, pensively, always, in deep sadness, often O God help me; is all my cry. Yet I have very little faith in the paternal love, I need; the government of the earth does seem so ruthless or so negligent.

I am tired of seeing men err and bleed. I am tired of thinking, tired of hoping. I take an interest in some plans, *our* socialism, for instance, for it has become mine, too, but the interest is shallow as the plans. They are needed, they are even good, but man will still blunder and weep, as he has done for so many thousand years.

Coward and footsore, gladly would I creep into some green recess, apart from so much meddling and so much knowing, where I might see a few not unfriendly faces, where not more wretches would come than I could relieve.

Yes! I am weary, and faith soars and sings no more. Nothing is left good of me, except at the bottom of the heart, a melting tenderness. She loves much.

Thus I now die daily, and well understand the dejections of other troubled spirits with whom in times past I have communed.

MsCfr (MB: Ms. Am. 1450 [103]); MsCfr (MH: bMS Am 1280 [111, pp. 273–74]). Published in part in *Memoirs*, 2:302, and *JMN*, 11:503.

805. To Ellen Fuller Channing

Rome
13th March, 1849.

My dear Ellen,

It is more than a year since I heard from you, and more than a year since I sent your pin and the little cross for Greta. I rather wonder you have never written a word, to tell me whether you liked them or not. I never even knew whether they reached you. I sent your pin by Mrs. Gardiner, a mosaic for Mother by Mr. Hillard.

I never recd from you money to buy you engravings!

I am now so neglected by my old friends that it quite takes away disposition on my side to write to them. Perhaps some letters are lost but I cannot know.

When I do get a letter there is generally forgetfulness how little I am likely to know of details as to your affairs in U.S. Of you I know nothing, except, as Charles Newcomb mentioned you were not at home when he was in Concord, I suppose you were then well.

I inclose some little pictures for Greta; if I were there, I could tell her stories about them all, and teach her to pronounce the Italian names.

All these costumes I have seen often; they animate the streets and squares of Rome on festival occasions. The Eminente is the Roman Transteverini, the descendant of the old blood, many of these women are very handsome and proud. The first autumn I was here I went often to see them dancing with their tamberines, and hear them sing their frank love-songs. I am now [r]id of all these women; [th]ey are so very unintellectual; at first one likes the naiveté but people always tire, when it is impossible to draw them one single step beyond their habitual limits. I have passed in Rome a winter nearly as lonely as you can in your little brown cottage, but then how different, when I can always have the delight" of going into the galleries or among the great remains, and every day the public events bring so much excitement. Yet now I mean to seek people a little. Sometimes I go apart because in their faces there is so little comfort, in their hearts so little warmth, but after awhile I must always return for it is my nature to expe[rience] and love a great many [hum]an beings, and I feel blighted in a narrow life.

The Crawfords take you this. Mrs. C. thinks herself very poor because she has only three thousand dollars a year and cannot keep a carriage; she comes here into my garret to tell me these distresses; how they must economize severely to have a thousand dollars in pocket when they leave Rome. They are going through France and by steamer. I fear when I come, it must be by sail-ship. I dread the voyage" exceedingly so long an one would be very terrible to my poor head. However I hope 'tis far enough off. I shall not come this year unless driven, yet dont let people forget me quite, twould be sad to come home and find nobody to greet poor affectionate

MARGARET.

ALS (MH: fMS Am 1086 [9:174]).
the delight] the ⟨excitement⟩ ↑ delight ↓
the voyage] the ⟨?⟩ ↑ voyage ↓

806. To Caroline Sturgis Tappan

16th March, 1849.

My loved Caroline

Your letter received yesterday, so full of sweetness and acquainting me so well with the facts of your life brought true consolation: forgive, if in the inclosed, I utter something like a reproach, that I knew through others first this great fact in your life. I ought not to have felt so, But all the while I was hoping myself, I thought of you too, and expected this news from your next letter. When it told me nothing, I thought it was not so, then when others came and told me, I felt sad. Since I have had this troubled feeling, I will not suppress it, but send the inclosed letter, otherwise not of worth, that you may know me no better than I am.

Now then your little one is there. Will not William write me the day and hour and what kind of weather there" was when it came. I hope to hear soon.

I am very glad to hear how your life is likely to be and that you will be with your baby among mountains. Mine too saw mountains when he first looked forward into the world. Rieti, not only an old classic town of Italy, but one founded" by what are now called the aborigines, is a hive of very ancient dwellings with soft-colored" red brown roofs, a citadel and several towers. It is in a plain twelve miles in diameter one way, not much less the other," entirely encircled with mountains of the noblest form, casinos and hermitages gleam here and there on their lower slopes. This plain is almost the richest in Italy and full of vineyards. Rieti is near the foot of the hills on one side, the rapid Velino makes almost the circuit of its walls on its way to Terni. *I too had my apartment, shut out from the family on the bank of this river. I too* saw the *mountains,* as I lay on my restless couch. I had a *piazza, or as they call them here loggia which hung over the river,* where I walked most of the night, for I was not like you, I could not sleep at all those months. I do not know how I lived.

In Rieti the ancient Umbrians were married thus. In presence of friends the man and maid received together the gifts of *fire and water.* The bridegroom then conducted to his house the bride. At the door he gave her the keys and entering threw behind him nuts as a sign that he renounced all the frivolities of boyhood.

But I intend to write all that relates to the birth of Angelino in" a little book, which I shall, I hope, show you sometime. I have begun it and then stopped; it seemed to me he would die. If he lives, I shall finish it, before the details are at all faded in my mind.

Rieti is a place where I should have liked to have him born, and where I should like to have him now, but 1st" the people are so wicked, the most ferocious and mercenary population of Italy. I did not know this when I went there." I expected to be solitary and quiet among poor people. But they looked on *the marchioness* as an ignorant *Inglese,* and they fancy all *Inglesi* have wealth untold. Me they were bent on plundering in every way; they are so still. They made me suffer terribly in the first days and disturb me greatly still in visits to my darling. To add to my trouble, the legion Garribaldi is now stationed there, in which so many desperadoes are enlisted.[1] The Neapolitan troops 6 miles off are far worse, and in case of conflict I should fear for the nurse of Angelino, the loveliest young woman there. I cannot take her from her family. I cannot change him to another place without immense difficulty in every way. That I could not nurse him was owing to the wickedness of these people, who threw me into a fever the first days. I shall tell you about it sometime. There is something very singular and fateful in the way all has wrought to give me more and more sorrow and difficulty. Now I only live from day to day watching the signs of the times; when I asked you for the money I meant to use it to stay with him in Rieti, but now I do not know whether I can stay there or not. If it proves impossible, I shall at all risks, remove him. I may say every day is to me one of mental doubt and conflict; how it will end, I do not know. I try to hold myself ready every way body and mind for any necessity.

You say no secret can be kept in the civilized world and I suppose not long, but it is very important to me to keep this, for the present, if possible, and by and by to have the mode of disclosure at my option. For this, I have made the cruellest sacrifices; it will, indeed, be just like the rest, if they are made of none effect.

After I wrote to you I went to Rieti. The weather was mild when I set out, but by the fatality that has attended me throughout, in the night changed to a cold, unknown in Italy and remained so all the time I staid. There was, as is common in Italy, no fireplace except in the kitchen. I suffered much in my room with its brick floor, and windows through which came the cold wind freely. My darling did not suffer, because he was a little swaddled child like this and robed in wool beside, but I did very much. When I first took him in my arms he made no sound but leaned his head against my bosom, and staid so, he seemed to say how could you abandon me, what I felt you will know only when you have your own. A little girl who lived in the house told me all the day of my departure he could not be comforted, always refusing the breast and looking at the door; he has been a strangely precocious infant; I think it was through sympathy with me, and that in that regard it may be a happiness for him to be with these more plebian, instinctive, joyous natures. I saw he was more serene, that he was not sensitive as when with me, and slept a great deal more. You speak of my being happy; all the solid happiness I have known has been at times when he went to sleep in my arms. You say when Ellen's beautiful life had been so wasted, it hardly seemed worthwhile to begin another. I had all those feelings too. I do not look forward to his career and his manly life; it is *now* I want to be with him, before passion, care and bafflings begin. If I had a little money I should go with him into strict retirement for a year or two and live for him alone. This I cannot do; all life that has been or could be natural to me is invariably denied. God knows why, I suppose.

I receive with profound gratitude your thought of taking him, if any thing should happen to us. Should I live, I dont know whether I should wish him to be an Italian or American citizen; it depends on the course events take here politically but should we die, the person to whom he would naturally fall is a sister of his father a person of great elegance and sweetness but entirely limited in mind. I should not like that. I will think about it. Before he was born I did a great deal having the idea I might die and all my spirit remain incarnated in him, but now I think I shall live and carry him round myself as I ride on my ass into Egypt. We shant go so mildly as this yet.

You talk about your mangers, Carrie, but that was only for a little, presently came Kings with gold cups and all sorts of things. Joseph pawned them; with part of the money[n] he bought this nice donkey for the journey; and they lived on the rest till Joseph could work at his trade, we have no donkey and it costs a great deal to travel in diligences and steamers, and being a nobleman is a poor trade in a ruined despotism just turning into a Republic. I often think of Dickens's marchioness playing whist in the kitchen.[2] So I play whist every where.

Speaking of the republic, you say do[n] I not wish Italy had a great man. Mazzini is a great man; in mind a great poetic statesman, in heart a lover, in action decisive and full of resource as Cesar. Dearly I love Mazzini, who also loves me. He came in just as I had finished this first letter to you. His soft radiant look makes melancholy music in my soul; it consecrates my present life that like the Magdalen I may at the important hour shed all the consecrated ointment on his head. There is one, Mazzini, who understands thee well, who knew thee no less when an object of popular[n] fear than now of idolatry, and who, if the pen be not held too feebly, will make that posterity shall know thee, too.

Ah well! what is the use of writing, dear Caroline. A thousand volumes would not suffice for what I have to say. Pray for You? oh much I have, for my love for you is deep, I trust immortal. May you hold a dear one safe in your arms! and all go sweetly as it has[n] gone

I could not wish thy better state
Was one of my degree
But we may mourn that evil fate
Made such a churl of me.

Could I envy it would be this peace with the own one, but God grant it to Carrie, since thou wert such a niggard as to steal it from me. At least make some good use of it; don't give it to fools only.

Adieu, love, my love to William your husband with the fair noble face. You can always show him my letters if he cares to read them, then burn—and when you are once more able [   ] to

[M]ARGARET

Although I think y[r]emember that I shall be [   ] for it is, indeed, a great physical crisis.

No American" here knows that I ever was in Rieti. They suppose I passed the summer at Subiaco.

ALfrS (MH: fMS Am 1086 [9:170]); MsCfr (MH: bMS Am 1280 [111, p. 213]). Published in part in *Memoirs*, 1:226 and 2:266–67, 279–81, 300; *At Home and Abroad*, p. 436; Higginson, *MFO*, pp. 268–70; Van Doren, p. 299; Miller, pp. 282–86, 297–98; *JMN*, 11:492; and Chevigny, pp. 470–72.

weather there] weather ⟨it⟩ ↑ there ↓
one founded] one ⟨inhabited⟩ ↑ founded ↓
soft-colored] soft- ↑ colored ↓
less the other,] less ⟨than another⟩ ↑ the other ↓ ,
Angelino in] Angelino ⟨a⟩ in
now, but 1st] now, ⟨if⟩ ↑ but 1st ↓
this when I went there.] this ↑ when I went there ↓ .
part of the money] part ↑ of the money ↓
say do] say ⟨Maz⟩ do
of popular] of ↑ popular ↓
it has] it ⟨was⟩ has
No American] No ⟨one⟩ ↑ American ↓

1. Toward the end of January 1849, Garibaldi went to Rieti to reorganize and train his army of 1,500 men (*Memoirs of Garibaldi*, pp. 217–20).
2. Charles Dickens, *The Old Curiosity Shop* (London, 1841). In chap. 57 Dick Swiveller promotes his "small servant" to a "marchioness" and teaches her to play cribbage.

807.   To Richard F. Fuller

Rome
17th March, 1849.

My dear Richard,

I am very glad to get from you the letter inclosing Caroline's in time to write by Mrs. Crawford. I give her my packet of letters the

20th but am afraid you will not get them before the 1st May as she will be sometime on the road.

I take occasion to inclose this seal as a little birth-day present for I think you are 25 in May. I have used it a good deal, the design is graceful and expressive; the stone of some little value.

It is strange that I should ever have said a word that could give you pain. I think I have been very guarded. Your letters have announced great variations of feeling and plan, probably your states have changed so much between one and the other that you do not remember at all in receiving the answer" what impression you last must have made on me.[1]

You wrote of staying in Boston as if you wished my advice and said you could not without aid from Mother and Arthur!" I told you I feared it was rash. — You wrote of being in a "Stygian pool of dejection" that you were "afflicted that you must live" I answer to this and you seem ever displeased.

If you cannot allow me freedom" of reply, it would be better I should make none. Could you read over your letters to me you would see that I had been singularly guarded and tender in my replies, indeed, I have used far more care than ought to be needed in a friendly intercourse. It is impossible, corresponding at such a distance, and with imperfect knowledge of motives and circumstances, to speak always to the point; allowance must be made on both sides, or" freedom and truth of expression will cease.

I should *prefer* not to reply to what you tell me of your movements, only I hope you will not misconstrue *this* in any way, but, confiding in my intelligence and affection, will continue to speak freely of your life, as I will do, so far as I can, of mine. I think my judgment can no longer aid you, or yours me, but we do not wish to become strangers to the course of one another's lives, while hoping" that an interview may renew a better communion.

A year ago you wrote me that you did not think you ever should marry. I considered this as a transient feeling and should have been very sorry if it had not proved so. Still I did not expect so soon and so suddenly to hear that you *are* married. In no letter that I have received have you ever even named to me her who is now your wife. I am entirely unprepared and ignorant. I *could* have no feeling from your letter but of painful surprize. Still, I shall not fail, as you wish, to postpone all fixed thought or feeling, until we meet, nor can you doubt that, if this step is for your permanent happiness, it will find full sympathy with me, nor that I shall be entirely disposed to love the person who proves to you a source of joy and consolation.

Meanwhile this news makes me even more indisposed to go back than I was before. I wish to see you all, but I feel sure now that in my family I can never find a tranquil abode. They have all their destinies to work out independent of me, and I must sustain myself alone as well as I can. For you, I would rather you passed some time in this domestic life before we meet again.

I have renounced the greater part of the privileges which opened for me as they did for no other American, seeing that I could not follow them up for want of money. I live with the severest economy consistent with my health. I could not live for less any where. I have renounced much, have suffered more. I trust I shall not find it impossible to accomplish at least one of my desires.

This is to see the end of the political struggle in Italy and write its history. I think it will come to its crisis within this year. But to complete my work as I have begun I must watch it to the end.

This work, if I can accomplish it will be a worthy chapter in the history of the world, if written in the spirit which breathes through me, and with sufficient energy and calmness to execute well the details, would be what the motto on my ring indicates "*a possession forever for man.*"

It ought to be profitable to me pecuniarily, but in these respects fate runs so uniformly counter to me, that I dare not expect ever to be free from perplexities and uncongenial labor. Still they will never more be so hard to me, if I shall have done something good which may survive my troubled existence. Still it would be like the rest if by ill health, want of means or being driven prematurely from the field of observation this hope also should be blighted. I am prepared to have it so. Only my efforts tend to the accomplishment of my object and should they not be baffled, you will not see me before the summer of 1850.

Meantime, let the future be what it may I live as well as I can in the present. My social advantages are very much limited by poverty. I live in a chamber and thus cannot receive many persons whose society would be valuable to me. I cannot afford to dress or to ride, so that I can visit others very little. I cannot afford reference books, little journeys, many things that would be of great use. When I return, I shall not be able to buy engravings &c to illustrate what I have seen for classes or otherwise. Still life in Italy, above all in Rome, is under any" circumstances full of means of culture, and refining delight. As far as I can I make use of these and the days are often very precious.

I must not write any more. Only 3 days remain and I wish to write a letter to the Tribune and close up many others.[2] This done, I shall probably go out of town for a time; the hire of my chamber being up. It is cheaper out[n] of town and I need for a time exercise in freer air. The mountain air does me good; that of Rome is always heavy and I have too little appetite here; change does me good. Farewell, my dear Richard. Receive whatever I have written in the spirit you have always known in me. You know that, while I viewed you with the sympathy of a sister and acted towards you with the good-will of a parent, I always left you to yourself. Even in very young years, you often, if not generally, acted against my judgment. I always hoped you knew better than I what was best for yourself. I do so now. That you may lead a peaceful, aspiring and generous life was ever and must ever be [the p]rayer from the soul of your sister

MARGARET.

Write me your exact address. I mean the no. and street of your office.

ALS (MH: fMS Am 1086 [9:255]); MsCfr (MH: fMS Am 1086 [Works, 2:889–97]). Published in part in *At Home and Abroad*, pp. 432–33. *Addressed:* Mr. / Richard Fuller / Boston / Mass.

all in receiving the answer] all ↑ in receiving the answer ↓
advice. and said you could not without aid from Mother and Arthur!] advice. ↑ and said you could not without aid from Mother and Arthur! ↓
me freedom] me ⟨any⟩ freedom
sides, or] sides, ⟨a⟩ or
while hoping] while ⟨expecting⟩ ↑ hoping ↓
under any] under ⟨?⟩ any
cheaper out] cheaper ↑ out ↓

1. As often happened, Richard took offense at his sister's advice. In his letter of 9 February (MH), he said that he was "afflicted" by her comments on his plan to go into law practice for himself.
2. Her letter to the *Tribune* of 20–21 March was published on 16 May.

808.   To Sarah Shaw

Rome, 18th March
1849.

Dear Sarah Shaw

I take your gold pen to write never yet having had to renew its nib. You can't think what a luxury it has been to me. I had another given me last winter, but I never felt at home with it as with yours; the thoughts did not flow freely from its point. In the Spring time I gave it to the German physician who had taken all the wet dreary winter such care of me.

I hear only incidentally of you, but in a way that leads me to hope you have no longer trouble with your eyes. I thought perhaps you would use them to see Europe. Does your flock seem too large; if you came while I was this side the big water I would help you to fold it.

I should think Frank would like to live awhile in Paris to have intercourse with the French Socialists, thought seems in such vigour there, and the advance made by the cause has been so great, I consider it quite settled now that that idea will organize its forms every where for the coming age.

George Sand too you would find and I should think you would want to see her before she grows old, for even her fire must wane at last. This book of hers I have read "Il Piccinino," is very feeble, but I hope the cause may be found in the distractions, the family distresses to which she has been subject since I was in Paris and not to any declension yet. I understand she impoverished herself entirely to settle her daughter and has been requited, as is so often the case, with entire ingratitude.[1]

Ardently as I am attached to Rome, my thoughts sometimes turn towards Paris. For each place has what the other wants. Beside I do not want to get entirely enchained by the Genius Italia.

Germany I could not see, the little stream of gold needed to float the lightest bark failing. I should have liked to take even that superficial look at it that has been granted of France and England. Yet in Germany also one would need to live two or three years and see the leading men to know much that is valuable.

Of [I]taly I know a good de[al.] I have looked on the life here the old and the new with love and reverence. I have, I think, caught some of its best spirits. I shall have somewhat to tell you when we meet again. Meanwhile will you not write and tell me of yourself and Frank, of dear Sarah Russell, dear Anna and the children of all.[2] I love you all even more than when I went away and prize you more; there are few in this world so generous in aspiration and so loyal in[n] act so open to truth and yet so tolerant of mixed characters as my friends of the race of[n] Shaw. I hope you all still care for me. Should my plans not be compulsorily relinquished, more than a year will pass before we meet again, but meanwhile keep the place for your friend.

MARGARET.

ALS (MH: bMS Am 1417 [182]). *Addressed:* Mrs. Shaw / Care F. G. Shaw Esq. / Inquire at 13 West St.

Sarah Sturgis Shaw and her husband, Francis Shaw, were friends of Fuller who

lived in West Roxbury. She was a cousin of Caroline Tappan; he was a retired businessman who translated George Sand's novels and worked for Fourierite socialism.
    loyal in] loyal ⟨an⟩ in
    friends of the race] friends ⟨that bear the name⟩ ↑ of the race ↓
    1. On 19 May 1847 Solange Dudevant married Jean-Baptiste Auguste Clésinger.
Almost immediately George Sand was embroiled in financial troubles with her daughter and son-in-law. As a dowry, Sand gave Solange a town house that, although worth
200,000 francs, was not readily convertible into cash. During the next six months the
young people and Sand had repeated bitter quarrels. In October, Sand invested 50,000
francs in an annual pension for Solange and paid an 8,000-franc debt that Clésinger
had contracted during the summer. Still, by the end of 1848 the town house was sold
for failure to pay the interest on its mortgage (Curtis Cate, *George Sand* [Boston, 1975],
pp. 556–609).
    2. Sarah Shaw, Frank's sister, married George Robert Russell; Anna, another sister,
married William Batchelder Greene. The Shaws had five children; the Russells had
seven.

809.   To Anna Barker Ward

Rome, 18th March,
1849.

My dear Anna,

I thought of you in your mountain home, enjoying life peacefully
with Sam and your children when a letter comes to tell me that you
have for months been separated from them, and are under a physician's care in New York.

Thus some strange worm comes in every bud; there is nothing
quite untouched and wholesome in this world.

You will receive this about May and then I want Sam to make for
me the yearly bulletin of your affairs, and be more particular as to details than heretofore. For of you especially I should like to know exactly how you fare and what are the prospects of recovery.

Caroline writes me that she too is likely to live in Lenox, so, if you
are well enough to be there and I ever come there," I shall see several
of my friends near together. But it must not be as it was in a dream I
had here in Rome. I dreamed that I came to your house; the place
seemed quite beautiful to me and I saw the mountains from the window. While I was looking, you and Sam came in with a number of
persons I did not know. You all talked of things about which I knew
nothing and nobody spoke to me or drew me from my window. At

216

last I suggested that I had been gone a long time and you replied carelessly "O yes, I think I have not seen you since Wednesday."—You must not be so indifferent when I *do* come, for it is really a long time since we have met and your home I have never seen.

Ellen Hooper is gone to a fitter sphere. I hope, more equal companionship. Is not Sam sorry to miss her? She cared a great deal for him.

I have passed the sunny winter in Rome, beset by cares and perplexities in strange combination, yet ransoming many hours when I could forget myself and learn from every part and live in the whole. I know not how I shall find myself in America separated from objects that have been so much to me. Rome as an abode has taken the strongest hold on my affections. Could I live here very simply with one or two objects of affection and what it is always so easy to find here two or three intellectual companions, sometimes publishing a few thoughts or impressions selected from the many, I should be content. But every plan I have made to secure by my own exertions the slender means needed for such a life has failed owing to[n] the negligence of those to whom I trusted in the distance. This seems to me very sad. I am here at a most important crisis. I am fitted to observe and communicate my observations. Yet owing to the carelessness of those who had made me every vow of love and service, I have suffered cruel suspense and at last more cruel disappointment,—I cannot tell you how weary I am of striving in the world. More weary than I ought, but my strength was prematurely exhausted, and the baffling of hope all through life will sadden the most ardent nature at last so that it gives smoke easier than flame.

Adieu! these lines I send by a private hand. They will not reach you before the 1st May; then I hope you will write, you or Sam to your friend

MARGARET.

Should I be able to remain, you will not see me before the Summer of 1850. Important objects as well as my wishes urge my remaining here a year more.

ALS (MH: bMS Am 1465 [930]).
come there,] come ⟨her⟩ there,
owing to] owing ↑ to ↓

810. To Giovanni Angelo Ossoli

Rieti

27 Marzo. [1849]

Mio caro,

Trovavo nostro amore in ottima salute, e adesso si buono, va dormire tutto solo in letto, giorno o notte. Dorme adesso sugando sua piccola mano. E molto grasso, ma stranamente piccolo. Suoi capelli non crescon niente, e porta ancora quelle scuffie nere, orrende.

Al primo tutti parlavan si forte lui mi reguardava tutto sorpreso e piangeva un poco. Ma quando[n] era solo con[n] mi, sembrava riconoscermi e inchinava e grottava sua fronte come negli primi giorni.

Scrivero più un altro giorno ma adesso[n] sto si soffrente cogli denti, non posso. pensare ni scrivere. Pioveva sul viaggio, e piove ancora. Io son come in agonia col pena negli orecchi, testa denti. Spero sentire che tu non stai male dopo quella cattiva notte e son sempre la tua

M.

RIETI

27 March. [1849]

My dear,

I found our child in excellent health, and now he is so good that he sleeps in bed alone, day or night. He sleeps sucking his little hand. He is very fat, but, strange enough, small. His hair does not grow, and he always wears those horrible black caps.

At first everybody spoke very loudly and he looked at me with surprise and cried a little. But when he was alone with me, he seemed to recognize me and bent his head and frowned as he did in the first days.

I will write more another day, because now I am suffering very much with my teeth, and I am not able to think nor to write. It rained during the trip, and it is still raining. I feel like I am in agony, as my ears, head and teeth hurt me. I hope to hear that you are not bad after that terrible night. And I am always your

M.

ALS (MH: fMS Am 1086 [9:194]); MsC in English (MH: fMS Am 1086 [Works, 2:205–7]). English copy published in part in Higginson, *MFO*, p. 262. *Addressed:* Sigr Mse / Gio. Angelo Ossoli / Roma. *Postmark:* Rieti.

Ma quando] M⟨?⟩a quando
solo con] solo ⟨?⟩ con
ma adesso] ma ⟨?⟩ adesso

811. To Giovanni Angelo Ossoli

Rieti
30 Marzo, 1849.

Mio caro,

Ricevo questa mattina i fogli e tua lettrina dal Castello. Mi rincresce trovarti si presto rinviato in servizio duro, e dopo quello cattiva notte con mi anche. Scrivi in dettaglio come stai.

Io commincio stare meglio cogli denti, e bisogna stare[n] grata, peraltro non sarei capace di niente.

Ieri la famiglia stava giù al pranzo, e nostro caro dormendo sopra in letto, io sedeva al suo lato pensando come era caro, perche lo aveva bagnato e vestito bene, e sembrava un altro bambino. Subito sentivo tavole e sedie cascando[n] giù e le donne strillando terribile "*aiiuto*". Io volavo giù e la stavan Niccola e Pietro cercando ammazzare un a l'altro. Io parlava a Niccola, lui non rispond[e]va ma mi riguardava come una bestia selvatica; le donne tenevan suo braccio che non poteva tirare suo coltello lui prendeva loro capelli. Pietro chi non aveva coltello buttava legna; un grande pezzo mancava poco mia testa. Subito correvan tutti i vicini; il padrone di Niccola levava suo coltello, ma si nostro bambino e stato giù, probabile sarebbe morto.

Io son convinta che Niccola e un ubbriacone.

Non posso scrivendo[n] dirti gli dettagli, ma voglio vederti. Pensi si[n] tu puoi venire *Martedi* prendere con mi consiglio. Tu allora potevi ritornare Sabato, e avere Sabato pel zio. Si non, che puoi fare per venire?—

Cerca di Antonia lunedi che lettere, fogli, o libri lei a per mi, e si non puoi venire Martedi inviagli[n] perla diligenza.

Non senti pel momento ansietà per nostro caro io non lo lascio più. E io credo quando tu lo vedi tu pen[s]erai come io penso, che [   ] vale tutto che bisogna per nio soffrire per lui.

Chiara e buona come sempre, a fatto suo possibile per lui Dio l'ha conservato e sta in ottima salute. Io sento calma, spero che possiamo trovare qualche buon consiglio. Si bisogna per lui noi direm nostro segreto, chi sa si non sara meglio infine? Ma bisogna pensare di tutto, perche tutto l'avvenire di nostre vite dipende sopra la discrezione di questo momento.

Addio caro, fido sentire da ti Domenica e son sempre tua

M.

Si vieni, potevi andare in albergo, o provare l'appartamento di Petruccio

Non voglio questo *Speranza* comprai[n] *Pallade* per inviarmi[n]

Rieti
30 March, 1849.

My dear,

This morning I receive the papers and your letters from the Castle. It makes me unhappy to find you returned to hard service so quickly and after that bad night with me. Write how you are in detail.

My teeth are starting to feel better, and I must be grateful, because otherwise I could do nothing.

Yesterday the family was downstairs for dinner, and our child was sleeping upstairs in bed, I sat at his side thinking how dear he was, because I had bathed and dressed him well, and he seemed another child. Soon I heard tables and chairs falling down and the women screaming terribly "*aiiuto.*" I rushed down and there were Niccola and Pietro trying to kill each other. I spoke to Niccola, he did not answer me but looked at me like a wild beast; the women held his arm so that he could not throw his knife[;] he grabbed them by their hair. Pietro[,] who did not have a knife[,] threw wood; a big piece just missed my head. Immediately all the neighbors arrived; Niccola's master took away his knife but if our child had been down there he probably would have been killed.

I am convinced that Niccola is a drunkard.

I am not able to tell you in writing all the details, but I want to see you. Do you think you can come *Tuesday* to take counsel with me? You can then return Saturday and have Saturday for your uncle. If not, what can you do about coming?

Monday ask Antonia what letters, papers or books she has for me, and if you cannot come Tuesday send them by coach.

Do not feel anxious about our child for a moment, I no longer leave him. And I believe that when you see him you will think as I think that [   ] he is worth all that we must suffer for him.

Chiara is good as always, she did everything possible for him[;] God has protected him[,] and he is in excellent health. I feel calm, I hope that we can find some good advice. If it is necessary for him, we will tell our secret, who knows if it will not be the best thing in the end? But it is necessary to think of everything, because our whole future lives depend upon the discretion of this moment.

Goodbye my dear, I hope to hear from you on Sunday and I am always your

M.

If you come you could go to the hotel, or try Petruccio's apartment. I do not want this *Speranza*[;] buy *Pallade* to send me

ALS (MH: fMS Am 1086 [9:194]); MsC in English (MH: fMS Am 1086 [Works, 2:207–11]). English copy published in part in Higginson, *MFO*, p. 263. *Addressed:* Sigr Mse / Gio. Angiolo Ossoli / Roma. *Postmark:* Rieti.
bisogna stare] bisogna st(?)are
sedie cascando] sedie ⟨versate⟩ ↑cascando↓
posso scrivendo] posso ⟨sulla carta⟩ ↑scrivendo↓
Pensi si] Pensi ⟨che⟩ ↑si↓
Martedi inviagli] Martedi ⟨?⟩ inviagli
Speranza comprai] *Speranza* ⟨?⟩ comprai
per inviarmi] per ⟨?⟩ inviarmi

812. To Giovanni Angelo Ossoli

domenica delle palme.
[1 avrile 1849]

Mio Caro

Scrivo senza avendo inviato alla posta avere tue notizie, perche tutte stan si confus[e] qui. Niccola e gravemente malato dopo sua furia. Si tu" non vieni Martedi io scrivero di tutto Mercoledi Adesso io sto bene cogli denti e tutto nostro caro benissimo e si caro voglio molto per ti vederlo Sempre tua

M.

Palm Sunday
[1 April 1849]

My Dear

I am writing without having sent to the post office to have your news because everything here is so confused. Niccola is seriously ill after his rage. If you do not come on Tuesday I will write on Wednesday about everything. Now my teeth are well and our dear one is splendid, and so dear that I want very much you to see him Always your

M.

ALS (MH: fMS Am 1086 [9:213]); MsC in English (MH; fMS Am 1086 [Works, 2:215–17]). *Addressed:* Sigr Mse Gio. Angiolo Ossoli / Roma.
Si tu] Si ↑tu↓

813. To Giovanni Angelo Ossoli

Rieti,
4th Avrile 49.

Mio caro,

Quanto e strana che noi non possiamo passare questo giorno insieme.[1] Bisogna pregare essere piu felici un altro anno. Ieri[n] avevo comprato uccelletti per nostra cena e speravo molto vederti come non sei venuto non mangiavo io.[n] Ma oggi non mi dispiace che non sei venuto perche ancora piove forte, e Angelino, che e stato avanti[n] si felice, si grazioso che volevo tutti i momenti per ti vederlo[n] oggi sta male. Ha sofferto tutta la notte cogli denti, e oggi, poverino, non puo trovare pace. Speriamo che stara bene quando hai[n] potete venire.

Mi pare che ero[n] inviato per Dio[n] proteggerlo in questi giorni terribili. Niccola stavo pazzo più che quaranta ore, Chiara sempre piangendo disperata. Ieri notte Niccola[n] ha dormito e oggi sta in suoi sensi.

Garribaldi non ha passato la frontiere, altro son venuti più truppe Napolitane in Aquila e qui vengon adesso piu truppe Romane da Terni rinforzare Garribaldi.[2] Ma non si crede qui che Napolitani pensan entrare, ma che fan questi dimostrazioni per levare una parte delle forze Romane da Terracina, che probabile van entrare per Terracina

Garribaldi non ha nul comando sopra questi desperati di sua banda, la Domenica amazzavan un frate, due cittadini e fra[n] se nove, si dice. Due corpi eran trovati nel fiume. La presenza della truppa regolare puo prevenire questi eccessi. Ma io adesso non ho, sicuro, coraggio sortire sola. Sta vicino da qui un piccolo giardino dove vado con Angelino negli begli giorni, in strada non sorto mai.

Domandi di Antonia si qualche persona mi ha cercato e fa mi piacere mettere questa lettrina subito a la posta per Firenze. Quanto mi dispiace che tu hai questo servizio terribile per la notte. Sara una rovina per tua salute e quanto e fatta scioccamente e senza calcolo come tutte le cose di Roma come si cercavan disgustare. Prendi per mi subito il foglio di Mazzini, si tu hai denaro per un mese si non pel sei mese. Son perfettamente disgusta con questa Epoca è divenuto[n] foglio reazionario. Addio, mio bene, Dio ti benedica e ti conserva prego questo 4 Avrile la tua

M.

Aspetto tue nuove Venerdi.

Non vieni qui la notte, vieni per la diligenza e prendi posta in cabriolet, di bon ora.

Rieti

4th April 49.

My dear,

How very strange it is that we cannot spend this day together.[1] We must pray to be happier another year. Yesterday I had bought little birds for our dinner and I hoped very much to see you[;] since you did not come, I did not eat. But today I am not sorry that you did not come because it is still raining hard, and Angelino, who was before so happy, so nice that I wanted you to see him every moment is not well today. He suffered all night because of his teeth and today, poor baby, he cannot find any peace. I hope he will be well when you are able to come.

I think I was sent by God to protect him in these terrible days. Niccola was crazy for more than 40 hours, Chiara always crying with desperation. Last night Niccola slept and today he is no longer delirious.

Garribaldi has not crossed the frontier, but more Neapolitan troops went to Aquila and more Roman troops are coming here from Terni to reinforce Garribaldi.[2] Nobody here believes that the Neapolitans think to enter, but they are making these maneuvers in order to move a part of the Roman forces from Terracina, and probably they are going to enter through Terracina.

Garribaldi has no control over these desperados of his band, it is said that on Sunday a friar, two citizens and 9 of their own were killed. Two bodies were found in the river. The presence of the regular troop can prevent these excesses. But now I surely do not have courage to go out alone. Near here there is a small garden where I go with Angelino on nice days, I never go out into the street.

Ask Antonia if someone has looked for me and please do me the favor to put this letter quickly into the mail for Florence. I am so sorry that you have that terrible night duty. It will ruin your health and it is done as foolishly and senselessly as everything else in Rome[,] as if for the purpose to try to disgust. Get Mazzini's paper for me at once, if you have money for one month if not for six months. I am really disgusted with this Epoca[;] it has become a reactionary's paper. Goodbye my dear, on this 4 April God bless and protect you prays your

M.

I forward your news on Friday.

Do not come here in the night, come by stagecoach and take a seat in the carriage early.

223

ALS (MH: fMS Am 1086 [9:196]); MsC in English (MH: fMS Am 1086 [Works, 2:211–15]). English copy published entire in Chevigny, pp. 472–73. *Addressed:* Sigr Mse / Gio. Angiolo Ossoli / Roma. *Postmark:* Rieti.

Ieri] ⟨?⟩ Ieri
vederti come non sei venuto non mangiavo io.] vederti. ↑ come non sei venuto non mangiavo io ↓
stato avanti] stato ↑ avanti ↓
ti vederlo] ti ve⟨?⟩derlo
quando hai] quando ⟨noi possiamo⟩ hai
che ero] che ⟨son⟩ ero
per Dio] per ⟨d⟩ Dio
notte Niccola] notte ↑ Niccola ↓
e fra] e f⟨?⟩ra
è divenuto] è diven⟨?⟩uto

    1. On 3 April Ossoli wrote: "Dear, how much I wish to spend tomorrow with you, since I well believe you will remember that it is the 4th April" (MH). Their commemoration of the date strongly suggests that it was their wedding anniversary.

    2. On 12 March Charles Albert renounced the Salasco truce and once again attacked the Austrians. On 23 March the two armies met at Novara, where the Piedmontese were again defeated. Charles Albert immediately abdicated and went into exile. Meanwhile, the Romans, not believing the war to be over, voted on 29 March to send troops to aid Piedmont. Garibaldi's army remained near Rieti until 26 April, when the army arrived in Rome to prepare to meet the French (King, *Italian Unity*, 1:304–6; Farini, 347–49; *Memoirs of Garibaldi*, p. 216).

814.   To Giovanni Angelo Ossoli

Rieti
venerdi
6th [avrile 1849]

mio caro,

    non volevo per ti venire la notte, perche pensavo che era cattivo per tua salute, ma, si bisogna ritornare mercoledi, va meglio cosi, ti aspetto domenica la mattina.

    Spero che allora Angelino stare bene; ha sofferto molto; la notte ho passato guarir tutto a piedi con lui; ma oggi ricomminciaⁿ ridere e giuocare. Son forzataⁿ scrivere sopra questa carta, ho versata la lampa sopro tutta mia carta. Volendo tanto vederti sempre law tua

M.

Rieti
Friday
6th [April 1849]

my dear,

    I did not want you to come in the night, because I thought it was bad for your health, but, if you must go back on Wednesday, it is better this way I will wait for you Sunday morning.

I hope that Angelino will be well at that time; he has suffered much; I have been up all night taking care of him; but today he starts again to laugh and play. I am forced to write on this paper, I spilled the lamp on all of my paper. Wanting so much to see you always your

M.

ALS (MH: fMS Am 1086 [9:197]); MsC in English (MH: fMS Am 1086 [Works, 2:217]). *Addressed:* Sigr Mse / Gio Angiolo Ossoli / Roma. *Postmark:* Rieti.
    oggi ricommincia] oggi ↑ ricommincia ↓
    Son forzata] Son forza⟨z⟩ta

815. To Giovanni Angelo Ossoli

[R]ieti
13 Avrile [1849]

Mio caro, Mi piace sentire che sei arrivato bene in Roma. Qui sta sempre pessimo tempo molto piove e una aria rigida chi mi da soffrire molto.

Nino e ancora rinfreddato ha tosse la notte, ma il giorno e molto e caro ridendo sempre, ha voluto vostra lettrina ma era per metterla in bocca. Si possibile vengo lunedi; soffro troppo qui, ma spero sentire da ti la Domenica e scrivero anch'io un altra volta sempre la tua

M.

Rieti
13 April [1849]

My dear, I am happy to hear that you arrived safely in Rome. Here the weather is still very bad; it rains very much and the chilly air makes me suffer very much.

Nino still has a cold; he coughs at night, but in the day he is very dear always laughing, he wanted your letter, but it was to put it into his mouth. If it is possible I will come on Monday; I am suffering too much here, but I hope to hear from you on Sunday and I will also write to you another time always your

M.

ALS (MH: fMS Am 1086 [9:197]); MsC in English (MH: fMS Am 1086 [Works, 2:217–19]). *Addressed:* Sigr Mse / Gio Angiolo Ossoli / Roma. *Postmark:* Rieti.

816. To Giovanni Angelo Ossoli

Domenica 15 avrile [1849]

Caro mio,

ho ricevuta scudi 3, per Petrucchio.

Penso venire domani Nino non sta male, avvertiti Antonia chi può avere letto e una minestra preparati per mi.

La resta quando vengo.

Sempre la vostra

M.

Sunday 15 April [1849]

My dear,

I received 3 scudi through Petrucchio.

I think to come tomorrow Nino is not bad, tell Antonia to have a bed and soup prepared for me.

The rest when I come.

Always your

M.

ALS (MH:fMS Am 1086 [9:209]); MsC in English (MH: fMS Am 1086 [Works, 2: 219]). *Addressed:* Sigr Mse Gio. Angiolo [   ]oli / Roma. *Postmark:* Rieti.

817. To Giovanni Angelo Ossoli

Casa Diez
venerdi 4 Maggio [1849]
2 p.m.

Mio caro,

Sorto alle 4, e rientro alle 6, e sto qui un ora. Alle 7 1/2 vado al spedale e spero ritornare alle 9. Si tu vieni quando son sortita mi aspetta si è possibile, si non, venite su e lascia una parola dire quando puoi venire domani mattina. Non manchi vedermi, prego, e terribile passare tante ore incerte senza rincontrare. Si dice che i Napoletani non avanzan, ma tutto pare si incerta.[1] Sempre, sempre la tua

M.

Si mai tu hai bisogno invia qualche duno subito mio amore, noi possiamo pagare per questo.

Casa Diez
Friday 4 May [1849]
2 p.m.

My dear,

I go out at *4* o'clock; return at *6*, and will say here for an hour. At 7 1/2 I will go to the hospital and I hope to come back at *9*. If you come when I am out, wait for me if it is possible, if not, come upstairs and leave a message saying when you will come tomorrow morning. Please, do not fail to see me, it is terrible to spend so many anxious hours without seeing you again. They say that the Neapolitans are not advancing, but all seems so uncertain.[1] Always, always your

M.

If you ever have need[,] send someone at once my love, we can pay for this.

ALS (MH: fMS Am 1086 [9:214]); MsC in English (MH: fMS Am 1086 [Works, 2:219–21]). English copy published entire in Higginson, *MFO*, p. 263. *Addressed:* Sigre Marchese / Gio Angiolo Ossoli.

1. On 31 March the French Chamber of Deputies authorized the government to invade Italy as a move against Austria. The expedition, under the command of General Nicolas Charles Victor Oudinot (1791–1863), duc de Reggio, arrived at Civita Vecchia on 24 April, deceitfully professing to be on a mission to save the Roman people. On 30 April the French attacked the Roman defenses outside the city, only to be routed by Garibaldi, The unexpectedly determined Roman resistance stalled the French. Two days before the French attack, Ferdinand II of Naples crossed the border with 9,000 men and established a headquarters at Albano on 4 May, the day Fuller wrote this letter. That same evening, taking advantage of a truce with the French, Garibaldi left Rome to attack the Neapolitans (King, *Italian Unity*, 1:333–34; Farini, 4:19–21; *Memoirs of Garibaldi*, p. 230; Acton, *Last Bourbons*, p. 285).

818. To Giovanni Angelo Ossoli

[ca. 6 maggio 1849]

Mio Caro,

Io sorto alla Posta e al Spedale. Non posso stare cosi in casa tutto il giorno, sento troppo ansieta. Si per disgrazia tu vieni quando non sto qui, prego cerci venire un momento la sera e lascia col portiere si tu puoi.

M.

[ca. 6 May 1849]

My Dear,

I am going to the post office and to the hospital. I cannot stay at home all day because I am too anxious. If by accident you come here while I am out please try to come back for a while this evening and leave word if you can.

M.

ALS (MH: fMS Am 1086 [9:213]); MsC in English (MH: fMS Am 1086 [Works, 2:223]). English copy published in part in Higginson, *MFO*, pp. 264–66; English copy published entire in Wade, p. 583. *Addressed:* Marchese Ossoli.

819. To Lewis Cass, Jr.

Casa Diez, May 20, 1849.

Dear Sir,

The news contained in your letter disappoints, but does not surprise me. I feared a conciliation was impossible. Should you hear anything farther, perhaps you will find time to call and see us. I am perplexed with many doubts, especially as to remaining in Rome. If likely to be shut up long here, I might resolve to go now, as the heat would be too much for my health a little later.

With thanks and best respects, yours,

S. M. Fuller.

MsC (MH: fMS Am 1086 [Works, 1:341]).

Lewis Cass, Jr. (1813?–78), son of Lewis Cass, the Democratic politician, was appointed the American chargé d'affaires to the Papal States after the death of Jacob Martin (*Detroit Society for Genealogical Research* 15 [December 1954]: 52). On 31 May 1854 he married Mary Ludlum of New York, who died the following March, age 20 ("Marriages and Deaths in the New York Evening Post," NEHGS, vols. 14 and 31).

820. To Lewis Cass, Jr.

Casa Diez
Tuesday.
[22? May? 1849]

Dear Sir,

In the *Democratic* you will find a letter of Madame Belgioioso, which

seems to answer very well to the idea you have of her. Me it has somewhat surprized. Salut et fraternité!!

MARGARET FULLER

ALS (MH: fMS Am 1086 [9:193]); MsC (MH: fMS Am 1086 [Works, 1:339]).

821. To Richard F. Fuller

Rome, May 22, 1849.

My dear Richard,

I received safely both your letter, and dear Eugene's, containing
the note of exchange on the Genoa house.[1] Will you write to Eugene
that I have done so? but that in the present distracted state of things I
have not been able to ascertain if I can get the money. I suppose yes,
but should any difficulty intervene, I am in no immediate want; I
have still some money; and a friend here, an excellent man, who takes
an interest in my welfare and regrets that he must go to leave me, has
given me a note by which I can have money at once.

I can draw on the other money I have in the bank but it is at such a
discount, I cannot afford it. I hope when the fate of Rome is decided,
one way or another, these difficulties will at least diminish.

I do not write to Eugene yet, because around me is such excitement
I cannot settle my mind enough to write a letter good for anything.
The Neapolitans have been driven back, but the French seem to be
amusing us with a pretence of treaties, while waiting for the Austrians
to come up.[2] The Austrians cannot, I suppose, be more than three
days' march from us. I feel but little about myself. Such thoughts are
merged in indignation, and the fears I have that Rome may be bom-
barded. It seems incredible that any nation should be willing to incur
the infamy of such an act,— an act that may rob posterity of the most
precious part of its inheritance,—only so many incredible things have
happened of late. I am with William Story, his wife and uncle, very
kind friends they have been in this strait. They are going away, so
soon as they can find horses,—going into Germany. I remain alone in
the house, under our flag, almost the only American, except the Consul and Ambassador.[3] But Mr Cass, the envoy, has offered to do any
thing for me; and I feel at liberty to call on him as I please.

But enough of this, dear Richard; you say truly, we lose the clues to each other's minds; but I hope we shall find them again on meeting. Do not feel coldly if I do not say much about your affairs. I feel at this distance that I cannot speak to the point, but all hints from you are most welcome, and when we meet, I do not believe you will find me unintelligent. You know well how I prize and need your affection. I think you feel the same towards me; let us implore of Fate another good meeting, full and free, whether long or short. Love to dearest Mother, Arthur, Ellen, Lloyd. Say to all that should any accident, possible to these troubled times, transfer me to another scene of existence, they need not regret it. There must be better worlds than this,—where innocent blood is not ruthlessly shed, where treason does not so easily triumph, where the greatest and best are not crucified. I do not say this in apprehension, but in cast of accident, you might be glad to keep this last word from your sister

MARGARET.

MsC (MH: fMS Am 1086 [*Works*, 1:243–47]). Published in part in *At Home and Abroad*, pp. 433–34, and Phillips, *Reminiscences*, p. 95.

1. In his letter of 5 April (MH), Richard sent 1,041 francs from Eugene.

2. On 9 May Garibaldi met and defeated a Neapolitan force near Palestrina, then returned to Rome on the 12th. On 16 May the entire Roman army, freed by a truce with the French, left Rome to fight Ferdinand, who began to withdraw from the Roman states the following day. On 19 May the Romans marched on Velletri and defeated the Neapolitans. Having dispatched Ferdinand and his troops, the Romans returned home on 24 May to await the French moves (*Memoirs of Garibaldi*, pp. 234–37, 239–41; Acton, *Last Bourbons*, p. 286). Ferdinand Marie de Lesseps (1805–94), later famous as the builder of the Suez Canal, arrived in Rome on 15 May as a minister extraordinary from the French to the Romans. Lesseps apparently acted in good faith in his attempts to negotiate a mutually acceptable compromise, but Oudinot and Louis Napoleon had no intention of allowing the republic to survive. Despite Lesseps' attempts to educate his superiors about the legitimacy of the republic, Oudinot was eager to move, in part because the malaria season was upon him. Rome was threatened on its flanks by 5,000 troops that Spain landed at Fiumicino and by Austria, which had invaded the Papal States early in May and forced Bologna into submission on the 16th (King, *Italian Unity*, 1:336; Farini, 4:87, 104).

3. Cass was the ambassador; Nicholas Brown 3d (1792–1859) was the United States consul at Rome. A graduate of Brown in 1811, he succeeded George Washington Greene in 1845. Brown, who had wanted the ambassadorship that went to Jacob Martin, discharged the duties between Martin's death and Cass's arrival. A supporter of the Italian Republicans, Brown resigned in June. On 29 May, however, he had officially been replaced by William Carroll Saunders (*The Biographical Cyclopedia of Representative Men of Rhode Island* [Providence, 1881], 1:227; Stock, *Consular Relations*, p. xxvii).

822.   To Lewis Cass, Jr.

Casa Diez, Thursday.
[24? May? 1849]

Dear Sir,

I was sorry to miss your visit; can you not take the trouble to come again this evening?

MARGARET FULLER.

MsC (MH: fMS Am 1086 [Works, 1:341]).

823.   To Richard F. Fuller

Rome
28th May, 1849.

My dear Richard,

I wrote you a day or two since a letter and including one for Mrs. Farrar, now, at the moment of closing for the mail, it cannot be found. Possibly it has by some mistake gone to the post and you will receive it, if not, we will consider it a destiny and not repent its contents. I believe they were very affectionate and altogether too dolorous, for amid the apparatus of war and fresh from the sight of blood, it seemed as if some accident might [p]revent my ever again seeing my kindred. Enough! leave them unsaid. If you love me, and are faithful, (how strangely rare that faithfulness on earth:) we shall meet again in some sphere or other.

I have recd your letter containing the bills of exchange, also one from dear Eugene with same. I hope to write to him by next mail, but, in case any thing should prevent me, want you to warn him it is recd. I have not yet been able to ascertain if there is any thing in the recent disasters of Genoa that might affect it, my banker being absent, but suppose not.[1]

I shall as soon, as I can, answer the questions of Mr E. Clarke[n] (of N. E. Bank)[2] He has every claim on me that many little kind acts can give, and if he had none, of course I should like to aid him or any one that I could, "Mankind is one" We need not calculate, but just do what we can for others.

231

God bless you, my dear Richard, in your heart and works. My sisterly remembrance to your wife. I hope we may meet in peace some day "here or elsewhere" ever yours

M.

Please take care that t[he] enclosed little notes arrive safe. They are of importance. Love to Arthur and dearest Mother, beg the latter to write again. I am anxious to hear how Arthur is this summer and if Ellen is safely delivered of her babe.

ALS (MH: fMS Am 1086 [9:160]); MsC (MH: fMS Am 1086 [Works, 2:601–5]). *Addressed:* Mr / R. F. Fuller / Boston / Mass. *Postmark:* New York 22 Jun.

E. Clarke] E. ⟨B⟩ Clarke

1. After the battle of Novara on 23 March, the Genoese revolted against Victor Emmanuel, the new king of Piedmont, who sent General Alfonso La Marmora to restore order. After a brutal bombardment, La Marmora allowed his troops to loot the city (King, *Italian Unity*, 1:354).

2. Elijah Pope Clark (1791–1859) was the cashier of the New England Bank in Boston (MVR 139:44). An enthusiastic reader of Carlyle, Clark served as his American agent after 1847. He compiled an album of several volumes of material relating to Carlyle (*The Correspondence of Emerson and Carlyle*, ed. Joseph Slater [New York, 1964], pp. 27, 347). In 1835 he married Sarah Ann Wilby (1807–89) (Boston City Records: Index to Marriages; Cambridge VR; MVR 402:140).

824. To Emelyn Story

Rome, May 29th, 1849.

I flatter myself, dear Emelyn, you will not be sorry to find a letter from me awaiting you at Florence, and I on my side, wish to write, because I miss you so much. Familiar as I am with the sorrows as well as the joys of solitude, I think I never felt it so intense as in this house now. At evening the house seems perfectly ghostly. When you all were here, although my thoughts were often painfully distracted and always I felt as if I did not belong to the party, yet the sight of your hopeful interest in Life and mutual enjoyment of one another's society was cordial, while the generous and delicate affection shown to me was consoling to my tired and perplexed spirit. Now at evening all seems so blank; the little moon looks in with an air of pensive amore, strange noises haunt the rooms, I start from my book and my sleep, seeming to hear the rustling of garments and the opening of doors, then all is silent, but black shadows here and there seem about to take form and advance upon me.

I think you will be in Florence on Thursday. I hope W has made two or three good sketches by the way. Am sorry I cannot hear his impressions of this journey, by me remembered with unmingled delight. I fear you have enjoyed yourself very little. Most vetturas roll up at the sides, allowing free passage to the air, and free look out; when I saw you had only the window I felt quite disturbed. Have you heard from the Mrs H. Frank offered to write to me from Civita Vecchia but naturally that vow dispersed in empty air. He was exceedingly surprized to find what a great trouble it is to part, said he could not have realised it before. They had still great difficulty in getting off, the veturino, it seems had a plan for getting away their passports for the use of other persons leaving them in the lurch. They had to go to the Police as late as 3 o'clock, and did not get off earlier than 5. I did not see them go, as I went out to drive with Mrs. Black. It was an ugly day, chilly and great gusts of wind carrying clouds of dust, but I climbed by a stair to the tops of the gate Santa Maria Maggore. Coming back we saw a crowd in Piazza Colonna, I went there, thinking there was some great news, but it was a pompeire getting down from the Column with the aid of his ladders, a poor dog, who had gone up within and was crying piteously not understanding the way back. He was dexterously persuaded and bravely carried down by the pompeire. The risk was great, as the dog was very large and often struggled not understanding about the ladder and the crowd. The people showed all the sympathy of young children.

Who should indulge me with a visit the next day at breakfast hour but Mr. Consul Brown? He said he came *first* to ask if he or Mrs. B. could be of use to me.[1] Mr. Brown said several good things about affairs here; indeed I think there is a spark of goodness even of generosity amid all his rubbish. The princess has the fever, but she keeps up, sticking to her purpose.

The handsom Garribaldi man has not your flowers yet. I have not been able to get fresh ones on my way to the hospital, but it shall be done. At the Valle, I have seen the "Tartuffe" of Moliere extremely well performed and greatly applauded. Read the letter of the triumvirate to Lesseps, dated *May 25th.*[2]

Who can resist the obvious sincerity, the mild and elevated tone of that can resist all. I hope you will not fail to write me a little letter and give your address for the future. Mention if Cranchs are gone and Moziers returned. You find the Austrians in Florence, tell me how it seems.[3] Love to William (I am very glad we know one another at last,) Mr. Wetmore and the dear children. I kiss the paper for Edie and you too, dear Emelyn,

MARGARET.

Last moment I saw Frank, he looked very beautiful, younger than ever, from the soft light of feeling that had been roused parting from his friends. He had in his cheeks that are so thin now a really rose flush.

MsC (MH: fMS Am 1086 [9:225]); MsC (MH: fMS Am 1086 [Works, 1:247–53]).

1. Caroline Matilda Clements (d. 1879), who married Brown on 22 November 1831, was the daughter of Pierce and Louisa Mendum Clements of Portsmouth, New Hampshire (Abby Isabel Bulkley, *The Chad Browne Memorial* [Brooklyn, 1888], p. 73; Percival Wood Clement, *Ancestors and Descendants of Robert Clements* [Philadelphia, 1927], p. 253).

2. Lesseps' mission was at a critical stage. On 25 May the triumvirs addressed a letter to him in which they reviewed the decisions by the great powers to restore the pope's temporal authority. They argued that the French had been misled by false reports of anarchy in Rome and claimed their right and duty to preserve their liberty. They pledged complete resistance to the French, saying that the citizens would "be massacred from barricade to barricade before [they would] submit." Finally, they offered to allow the French to remain at Civita Vecchia as a neutral presence, but they firmly refused to allow them to enter the city. Lesseps replied: "Friendship and Violence are incompatible. Thus it would be inconsequent on our part to begin by firing our cannon upon you to make you natural protectors" (Farini, 4:135–40; *New-York Daily Tribune*, 24 July 1849). On 29 May he offered the Romans a four-part compromise that called for the peaceful entry of the French army as a defense against the other invading armies. In return, Lesseps promised not to contest the right of the Romans to form a government of their choosing. However, that same night Oudinot, who disdained Lesseps and his mission, moved troops across the Tiber. Finally, on 31 May Lesseps made yet another offer; the Romans accepted it, but Oudinot furiously denounced Lesseps' pledges. That same day Lesseps received his recall from Paris. He set out for home on 1 June and Oudinot declared war on Rome (Farini, 4:167–74).

3. On 5 April the Austrian field marshal Konstantin d'Aspre crossed the Tuscan border under an agreement with the grand duke, who was too craven to acknowledge the fact. Although Leopold tried to keep the Austrians out of Florence, they occupied the city on 25 May (King, *Italian Unity*, 1:371–72).

825. To Emelyn Story

[ca. June 1849]

I want William to go to Fenzi and Hall and see if he can find the present address of Marchesa Arconati and if he can, for you to enclose it to me.[1] They used to be her bankers, and may, probably, know where she is now.

Write often, if you can, dear E. but don't write under envelope; it makes the letter cost double, and I have to *screw* in these for me very hard days.

Ossoli salutes you; hopes to see you in Rome again. I am glad William has got Mr. Mozier's good studio. I wish he would write what he thinks of the Lorenzo de Medichi I entirely agree with him about the

I was on Pincian yesterday evening, it was perfectly full of the Roman society, a real flower garden. Nobody could have dreamed there was any difficulty in Rome. I wished much you were with me and Edith and Joe. With kisses to them and much affection for you,

MARGARET

My best regards to Katy.

MsCfr (MH: fMS Am 1086 [9:234]).

1. Emanuele Fenzi was a Florentine banker (Greenough, *Letters*, p. 183).

826. To Giovanni Angelo Ossoli

[guigno 1849]

Quanto m'incresce, amore, mancar ti ieri e possibile anch, oggi, si tu puoi" venire. Vado a Casa Diez, si possibile cerchi la, ultimo piano, si sto la ancora o son andato al spedale. Dio ti conserva Quanto ho sofferta a vedere i feriti, e non posso conoscere si qualche" cosa ti accade, ma bisogna sperare. Ho ricevuta la lettera di Rieti, nostro Nino sta perfettamente bene," grazia per questo."

[M]i fa di bene che almeno i Romani han fatto qualche cosa, si solamente tu puoi stare. In evento del morte di tutti dui ho lasciata una carta col certificato" di Angelino e alcune righe pregando i Sto curare per lui. Si per qualche accidente io moriro tu puoi riprendere questa carta si vuoi da me, come da tua moglie. Ho voluta per Nino andare in America, ma tu farari come ti pare. Era nostro dovere combinare questo meglio. Ma speriamo che non sara bisogno. Sempre benedicendo la tua

MARGHERITA

Si tu vivi e io moro, stai sempre devotissimo per Nino. Si tu ami mai un altra, ancora pensi primo per lui, io prego, prego, amore.

[June 1849]

How sorry I am, love, to miss you yesterday and possibly also today, if you can come, I [will] go to Casa Diez, if possible inquire for me there, on the last floor, if I am still there or if I went to the hospital. God keep you How much I suffered at the sight of those wounded

235

people, and I have no way of knowing whether something happens to you, but one must hope. I received the letter from Rieti, our Nino is perfectly well, thanks for this.

It does me good that at least the Romans have done something, if only you can survive. In the event of the death of both of us I have left a paper with Angelino's birth certificate and a few words praying the Sto[rys] to take care of him. Should I by any chance die you can take back this paper from me, if you want, as from your wife. I wanted Nino to go to America, but you will do as you wish. It was our duty to arrange this better, but let's hope that there will not be need for it. Always blessing you your

MARGARET

If you live and I die, be always very devoted to Nino. If you ever love another woman, always think first of him, I beg you, beg you, love.

ALS (MH: fMS Am 1086 [9:215 1/2]); MsC in English (MH: fMS Am 1086 [Works, 2:223–25]). English copy published entire in Higginson, *MFO*, pp. 264–65, and Wade, p. 583. *Addressed:* Sigr Mse / Gio Angiolo Ossoli / Roma.

tu puoi] tu p⟨?⟩uoi
si qualche] si qua⟨c⟩lche
perfettamente bene,] perfettamente be⟨?⟩ne,
per questo.] per qu⟨s⟩esto.
col certificato] col ⟨s⟩ certif⟨a⟩icato

827. To Arthur Hugh Clough

Casa Diez
Thursday [June? 1849]

Dear Mr Clough,

It was very kind of you to give the Cologne; there will fall from these bottles many drops of comfort for these hot, tired, but most patient patients. I should have written yesterday but fancied you would come here to accompany me: will you not to day? I shall go a little after 5.

MARGARET—

ALS (Bodleian Library). Published in Clough, *Correspondence*, 1:262.
Arthur Hugh Clough (1819–61), the English poet, had arrived in Rome on 16 April.

His journal records six meetings with Fuller from 18 May to 30 June (*DNB;* Arthur Hugh Clough, *Amours de Voyage,* ed. Patrick Scott [St. Lucia, Queensland, 1974], pp. 77–78).

828. To Giovanni Angelo Ossoli

lunedi
4 guigno [1849]

mio caro,

Questa mattina" andavo al giardino del Vaticano all 9 e 1/2 ti cercavan e ritornando dicevan che tu sei sortito. Io ritornavo subito in casa ma come tu non sei venuto mai qui credo era sbaglio Questa sera spero staro" in casa alle 8, questa sera si tu vieni primo aspetta ti prego. Grazia a Dio che tu stai ancora vivente. Quanto ho sofferta ieri" tu puoi credere a rivedere carissimo *consorte,* come scriveva sempre il cattivo su Giovanni

sorto perche e dovere andare al spedale.

Monday
June 4 [1849]

my dear,

This morning I went to the Vatican garden at 9 1/2[;] they looked for you and when they came back they said you had left. I came back home right away but since you never came here I think it was a mistake. This evening I hope I will be home at 8, this evening if you arrive first please wait. Thank God you are still alive. You can believe how I suffered yesterday to see again the dearest *husband,* as that bad woman always wrote about Giovanni

I am leaving because I must go to the hospital.

AL (MH: fMS Am 1086 [9:215]); MsC in English (MH: fMS Am 1086 [Works, 2: 221]). English copy published entire in Higginson, *MFO,* p. 264. *Addressed:* Sige Mse / Gio. Angiolo Ossoli / Roma.

Questa mattina] Qu⟨s⟩esta mattina
spero staro] spero star⟨e⟩o
8, questa sera] 8, ↑ questa sera ↓
sofferta ieri] sofferta ↑ ⟨Casa⟩ ↓ ier⟨e⟩i

829. To Emelyn Story

Rome, 6 June 1849

The help I needed was external, practical. I knew myself all the difficulties and pains of my position; they were beyond present relief; from sympathy I could struggle with them, but had not life enough left, afterwards, to be a companion of any worth. To be with persons generous and refined, who would not pain; who would sometimes lend a helping hand across the ditches of this strange insidious marsh, was all I could have now, and this you gave.

On Sunday, from our loggia, I witnessed a terrible, a real battle. It began at four in the morning; it lasted to the last gleam of light. The musket-fire was almost unintermitted; the roll of the cannon, especially from St. Angelo, most majestic. As all passed at Porta San Pancrazio and Villa Pamfili, I saw the smoke of every discharge, the flash of the bayonets; with a glass could see the men. Both French and Italians fought with the most obstinate valor. The French could not use their heavy cannon, being always driven away by the legions Garibaldi and——, when trying to find positions for them. The loss on our side is about three hundred killed and wounded; theirs must be much greater. In one casino have been found seventy dead bodies of theirs. I find the wounded men at the hospital in a transport of indignation. The French soldiers fought so furiously, that they think them false as their general, and cannot endure the remembrance of their visits, during the armistice, and talk of brotherhood. You will have heard how all went:—how Lesseps, after appearing here fifteen days as *plenipotentiary,* signed a treaty not dishonorable to Rome; then Oudinot refused to ratify it, saying, *the plenipotentiary had surpassed his powers:* Lesseps runs back to Paris, and Oudinot attacks:—an affair alike infamous for the French from beginning to end.[1] The cannonade on one side has continued day and night, (being full moon,) till this morning; they seeking to advance or take other positions, the Romans firing on them. The French throw rockets into the town; one burst in the court-yard of the hospital, just as I arrived there yesterday, agitating the poor sufferers very much; they said they did not want to die like mice in a trap.

ELfr, from *Memoirs,* 2:261–62.

1. When he declared war on 1 June, Oudinot announced that he would not attack until Monday, 4 June, in order to allow foreign nationals to leave Rome. The attack came, however, at 3 A.M. on Sunday, 3 June. In the first battle since 30 April, the Romans fought for sixteen hours outside the city walls, only to be forced to retreat within.

The failure of the smaller Roman force to keep the French at bay allowed Oudinot to lay siege to the city, beginning on 13 June (*Memoirs of Garibaldi*, pp. 246–47; King, *Italian Unity*, 1:337–38).

830.   To Ralph Waldo Emerson

Rome, 10 June 1849

I received your letter amid the round of cannonade and musketry. It was a terrible battle fought here from the first till the last light of day. I could see all its progress from my balcony. The Italians fought like lions. It is a truly heroic spirit that animates them. They make a stand here for honor and their rights, with little ground for hope that they can resist, now they are betrayed by France.

Since the 30th April, I go almost daily to the hospitals, and, though I have suffered,—for I had no idea before, how terrible gunshot-wounds and wound-fever are,—yet I have taken pleasure, and great pleasure, in being with the men; there is scarcely one who is not moved by a noble spirit. Many, especially among the Lombards, are the flower of the Italian youth. When they begin to get better, I carry them books, and flowers; they read, and we talk.

The palace of the Pope, on the Quirinal, is now used for convalescents. In those beautiful gardens, I walk with them,—one with his sling, another with his crutch. The gardener plays off all his water-works for the defenders of the country, and gathers flowers for me, their friend.

A day or two since, we sat in the Pope's little pavilion, where he used to give private audience. The sun was going gloriously down over Monte Mario, where gleamed the white tents of the French light-horse among the trees. The cannonade was heard at intervals. Two bright-eyed boys sat at our feet, and gathered up eagerly every word said by the heroes of the day. It was a beautiful hour, stolen from the midst of ruin and sorrow; and tales were told as full of grace and pathos as in the gardens of Boccaccio, only in a very different spirit,— with noble hope for men, with reverence for woman.

The young ladies of the family, very young girls, were filled with enthusiasm for the suffering, wounded patriots, and they wished to go to the hospital to give their services. Excepting the three superintendents, none but married ladies were permitted to serve there, but their services were accepted. Their governess then wished to go too, and, as she could speak several languages, she was admitted to the rooms of the wounded soldiers, to interpret for them, as the nurses knew nothing but Italian, and many of these poor men were suffering, because they could not make their wishes known. Some are French, some German, and many Poles. Indeed, I am afraid it is too true that there were comparatively but few Romans among them. This young lady passed several nights there.

Should I never return,—and sometimes I despair of doing so, it seems so far off, so difficult, I am caught in such a net of ties here, —if ever you know of my life here, I think you will only wonder at the constancy with which I have sustained myself; the degree of profit to which, amid great difficulties, I have put the time, at least in the way of observation. Meanwhile, love me all you can; let me feel, that, amid the fearful agitations of the world, there are pure hands, with healthful, even pulse, stretched out toward me, if I claim their grasp.

I feel profoundly for Mazzini; at moments I am tempted to say, "Cursed with every granted prayer,"—so cunning is the daemon. He is become the inspiring soul of his people. He saw Rome, to which all his hopes through life tended, for the first time as a Roman citizen, and to become in a few days its ruler. He has animated, he sustains her to a glorious effort, which, if it fails, this time, will not in the age. His country will be free. Yet to me it would be so dreadful to cause all this bloodshed, to dig the graves of such martyrs.

Then Rome is being destroyed; her glorious oaks; her villas, haunts of sacred beauty, that seemed the possession of the world forever,— the villa of Raphael, the villa of Albani, home of Winkelmann, and the best expression of the ideal of modern Rome, and so many other sanctuaries of beauty,—all must perish, lest a foe should level his musket from their shelter.[1] *I could not, could not!*

I know not, dear friend, whether I ever shall get home across that great ocean, but here in Rome I shall no longer wish to live. O, Rome, *my* country! could I imagine that the triumph of what I held dear was to heap such desolation on thy head!

ELfr, from *Memoirs*, 2:264–66. Published entire in *At Home and Abroad*, pp. 434–36; Van Doren, pp. 296–98; and Miller, pp. 295–97; published in part in Chevigny, pp. 476–77.

1. The Villa of Raphael, near the west entrance of the Villa Borghese, was destroyed in the siege. The Villa Albani, however, which lies just outside the city walls on the Via Salaria, was not. Johann Joachim Winckelmann (1717–68) was an art historian and archaeologist who went to Rome in 1755 and became librarian for Cardinal Albani (Harold Osborne, ed., *The Oxford Companion to Art* [Oxford, 1970]).

831. To Elizabeth Hoar

17th June [1849].

[   ] I copy this from the Roman Monitor of this week, as a natural appendix to my letter.[1]

I feel an inexpressible weariness of spirits today. The state of seige is very terrible, such continual alarms, then to hear the cannonade day and night and to know with every shot, some fellow man may be bleeding and dying. Sometimes I cannot sleep, sometimes I do again from sheer exhaustion. I did think, since this world was so full of ill, I was willing to see it all. I did not want to be cowardly and shut my eyes. Nor is this perpetual murder of men so bad as to see them indolently lying in the mud. The sad night is cheered by sparklings of pure fire. Yet it *is* very sad, and oh, Rome, *my* Rome, every day more and more desecrated! One of the most gentle hallowed haunts, La Maria di Trastevere, is I hear almost ruined by the bombs of day before yesterday.[n] Almost nightly I see burning some fair cascine. Adieu, dear Lizzie, prize the thoughtful peace of Concord.

"Martyrology of Italian liberty"[n]

Colemba Antonietti di Fuligno has followed for two years her husband Luigi Porzio, lieutenant in the 2d regiment of the Line, sharing with him fatigues and dangers, the long marches and the fire of the enemy.

She was only 21 years old, of most generous heart, of the highest Italian sentiment. She fought like a man, rather say a hero, in the battle of Volletri, worthy of her husband, worthy of her cousin, the colonel Luigi Masi. Yesterday 13th June, she was near the wall San Pancrazio, threatened by the French fire. There while she passed to her husband what he wanted while working at the breach, a cannon ball struck her in the side. She joined her hands, looked up and died crying *Viva l'Italia* Frenchmen if Italian men "do not fight"[n] let our women teach you respect for the name and valor of Rome.

Fire, barbarians, but incline yourselves!

ALfr (NNPM).

bombs of day before yesterday.] bombs. ↑ of day before yesterday. ↓

Fuller copied this extract on the back of the letter.

Here Fuller made an x to mark an addition that she wrote at the end: quoted from sneers of the French newspapers.

1. The report appeared in the *Monitore Romano: Giornale officiale della repubblica* on 14 June 1849 under the headline: "Martirologio della Libertia Italiana."

832. To Lewis Cass, Jr.

[ca. 17 June 1849]

Dear Mr Cass,

My journal, the Democratic is stopped, its bureaux having been broken open, and Considerant put under arrest.[1] Have you not seen that the most liberal journals are all suspended? I was hoping to hear through you, some news from Paris. Will you not come this evening to see me, if you can? I shall be at home at 9. P.M.

MARGARET F.

MsC (MH: fMS Am 1086 [*Works*, 1:339]).

Dated by the reference to the newspaper, which was suspended from 12 June to August 1849.

1. Prosper-Victor Considérant (1808–93), a Fourierite socialist, founded *La Democratie pacifique* in 1843 (*Dictionnaire de biographie française*).

833. To Ellen Fuller Channing

Rome, 19 June 1849

As was Eve, at first, I suppose every mother is delighted by the birth of a man-child. There is a hope that he will conquer more ill, and effect more good, than is expected from girls. This prejudice in favor of man does not seem to be destroyed by his shortcomings for ages. Still, each mother hopes to find in hers an Emanuel. I should like very much to see your children, but hardly realize I ever shall. The journey home seems so long, so difficult, so expensive. I should really like to lie down here, and sleep my way into another sphere of existence, if I could take with me one or two that love and need me, and was sure of a good haven for them on that other side.

The world seems to go so strangely wrong! The bad side triumphs; the blood and tears of the generous flow in vain. I assist at many saddest scenes, and suffer for those whom I knew not before. Those whom I knew and loved,—who, if they had triumphed, would have opened for me an easier, broader, higher higher-mounting road,—are every day more and more involved in earthly ruin. Eternity is with us, but there is much darkness and bitterness in this portion of it. A baleful star rose on my birth, and its hostility, I fear, will never be disarmed while I walk below.

ELfr, from *At Home and Abroad*, p. 437. Published entire in Miller, pp. 298–99.

834. To Lewis Cass, Jr.

[ca. 8 July 1849]

My dear Mr. Cass,—

I beg you to come and see me, and give me your counsel, and, if need be, your aid, to get away from Rome. From what I hear this morning, I fear we may be once more shut up here; and I shall die, to be again separated from what I hold most dear. There are, as yet, no horses on the way we want to go, or we should post immediately.

You may feel, like me, sad, in these last moments, to leave this injured Rome.[1] So many noble hearts I abandon here, whose woes I have known! I feel, if I could not aid, I might soothe. But for my child, I would not go, till some men, now sick, know whether they shall live or die.

ELfr, from *Memoirs*, 2:271.
Dated by her plans to leave Rome.
1. The Roman republic defended itself from 3 June until the night of 21–22 June, when the French pierced its defenses. On 30 June the Roman assembly voted to end the resistance; Garibaldi left the city with his legion on 2 July. The French army entered the defeated city the next day (Farini, 4:209–26).

835. To Richard F. Fuller

Rome
8th July, 1849.

My dear Richard,

I received two or three weeks ago your letter of the 4th May. Probably I shall answer it, sometime, if[n] I should ever again find myself tranquil and recruited from the painful excitements of these last days. But amid the ruined hopes of Rome, the shameful oppressions she is beginning to suffer, amid these noble bleeding martyrs, my brothers, I cannot fix my thoughts on any thing else.

I write that you may assure Mother of my safety, which in the last days began to be seriously imperilled. Say that so soon as I can find means of conveyance, without an expense too enormous, I shall go again into the mountains. There I shall find pure bracing air and I hope stillness for a time. Say she need feel no anxiety if she does not hear from me for sometime. I may feel indisposed to write, as I do now, my heart is too full.

243

Private hopes of mine are fallen with the hopes of Italy. I have played for a new stake and lost it. Life looks too difficult. But, for the present, I shall try to waive all thoughts of self, and renew my strength.

Say to dear Eugene when you write that the hour is not yet come for me to write to him as I would.

On the last page is the answer to Mr E. B. Clarke about the engraving it is put apart so that you can tear it off and give it him. I do not feel as if I could write any more. Your affectionate sister

M.

I have found a conveyance and hope to be in the country tomorrow. Radetsky is expected here on Sunday.[1]

ALS (MH: fMS Am 1086 [9:160]); MsC (MH: fMS Am 1086 [Works, 2:879–83]). Published in part in *Memoirs*, 2:267, and Van Doren, pp. 299–300. *Endorsed:* F. Ma / Margaret / 8. July / 49.

sometime, if] sometime, ↑ if ↓

1. Austria conquered Ferrara, Bologna, and Ancona and so held the entire northern portion of the Papal States. It did not, however, choose to contest France for Rome. Radetzky visited Florence on 7–10 June but he did not go to Rome (William A. Jenks, *Francis Joseph and the Italians, 1849–1859* [Charlottesville, 1978], pp. 84–85, 98–99).

836. To Lewis Cass, Jr.

Tuesday 10th July. [1849]

Dear Mr Cass,

I came in so late last eveg that I could not answer your note then. Thanks as ever. Am I to understand we have carriage and horses for 18 scudi,[n] and a carriage that accomodates as the vetturras usually do 6 persons. If so, there are four would like to go with us, and we could make the journey at about the usual expense[n] you said you could come to see me today if it could be before 5 or 6 oclock, I[n] could see the other persons before evening and make our arangements to go Thursday morng. I could not well be ready for tomorrow. And in that case ought we not to have the passports today; are not other viseés to be procured tomorrow morng? Pardon all trouble, I will do as much for you sometime, I hope.

If your servant could have the passports viseéd we should be glad; then Ossoli would not have to present himself. If we could have your card for the vetturino, we could arrange that. Perhaps if at home, you will write a word to tell when I am likely to see you.

MARGARET—

ALS (MH: fMS Am 1086 [9:159]); MsC (MH: fMS Am 1086 [Works, 1:343−45]).
    18 scudi,] 18 scu⟨?⟩di,
    usual expense] usual expense⟨s⟩
    oclock, I] oclock, ⟨we⟩ ↑ I ↓

837. To Lewis Cass, Jr.

Rieti
19th July, 1849.

Dear Mr Cass,

I seem to have arrived in a different world, since passing the mountains. This little red-brown nest, which those we call the aborigines of Italy made long before Rome was, lies tranquil amid the net-work of vineyards, its casines and convents gleam pleasantly from the hillsides, the dirt accumulates undisturbed in its streets, and pigs and children wallow in it, while Madonna-veiled bare-legged women twirl the distaff at every door and window, happy if so they can earn five cents a day. We have not been able to find an apartment, so we have rooms at the rustic *locanda*, which is on the piazza, clean and airy and where may be studied all the humours of the place. There is the fountain where come the girls in their corset, long shift-sleeves, and coloured petticoat, the silver needle in their fine hair, attractive they look from my window for the dirt disappears in distance. Near, it not dismays their lovers, who help them to adjust the water-vase on their heads. (N. B. no husband does this.) All the dandies of Rieti in all kinds of queer uniforms are congregated below, at the barber's[n] the druggists, the caffé, they sit and digest the copious slander, chief product of this, as of every *little* hive of men. The Baronesses and Countesses, in the extreme of Italian undress, are peeping through the blinds, at half past seven, if the band plays, they will put on their best dresses, (alas! mongrel French fashions prevail here,) and parade on foot, fanning themselves whether the weather be hot or cold, on foot, for the Corso of Rieti is nominal. At present the scene is varied by the presence of the Spanish force, who promise to stay only three days, and I hope they will not, for they eat every thing up like locusts.[1]

For the moment it pleases to see their foreign features, and hear the noble sounds of their language. We have performed our social duties, have called on the handsome doctor's wife, whom we [fo]und ironing in her antichamber. [Mad]ame, the Gonfaloniere's sister, who had just had a child, and recd us in her chamber, and on the father guardian of the beautifully placed monastery of St Antonio, who insisted on making us excellent coffee, which we must take under the shade of the magnificent cypresses, for women must not enter, "only" said he chuckling, "Garribaldi obliged us to let his enter, and I have even seen them braiding their hair!" Maria of the Episcopal garden has left her card in the form of a pair of pigeons. I could find much repose for the moment in these simple traits of a limited life and in this pure air, were it not for the state in which I find my baby. You know, my dear Mr Cass, I flattered you with the thought you would be happy in having a child, may you never know such a pang as I felt in kissing his poor pale little hand which he can hardly lift. He is worn to a skeleton, all his sweet childish graces fled; he is so weak it seems to me he can scarcely ever revive to health, if he cannot, I do not wish him to live; life is hard enough for the strong it is too much for the feeble. Only, if he dies, I hope I shall, to[o.] I was too fatigued before, and this last shipwreck of ho[pes] would be more than I could bear.

Adieu, dear Mr Cass, write when you can; tell me of the world, of which I hear nothing here, of suffering Rome, always dear, whatever may oppress me, and of yourself. Ever yours

M. O.

ALS (MB: Ms. Am. 1450 [29]). Published entire in Higginson, *MFO*, pp. 266–68. *Addressed:* Mr Cass / Charge d' Affaires / des Etats-Unis d'Amerique / Rome. *Postmark:* Rieti.

the barber's] the ⟨B⟩barber's

1. The Spanish troops were pursuing Garibaldi, who had completely fooled them. Upon leaving Rome, Garibaldi marched toward Tivoli as though he were retreating to Rieti, where he had trained his army before the French invasion. On 4 July the Spaniards set off after him along the eastern flank of the mountains. Garibaldi, however, stayed on the western side and marched undetected toward Monte Rotondo. Had the Spaniards or the French been aware of his presence, either might easily have intercepted his troops (George Macaulay Trevelyan, *Garibaldi's Defence of the Roman Republic* [London, 1910], pp. 242–48).

838. To William H. Channing

[I] [ca. late] July 1849

I cannot tell you what I endured in leaving Rome; abandoning the wounded soldiers; knowing that there is no provision made for them, when they rise from the beds where they have been thrown by a noble courage, where they have suffered with a noble patience. Some of the poorer men, who rise bereft even of the right arm,—one having lost both the right arm and the right leg,—I could have provided for with a small sum. Could I have sold my hair, or blood from my arm, I would have done it. Had any of the rich Americans remained in Rome, they would have given it to me; they helped nobly at first, in the service of the hospitals, when there was far less need; but they had all gone. What would I have given that I could have spoken to one of the Lawrences, or the Phillipses; they could and would have saved the misery.[1] These poor men are left helpless in the power of a mean and vindictive foe. You felt so oppressed in the slave-states; imagine what I felt at seeing all the noblest youth, all the genius of this dear land, again enslaved.

[II] After the attempt at revolution in France failed, could I have influenced Mazzini, I should have prayed him to capitulate, and yet I feel that no honorable terms can be made with such a foe, and that the only way is *never* to yield; but the sound of the musketry, the sense that men were perishing in a hopeless contest, had become too terrible for my nerves. I did not see Mazzini, the last two weeks of the republic. When the French entered, he walked about the streets, to see how the people bore themselves, and then went to the house of a friend. In the upper chamber of a poor house, with his life-long friends,—the Modenas,—I found him. Modena, who abandoned not only what other men hold dear,—home, fortune, peace, —but also endured, without the power of using the prime of his great artist-talent, a ten years' exile in a foreign land; his wife every way worthy of him,—such a woman as I am not.[2]

Mazzini had suffered millions more than I could; he had borne his fearful responsibility; he had let his dearest friends perish; he had passed all these nights without sleep; in two short months, he had grown old; all the vital juices seemed exhausted; his eyes were all blood-shot; his skin orange; flesh he had none; his hair was mixed with white; his hand was painful to the touch; but he had never flinched, never quailed; had protested in the last hour against surrender; sweet and calm, but full of a more fiery purpose than ever; in him I revered the hero, and owned myself not of that mould.

You say truly, I shall come home humbler. God grant it may be entirely humble! In future, while more than ever deeply penetrated with principles, and the need of the martyr spirit to sustain them, I will ever own that there are few worthy, and that I am one of the least.

A silken glove might be as good a gauntlet as one of steel, but I, infirm of mood, turn sick even now as I think of the past.

[III] I am so much merged now in the young growth of my child. For I am a mother now, and the spirit of my little one embellishes more and more its frail temple, so frail it requires great care from me to keep it fixed here on earth. His smiles are an exceeding rich reward, and often give my heart amid the cries of carnage and oppression an even bird like joy Yet for his possession also, whether given or lent, a great price is exacted.

What shall I say to you of his father? If earthly union be meant for the beginning of one permanent and full we ought not to be united, for the time was gone by when I could more than *prefer* any man. Yet I shall never regret the step which has given me the experience of a mother and satisfied domestic wants in a most sincere and sweet companion.

Once you said to me in speaking of your two natures "Sometimes I feel as if I would fain have been a violet, stilly growing in the precincts of the ancient forest." That is exactly true of him, my gentle friend, ignorant of great ideas, ignorant of books, enlightened as to his duties by pure sentiment and an unspoiled nature, but never failing in the degree his nature has once promised.

The tie leaves me mentally free, as I wish him also to remain. I trust in the midst of a false world, we may be able to sustain some degree of truth, though indeed children involve too deeply, in this corrupt social contract and truth is easier to those who have not them. I however pined too much and my heart was too suffocated without a child of my own. I say again I am not strong as we thought.

I: ELfr, from *Memoirs*, 2:269; II: Elfr, from *Memoirs*, 2:267–69; III: MsCfr (MB: Ms. Am. 1450 [104]). Published in part in *At Home and Abroad*, pp. 437–38, and Chevigny, p. 493.

1. Probably a reference to Amos, Abbot, and William Lawrence, formerly of Groton, who made fortunes in retail trade and textile manufacture. Jonathan Phillips, son of Governor William Phillips, also made a fortune in trade (*"Our First Men": A Calendar of Wealth, Fashion, and Gentility* [Boston, 1846], pp. 29–30, 36; *DAB*).

2. Gustavo Modena (1803–61), son of Giacomo and Luigia Bernaroli Modena, was an author and actor who was active in revolutionary politics. He took part in the uprising in Romagna in 1831. Exiled to Marseilles, he met Mazzini, joined Young Italy in the aborted attack on Savoia in 1834, and endured an exile in London. After his return to Italy he took part in the revolution in Milan. Modena married Giulia Calame, whom he met in Berne (Nardo Leonelli, *Attori tragici, attori comici* [Milan, 1940–44], 2:98–99).

839.   To Lewis Cass, Jr.

Rieti 30 July, 1849.

To Mr. Cass—

We have now the most glorious moon, and as I walk beside the river in its light, or sometimes by day in the little vineyard paths of this great rich valley where gleams of the mountains in prismatic hues are caught every now and then betwixt the bright leaves. I regret you should be staying in Rome at this season, when its air is so oppressive and unhealthy. I should urge you much to make the little journey— come here, at least for a day or two, only my little boy is still so ill; his moans would annoy you and I could not see you freely. He still wanders feebly on the surface between the two worlds, inclining, I fear me, most over the abyss. His nurse who seemed so lovely and innocent, betrayed him for the sake of a few scudi, and gave all the nourishment to her own child. The one I have at present a fine healthy girl (with a heart such as you may imagine, since she has two children already at the Foundling Hospital) is always trying not to give him milk, for fear of spoiling the shape of her bosom! Since I have known the lower women of Italy, the bosom of woman, that once seemed to me the invariable home of angelic pity, seems almost a shrine for offerings to moloch. When the lower are so loveless, we ought not to hope much good of the higher. Take not to heart, my friend, any Italian woman. As to "flirtation," I fancy with the maidens here, some of them quite pretty ones, their swains pursue it principally by lounging in the streets before the house, or peeping up at their windows. Nearer approaches bring papa immediately into question, with "what have you to offer"—or "what dowry do you expect"—or "Off with you, you compromise the reputation of my daughter"—but married ladies seem more accessible—

MsCfr (MB: Ms. Am. 1450 [30]).

840.   To Costanza Arconati Visconti

[August, 1849]

[I] Reading a book called "The Last Days of the Republic in Rome," I see that my letter, giving my impressions of that period, may well have seemed to you strangely partial. If we can meet as once we did, and compare notes in the same spirit of candor, while making mutual allowance for our different points of view, your testimony and opinions would be invaluable to me. But will you have patience with my democracy,—my revolutionary spirit? Believe that in thought I am more radical than ever. The heart of Margaret you know,—it is always the same. Mazzini is immortally dear to me,—a thousand times dearer for all the trial I saw made of him in Rome;—dearer for all he suffered. Many of his brave friends perished there. We who, less worthy, survive, would fain make up for the loss, by our increased devotion to him, the purest, the most disinterested of patriots, the most affectionate of brothers. You will not love me less that I am true to him.[1]

Then, again, how will it affect you to know that I have united my destiny with that of an obscure young man,—younger than myself; a person of no intellectual culture, and in whom, in short, you will see no reason for my choosing; yet more, that this union is of long standing; that we have with us our child, of a year old, and that it is only lately I [II] acquainted my family with the fact.

If you decide to meet with me as before, and wish to say something about the matter to your friends, it will be true to say that there have been pecuniary reasons for this concealment. But *to you* in confidence I add, this is only half the truth; and I cannot explain or satisfy my dear friend farther—I should wish to meet her independent of all relations; but as we live in the midst of "society," she would have to enquire for me now as *Margaret Ossoli* that being done, I should like to say nothing farther on the subject.

However you may feel about all this, dear Madame Arconati, you will always be the same in my eyes. I earnestly wish you may not feel estranged, but only, if you do, I would rather for you to act upon it. Let us meet as friends, or not at all—In all events I remain ever yours,

MARGARET

I: ELfr, from *Memoirs*, 2:314–15; II: MsCfr (MH: fMS Am 1086 [9:232]). Published in part in Chevigny, pp. 485–86.

1. In her reply of 5 October, Arconati Visconti said: "I know ... that you are republican & radical, & as it is not Mazzini whom you have married, we shall not be more separated by the differences of *our politics* than we have been heretofore" (MH).

841. To Ellen Fuller Channing

[ca. August 1849]

I felt much what you wrote, "*if it were well with my heart.*" How seldom it is that a mortal is permitted to enjoy a paradisaical scene, unhaunted by some painful vision from the past or the future! With me, too, dark clouds of care and sorrow have some times blotted out the sunshine. I have not lost from my side an only sister, but have been severed from some visions still so dear, they looked almost like hopes. The future seems too difficult for me. I have been as happy as I could, and I feel that this summer, as last, had I been with my country folks, the picture of Italy would not have been so lively to me. Now I have been quite off the beaten track of travel, have seen, thought, spoken, dreamed only what is Italian. I have learned much, received many strong and clear impressions. While among the mountains, I was for a good while quite alone, except for occasional chat with the contadine, who wanted to know if Pius IX. was not *un gran carbonaro!*—a reputation which he surely ought to have forfeited by this time. About me they were disturbed: "*E sempre sola soletta,*" they said, "*eh perche?*"

Later, I made one of those accidental acquaintances, such as I have spoken of to you in my life of Lombardy, which may be called romantic: two brothers, elderly men, the last of a very noble family, formerly lords of many castles, still of more than one; both unmarried, men of great polish and culture. None of the consequences ensued that would in romances: they did not any way adopt me, nor give me a casket of diamonds, nor any of their pictures, among which were originals by several of the greatest masters, nor their rich cabinets, nor miniatures on agate, nor carving in wood and ivory. They only showed me their things, and their family archives of more than a hundred volumes, (containing most interesting documents about Poland, where four of their ancestors were nuncios,) manuscript letters from Tasso, and the like. With comments on these, and legendary lore enough to furnish Cooper or Walter Scott with a thousand romances, they enriched me; unhappily, I shall never have the strength or talent to make due use of it. I was sorry to leave them, for now I have recrossed the frontier into the Roman States. I will not tell you where,—I know not that I shall ever tell where,—these months have been passed. The great Goethe hid thus in Italy; "Then," said he, "I did indeed feel alone,—when no former friend could form an *idea* where I was."[1] Why should not——and I enjoy this fantastic luxury of *incognito* also, when we can so much more easily?

I will not name the place, but I will describe it. The rooms are spacious and airy; the loggia of the sleeping room is rude, but it overhangs a lovely little river, with its hedge of willows. Opposite is a large and rich vineyard; on one side a ruined tower, on the other an old casino, with its avenues of cypress, give human interest to the scene. A cleft amid the mountains full of light leads on the eye to a soft blue peak, very distant. At night the young moon trembles in the river, and its soft murmur soothes me to sleep; it needs, for I have had lately a bad attack upon the nerves, and been obliged to stop writing for the present. I think I shall stay here some time, though I suppose there are such sweet places all over Italy, if one only looks for one's self. Poor, beautiful Italy! how she has been injured of late! It is dreadful to see the incapacity and meanness of those to whom she had confided the care of her redemption.

ELfr, from *Memoirs*, 2:254-56.

1. "Heut abend setzt' ich mich in einem Winkel un hatte meine stille Betrachtung; da fühlt' ich mich recht allein, denn kein Mensch in der Welt, der in dem Augenblick an mich gedacht hätte, würde mich hier gesucht haben" (Tonight I sat there meditating in a corner. I felt very alone, since no one in the world, even had he thought of me at that moment, would have looked for me in such a place") (Goethe, *Gedenkausgabe*, 11:68; Goethe, *Italian Journey*, p. 57).

842. To Lewis Cass, Jr.

Rieti
8th August, 49.

Dear Mr Cass

This letter will be presented by *Don Alfonso Zeuli* of *Aquila*.[1] He has been much compromised in political affairs, and takes refuge with the French from the tender mercies of King Bomba. He supposes he shall be obliged to leave Italy, and, as all other countries are being closed against the exile, may need to seek America; if so, perhaps you will recommend him to Freeman for a passport.[2] I know nothing of him, except that he is considered good and gentlemanly; his brother I knew a little in Aquila, and, as he prayed to be presented to you, in case he could not find other outlet from Italy, I thought I ought not to decline at this moment of trouble. More I do not say here,[n] as perhaps he may never present the letter, and it is better to write by post. Most truly yours

M. O.

ALS (MH: fMS Am 1086 [9:164]); MsC (MH: fMS Am 1086 [Works, 1:345–47]).
Addressed: Mr Cass / Hotel de Russie / Rome.

say here,] say ↑ here ↓,

1. Alfonso Zeuli (1822–56), the principal landowner in Aquila, actively opposed the Neapolitan Bourbon regime. In 1851 he was arrested, tried, and sentenced for his political activities (*Dizionario del risorgimento nazionale*).

2. James Edwards Freeman (1808–84) had moved in 1836 from New York City to Italy, where he lived for the rest of his life. From 1840 to 1849 he was the American consul at Ancona. In 1845 he married Augusta Latilla (b. 1826), a sculptor (*DAB*; Albert Teneyck Gardner, *Yankee Stonecutters* [New York, 1945], p. 64). George Curtis wrote in a letter of 1 July 1847 to Christopher Pearse Cranch that Fuller "detested" Freeman (MHi).

843. To Giovanni Angelo Ossoli

Rieti
9 Agosto 49.

Mio Caro,

Potete pensare in quel pena ho passata la notte; non riceveva mai tua lettera; era solamente questa mattina che prendevo l'idea che tu sei per sbaglio entrato nel Regno. Andava col Gonfaloniere da Monsignor Bella e m'assicura che come tue carte son in regola, tu puoi ritornare subito;[1] egli scrive al Intendente di Citta Ducale; io spero possibile tu puoi ritornare al pranzo. Nino sta bene. Pensavo un poco prendere un legno cercarti, ma temevo che sia un affare lunga; e che devo lasciar Nino troppo. Ma si tu sei stanco e non trovi legno o altro mezzo di venire scrivi in risposta che devo fare, sempre la tua

M.

Si tu vuoi per mi venire in legno, cercaro farlo subito quando ricevo una riga.

lascio aperta la lettera, che sia più sicura arrivare in tue mani

Rieti
9 August 49.

My Dear,

You can imagine in what torment I passed the night; I never received your letter; it was only this morning that I got the idea you had entered the Kingdom by mistake. I went with the Gonfaloniere to Monsignor Bella and he assured me that since your papers are in order, you can come back immediately;[1] he will write to the Intendente of Citta Ducale; I hope it is possible that you will come back at dinner.

Nino is well. I had thought a little to take a stagecoach and come to look for you, but I was afraid it would take too long a time and I had to leave Nino for too long. But if you are tired and you cannot find a stagecoach or other means of travel, write [me about] what I should do. Always your

M.

If you want me to come by stagecoach, I will try to do that as soon as I receive a word from you.

I leave open the letter, so that I can be more sure it will arrive in your hands

ALS (MH: fMS Am 1086 [9:202]); MsC in English (MH: fMS Am 1086 [Works, 2:225–27]). *Addressed:* al Sigr Mse / G.A. Ossoli / Citta Ducale.
1. Tancredi Bellà served in a number of diplomatic positions (Stock, *United States Ministers*, p. 189).

844. To Lewis Cass, Jr.

Rieti, 13th Aug, 1849.

To Mr Cass.—

My little boy is again peaceful and gay as is his nature, though still a skeleton, and requiring great care

Ossoli the other day happening to stray without knowing it into the kingdom of Naples, was arrested on suspicion of being one of the followers of Garribaldi. To get the needed papers for his liberation, I was obliged to go to Monsigneor Bella, the new delegate. This led to my acquintance with Cavalier Ricci one of the old fashioned literati courtiers and pietists, an interesting person in his way to know, and of a class which will not long endure.[1] He has in his collection several exquisite pictures, three by Raphael in the finest manner which have been always in his family and never retouched—and two fine Claudes. He is a person could tell much to me who wants to know well Italy prelatic, Italy artistic; the young Italy he of course abhors, but never dreams that I could have any sympathy with it—

I wish you could be here for the fair of Rieti, for which they are making preparations before my window, and which will make a bright show of all that is characteristic in this part of the country.

We think of staying here about three weeks longer—We might be very happy now if we had only a little fortune, living peaceably in one beautiful provincial town after another. The tastes of us both are very simple, our habits independent it is easy to fill up the day to our mind; but there is always something to prevent being happy—

MsCfr (MB: Ms. Am. 1450[31]).

1. Probably Angelo Maria Ricci (1776–1850), an author of several volumes of poems and a former professor of eloquence at the University of Naples (*Dizionario enciclopedico*).

845. To Horace Greeley

Rieti, August 25, 1848. [1849]

My Beloved Friend:

Bitterest tears alone can answer those words—*Pickie is dead.*[1] My heart has all these years presaged them. I have suffered not a few sleepless hours thinking of our darling, haunted with fears never again to see his sweet, joyous face which on me, also, always looked with love and trust. But I always thought of small-pox. Now how strangely snatched from you, oh poor mother; how vain all your feverish care night and day to ward off the least possible ill from that fair frame. Oh, how pathetic it seems to think of all that was done for dear, dear Pickie to build up strong that temple from which the soul departed so easily.

You say I left him too soon to know him well, but it was not so. I had spiritual sight of the child, and knew his capacities. I hoped to be of use to him if he lived, for sweet was our communion beside the murmuring river, and when he imitated the low voices of the little brook, or telling him stories in my room, which even then he well understood. A thousand times I have thought of the time when he first said the word *open* to get into my room, and my heart always was open to him. He was my consolation in hours sadder than you ever guessed—my spring-flower, my cheerful lark. None but his parents could love him so well; no child, except little Waldo Emerson, had I ever so loved. In both I saw the promise of a great future; its realization is deferred to some other sphere; ere long may we follow and aid it there.

Ever sacred, my friend, be this bond between us—the love and knowledge of the child. I was his aunty; and no sister can so feel what you lose. My friend, I have never wept so for grief of my own, as now

255

Horace Greeley. Courtesy of the National Portrait Gallery, Smithsonian Institution, Washington, D.C.

for yours. It seems to me *too* cruel; you are resigned; you make holy profit of it; the spear has entered and forced out the heart's blood, the pure ichol follows. I know not yet how to feel so; I have not yet grieved away the bitter pang.

My mother wrote me he said sometimes he would get a boat and carry yellow flowers to his Aunty Margaret. I suppose he had not yet quite forgotten that I used to get such for him. I often thought what I should carry him from Europe—what I should tell him—what teach? He had a heart of natural poetry; he would have prized all that was best.

Oh, it is all over; and indeed this life is over for me. The conditions of this planet are not propitious to the lovely, the just, the pure; it is these that go away; it is the unjust that triumph. Let us, as you say, purify ourselves; let us labor in the good spirit here, but leave all thought of results to Eternity.

I say this, and yet my heart is bound to earth as never before; for I, too, have a dearer self—a little son. He is now about the age Sweet Pickie was when I was with him most; and I have thought much of the one in the dawning graces of the other. But I accept the lesson, and will strive to prepare myself to resign him. Indeed, I have the warning before; for, during the siege of Rome, when I could not see him, my mind, agonized by the dangers of his father, as well as all the overpowering and infamous injuries heaped upon the noble, sought refuge in the thought of him safe in his green nook, and, as I thought, in care of worthy persons, When at last we left, our dearest friends laid low, our fortunes finally ruined, and every hope for which we struggled, blighted, I hoped to find comfort in his smiles. I found him wasted to a skeleton; and it is only by a month of daily and hourly most anxious care (in which I was often assisted by memories of what Mrs. Greeley did for Pickie) that I have been able to restore him. But I hold him by a frail tenure; he has the tendency to cough by which I was brought so low.

Adieu. You say, pray for you; oh, let us all pray together. I hope we shall yet find dear Pickie where he is; that earthly blemishes will be washed out, and he be able to love us all. Till then, God help and guide us, dear friend. Amen.

M. F. O.

You may address me in future as Marchioness Ossoli.

EL, from Cecilia Cleveland, *The Story of a Summer* (New York, 1874), pp. 243–46.
1. In his letter of 23 July 1849 (MH), Greeley described his son's death.

846.   To William H. Channing

Rieti, 28 August 1849

You say, you are glad I have had this great opportunity for carrying out my principles. Would it were so! I found myself inferior in courage and fortitude to the occasion. I knew not how to bear the havoc and anguish incident to the struggle for these principles. I rejoiced that it lay not with me to cut down the trees, to destroy the Elysian gardens, for the defense of Rome; I do not know that I could have done it. And the sight of these far nobler growths, the beautiful young men, mown down in their stately prime, became too much for me. I forget the great ideas, to sympathize with the poor mothers, who had nursed their precious forms, only to see them all lopped and gashed. You say, I sustained them; often have they sustained my courage: one, kissing the pieces of bone that were so painfully extracted from his arm, hanging them around his neck to be worn as the true relics of to-day; mementoes that he also had done and borne something for his country and the hopes of humanity. One fair young man, who is made a cripple for life, clasped my hand as he saw me crying over the spasms I could not relieve, and faintly cried, "Viva l'Italia." "Think only, *cara bona donna*," said a poor wounded soldier, "that I can always wear my uniform on *festas*, just as it is now, with the holes where the balls went through, for a memory." "God is good; God knows," they often said to me, when I had not a word to cheer them.

ELfr, from *Memoirs*, 2:269–70. Published entire in Miller, pp. 299–300, and Chevigny, p. 483.

847.   To Caroline Sturgis Tappan

Rieti 28 Aug 49.

I have been on the brink of losing my little boy. During all the siege of Rome I could not see him, and though the Physician wrote reassuring letters I often seemed to hear him calling me amid the roar of the cannon, and he seemed to be crying. When I came I found mine own fast waning to the tomb. All that I have undergone seemed little to what I felt seeing him unable to smile or lift his little wasted hand

Now by incessant care day and night I have brought him back (who knows if indeed that be a deed of love?) into this difficult world. I hope that the cruel law of my life will at least not oblige me to be separated from him—

MsCfr (MB: Ms. Am. 1450 [152]). Published in part in *Memoirs*, 2:301.

848. To Margarett C. Fuller

[31 August 1849]

Dearest Mother,

I received your letter a few hours before leaving Rome. Like all of yours, it refreshed me, and gave me as much satisfaction as anything could, at that sad time. Its spirit is of eternity, and befits an epoch when wickedness and perfidy so impudently triumph, and the best blood of the generous and honorable is poured out like water, seemingly in vain.

I cannot tell you what I suffered to abandon the wounded to the care of their mean foes; to see the young men, that were faithful to their vows, hunted from their homes,—hunted like wild beasts; denied a refuge in every civilized land. Many of those I loved are sunk to the bottom of the sea, by Austrian cannon, or will be shot. Others are in penury, grief, and exile. May God give due recompense for all that has been endured!

My mind still agitated, and my spirits worn out, I have not felt like writing to any one. Yet the magnificent summer does not smile quite in vain for me. Much exercise in the open air, living much on milk and fruit, have recruited my health, and I am regaining the habit of sleep, which a month of nightly cannonade in Rome had destroyed.

Receiving, a few days since, a packet of letters from America, I opened them with more feeling of hope and good cheer, than for a long time past. The first words that met my eye were these, in the hand of Mr. Greeley:—"Ah, Margaret, the world grows dark with us! You grieve, for Rome is fallen;—I mourn, for Pickie is dead."[1]

I have shed rivers of tears over the inexpressibly affecting letter thus begun. One would think I might have become familiar enough with images of death and destruction; yet somehow the image of Pickie's little dancing figure, lying, stiff and stark, between his parents, has made me weep more than all else. There was little hope he could do justice to himself, or lead a happy life in so perplexed a world; but never was a character of richer capacity,—never a more charming child. To me he was most dear, and would always have been so. Had he become stained with earthly faults, I could never have forgotten what he was when fresh from the soul's home, and what he was to me when my soul pined for sympathy, pure and unalloyed. The three children I have seen who were fairest in my eyes, and gave me most promise of the future, were Waldo, Pickie, Hermann Clarke;—all nipped in the bud.[2] Endless thoughts has this given me, and a resolve to seek the realization of all hopes and plans elsewhere, which resolve will weigh with me as much as it can weigh before the silver cord is finally loosed. Till then, Earth, our mother, always finds strange, unexpected ways to draw us back to her bosom,—to make us seek anew a nutriment which has never failed to cause us frequent sickness.

This brings me to the main object of my present letter,—a piece of intelligence about myself, which I had hoped I might be able to communicate in such a way as to give you *pleasure*. That I cannot,—after suffering much in silence with that hope,—is like the rest of my earthly destiny.

The first moment, it may cause you a pang to know that your eldest child might long ago have been addressed by another name than yours, and has a little son a year old.

But, beloved mother, do not feel this long. I do assure you, that it was only great love for you that kept me silent. I have abstained a hundred times, when your sympathy, your counsel, would have been most precious, from a wish not to harass you with anxiety. Even now I would abstain, but it has become necessary, on account of the child, for us to live publicly and permanently together; and we have no hope, in the present state of Italian affairs, that we can do it at any better advantage, for several years, than now.

My husband is a Roman, of a noble but now impoverished house. His mother died when he was an infant, his father is dead since we met, leaving some property, but encumbered with debts, and in the present state of Rome hardly available, except by living there. He has three older brothers, all provided for in the Papal service,—one as Secretary of the Privy Chamber, the other two as members of the Guard Noble. A similar career would have been opened to him, but he embraced liberal principles, and, with the fall of the Republic, has lost all, as well as the favor of his family, who all sided with the Pope. Meanwhile, having been an officer in the Republican service, it was best for him to leave Rome. He has taken what little money he had, and we plan to live in Florence for the winter. If he or I can get the means, we shall come together to the United States, in the summer; —earlier we could not, on account of the child.

He is not in any respect such a person as people in general would expect to find with me. He had no instructor except an old priest, who entirely neglected his education; and of all that is contained in books he is absolutely ignorant, and he has no enthusiasm of character. On the other hand, he has excellent practical sense; has been a judicious observer of all that passed before his eyes; has a nice sense of duty, which, in its unfailing, minute activity, may put most enthusiasts to shame; a very sweet temper, and great native refinement. His love for me has been unswerving and most tender. I have never suffered a pain that he could relieve. His devotion, when I am ill, is to be compared only with yours. His delicacy in trifles, his sweet domestic graces, remind me of E——. In him I have found a home, and one that interferes with no tie. Amid many ills and cares, we have had much joy together, in the sympathy with natural beauty,—with our child,—with all that is innocent and sweet.

I do not know whether he will always love me so well, for I am the elder, and the difference will become, in a few years, more perceptible than now. But life is so uncertain, and it is so necessary to take good things with their limitations, that I have not thought it worth while to calculate too curiously.

However my other friends may feel, I am sure that *you* will love him very much, and that he will love you no less. Could we all live together, on a moderate income, you would find peace with us. Heaven grant, that, on returning, I may gain means to effect this object. He, of course, can do nothing, while we are in the United States, but perhaps I can; and now that my health is better, I shall be able to exert myself, if sure that my child is watched by those who love him, and who are good and pure.

What shall I say of my child? All might seem hyperbole, even to my dearest mother. In him I find satisfaction, for the first time, to the deep wants of my heart. Yet, thinking of those other sweet ones fled, I must look upon him as a treasure only lent. He is a fair child, with blue eyes and light hair; very affectionate, graceful, and sportive. He was baptized, in the Roman Catholic Church, by the name of Angelo Eugene Philip, for his father, grandfather, and my brother. He inherits the title of marquis.

Write the name of my child in your Bible, Angelo Ossoli, *born September 5, 1848*. God grant he may live to see you, and may prove worthy of your love!

More I do not feel strength to say. You can hardly guess how all attempt to express something about the great struggles and experiences of my European life enfeebles me. When I get home,—if ever I do, —it will be told without this fatigue and excitement. I trust there will be a little repose, before entering anew on this wearisome conflict.

I had addressed you twice,—once under the impression that I should not survive the birth of my child; again during the siege of Rome, the father and I being both in danger. I took Mrs. Story, and, when she left Rome, Mr. Cass, into my confidence. Both were kind as sister and brother. Amid much pain and struggle, sweet is the memory of the generous love I received from William and Emelyn Story, and their uncle. They helped me gently through a most difficult period. Mr. Cass, also who did not know me at all, has done everything possible for me.

ELfr, from *Memoirs*, 2:271–76. Published entire in Van Doren, pp. 301–6; published in part in Chevigny, pp. 484–85.

In a letter postmarked 3 November (MH), Mrs. Fuller acknowledged this letter of 31 August.

1. In a letter of 21 May (MH), Mrs. Fuller described Pickie as a beautiful but tormented child who sowed dissention between his parents. Pickie had, said Mrs. Fuller, "the habit of throwing every thing he thought he could break out of the window, pulling the paper from the walls."

2. Herman Clarke, the son of James Freeman and Anna Huidekoper Clarke, died on 15 February 1849.

849. To Emelyn Story?

31 August. 1849.

Feel no immediate anxiety about me. Our plans are laid till next April, and we think we have money sufficient to last till then. Meanwhile Ossoli will make an effort to have a sum of ready money from his family for renunciation of claims on a vineyard, houses etc; but I hardly hope he will succeed. They are angry (the brother who is administrator having been obliged to hide in a cellar and troops quartered in his house during the Rule of the Republic) beside, ready money is very hard to raise in Rome at present.

It is odd how peculiarly things have turned against us. You have read that the dispatches of Oudinot are dated from *Villa Santucci*: that beautiful place was the property of Ossoli's grandmother, which, in the religious weakness of her last hours she gave to M. Santucci, then her confessor. As he is Godfather to my husband there was reason to hope he might restore the unjust acquisition at his death; but he has had to fly and hide, his property has been ravaged by the war, and he will feel little love for a godson who served on the Republican side.

MsCfr (MB: Ms Am. 1450 [148]).

850.   To Edgar T. Welby

Rieti
31st August 1849

Dear Sir,

The money for which I send I must take in gold; please put the necessary charge to my acct and write a line to tell me what it is. I am going now to Perugia, and thence to Florence where if[n] I resolve on passing the winter, I shall write and request that whatever balance remains for me may be transferred to Maquay and Pakenham, there.

Be so kind as to give the bearer any letters or papers you may have for me— If I stay long in Perugia and find safe means, I shall send for them once more before I go to Florence.

Will you allow these parcels to remain at the bank for Mr Crawford and Macpherson or if Mr Hooker has Mr C's keys, his book could be replaced in the library of Villa Negroni.[1]

Respectfully yours

S. M. FULLER.

ALS (MH:fMS Am 1086 [9:173]). *Addressed:* E. Welby Esq. / 20 Piazza di Spagne. *Endorsed:* 1849 / Rieti 31 Aug / S. M. Fuller.

Edgar T. Welby was an English banker. In 1860 he served as the United States consul at Civitavecchia (Stock, *Consular Relations*, p. 217; Stock, *United States Ministers*, p. 179).

where if] where ↑ if ↓

1. Julia Ward Howe described the Villa Negroni as "an old-time papal residence. This was surrounded by extensive gardens, and within the inclosure were an artificial fish pond and a lodge." Thomas Crawford later had a studio there (Howe, *Reminiscences*, p. 192).

851. To Lewis Cass, Jr.

[September 1849]

Heaven has always blessed me with some generous tender friend; fervently I acknowledge that beneficence. Those whom I have once loved have rarely failed me, and I hope to love them eternally.

Your letter was dated *5th September*. I wish I had received it then; that was the birthday of my little boy; and I had instead the letter of the London publishers, which indeed I had foreseen from previous advices, or rather perhaps from a feeling of fate. It has been my fate that when I worked for others I could always succeed; when I tried to keep the least thing for myself, it was not permitted. Must this schooling be life-long? But let us not always be thinking of my fate; indeed, I hope never to say so much about it again—but tell me of yours.

MsCfr (MB: Ms. Am. 1450 [171]); MsCfr (MH:bMS Am 1280 [111, p. 210]). Published in part in *JMN*, 11:492.

852. To Edgar T. Welby

Perugia
21st Septr 1849.

Dear Sir

I wrote some days ago to Mr Cass asking, if he would inquire if there were" letters for me at the bank; in case he came for a day or two to Perugia. But I hear nothing from him and think perhaps he was not in Rome. Will you now have the kindness to send whatever may be in your care for me to Maquay and Pakenham Florence and also to transfer whatever balance remains for" me, after settling our account up to this time, to them. All letters that come in future may be forwarded there, as I shall probably remain some months but it must be to another name as I now write myself

M. OSSOLI

P. S.

I go upon the supposition that Mr Welby knows my unhappy handwriting, perhaps I ought to sign late

MARGARET FULLER.

ALS (MH:fMS Am 1086 [9:175]).
inquire if there were] inquire ⟨for⟩ ↑ if there were ↓
remains for] remains ⟨to⟩ for

853. To Lewis Cass, Jr.

Florence, 30 Sept. 49

I am very sorry you could not come to Perugia—it was so pleasant there. The pure mountain air was a perfect elixir; the walks are so beautiful on every side, and there is so much to see which excites generous and consoling feelings. I think the works of the umbrian school are never well seen except in their home—they suffer by comparison with works more full in coloring, more genial, more full of common life. The depth and tenderness of their expression is lost on the observer, stimulated to a point out of their range. Now I could prize them. We went every morning to some church rich in pictures, returning at noon for breakfast. After breakfast we went into the country, or to sit and read under the trees near St Pietro, as you will do, if you stay in Perugia. Thus I read "Nicolo Di' Lapi," a book unenlivened by a spark of genius; but it interested me as illustrating Florence.[1]

Our little boy gained strength rapidly, there; every day he was able to go out with us more; he is now full of life and gaiety. We hope he will live and grow into a strong man yet.

Our journey here was delightful; it is the first time I have seen Tuscany when the purple grape hangs garlanded from tree to tree. We were in the first days of the vintage; the fields were animated by men and women, some of the latter with such pretty little bare feet, and shy soft eyes under the round straw hat! They were beginning to cut, but had not done enough to spoil any of the beauty.

Here too I feel better pleased than ever before. Florence seems so cheerful and busy after ruined Rome. I feel as if I could forget the disasters of the day for awhile in looking on the treasures she inherits—

MsCfr (MH:fMS Am 1086 [9:236]). Published in part in *Memoirs*, 2:303–4.

1. Massimo Tapparelli, marchese d'Azeglio (1798–1866), a Piedmontese statesman, was a painter, a novelist, and Manzoni's son-in-law. His second novel, *Niccolò de' Lapi* (Milan, 1841), was set in sixteenth-century Florence.

854. To [?]

[ca. Autumn 1849]

our little boy wakes, he always beckons and cries to come into our room. He draws the curtains himself with his little dimpled hand; he laughs, he crows, he dances in the nurse's arms, he shows his four teeth, he blows like the bellows, pretends to snuff candles, and then having shown off all his accomplishments, calls for his playthings. With these he will amuse himself on the floor while we are dressing, sometimes an hour after. Then he goes to the window to hear the Austrian drums, to which he keeps time, with head and hand. It is soon eleven, and he sleeps again. Then I employ myself—When he wakes, we go out to some church or picture gallery or museum, almost always taking him.

MsCfr (MB: Ms. Am. 1450 [170a]). Published entire in Higginson, *MFO*, p. 270.

855. To Elizabeth Hoar?

[ca. Autumn 1849]
Never blame him for ills I may have to undergo; all that he could he has done for me, all that he had has given. When we look on the sweet face of our child, we think if we can keep him, we shall have courage for whatever we may have to do or endure—

MsCfr (MB: Ms. Am. 1450 [83]).

856. To William H. Channing?

[ca. Autumn 1849]
she will not live to bear a great deal; and, (it may be merely from a habit of feeling, formed in those past years of ill health,) I cannot realise that I shall be here long either, though I feel perfectly willing now to stay my three-score years, if it be thought I need so much tuition from this planet.

MsCfr (MB: Ms. Am. 1450 [109, 110]). Published in part in *Memoirs*, 2:337, and Miller, p. 316.

857.   To Lewis Cass, Jr.

Florence 4 Oct. 1849.

To Mr. Cass—

The Police talk of sending us away out of Tuscany. Because Ossoli has an American passport they have taken the impression that he was obliged to fly from Rome. In vain have we made them observe, that, at that moment of confusion, it was natural to take such, I being an American; that we lived two months undisturbed under the Pontifical Authorities at Perugia. They insist on fresh papers for Ossoli as a Roman, by the Tuscan authorities in Rome, or they will not let us stay. To go would be to us a source of great pain and annoyance. Indeed we know not where to go, and have not yet the money to go with, especially as we should have to pay for the apartment here taken for six months, we having entertained no doubt we could stay, and the Police only yesterday beginning thus to harass us.

MsCfr (MB: Ms. Am. 1450 [32]).

858.   To Lewis Cass, Jr.

Florence
8 Octr 1849.

Dear Mr Cass,

Yesterday I recd your letter of the 5th and today that of the 7th. I thank you very much and hope your interposition will put an end to our troubles. I should feel sure of it, but for the bitter malevolence shown by the director in this department of the Police. I suppose he is one of those who were chased away and are now anxious to revenge themselves on all they suspect to have had the least share in the democratic movement. Mr Horatio Greenough has shown the kindest sympathy here; he has seen the Duke of Casigliano whom he personally knows.[1] And at his request to day presents a memorial as to the facts which he thinks will be favorably recd. I hope this, with the letter you have[n] induced the Tuscan Consul to write, will be sufficient, if not, we shall beg for further delay as you advise.[2] Mr Ombressi is not considered by the Amessio as a sufficient agent, not being really and regularly Consul here but Mr Gammage, named Consul General for Tuscany, is daily expected.[3]

I feel afraid the exertion you made for me may have hurt you; how very sorry I am you were detained in Rome so as to take the fever; be very careful or it will hang upon you during the winter. How very sad that you were ill there all alone! Is not a change of air generally considered the best means of breaking up the remains of fever, and, if so, and we stay, will you not come here, so soon as you are strong enough. The air seems at this season[n] delightfully pure and animating; it is a great relief after the heavy depressing atmosphere of Rome. You could take some cheerful lodging where it flows free, and when you get better you will enjoy going on horseback to the heights and that would do you good. The Amern society is composed at present only of three or four families, but they are good and pleasant people. My friend, Mrs Black, is also here in a delightful house. Do come, as soon as you are able, do not stay constantly in Rome; it is not a climate which one of our race can live in constantly with impunity. And I want to see and talk with you! Think a little of that.

I am not at liberty to name the person from whom I heard about the passports, but if you have given only three and in that guarded way it is impossible you should be subjected to annoyance. Only as I think the remarks were occasioned by some foolishness of Bonaparte in London about his having from you an Amern passport, it might be well to possess some friend, who acts for you [n]ear the govt in U. S., with the exact facts, not doing any thing yourself, only that such a friend, if he hears misrepresentation may contradict it.[4] When I said *ill-willers*, I meant no more than by way of party opposition, to yr father[n] or wanting your place for themselves for I never heard that personally you have enemies and certainly think you ought not.[5] Pray write soon again to tell me how you are, but only a line; don't fatigue yourself to make a letter for me or others, relapse from the fever is very bad. I feel grieved you have not some friend with you to watch that you do not over-exert yourself. With[n] affece good-wishes that all may go well at any rate yours

M. O.

ALS (MH:fMS Am 1086 [9:165]); MsC (MH: fMS Am 1086 [Works, 1:347–51]). *Addressed:* Mr Cass / Chargé d' Affaires des / Etats Unis d' Amerique / Rome. *Postmarks:* Fierenzi 8 Ott. 1849; Roma 10 Ott. 49.

letter you have] letter ⟨you have⟩ ↑ you have ↓
seems at this season] seems ↑ at this season ↓
opposition to yr father,] opposition, ↑ to yr father ↓
yourself. With] yourself. ⟨Most⟩ With

1. Andrea Corsini (1804–68), duke of Casigliano, was the son of Prince Tommaso Corsini. The duke was nominated for the Tuscan senate in 1848 and became minister

of foreign affairs upon the return of the grand duke in 1849 (Vittorio Spreti, *Enciclopedia storico–nobiliare italiana* [Milan, 1928], 2:554).

2. James Ombrosi (1777?–1852), a Tuscan lawyer, was the first United States consul at Florence, but he was not recognized by the Florentine government (Greenough, *Letters*, p. 26; Stock, *Consular Relations*, p. 9).

3. Edward Gamage (d. 1853), son of Samuel and Mary Ellise Gamage, had been named consul for both Leghorn and Florence on 27 June 1849 (*South Carolina Historical Magazine* 59 [1958]: 115; 67 [1966]: 157; Arabella L. G. Morton, *Descendants of John Gamage of Ipswich, Massachusetts* [Worcester, 1906], p. 24).

4. In a dispatch of 20 September 1849 to Secretary of State John Clayton, Cass denied having issued a passport to Prince Carlo Bonaparte. He said Brown had issued passports to a number of Italians immediately after Rome's fall but that "in no instance was the title of American citizen conferred upon a foreigner. The passports were of a simple form, framed, as I understood, especially for the occasion, praying that the holder might be permitted to pass without molestation." Cass had, however, issued "open letters" not only to Bonaparte but to Mazzini and General Giuseppe Avezzana (Stock, *United States Ministers*, p. 59).

5. Lewis Cass, Sr. (1782–1866), had been a soldier, governor of the Michigan territory, minister to France, and senator. An expansionist Democrat, he was the party's presidential nominee in 1848. Like Daniel Webster, Cass placed union over his antislavery sentiments, thus positioning himself between the more active extremes that had been created by acquisition of the former Mexican territories (*DAB*; Frank B. Woodford, *Lewis Cass* [New Brunswick, N.J., 1950], pp. 272–75).

859. To Costanza Arconati Visconti

[I]Florence 16 Oct 49

My loved friend, I read your letter with greatest content.[1] I did not know but there might seem something offensively strange in the circumstances I mentioned to you. Goethe says, there is nothing men pardon so little as singular conduct for which no reason is given; and remembering this, I have been a little surprised at the even increased warmth of interest with which the little American society of Florence has received me, with the unexpected accessories of husband and child, asking no questions, and seemingly content to find me so. With you I indeed thought it would be so, because you are above the world; only, as you have always walked in the beaten path, though with noble port and feet undefiled, yet I thought you might not like your friends to be running about in these blind alleys. It glads my heart indeed that you do not care and we may meet in love.

You speak of our children. Ah, dear friend, I do, indeed, feel we shall have deep sympathy there. I do not believe mine will be a brilliant child, like Gian Martino.[2] Indeed, I see nothing particular about him, yet he is to me a source of ineffable joys, far purer, deeper than any thing I ever felt before, like what Nature had sometimes given, but more intimate, more sweet. He loves me very much, his little heart clings to mine. I trust, if he lives to sow there no seeds which are not good, to be always growing better for his sake. His father, too, will be a good father. He has very little of what is called intellectual development, but unspoiled instincts, affections pure and constant, a quiet sense of duty, which to me, who have seen much of the great faults in characters of enthusiasm and genius, seems of highest value.

[II] When you write by post, please direct *Marchesa Ossoli*, as all the letters come to that address. I might lose yours without it. I did not explain myself on that point. The fact is, it seems to me silly for a radical like me, to be carrying a title; and yet, while Ossoli is in his native land, it seems disjoining myself from him not to bear it. You spoke of my always addressing you in form: now for you, it seems appropriate, and, though the least of your honors, it would pain me to have it omitted. You were born so. You are really the lady of large lands; you and your husband both feel the duties that come with position of command, and, I am sure, if you look back with pride to ancestors, it is not, as many do, to lean upon their merits, but to emulate them. For me, it [III] is a sort of thing that does not naturally belong to me, and unsustained by fortune, is but a *souvenir* even for Ossoli. Yet it has seemed to me for him to drop it, an inherited title, would be in some sort to acquiesce in his brothers' disclaiming him, and dropping a right he may possibly wish to maintain for his child. How does it seem to you? I am not very clear about it. If O. dropt the title, it would be a suitable moment in becoming an inhabitant of republican America.

I: MsCfr (MH:fMS Am 1086 [9:232]); II: MsCfr (MH:bMS Am 1280 [111, pp. 19–20]); III: MsCfr (MH:fMS Am 1086 [9:232]). Published entire in *Memoirs*, 2:316–17; published in part in *JMN*, 11:462.

Emerson dates his fragment 6 April 1850, but the contents place the letter at an earlier period, for by April Fuller had made firm plans to leave Italy. She would not then have needed to give mailing directions to Florence.

1. In her letter of 5 October (MH), Arconati Visconti said: "I wish I could give wings to my assurance that I see nothing in your change of state which need alter our relations—On the contrary there will be one more bond between us, since we shall have in common our maternal affections."

2. Giovanni Arconati Visconti (1839–89) became a soldier in the Piedmontese army and was decorated for his valor in the campaign of 1860–61 (*Dizionario del risorgimento nazionale*).

860. To Samuel G. and Anna Barker Ward

Florence
21st Octr 1849.

My dear Sam,

I saw with great pleasure your writing on one of the letters brought by Mr Mozier and opened that one first; it was a disappointment to find only a few lines about the money, though I thank you much for your affectionate thoughtfulness of me which induced your sending that; it was welcome at this period, though I am sorry to need such aid and should not but for the violation of pledges" in those who had not only promised but offered to secure me employment ample for my maintenance in remaining abroad. But I will not stain this brief page with any notice of the bitter cares and disappointments I have been made to suffer at a time when a little peace would have been so precious. Ere reading this you will know that I am married and that my husband is not better situated than myself; indeed worse for he must be for the present separated from his natural friends and career. He will have by and by a little money from the paternal estate, but, in the present condition of the Roman dominion, it is not easy to raise, we may have to wait several years. Every thing has turned against us; we are not disposed to complain amid the desolation of other homes, and the deep griefs the noblest we know are suffering, yet our causes for anxiety are great, the rather as we have a little tender one to care for, and I confess I do not feel much courage when I think of privation for him. I would wish him the shelter of a secure roof, good care and a serene environment in his earliest days. I thought I had loved the children of others as much as I could love a child, but find the thrill far more vital with my own; You may perhaps look for me to say something of my companion and to you I should like to, but it is too difficult; you are among the very few of my friends who I think may be able to see why we can live together, and may appreciate the unspoiled nature and loveliness of his character; he is entirely without what is commonly called culture, educated by a tutor and that tutor an old priest, he knows readin ritin and" rithmetic, but the first I think he never used to go through with a book; nature has been his book; of that some lines he has spelled thoroughly. To me the simplicity, the reality, the great tenderness and refinement of his character make a domestic place in this world and as it is for my heart that he loves me, I hope he may always be able to feel the same, but that is as God pleases. It seems to us now

Samuel Gray Ward. By permission of the Houghton Library, Harvard University.

that, if we were sure of a narrow competency, we could have a good deal of happiness together in what remains of life; however it is not worth-while to trouble too much, life itself is so uncertain; we both had a narrow escape during the seige of Rome; our little one has since been very near death, and now the Cholera is as near as Bolgona.

I will now turn to Anna from whom I have a letter since receiving yours—you speak dear Anna of my not having answered some letter, probably some one has been lost, as many were in the more convulsed days; here five have come to me that have been *perdus* in some corner for more than a year but none was from you; it was I know not how long since I had heard. Now I thank you for this one which gives me the real facts as to your health, Sam's new life &c. I had heard before that you bore your imprisonment beautifully but had been led to fear you would not be able to walk any more, but lose the benefit and joy of free motion entirely as Mrs Spring did when I knew her; you do not say positively, but I infer from your letter it is nothing so, for you talk of climbing the hills with me. Your hills and all objects in America look very far off to me; at times I cannot realize that I shall ever see the old familiar faces again; very dear and lovely they seem in the distance, especially now as in the sad reflux of that great tide of life in which my heart had gone forward with as much force as was left it I have more time to think of lang syne. It makes me weep to think of it; life was so fatiguing then and is so now, beyond my strength; happy are those who have a childhood of play beneath the trees; I hope your little ones will have it in their mountain home, and that if I do not see you or them there we shall meet in Elysium—But perhaps we shall meet in some very different place; I have some vague idea of returning next summer, though ways means and prospects are yet to be discovered. At present we are moored in Florence, I hope till April or May. I wrote to you the day I recd your letter, but before finishing, the Police began to trouble us, and I have been uncertain if we should not have to go away. Now we have permission to stay for two months and I suppose they will make no difficulty about renewing it. So I hope you will write here to Margaret Ossoli, care J. Mozier Esq. Although a green retirement and still country life seem now to me so sweet, I felt glad to hear that Sam is to leave it for a time; it is better to mix often with the struggling suffering crowd; it is a more generous life and culture. Happy those who can alternate the two lives at pleasure. I like to see Dante as he stands here on the wall of the Cathedral[1] Heaven and Hell are in the near view, he touches the walls of Florence. Yet it is not Florence I would have chosen to touch. Florence is a kind of Boston: it has not the poetic greatness of the other Italian cities; it is a place to work and study in; simple life does not seem so great. I feel reconciled[n] to be here now as the place most economical and convenient and where I still have two or three friends. I begin to feel interested again[n] in looking at Art and I like walking on the heights, beside the air agrees with the baby; who seems to grow better every day; still this place will never charm me as have (I do not speak of Rome, which was my *home*) but Venice, Milan Bologna, Brescia in fact almost all Italian towns. The end of my sheet bids me come to an end; you asked me to write a *real* letter. I fear this will give you no satisfaction, if so, pardon dear Anna, so great has been the passion of my life since you knew me, it is difficult to speak. My friends remain in their place I seem to have more clue to their state than they to mine. Across the stream I see them; they look fair and tall, but I must go to them; they cannot come to me. Farewell.

AL (MH:bMS Am 1465 [931]).

pledges] *Here Fuller marked the sheet with an* x *and crosshatched:* I do not refer to Mr Greeley who has always urged me to return.

readin ritin and] readin⟨g⟩ ritin⟨g⟩ and

feel reconciled] feel reconci(i)led

interested again] interested ↑ again ↓

1. A statue of Dante, one of a group of 14 devoted to artists and poets, stands below the pediment of the facade on the Duomo (Santa Maria del Fiore) in Florence (Augusto Conti, *Illustrazione delle sculture e dei mosaici sulla facciata del duomo di firenze* [Florence, 1887], p. 36).

861. To George W. Curtis

Florence
25th Octr 1849.

Dear George

I was just regretting I had not asked you to write when your letter came. I am every day longing to hear from Rome; home-sick for Rome, though I would not, for the world, be there to see her lying shrouded in the trance. *You* cannot dream what life was there during the glorious dream of hope.[1] The weather was all those months the most beautiful, the artistic genius of the people displayed itself at every moment by some refined symbol, some glorious pageant; never in any place or time was every day life so poetical; all others must ever after seem flat and unprofitable. The walks here are beautiful, there are many objects worth sight and study. I am like to have the society of several persons I highly value we both need repose after much pain and to nerve ourselves to encounter many difficulties. Our little boy grows better in the air; all reasons with me to be contented, but oh Rome, *my* Country!

I think you must have the same apartment I occupied at Casa Diez, since you are served by that atrocious Virginia who combines all the faults of French Italian and American servants. Imagine only that when Clough (Cluff was the name) used to establish himself for a poetic moonlight reverie upon the loggia, she used to place herself in the same attitude quite fondly at his side, wringing from even his gentleness the apostrophe of "Brute" Fortunately she goes away now[n] in the eveg. From that loggia I saw day and night how went the battle. I am glad the Diez have nobody in their house, though they treated me well; they were so delighted when the French entered

I dont understand how it is there are duplicates of these papers, if they are all from Paris: are they all Democratics? I long to see them.

I have exchanged visits with the Brownings, like Mr B. already very much and expect to like her, though she seems too gentle and faded at first sight to excite positive feeling of any kind. They have the prettiest little baby; it is so fat and laughing and violet eyed; it looks as if it was created fresh after a flood, and could not be the child of two people who had written books and such thoughtful sad books too.[2] They were full of serious regret at not seeing you. Browning seems to have taken a fervent interest in the Italn revolution, but feels the greatest contempt for the Florentines.

The Barberina has called and we have been to dine with her in her garden house a very pleasant time we had she often wishing that you and Quincy were there, wishes which Fanny *loudly* echoed.[3] Indee[d] tis pity you could not have staid a wh[ile] longer; though Rome is better, infinitely better, but still to have both! The Barber left a pretty little picture of himself in that little Florence, though I dont think she will turn out very good. The birds of the first nest are no cuckoo-brood, but have the right May-voice, clear and strong.

As I was coming past the Duomo the other day at set of sun, I saw a pale, erect, narrow little figure, which made all my nerves tingle with old associations. This was explained by his accosting me and naming himself as Horace Sumner.[4] Imagine Brook Farm walking the streets of Florence; every body turned to look at him Ossoli who had not understood what he said thought he was some insane person and kept touching my arm for me to stop somewhere, while I was listening with

George William Curtis. Courtesy of the Library of Congress.

a sort of pleasure to the echo of the old pastoral masquerade, or masquerade pastoral. He "had been walking into the country to see the green" (being just come from Mata), he "reads Cowper in his room at e'en." He has since been to see me and talked of Mr Power and asked if Greenough was not a sculptor. He also[n] mourns not to see you and Quincy. Where has he been living Is it a dream or did I hear he was married to Cornelia Hall?[5] He seems as if something strange perhaps sad had happened to him and inspires me with a friendly wish to serve, but I should like to know something about him. Adieu; write again, if you can spare a half hour. My love to Quincy. Ossoli salutes you both in all friendship; he would like to have seen you more. Tell Mr Cass I expect him at Florence and will take him, if he will only come, to the attic window of the Convent at St Miriato, from which the ideal Florence may be seen Affecy your friend

M.—

Mr Cass knows two ladies famed in the Roman scandalous chronicle great possidenti they are too in the Duchy of Spolito, Countesses Pianciani, perhaps he will present you; they might be worth knowing to one who has a curiosity to see that sort of thing.[6] For my part, mine was easily satisfied I found troubled water no deeper, because you could not count the pebbles at the bottom.

ALS (MHarF). *Addressed:* Mr George Curtis / Packenham Hooker & Co / 20 Piazza di Spagna / Rome. *Postmark:* Firenzi 26 Otr 48. *Endorsed:* M. Fuller / Florence Oct 25. / Rome—Oct 28 49.

away now] away ↑ now ↓
He also] He ↑ also ↓

1. Curtis, who was unsympathetic to the revolution, had spent the months during the war in Germany, Switzerland, and Paris (Milne, *George William Curtis*, pp. 38–48).

2. Robert Wiedeman Barrett Browning (1849–1912) had been born on March 9. Called "Pen" or "Penini," Browning studied at Oxford but did not take a degree. He became a painter and sculptor (Gertrude Reese, "Robert Browning and His Son," *PMLA* 61 [1946]: 784–803).

3. Quincy Adams Shaw (1825–1908), Frank Shaw's younger brother, was in Europe with Curtis. A Harvard graduate in 1845, Shaw accompanied Francis Parkman on his Oregon Trail expedition, organized the Calumet and Hecla mining company and was, at his death, said to be the wealthiest man in New England. In 1860 he married Pauline Agassiz (1841–1917), daughter of Louis Agassiz, the geologist (Harvard archives; MVR 1917 1:132). Curtis and Shaw met first in Paris and again in Geneva in the summer of 1849 (Milne, *George William Curtis*, pp. 47–48).

4. Horace Sumner (1824–50), Charles Sumner's brother, sailed with the Ossolis on the *Elizabeth* and died in the wreck (*NEHGR* 8 [1854]: 128k).

5. Cornelia Romana Hall (1807–83), eighth child of James and Catharine Davis Hall of Medford, had boarded at Brook Farm, where she gave "remarkable dramatic readings." On 12 December 1847 she married Henry Sumner (1815?–52), not Horace, who never married (David Brainard Hall, *The Halls of New England: Genealogical and*

Biographical [Albany, 1883], p. 324; Lindsay Swift, *Brook Farm* [New York, 1900], p. 59; *NEHGR* 6 [1852]: 310; Suffolk probate, no. 69859).

6. Fuller's reference is unclear. The Pianciani family had one nobleman who was active in the Italian cause: Luigi Pianciani (1810–90), son of Count Vincenzo and Amalia, princess Ruspoli Pianciani, had been a conspirator against the pope, a member of the Costituente, and a disciple of Mazzini (Salvatore Fratellini, *Spoleto nel risorgimento nazionale* [Spoleto, 1910], pp. 53–55; *Annuario della nobiltà italiana*, p. 418). He appears to have had no sisters.

862.   To Samuel G. Ward

31st Octr, [1849]

My dear Sam,

This morng I receive your letter of the 9th, thank you for writing at once and with such true sympathy. I will now send the inclosed which I have been keeping with the idea of making up a parcel for America, but many interruptions prevent. I am glad I have kept it thus long, for now I feel better than when it was written; when I am suffering it is always somewhat exaggerated by the feeling of fatigue I mentioned to Anna. I had so much fatigue of soul, even in childhood, I have more need of repose and light than would otherwise be natural, however a few good days always recruit me," so that no one that sees me would imagine I had ever had any care; it is only I who inly feel the trembling of the chord. Ossoli is a good companion to me here he has suffered enough to understand what I feel, at the same time his disposition is so gentle and I may say in the strictest sense so pious, that it reacts easily. We have been very happy these last days in going to the churches, and on the sunny heights near Florence; we can always be happy together when there is not too much to disturb us. I feel now like studying more in detail objects around me. Mr Mozier has a plan for trying to get me an adequate compensation for a series of Letters from Florence. should he succeed in this we may stay here longer than originally proposed. I should like it much, for it would be a *natural* way for me to earn money. Without" a great deal of exercise and life in the open air I am the slave of headach, but if, after the morning care of my baby, and an hour's study we went out and at the end of our walk, saw with care and love something good, then I gave the later hours of the eveg to writing some remarks upon it;" it would suit us exactly and be the amount of exertion my mind requires and health will bear. But I hardly dare hope any plan will succeed; so many have failed. Should it we shall live pleasantly here with a few

friends. Mr Mozier I like much, the Mrs Greenough are very agreeable. There is an English family who love me much and the husband
a really accomplished scholarly man. I like Mr and Mrs Browning extremely, and a dear and (as a companion) most highly prized) friend
whom perhaps I have mentioned to you, Madame Arconati is to pass
the winter here. With all these persons I am on a footing so sincere
that I can associate with them and not transgress the bounds of that
rigid economy we must observe. I have now filled the sheet write
again, dear Sam, and more words if you can. I know so very little, except by divination of your life for a long time past. When you are in
N. Y. do me the pleasure of visiting the studio of Hicks and seeing
him, if you can. I have loved him very much; we have been very intimate; I should like to have you see him; perhaps an acquaintance will
spring up; in his soul is real greatness; his life has been a battle but
waged on his side with great calmness; I will not say more; you will
see him for your self. Ossoli salutes and thanks you; if you please ask
M. Channing to show you the daguerrotype of Ossoli.[1] Ever affecty

M.

ALS (MH:bMS Am 1465 [932]). *Addressed:* S. G Ward / Care T. W. Ward Esq / Boston, Mass / U. S. A. *Postmarks:* Sard 8 Nov 49 Pont US-B; Firenzi 1849; Bureau Maritime 9 Nov 49 Havre. *Endorsed* 1849 / S. M. Fuller / Octr. 21.

recruit me,] recruit⟨s⟩ me,
money. Without] money. ⟨w⟩ Without
writing some remarks upon it;] writing ↑ some remarks upon it ↓ ;

1. Mary Channing, daughter of Dr. William Ellery Channing, had known Fuller
since their youth.

863.   To Emelyn Story

[ca. November 1849]
talk with Mrs. S. Today we have been out to the casa di Ogli and
found its little chapel full of contadine (their lovers were waiting outside the door); they looked charming in their black veils, their straw
hat was worn to the door and then hung on the arm with shy glancing
eyes and cheeks pinched rosy by the cold. For it is cold here as N England. On foot we have explored a great part of the environs, before
I had no idea of their beauty. When here with the Springs I took only
the regular drives, as prescribed for all ladies and gentlemen that

travel. This evening we came home by a path that led to the banks of the Arno; the dome, the snowy mountains, were glorious in the rosy tint and haze just before sunset. What a difference it makes to come home to a child; how it fills up all the gaps of life, just in the way that is most consoling, most refreshing. I used to feel sad at that time; the day had not been nobly spent, I had not done my duty to myself and others; then I felt so lonely, now I never feel lonely, for even if my little boy dies, our souls will remain eternally united. then I feel *infinite* hope for him, hope that he will serve God and man more loyally than I have and seeing how full he is of life, how much he can afford to throw away, I feel the inexhaustableness of nature and console myself for my own incapac[   ]

I see Mr and Mrs Browning often, but Mrs B. will not be able to go out any more, being again *enceinte*, their baby is surpassingly pretty.[1] Our intercourse as yet has not amounted to much, being taken too much in snatches. She seems to me just as you described her. Mr B. is entertaining, very cordial in his manner, but my intercourse with him I find singularly external. I know not that I ever had such with any person of substance. They speak of you both with very great partiality (let not that word read as equivoque) and desire to be commended unto you.

Madame Arconati is near me; we have had some hours of great content together, but in the last weeks her only child has been dangerously ill. I have no other acquaintance except in the American Circle, and should not care to make any unless singularly desirable, for I want all my time for the care of my child, for my walks and visits to objects of art, in which again I can find pleasure, and in the evening for study and writing. Ossoli is forming some taste for books, which I never expected, also he is studying English. He learns it of Horace Sumner to whom he teaches Italian in turn.

MsCfr (MH:fMS Am 1086 [9:230]);MsCfr (MH:fMS Am 1086 [Works, 1:325–29]). Published in part in *Memoirs*, 2:304.

1. The pregnancy ended in a miscarriage late in October, though the Brownings were not convinced of the fact until sometime late in 1849 or early in 1850 (*The Letters of Elizabeth Barrett Browning to Mary Russell Mitford, 1836–1854*, ed. Meredith B. Raymond and Mary Rose Sullivan [Winfield, Kan., 1983], 3:83, 296). Like others, Elizabeth Browning was surprised at the Ossolis' marriage: "The American authoress Miss Fuller, with whom we had had some slight intercourse by letter, & who has been at Rome during the siege, as a devoted friend of the republicans & a meritorious attendant on the hospitals, has taken us by surprise at Florence, .. retiring from the Roman field with a husband & child above a year old!—Nobody had even suspected a word of this underplot, & her American friends stood in mute astonishment before this apparition of them here" (ibid., p. 285).

864. To Miss Erbeau

Casa Libri—
8th Novr 49.

Dear Miss Erbeau
  I hope if the day is good, you will come and see me next Sunday morng.

M. OSSOLI.

ALS (ViU). *Addressed:* Miss Erbeau. *Endorsed:* Mme Ossoli.

865. To Sarah Ann Clarke

Florence
Eveg of 18th Novr
1849.

My dearest Sarah,
  Since the reception of yours by Mr Mozier, I have been constantly wishing to write, but entire uncertainty about my prospects has prevented. Now having unexpectedly oppy by an Amern going direct tomorrow morng I will write as well as I can, it must be only about yr coming to Europe not a superfluous word. As to *Peace*; it is quite uncertain, yet there is perhaps more likelihood of the stillness that wears its guise than later; the poor patient, is in a languor or swoon, after his blood-letting and agony struggle it seems he cannot have strength to rise again directly.[1] Sarah and William may have time to gaze on him meanwhile and perhaps he may not lie so still again while they do live on earth down here.[2] As to where I shall be. If I can; that is if we have any money, and the Police lets us as I think it will[n] I shall stay in Florence till June, later I yet see not decidedly. If you would arrive in March, you could be with me two months, you could even take an apartment with me, it would[n] be more economical for you; we would see to all your affairs the first days, you could practise Italian with us, and I would tell you all I could that would be useful to you.[3] I should like to do all I could for my dear Sarah, and should like to have some peaceful hours in Italy with her, but my guardian Angel, in fitting me out for the voyage of life forgot the purse and that is always impeding the plan of my travels. If you would come to Italy at any rate, it would

be worth trying to have these days with me. How I wish you had come this autumn. I should have written as soon as I could after leaving Rome and the distress that followed, but they sent me word you would sail at any rate in August. I did not think you could get a letter. Now write to William and see if we shall meet in Italy at all. Come in March, if you come in Spring they say the spring is so beautiful in Florence. The letter is snatched from ever your

MARGARET

direct to me Care of J. Mozier.

ALS (NjP). *Addressed:* Miss Sarah Clarke / Care Rev J. F. Clarke / Boston / Mass. / USA. *Postmark:* Boston 31 Dec 2.

money, and the Police lets us as I think it will] money, ↑ and the Police lets us as I think it will ↓

it would] it ⟨might⟩ ↑ would ↓

1. In her letter of 29 July (MH), Clarke said that she was not yet coming to Italy: "as I shall never cross the ocean but once I do not wish to go till peace prevails & I can go where I please."

2. William Clarke, Sarah's brother, whom Fuller knew well and with whom she corresponded.

3. In her reply of 5 March 1850 (MH), Sarah admitted that she had never learned Italian: "your exhortations about learning to speak & write Italian have all been thrown away—I have rather calculated I run upon making you my mouthpiece as I have often done before—However if we do not lose the use of our eyes through extreme old age I shall be contented to be dumb or make signs for food & fire."

866. To [?]

Florence, Casa Libri, Piazza Maria Novella
evening of 29th Nov., 1849.

It is an evening of cold, statue-like moonlight, such as we have in New England, such as I do not remember in all my life of Italy. That light falls most holy on the Bride of Michael Angelo,—the church to be near which I live in this piazza,—and great has been the delight of looking at it, and its background of mountains, every morning and evening. [   ] I crossed the river for my afternoon walk, to see Mr. and Mrs. Browning. They have a beautiful little baby, two or three months younger than mine, so we have this in common with so many other sympathies. [   ]

Now Ossoli is gone out, and I am alone in my little room, beside a bright fire. I have your letter before me, and I am thinking how much I wish for you instead. Though your letter is very dear, and does me good, you are one of the persons I have wished so much might know about me without being told. I have thought a great deal about you, and things you used to tell me, and remembered little traits and pictures of your children that would surprise you. How pleasant it would be to talk over all these now and here; for you are quite right, it is in Italy we should have met. [   ] I wish I did know how to write to you about myself, but it is exceedingly difficult. I have lived in a much more full and true way than was possible in our country, and each day has been so rich in joys and pains, actions and sufferings, to say nothing of themes of observation, I have never yet had time to know the sum total—to reflect. My strength has been taxed to the uttermost to live. I have been deeply humiliated finding myself inferior to many noble occasions, but precious lessons have been given, and made me somewhat better, I think, than when you knew me. My relation to Ossoli has been like retiring to one of those gentle, lovely places in the woods—something of the violet has been breathed into my life, and will never pass away. It troubles me to think of going to America. I fear he will grow melancholy-eyed and pale there, and indeed nothing can be more unfit and ill-fated outwardly than all the externals of our relation. I can only hope that true tenderness will soothe some of them away. I have, however, no regrets; we acted as seemed best at the time. If we can find a shelter for our little one, and tend him together, life will be very precious amid very uncongenial circumstances. I thought I knew before what is the mother's heart, I had felt so much love that seemed so holy and soft, that longed to purify, to protect, to solace *infinitely*; but it was nothing to what I feel now, and that sense for pure nature, for the eager, spontaneous life of childhood, was very partial in me before. My little one seems nothing remarkable. I have no special visions about him; but to be with him, to take care of and play with him, gives me such delight, and does me so much good, that it is only now I feel poverty a great evil, that it is to disturb me in these days, fetter me with toils for which I do not feel inclined, and harass with care the purest feelings of my life. Should I succeed in cutting my way through the thorns, and stand in a clear place at last, I shall be tired out and aged perhaps, or my little one will be dead. This last seems to me very probable, for Heaven has thus far always reclaimed the children I most loved. You ask my plans: they are very unsettled; there is no chance that we can return to Rome, or Ossoli get anything from a little property he has there, at present. I had a promise of employment here, but the promiser seems to have forgotten it. I suppose I will have to return to the U. S. I want to see my mother, and some of you, my dear ones; and if we had a little money and could live in obscure quiet, I should not be sorry to leave Italy till she has strength to rise again, and stay several years in America. I should like to refresh my sympathy with her great interests and great hopes. I should like to do anything I could for people there; but to go into the market, and hire myself out, will be hard as it never was before: my mind has been very high-wrought, and requires just the peace and gradual renovation it would find in still, domestic life. I hardly know how I am to get there, either; even in the most economical way, direct from Leghorn or Genoa, is two hundred dollars for us both. I am very sick, and suffer extremely in the head at sea. I suppose it would be worse with these poor accommodations than it was in the steamer, and Ossoli is untried. We cannot afford to take a servant, and what would become of the baby if we were both sick? [   ] I never think of the voyage without fearing the baby will die in it. [   ] These things look formidable in the distance, however they may diminish nearer.

ELfr, from *Century* n.s. 23 (1893): 930–31.

867.   To Emelyn Story

Florence. 30th Nov. 1849.

Dear Emelyn,

I am grieved indeed that after coming so near, you have turned from us again.[1] May it be better for you! for me I am very sorry.

Thanks for the true affection that breathes in your letter. I most warmly prize it and hope it will prove a life-long treasure to me, and that mine may sometimes have beneficient power towards you and yours.

Thus far my friends have received news, that must have been an unpleasant surprize to them, in a way that, à moi, does them great honor.[2] None have shown littleness or displeasure at wanting my confidence while they were giving theirs. Many have expressed the warmest sympathy, and only one has shown a disposition to transgress the limit I myself had marked and to ask questions, with her, I think, it was because she was annoyed by things people said and wanted to be able to answer them. I replied to her that I had communicated already all I intended to and should not go into detail as to the past that when unkind things were said about me, she should let them pass. You, dear E do the same. I am sure your affection for me will prompt you to add, that you feel confident whatever I have done has been in a good spirit and not contrary to *my* ideas of right; for the rest, you will not admit for me, as I do not for myself, the rights of the social inquisition of the U. S. to know all the details of my affairs. If my mother is content, if Ossoli and I are content, if our child when grown up is content, that is enough. You and I know enough of the U. S. to be sure that many persons there will blame whatever is peculiar, the lower persons everywhere, are sure to think that whatever is mysterious must be bad, but I think there will remain for me a sufficient number of friends to keep my heart warm and help me to earn my bread; that is all that is of any consequence. Ossoli seems to me more lovely and good every day; our darling child is well now and every day more gay and playful, for his sake I shall have courage and I hope some good Angel will show us the way out of our external difficulties.

I must keep the wet-nurse for the baby till Spring; we dispense with all other service, except a little daily from a donna di faccende but her we must pay and maintain well. I have taken Isabella, Mr. Mozier's only child, to study with me.[3] I regret very much that I may have to take some money for this as all I could do to serve him in this way would be inadequate compensation for his active and steady interest for me, but, if other plans fail, I shall take a little probably sufficient, to eke out the bread and salt and coffee till April, beyond that I do not yet look.

And now to turn to more pleasing themes or less *un*pleasing shall I say? There is some strange gap in my knowledge about you. I never received any letter after the first you wrote from Interlaken. Hooker has forwarded me none of late, all I have known till this from Venice has been through Mrs. Henry Greenough.[4] I like her sense of what is humorous, I like her loyalty. *Nous verrons.*

A great lesson against hasty judgments I received as to Mr Clough (Cluff is his name) who turned out so well as to tongue, pen and soul, so generous, tender, and advanced in thought.

I heard indirectly that Jane had sent a letter for me to your care;[5] is that inclosed with any you have sent me?

MsCfr (MH:fMS Am 1086 [9:226]); MsCfr (MH:fMS Am 1086 [Works, 1:253–57]). Published in part in *Memoirs*, 2:312–13, and Miller, p. 301.

1. The Storys had gone to Venice.
2. According to Story, Fuller told her of her marriage and motherhood during the Roman siege (*Memoirs*, 2:289). It is clear from Fuller's letter to William Story of 2 December 1849 that he had not known what his wife knew. A letter from Thomas Wetmore to Emelyn of 25 November 1849 (TxU) shows that he, too, had not known the facts until then.
3. Isabella Mozier (1836–1923) married James Lenox Banks (1832–83) (James Lenox Banks, *Genealogical Notes Concerning the Banks and Allied Families* [New York, 1938], pp. 20, 39).
4. Frances Boott (1809–97), daughter of Francis Boott, married Henry Greenough (1807–83) in 1837. Henry Greenough, Horatio's brother, was a painter and architect (Cambridge VR; Mt. Auburn records; *DAB*).
5. Jane Tuckerman King.

868. To William Wetmore Story

Florence. 2nd Dec. 1849

Dear William,

It was like you to receive with such kindness the news of my marriage.[1] A less generous person would have been displeased, that when we had been drawn so together, when we had talked so freely, and you had shown towards me such sweet friendship, I had not told you. Often did I long to do so, but I had for reasons that seemed important, made a law to myself to keep this secret as rigidly as possible, up to a certain moment, that moment came; its decisions were not such as I had hoped, but it left me at least without that painful burden of secret, which I hope never to bear again. Nature keeps so many secrets, that I had supposed the moral writers exaggerated about the dangers and plagues of keeping them, but they cannot exaggerate. All that can be said about mine is that I at least acted out with to me tragic th[o]roughness The wonder, a woman keeps a Secret. All that can be said of my not telling you is that I was keeping the same from my family and dearest friends at home, and had you remained near me a very little later, you would have been the very first person to whom I should have spoken as you would have been the first on [this s]ide the water to whom I should have written had I [known] where to address you. Yet I hardly hoped your sympathy dear William. I am very glad if I have it.

May brotherly love ever be returned unto you in like measure. Ossoli desires his love and respect to be testified to you both.[2] Should he meet you sometime in our land I doubt not the light of your eye will be consoling to him. I feel he will feel very strange and lonely there; indeed I feel much more anxious about his happiness than my own. Still his love for our child is so great and his pleasure in the wood and fields so simple and profound, I hope he will be able to make for himself a life in the unknown country till changes favor return to his own.

That changes must take place very soon within two or three years at farthest, there seems great reason to expect The conducts of the restored authorities is so very injudicious that it cannot be otherwise.

I am just reading Macaulay's new history which seems even more brilliant and fascinating than his previous writings.[3] He says James II was unable to get beyond this one idea "My father made concessions and was beheaded therefore the only safe way for me to do is to make no concessions." The Cardinals are just as stupid. But it is better for one not to write about these matters through the post. I suppose letters are not opened here as the mean espionage is not likely to reach the same he[ight as] in Rome, but cannot feel sure, and we study to give no umbrage, as the Police made difficulty about letting us stay, and the need to move would be a great evil at this moment.

The "*Volkerbund*" I suppose you will be able to see in Germany, and it will give you tidings of what the great disbanded are hoping and trying.[4] I do not expect to see it while here.

I deeply regret you did not decide on coming here this winter; it would have been such a pleasure to me and others to have you, but you would not have found your marble. If I can do anything about it by and by you will let me know, if I could not see about it myself, I might keep alive the interest of some capable person. Mr. Browning and Mr. Henry Greenough both speak in high praise of the statue; do not be too long before you put it into Marble.

I think you will have some opportunity of sending your poems as it is said there is a great tide of travel from Germany into Italy at present. I have been much pleased with Mr Clough's which he sent me and with those of two of his friends Burbidge and Arnold, they are of the Emersonian kind, entirely out of all rule, not of high power, but genuine though imperfect reflexes of the higher life of their writers.[5]

I think you will be amazed when you see the Highland [   ] will be hardly able to believe it written by our timidly [   ] of leading questions.[6] He is indeed spoken of in England as the new man. Mr Browning as was natural in a high professor of the Lyric art was annoyed by the defects in form, while he liked the substance.[7] I scarcely observed them it is so rare now a days to come so near in contact with the living soul as you may in some of these.

When you go to London do call on Mr. C. He is superior of University Hall Garden Square. Through him you will no doubt come in[n] contact with young men really alive like the best of us in America. Adieu, dear William. If you sometimes write me a little about what you are observing and doing I shall be very glad, but make no claims knowing well how thronged these European days are with claims and fascinations. I trust a solid friendship has now been founded which will last through our lives and that every now and then we shall meet and exchange some cordial words. I count it among the gains of these years to subscribe myself with grateful and hopeful affection Your friend

MARGARET.

MsC (MH:fMS Am 1086 [9:227]); MsC (MH:fMS Am 1086 [Works, 1:259–65]). Published in Wade, pp. 584–86; published in part in *Memoirs*, 2:313–14, and Miller, pp. 302–3.

come in] come in come in

1. In a letter to Caroline Tappan late in December, Fuller says Story found out about her marriage and son at the hotel in Venice. He had at about that time received a letter from George Curtis (TxU) written from Palermo on 26 November 1849:

> But what of Palermo and the East when I tell you that I have seen Margaret Fuller's husband & baby? The latter is some 18 months old. The former some 27 years, I should think. He is a dark-haired, quiet, modest man. He has no appearance of smartness. Does not seem, per esempio, as if he would ever learn to speak English. But he is very simple and affectionate & clings to Margaret with quite a touching confidence & affection.—
>
> The child is heavy & not handsome. But that was caused by a nurse who spite of madonna beauty served the devil & fed its undiscriminating innocence upon red wine instead of white milk.
>
> The Marchesa Ossoli herself seems as always— There was a vein of intense enthusiasm threading with fire her talk about Rome, which was fine & wonderful at the same time.
>
> She expressed great interest & curiosity about you & my lady, asking where you were to be & how she could communicate. She will remain in Florence for the winter, but her farther arrangements are unsettled. Her heart is now too much rooted in Rome, I think, ever to bear a long, never a life-long separation.

2. Story, who knew Ossoli in Rome, visited him on 3 May 1849 at the Roman fortifications during the French attack (William Wetmore Story diary, TxU).

3. Thomas Babington Macaulay had just published his *History of England from the Accession of James II* (London, 1849), in two volumes. A huge success, the work was expanded to four volumes in 1855. His *Lays of Ancient Rome* was published in 1842 (*DNB*).

4. Twelve issues of *Der Völkerbund* were published in Geneva, beginning in 1849 (*Bibliographie der Zeitschriften des Deutschen Sprachgebietes bis 1900*, ed. Joachim Kirchner [Stuttgart, 1977], 2:83).

5. Thomas Burbidge (1816–92) had published *Ambarvalia* with Clough in 1849 (Boase). Matthew Arnold (1822–88) had traveled in Italy and was interested in the revolutionary movement in Rome (*DNB*).

6. Clough's "The Bothie of Toper-na-fuosich," published in November 1848, a narrative poem in hexameters, was attacked by some critics, but it was praised by Thackeray and Charles Kingsley (Clough, *Correspondence*, 1:228).

7. So did Elizabeth Barrett Browning, who said that "The Bothie" was "written in loose and more-than-need-be unmusical hexameters, but full of vigour and freshness" (*The Letters of Elizabeth Barrett Browning*, ed. Frederic G. Kenyon [New York, 1897], 1:429).

869.   To Elizabeth Barrett Browning

Casa Libri
Thursday 6th Decr [1849]

Dear Mrs Browning,

Thanks for sending me the names. I find I had already the same cap pattern, but it looked so pretty on your baby's head I did not recognize it.

I am very sorry the nurse did not come upstairs with him; if you send her again will you tell her to do so, that he may exchange a few looks with mine. I think babies seem amazed at one another, they are not in haste to make acquaintance, probably they still feel what a world lies hidden in each person, they are not not yet made callous by those habits" of hasty unfeeling intercourse soon formed by what is called society.

It seemed to me when I was last at your house, as if a curtain fell down between us. A great sadness fell upon me, just after Mr Browning came in; it did not seem to come from him; he seemed cheerful and glowing after his walk, but some cause changed suddenly the temper of my soul, so that I could hardly realize what was passing and the cloud did not leave me" for several hours. Did you share any such influence. I think probably it was confined to me, but have noted the day and hour in my diary, in case any interpretation should later be tendered.

Those fragments expressed the almost universal feeling" towards Poe; several women loved him, but it seemed more with passionate illusion which he amused himself by inducing than with sympathy; I think he really had no friend. I did not know him, though I saw and talked with him often, but he always seemed to me shrouded in an assumed character. Still as I did not know him, and do not accept the opinions of others till my own impressions have confirmed them, as I did" know he had much to try his spirit I always treated him cordially.[1] He seemed to feel that *I* was not prejudiced against him; he once said that he had faith in me, that he thought me not only incapable of baseness, but incapable of understanding it; that this was from him a strong expression of esteem, shows what his life had been. He said in a sketch he published of me that he thought me capable of great affection.[2] Now, seeing these bitter waters poured out even upon his tomb, I have remembered these things and regretted that I never tried whether more friendliness from me might have been useful to him; but it is only the millionth time I have let occasions pass where suffering fellow men might have been soothed or helped[3] Pardon that the leaf is soiled. I had not observed it. Ever truly yours

M. Ossoli

ALS (VtMiM). Published in *American Literature* 9 (1937): 70–71. *Addressed:* Mr & Mrs Browning / via Massio.

those habits] those ha⟨f⟩bits
not leave me] not ⟨pass⟩ ↑ leave me ↓
universal feeling] universal ↑ feeling ↓
I did] I ↑ did ↓

1. Though Fuller was wary of Poe's combative criticism, she was evenhanded in her assessment of his strengths and weaknesses as a poet, and she praised his fiction. She found the tales "a refreshment, for they are the fruit of genuine observations and experience." "Even the failures," she said, "are those of an intellect of strong fibre and well-chosen aim" (*New-York Daily Tribune*, 11 July 1845). In her review of *The Raven and Other Poems*, Fuller said that the book indicated "a power to do something far better." She was, however, impressed by "To One in Paradise" (*New-York Daily Tribune*, 26 November 1845). When, however, Fuller wrote on American literature in *Papers on Literature and Art*, she omitted Poe entirely, even from her hasty list of those writers she had no room to discuss in detail.

2. In his fourth *Literati* essay, Poe praised Fuller's attack on Longfellow and her defense of Harro Harring. *Woman in the Nineteenth Century*, he said, "is a book which few women in the country could have written, and no woman in the country would have published, with the exception of Miss Fuller. . . . I need scarcely say that the essay is nervous, forcible, thoughtful, suggestive, brilliant, and to a certain extent scholar-like—for all that Miss Fuller produces is entitled to these epithets." In the final paragraph of the essay, Poe described Fuller's face: "the mouth when in repose indicates profound sensibility, capacity for affection, for love" (*Complete Works of Edgar Allan Poe*, ed. James A. Harrison [New York, 1902], 13:73–83). In his review of Lowell's *A Fable for the Critics*, Poe, bitter at his exclusion from the discussion, called Fuller's essay on American literature a "silly and conceited piece of Transcendentalism" (ibid., 13:169).

3. On 9 October 1849 Rufus Griswold, who acted as Poe's literary executor, published a defamatory article in Greeley's *Tribune*. Griswold maliciously used quotations from Bulwer's *The Caxtons* to describe Poe. When he reprinted the article, Griswold omitted the quotation marks from the passages and presented them as his own. "The damage this article did to Poe's reputation is incalculable" (Arthur Hobson Quinn, *Edgar Allan Poe* [New York, 1969 (1941)], pp. 646–47).

870.   To Ellen Fuller Channing

Florence.
11th Decr 1849

My dear Ellen

I find myself in the novel position of having no less than 3 letters of yours to answer, the one written after your visit to Mother, one by Mr

Mozier (with Napoleon, contribution of 2 dimes from my little loves of the rising generation, their hair and the Daguerrotype) and one a year and a half old which came to light with 3 dollars worth more of the same date tother day. This is the second time of my unexpectedly finding the gaps in correspondence filled up, in consequence of some bankers clerk feeling an unexpected twinge of conscience. I wish the fit would come upon them oftener than once a year. The Daguerro-type is beautiful. Mr Horatio Greenough was delighted with it; he says it is a true picture, another person of fine taste observed that the posi-tion and sentiment of the child are truly Raphaelesque. Several have observed that she looks like my Angelino. I do not see that it is so.

You are anxious, my dear Ellen, to know some details of my past history and I should like to gratify you, but I hardly know how. There are some reasons which I cannot explain, further than by the remark that Ossoli is still a member of the Roman Catholic church, why I do not go into all the matter of fact history. I cannot, at least at present, tell exactly the facts, so I choose to say nothing. I should be glad if he disengaged himself entirely from the Roman ritual, but I doubt he never will; his habitual attachment to it is strong, and I do not trouble myself about it as no priest has any influence over his mind.

About him I do not like to say much, as he is an exceedingly deli-cate person. He is not precisely reserved, but it is not natural to him to *talk* about the objects of strong affection. I am sure he would not try to describe me to his sister, but would rather she would take her own impression of me, and, as much as possible, I wish to do the same by him. I expect that to many of my friends Mr Emerson for one, he will be nothing, and they will not understand that I should have life in common with him. But I do not think he will care; he has not the slightest tinge of self-love; he has throughout our intercourse been used to my having many such ties; he has no wish to be anything to persons with whom he does not feel spontaneously bound, and when I am occupied is happy in himself. But *some* of my friends and my family who will see him in the details of practical life, cannot fail to prize the purity and simple strength of his character, and, should he continue to love me as he has done, to consider his companionship an inestimable blessing to me. I say *if*, because all human affections are frail, and I have experienced too great revulsions in my own not to know it, yet I feel great confidence in the permanence of his love. It has been unblemished so far, under many trials, especially as I have been more sick, desponding and unreasonable in many ways than I ever was before and more so, I hope, than I ever shall be again. But at all such times, he never had a thought except to sustain and cheer me; he is capable of the sacred love, the love passing that of women, he showed it to his father, to Rome, to me, now he loves his child in the same way. I think he will be an excellent father, though he could not speculate about it, or in fact about anything

Our meeting was singular, fateful I may say. Very soon he offered me his hand through life, but I never dreamed I should take it. I loved him and felt very unhappy to leave him, but the connexion seemed so every way unfit, I did not hesitate a moment. He, however, thought I should return to him, as I did. I acted upon a strong impulse. I could not analyze at all what passed in my mind. I neither rejoice nor grieve, for bad or for good I acted out my character Had I never connected myself with any one my path was clear, now it is all hid, but in that case my development must have been partial. As to marriage I think the intercourse of heart and mind may be fully enjoyed without entering in this partnership of daily life, still I do not find it burdensome. We get along very well and I find have our better intercourse as much as if we did not buy (unhappily we have nothing to sell) together. The friction that I have seen mar so much the domestic life of others does not occur with us, or at least has not. Then there is the pleasure of always being at hand to help one another. Still all this I had felt before in some degree. The great novelty, the immense gain to me is my relation with my child. I thought the mother's heart lived in me before, but it did not. I knew nothing about it. Yet before his birth I dreaded it. I thought I should not survive but if I did and my child[n] did, was I not cruel to bring another into this terrible world. I could not at that time get any other view. When he was born that deep melancholy changed at once into rapture, but it did not last long, then came the prudential motherhood, then came Mrs Edgworth, Mrs Smith.[1] I became a coward, a caretaker not only for the morrow, but impiously faithless twenty or thirty years ahead. It seemed very wicked to have brought the little tender thing into the midst of cares and perplexities we had not feared in the least for ourselves. I imagined every thing; he was to be in danger of every enormity the Croats were then committing on the babies of Lombardy. The house would be burned over his head, but if he escaped, how were we to get money to buy his bibs and primers. Then his father was to be killed in the fighting and I t[o] die of [   ]. Your hazarding the opinion dear Ellen, [tha]t it would have been best to tell Mother any part of th[is] till I arrived at some "clearing" however fruitless, and [w]aterless, only shows the impossibility of judging for others in these great trials. I have borne Mother much love, and shown her some, and never more than by standing quite alone, in those strangely darkening days. I grieve she should have suffered now, but that is nothing in comparison with anxiety she might have been made to feel.

During the siege of Rome I could not see my little boy. What I endured at that time in various ways not many would survive. In the burning sun I went every day to wait in the crowd for letters about him Often they did not come. I saw blood that had streamed on the wall close to where Ossoli was. I have here a piece of bomb that burst close to him. I sought solace in tending the suffering men. But when I saw the beautiful fair young men bleeding to death, or mutilated for life, I felt all the wo of all the mothers who had nursed each to that full flower to see it thus cut down. I felt the consolation too for those youths died worthily. I was the Mater Dolorosa, and I remembered that the midwife who helped[n] Angelino into the world came from the sign of the Mater Dolorosa. I thought, even if he lives, if he comes into the world at this great troubled time, terrible with perplexed duties, it may be to die thus at twenty years, one of a glorious hecatomb indeed, but still a sacrifice. It seemed then I was willing he should die But when I really saw him lingering as he did all August 2d and July 1st[n] between life and death, I could not let him go unless I would go with him. When I saw his first smile, his poor wan feeble smile and more than four weeks we watched him night and day before we saw it, new resolution downed in my heart, I resolved to live day by day and hour by hour for his dear sake and feed on ashes when offered. So if he is only treasure lent, if he must go as sweet Waldo did, as my little Pickie, as *my* children do, I shall at least have these days and hours with him. Now he is in the highest health and so gay— We cannot but feel happy in him, though the want of money is so serious a thing. I wish we had a little money, since we *have* lived, or knew better how to earn it. I suppose we shall find ways The governor of the world must have his alms days every now and then; we will eat the charity soup ourselves and buy pap for Nino. If I can but be well, there's the rub, always.

[G]ive love and kisses to the dear children, tell Marnie and Ittie I keep the dimes for Angelino.

He plays a great deal with their hair, talks to it, says *poor*, I hope they may all meet next summer, and Eugene's little one, too. My love to dear Elizh I wish she and Mr Emerson would write to me, but I suppose they dont know what to say Tell them there is no need to say anything about these affairs if they dont want to. I am just the same for them I was before and yr affect sister

M.

ALS (MH:fMS Am 1086 [9:171]); MsCfr (MH:bMS Am 1280 [111, p. 204]); MsCfr (MB: Ms. Am. 1450 [105]. Published in part in *Memoirs*, 2:276–79, 301; Miller, pp. 303–6; *JMN*, 11:491; and Chevigny, pp. 487–89. *Addressed:* Mrs Ellen Channing / Concord near Boston / Massachusetts / United States of N. America. / via Inghilterra / Liverpool Steamer. *Postmarks:* Firenzi 12 Dic 1849; [*illegible*] 19 Dec 49 Font de.—B.; [*illegible*] maritime 20 Dec 49.

and my child] and ⟨it⟩ ⟨he⟩ ↑ my child ↓
who helped] who ⟨bro⟩ helped
August 2d and July 1st] August ↑ 2d ↓ and July ↑ 1st ↓

1. Probably Maria Edgeworth (1767–1849), whose *Parent's Assistant* was published in 6 volumes in 1800, and Elizabeth Oakes Smith (1806–93), who had published a number of books of poems and stories, and who later became a noted feminist lecturer and writer (*DNB; NAW*).

871. To Marcus and Rebecca Buffum Spring

Florence 12 Dec 1849

Dear Marcus and Rebecca

A letter from Mr. Doherty, a notice in the paper of Miss Bremer's visit to the North American Phalanx, undoubtedly made in company with you brings you so forcibly to mind that I must e'en devote the last two hours and the best and quietest ones of the 24 to answering your letters.[1] For I have actually two letters from you to answer and excellent ones likewise—

Your letter, my dear Rebecca, was written in your noblest and most womanly spirit. I thank you warmly for your sympathy about my little boy. What he is to me, even you can hardly dream, you who have three, and in whom the natural thirst of the heart was earlier satisfied can scarcely know what my one ewe lamb is to me. That he may live, that I may find bread for him, that I may not spoil him by overweening love, that I may grow daily better for his sake are the ever recurring thoughts, say prayers, that give their hue to all the current of my life.

Yet in answer to what you say, that it is still better to give the world this living soul than a portion of my life in a printed book; it is true; and yet of my book I could know whether it would be of some worth or not, of my child I must wait to see what his worth will be. I play with him, my ever growing mystery, but from the solemnity of the thoughts he brings, is refuge only in God. Was I worthy to be parent of a soul with its eternal immense capacity of weal and woe. God be merciful to me a sinner comes so naturally to the mother's heart I think.— But I cannot write much about it; we shall meet sometime and see whether it is natural to communicate on these subjects. Meanwhile I doubt not you will feel for my child somewhat of the affectionate [   ] I do about yours. You say you wish I had not left you to hear these things from others and I wish so too, but the fact is never having heard from you of the birth of little Marcus,[2] never any answer to a letter addressed to you in November or December of the past year, under the pressure of heavy care and sorrow, never any line in answer to an effusion of feeling sent you just after Mazzini came to Rome in the spring, I felt as if your friendship to me was, not dead, indeed, but sleeping, and could not resolve to write on a subject so delicate and make my communication to any but hearts that seemed awake in love to mine at that time worn out and sensitive from much suffering. I wrote to Mr Greeley, my soul all opened towards him by the news of his great calamity— mine too it was— for the lost child was infinitely dear to me. I have been sadly disappointed that he should not answer that letter, but life is full of such things, truly hard is the travel to one who has but the "brain-unencompassed by nerves of steel"—[3]

My dear Marcus, your long letter was a grand one and did me good. It was like some few walks and talks we had in our travels one out of Birmingham I think, amid the green shrubberies of Edgbarton,— one climbing the Appenines to Pietra Mala. It imparted much of valuable facts more of your own true soul. I wish I could answer in kind but can only touch on some topics. I have become an enthusiastic Socialist; elsewhere is no comfort, no solution for the problems of the times. I rejoice in what you tell of some successful practical study at the N. A. Phalanx. I wish you had told more explicitly why you return to business in the common way. Was it because you needed more money? or because a truly congenial course was not yet clearly marked out for you? It is an excellent thing you have done about that washing house. Blessed be he who gets one such good thing done while the rest of us are only blundering observing, perhaps learning something. What you say is deeply true about the peace way being the best. If any one see clearly how to work in that way, let him in God's name. Only if he abstain from fighting against giant wrongs let him be sure he is really and ardently at work undermining them or better still sustaining the rights that are to supplant them. Meanwhile I am not sure that I can keep my hands free from blood. I doubt I have not the strength. Cobden is good, but if he had stood in Kossuth's place, would he not have drawn the sword against the Austrian?[4] You, Marcus, could you let a Croat insult Rebecca, carry off Eddie to be an Austrian serf; and leave little Marcus bleeding in the dust? Yet is true that while Moses slew the Egyptian, Christ stood to be spit upon and that Death to man could do no harm. You have the truth, you have the right, but could you act it, Marcus in all circumstances? Stifled under the Roman priesthood would you not have thrown it off with all your force? Would you have waited unknown centuries hoping the moment when you could use another method? If so, you are a Christian; you know I never pretended to be except in dabs and sparkles here and there. Yet the agonies of that baptism of blood I feel oh how deeply in the golden June days of Rome. Consistent no way I felt I should have shrunk back. I could not have had it shed. Christ did not have to see his dear ones pass the dark river; he could go alone; however, in prophetic spirit no doubt, he foresaw the crusades.

In answer to what you say of Harro, I wish indeed the little effort I made for him had been wiselier applied.[5] Yet these are not the things one regrets. It does not do to calculate too closely with the affectionate human impulse; we must consent to make many mistakes or we would move too slow to help our brothers much. I am sure you don't regret what you spent on Miani and other worthless people; as the circumstances looked then it would have been wrong not to risk the loss. To be sure one must learn prudence by degrees. If I ever have any thing to give again I hope to have better discretion than in past years. Yet I have been very fortunate a number of times when I have tried to help Efforts not very energetic have been crowned with a good deal of success. The little way I ever travelled on the road to Zion I have been borne along on flowery beds of ease, and other people have been fifty times better to me than I have been to my small pack of Lazaruses.

As to what you say of your wishes to mewards I want nothing of thee, dear Marcus, in the shape of dollars. I know you are not rich; that you have upon you many claims and make many more paying double tithes to the true church of fraternity— equality. What you have done for me I prize, the acts and the spirit in which they were done may like love ever be ready to cheer yourself if you should need it. What you may do for me now is—

1stly Pray to St Margaret, since she hangs in your parlour that I may somehow escape from the dragon of poverty which I have faced much in the same ecstatic mood as she seemed to feel, and now begin to fear lest it snatch my boy.[6] Pray that I may find some way to earn my daily bread, with milk and pearlbarley for my boy.

2ndly Go to Wiley and Putnam and ask if all that stuff published as my miscellanies is forever to be unprofitable as well as flat and stale.[7]

If so I don't think it is quite fair as certainly worse slate stones turn to gold in some hands. It is now the end of the third year and if you could squeeze for me even a very small sum from his publishing mercies, it would be most welcome. A fifty dollars would at least pay my postage bill when I leave Florence. I am now sore pressed; and we are like to be so for several years. Could we weather through these next years, we might have a little peace, joy perhaps. Yet worry not thyself for me. I dare say God who has got me on thus far through the bog of practical life will never let me sink in more than knee deep, and I shall get off with only a fright or two at last. Write of Miss Bremer. I think she will see many things in the U. S. to please her kind heart, and trust she will give the benefit of many wise suggestions and reproofs. Sauced by her kindly playfulness they will be digested even by the conceit of Jonathan.

Love to dear Eddie and Jeanie, and kiss to the baby. It all came right— a Marcus was better than a Margaret.

MsC (MH:fMS Am 1086 [9:219]); MsC (MH:fMS Am 1086 [Works, 1:265–77]); MsCfr (MH:bMSAm 1280 [111, p. 41]); MsCfr (NjHi); MsCfr (CSmH [46944]). Published entire in Wade, pp. 587–90; published in part in *WNC*, pp. 376–78; *Memoirs*, 1:302–3; *Critic* 48 (1906): 252; F. B. Sanborn, *Recollections of Seventy Years* (Boston, 1909), pp. 410–11; *JMN*, 11:466; and Chevigny, pp. 490–91.

1. Hugh Doherty was an English writer and editor who championed Fourier's socialism. Fredrika Bremer (1801–65) was born in the part of Finland that was then in Sweden. She wrote a number of novels in the 1830s and '40s, one of which, *Die Nachbarn*, Fuller reviewed in the *Dial*. On 4 October 1849 Bremer arrived in New York City, where she met the Springs and, according to the *Tribune* for 19 November, visited the North American Phalanx (Signe Alice Rooth, *Seeress of the Northland* [Philadelphia, 1955], pp. 7–33; Fredrika Bremer, *Homes of the New World* [New York, 1853], p. 73). The North American Phalanx had been formed in 1843 at Albany, then moved to a farm in Monmouth County, New Jersey, on 12 August 1843. It lasted until 1855 (John Humphrey Noyes, *History of American Socialisms* [Philadelphia, 1870], pp. 451, 461, 501).

2. Herbert Marcus Spring (1848–1908), third and last of the Spring children, had been born on 18 September 1848 (Beatrice E. Borchardt, "Heaven Comes Later," NjHi).

3. Shelley's "Reality," number 21 of the "Esdaile Poems":

> This world is the nurse of all we know,
>   This world is the mother of all we feel,
> And the coming of death is a fearful blow
>   To a brain unencompassed with nerves of steel;
> When all that we know, or feel, or see,
> Shall pass like an unreal mystery.

(*The Complete Poetical Works of Percy Bysshe Shelley*, ed. Neville Rogers [Oxford, 1972], 1:113.)

4. Richard Cobden (1804–65) was best known as a leader of the Anti-Corn Law League but by 1849 had already made himself known as an advocate of nonintervention. Lajos Kossuth (1802–94) had been imprisoned by Austria from 1837 to 1840. He

became a member of the Hungarian Diet and then led the revolution of 1848–49. On 14 April 1849 the Hungarians declared their independence from Austria and chose Kossuth as their governor-president. He resigned on 11 August after the battle of Temesvar, which Hungary lost to the Austrians (*Cambridge Modern History*, 11:207–12).

    5. Fuller had met, defended, and apparently lent money to Harro Harring, a Danish novelist and political agitator.

    6. Saint Margaret of Antioch (called also Marina) was reputed to be the daughter of a pagan priest; she became a Christian and was cast into prison. There Satan visited her in the form of a dragon and swallowed her. A cross opened the demon's belly, permitting her to escape (*Butler's Lives of the Saints*, 3:152).

    7. In 1846 Fuller had published *Papers on Literature and Art*, a two-volume collection of her essays. As she often does, Fuller uses the language of *Hamlet*, I.ii.133–34.

872. To Margarett C. Fuller

[I] Florence, [15? December] 1849

Weary in spirit with the deep disappointments of the last year, I wish to dwell little on these things for the moment, but seek some consolation in the affections of my little boy is quite well now, and I often feel happy in seeing how joyous and full of activity he seems. Ossoli, too, feels happier here. The future is full of difficulties for us; but having settled our plans for the present we shall set it aside while we may— "Sufficient for the day is the *Evil* thereof"[1]— and, if the *good* be not *always* sufficient, in our case it is; so let us say grace to our dinner of herbs.

Dearest Mother, of all your endless acts and words of love, never was any so dear to me as your last letter so generous, so sweet, so holy! What on earth is so precious as a mothers love; and who has a mother like mine?

I was thinking of you and father, all that first October, wishing to write only there was much to disturb me that day, (as the Police were threatening to send us away) It is only since I have had my own child that I have known how much I failed always to do what I might have for the happiness of you both. Only since I have seen so much of men and their trials, that I have learned to prize my father as he deserved. Only since I have had a heart daily and hourly testifying to me its love, that I have understood too late what it was for you to be deprived of it. We never sympathized with you as we ought, or tried as we ought to embellish and sustain your life as far as is possible after such an irreparable maim.

It will be terrible for me to leave Italy, uncertain of return. Yet when I think of you, beloved Mother, of brothers and sister and many friends, I wish to come. Ossoli is perfectly willing. He leaves in Rome a sister whom he dearly loves; his Aunt is dying now. He will go among strangers, but to him, as to all the young Italians, America seems the land of liberty. He hopes too, that a new revolution will favor return, after a number of years, and that then he may find really a home in Italy. All this is dark; we can judge only for the present moment the decision will rest with me. I shall wait till the last moment, as I always do, that I may have all the reasons before me.

[II] I thought, to-day, ah, if she could only be with us now! But who knows how long this interval of peace will last? I have learned to prize such, as the halcyon prelude to the storm. It is now about a fortnight, since the police gave us leave to stay, and we feel safe in our little apartment. We have no servant except the nurse, with occasional aid from the porter's wife, and now live comfortably so, tormented by no one, helping ourselves. In the evenings, we have a little fire now;— the baby sits on his stool between us. He makes me think how I sat on mine, in the chaise, between you and father. He is exceedingly fond of flowers;— he has been enchanted this evening by this splendid Gardenia, and these many crimson flowers that were given me at Villa Correggi, where a friend took us in his carriage. It was a luxury, this ride, as we have entirely renounced the use of a carriage for ourselves. How enchanted you would have been with that villa! It seems now as if, with the certainty of a very limited income, we could be so happy! But I suppose, if we had it, one of us would die, or the baby. Do not you die, my beloved mother;— let us together have some halcyon moments, again, with God, with nature, with sweet childhood, with the remembrance of pure trust and good intent; away from perfidy and care, and the blight of noble designs.

Ossoli wishes you were here, almost as much as I. When there is anything really lovely and tranquil, he often says, "Would not 'La Madre' like that?" He wept when he heard your letter. I never saw him weep at any other time, except when his father died, and when the French entered Rome. He has, I think, even a more holy feeling about a mother, from having lost his own, when very small. It has been a life-long want with him. He often shows me a little scar on his face, made by a jealous dog, when his mother was caressing him as an infant. He prizes that blemish much.

I:MsCfr (MH:fMS Am 1086 [9:236]); II: ELfr, from *Memoirs*, 2:306–7. Published in part in Van Doren, pp. 310–12, and Chevigny, p. 485.

Both the copyist and the Memoirs *editors misdate this letter. The copyist wrote "Florence, Oct 14, 1849"; the* Memoirs *editors give "Florence, Nov 7." Fuller, however, here answers the one from Mrs. Fuller postmarked 3 November (MH). Since mail took a full month to travel from New England to Florence, Fuller could hardly have answered it before mid-December. The* Memoirs *editors published the letter as two different ones; the copyist preserved it as one letter. Thus the first paragraph may, in fact, not belong to the body of the letter to Mrs. Fuller.*

1. Matt. 6:34: "Take therefore no thought for the morrow: for the morrow shall take thought for the things of itself. Sufficient unto the day is the evil thereof."

873.   To William H. Channing

[I] Florence 17th December 1849.

It is now a month since I had your little letter, and always I have been waiting to answer in vague expectation of some kind of a crisis. I know not what but it has long seemed that in the year 1850, I should stand on some important plateau in the ascent of life, should be allowed to pause for awhile, and take more clear and commanding views than ever before. I feel however no marked and important change as yet, and it is not worth while to wait too long.

[II] My love for Ossoli is most pure and tender, nor has any one, except little children or mother, ever loved me as genuinely as he does. To you, dear William I was obliged to make myself known; others have loved me with a mixture of fancy and enthusiasm excited by my talent at embellishing subjects. He loves me from simple affinity; he loves to be with me, and serve and soothe me. Our relation covers only a part of my life, but I do not perceive that it interferes with anything I ought to have or be; I do not feel any way constrained or limited or that I have made any sacrifice. Younger I might, because I should have been exposed to love some other in a way that might give him pain, but I do not now feel apprehensive of that. There is more danger for him, as he is younger than I; if he should, I shall do all that this false state of society permits to give him what freedom he may need. I have thought a great deal about this; there are things I do not wish to put on paper. I daresay I shall tell them to you when we meet. You speak as if I might return to America without him. I thought of it at one time, knowing it would be very trying for him to go with me, that when I first am with my former friends, he may have many lonely hours. Beside he had then an employment in Rome and we needed the money. I thought I would go and either write for him to come to me, or return to Italy. But now that cannot be. He could not at present reenter Rome without danger; he is separated from his employment and his natural friends, nor is any career open for him in Italy at present. Then I could not think of taking away the child for several months; his heart is fixed on the child as fervently as mine.

Then it would not only be very strange and sad to me to be without his love and care for weeks and months, but I should feel very anxious about him under present circumstances. I trust we shall find means to make the voyage together and remain together. In our country he will have for resources, his walks and quiet communings with nature, which is always so great a part of his life; he will have the child, and I think my family, expecially my mother, will love him very dearly and he will be learning the language with them. I suppose I must myself be engaged in the old unhealthy [III] way, life will probably be a severe struggle. I hope I shall be able to live through it, and not neglect my child, nor Ossoli. He has suffered enough; it has ploughed furrows in his life since first we met. He has done all he could and cannot blame himself. Our destiny is sad; we much brave it as we can. I hope we shall always feel mutual tenderness, and Ossoli has a simple child-like piety that will make it easier for him.

You speak of my whole future, that future here on earth now seems to me short. It may be terribly trying but it will not be so very long now. Indeed, now I have the child, I am often sad fearing I may not stay long enough

[IV] As to my writing do not expect any thing very good of it I suppose there are impressions worth the general hearing about as far as they are correct and I am anxious to do historical justice to some facts and persons, but I am not aware that there will be *that* of advantage to a thinker. I do not know for I cannot read it over, but believe I have scarce expressed what lies deepest in my mind. I take no pains about this or other things but let the Genius lead. I did struggle to lead a simple, natural life *at home*, and learning of my child, writing only when imperatively obliged by the mind that insisted on utterance, but was defeated and now I strive no more. Eternity is ours, beloved William— we will be true and full living beings yet—

Ever yours—

I: MsCfr (MB: Ms. Am. 1450 [107]); II: MsCfr (MB: Ms. Am. 1450 [109]); III: MsCfr (MB: Ms. Am. 1450 [115]); IV: MsCfr (MB: Ms. Am. 1450 [58]). Published in part in *Memoirs*, 2:334–35, 337.

874. To Caroline Sturgis Tappan

[ca. 17 December 1849]

[   ] I do not know what to write about him; he changes so

much; has so many characters; he is like me in that, his father's character is simple and uniform though not monotonous more than are the flowers of spring, flowers of the valley. He is now in the most perfect rosy health, a very gay impetuous, ardent, but sweet tempered child. He seems to me to have nothing in common with the first baby with its exstatic smiles, its exquisite sensitiveness and a distinction in the gesture and attitudes that struck every body. His temperament seems changed by taking the milk of these robust women. His form is robust but the feet and [   ] quite any [   ] make him some prettier dresses.

He is now come to quite a knowing age (fifteen months.) In the morng, so soon as dressed, he signs to come into our room, there draws our curtain, kisses me, rather violently pats my face, says *poor*, stretches himself and says *bravo*, then expects as a reward to be tied in his chair and have his play things. These engage him busily, but still he calls to us to sing and drum to enliven the scene. Sometimes he calls me to kiss his hand; he laughs very much at this. Enchanting is that baby laugh, all dimples and glitter, so strangely arch and innocent. Then I wash and dress him; that is his great time. He makes it as long as he can insisting to dress and wash me the while; kicking, throwing the water about full of all manner of tricks that I think girls nere dream of. Then is his walk; we have beautiful walks here for him, Lung-Arno by the bridges, or the sunny walk at the Cascine protected by fine trees always warm in mid-winter[n] the band playing in the distance and children of all ages walking and sitting with their nurses. His walk and sleep give me about three hours in the middle of the day, then at [nig]ht he goes to bed and we have the [   ] otherwise I am always engaged [with] him. Indeed I often walk [with] him, as Italn servants are [not] to be trusted and I feel now [the] need of seeing him at each [mo]ment.

[I] feel so refreshed by his young life. Ossoli diffuses such a peace and sweetness over every day, that I cannot endure to think yet of our future. Too much have we suffered already trying to command it. I do not feel force to make any effort yet. I suppose that very soon now I must do something. I hope I shall feel able when the time comes. I do not yet.

My constitution seems making an effort to rally by dint of much sleep. I had slept so little for a year and a half, during the last months of pregnancy never an hour in peace, after the baby's birth, such anxiety and anguish, when separated from him, I was consumed as by nightly fever. I constantly started up seeming to hear him call me. The last two months at Rome would have destroyed almost any woman then when I went to him, he was so ill and I was constantly up with him at night, carrying him about, feeding him. At Perugia he began to get better. Then w[hen] we arrived here the Police [   ] to send us away; it was as [   ] as three weeks before we coul[d] [get] permission to stay. Now for th[ree] months we have been tranquil; a[nd] have resolved to repose and enjo[y] being together as much as we cou[ld] in this brief interval, perhaps all we shall ever know of peace. It is very sad we have no money; we could have been so quietly happy awhile. I rejoice in all Ossoli did but the results in this our earthly state, are disastrous, especially as my strength is now so much impaired This much I do hope, in life or death to be no more separated from Angelino. Last winter I made the most vehement efforts at least to redeem the time hoping thus good for the future. But of at least two volumes written at that time, no line seems of any worth. I had suffered much constraint, much that was uncongenial, harassing, even agonizing, but this kind of pain found me unprepared. The position of a mother separated from her only child is too frightfully unnatural.

I do think to see you and your baby this coming year. You two I wish to see and some other friends and Mother. Eugene hopes to come to N. England. I have not seen him for 9 years and may not again if I do not take this oppory. There are many difficulties but I think we shall come. If we cannot place ourselves well there, it will be time to think where to go, when I have seen you all, and know whether Ossoli can learn English and to live with those of English blood. Perhaps I shall see you in your Lenox home. But what you say of the meddling curiosity of people repels me. It is so different here When I made my appearance with a husband and a child of a year old nobody did the least thing to annoy me. All were most cordial, none asked or implied questions. Yet there were not a few that might justly have complained that when they were confiding to me all their affairs and doing much to serve me, I had observed absolute silence to them. Others might for more than one reason be displeased at the choice I made. All have acted in the kindliest and most refined manner. An Italian lady with whom I was intimate who might be qualified in the court Journal as one "of the highest rank sustained by the most scrupulous decorum"!! when I wrote "Dear friend, I am married. I have a child There are particulars as to my reasons for keeping this secret I do not wish to tell. This is rather an odd affair, will it make any difference in our relations?" She answered "What difference can it make, except that I shall love you more now that we can sympathize as mothers?" Her first visit here was to me; she adopted at once Ossoli and the child to her love Emelyn Story wrote me that William was a little hurt at first that I did not tell him even in the trying days of Rome, but left him to hear it as he unluckily did at the table d' hote in Venice. But his second and prevailing" thought was regret that he had not known it so as to soothe and aid me, to visit Ossoli at his post, to go to the child in the country. Wholly in that spirit was the fine letter he wrote me, one of my treasures. His character has come out beautifully at times in Europe; he has had his ordeals. The little Amern society here have been most cordial and attentive; one lady who has been most intimate with me dropped a tear or two over the difficulties before me but she said "Since you have seen fit to take the step all your friends have to do now is to make it as easy for you as they can."

I am sorry it is known that I had written to you for one thing; it might give pain to Mother to know I had told any one in America before her. I had a letter from her in the Summer, when speaking of the fact that she had never been present at the marriage of one of her children, she said with a kind of sigh, "I think if Arthur were engaged he would tell me, but perhaps not"[1] A great pang came of remorse and I thought if Angelino dies I will not give her the pain of knowing that I have kept this secret from her. She shall hear of this connection as if it were something new. When I found he would live I wrote to her; it half killed me to write those few letters, and yet I know many are wondering I did not write more letters and more particularly. As soon as they were done, I went into bed, but soon had to rise for the baby cried

"Ah che giorni"! I often see Rossini here and think I could teach him to make a better Semiramide![2] But Mother received my communication in the highest spirit. She said she was sure a first object with me" had been now and always to save her pain She blessed as she rejoiced that she should not die feeling there was no one left to love me with the devotion she thought I needed. She expressed no regret at our poverty she offered me her feeble means to stead me. Her letter was a noble crown to her life of disinterested purifying love. I should be inexpressibly grieved now, if there is the least thing more to give her pain. Richard, too, never writes. I suppose he is deeply hurt at my silence, but he is young and strong and will feel differently when he has seen me.

29th An absurd number of days have passed without my getting time even to finish this little letter. Generally I go out little, but have taken my part in the Christmas holidays. They interest me now through my

child as they never did for myself. I like to go out and watch the rising generation who will be his contemporaries. On sunday I went with
the Italian friend I mentioned in her carriage to the Cascine, after we
had taken the drive we sat down on a stone seat in the sunny walk, to
see the people walk by. The Grand Duke and all his children, the ele-
gant Austrian officers who will be driven out of Italy when Angelino
is a man, Princess Demidoff with her hussars, Harry Sorrequer
(Sever) and his absurd brood, M de Corceilles who helped betray
Rome, many lovely children, many" little frisking dogs with their
bells.[3] The sun shone brightly on the Arno, a bark moved gently by
All seemed good to the baby, he laid himself back in my arms,
smiling, singing to himself, dancing his feet. I hope he will retain
some trace in his mind of the perpetual exhilarating picture of Italy.
You say you would like your child to have it; I hope she will, while yet
a child walk in these stately gardens full of sculpture and hear the
untiring music of the fountains. It is to childhood it must be most important. Christmas eve we went to the Annunziata for midnight mass,
but it is not splendid here like Rome. Still we enjoyed it, sitting in one
of the side chapels, at the foot of a monument, seeing the rich crowd
steal gently by, every eye gleaming every gesture softened by the influence of the pealing choir, of the hundred silver lamps, swinging
their full light in honor of the abused Emmanuel. But" the finest
thing was passing through the Duomo, no one was there, only the al-
tars lit up, the priests who were singing could not be seen, by this
faint light, the vast solemnity of the interior is really felt. The hour
was worthy of Brunelleschi.[4] I hope he has walked there so. You will
love the Duomo, it is far more divine than St Peters, worthy of Genius, pure and unbroken. St Peters is like Rome, mixture of sublimest
God, with corruptest Earth. I adore the Duomo, though no place can
now be to me like St Peters, where has been the splendidest part of
my life. My feeling was always perfectly regal, on entering
the piazza of St Peters, the calmest intoxication, no spot on earth is
worthier the sun light, on none does it fall so fondly. Christmas day I
was just up and Nino all naked on his sofa, when came some beautiful
large toys that had been sent him a bird, a horse, a cat that could be
moved to express different things. It almost made me cry to see the
kind of fearful rapture with which he regarded them, legs and arms,
extended, fingers and toes quivering, mouth made up to a little
round O, eyes dilated; for a long time he did not even wish to touch
them, after he began to he was different with all the three, loving the
bird; very wild and shouting with the horse, with the cat pulling her
face close to his, staring in her eyes, and then throwing her away. Af-

terwards I drew him in a lottery at a child's party given by Mrs Gree-nough a toy of a child asleep on the neck of a tiger. The tiger is stretching up to look at the child; this he likes best of any of his toys. It is sweet to see him when he gets used to them and plays by himself, whispering to them, seeming to contrive stories. You would laugh to know how much remorse I feel that I never gave children more toys in the course of my life. I regret all the money I ever spent on myself or in little presents for grown people, hardened sinners. I did not know what pure delight could be bestowed. I am sure if Jesus Christ had given, it would not have been little crosses. You must not show this letter to William he would certainly think it far funnier than yours. There is no use for me to write any more, I could write on all kinds of things a month, but I am very tired this very minute. There is snow all over Florence in our most beautiful piazza. La Maria No-vella, with its fair loggia and bridal church is a carpet of snow and the full moon looking down, I had forgotten how angelical all that is, how fit to die by. I have only seen snow in mountain patches for so long, here it is the even, holy shroud of a desired peace. God bless all good and bad tonight and save me from despair

I must not write any more. I am very glad I will have some money to buy you things, and I shall be pleased indeed if I can get the en-gravings for Elizh. I had one for her once, and was so silly as to give it away. I want you to specify how high I may go for your cameo, some of fine workmanship are as much as thirty dollars, the one I should once have liked to get for you was only six. There are many grades of excellence as to the cutting. Such an one as my Apollo that you re-member may sometimes be got for three or four dollars. Rome is the cameo place, still I hope to be able to please you here. You did not specify any other objects; I suppose you will when you send the money. Goodnight, I leave a little place open, if more words be needed on steamer day.

30th Decr I see I[n] have been writing with the most shameful ink; your eyes will be quite put out. This is Sunday I suppose you have been playing with your baby (you on your side do not tell me her age, but I suppose it 9 months,) mine has been walking to day. I have taken such pleasure in watching his little foolish legs. I am sorry to say he seems timid and yet a great bully. I hope these faults may be evoked up into respectable virtues by dint of steady maternal reason-ing. We have got your frightful news from Boston. Certainly there is no place like Boston for unexpected horrors. Imagination cowers, faints and dwines away in the attempt to depict Dr Parkman being murdered, Dr Webster murdering.[5] Mr Browning was here yesterday and inspired by this occasion we exchanged our chronicles of the kind. When you first showed me *Pippa passes* I did not foresee what pleasant hours I should pass with the writer, only that writer I never see. We talk too fast; he is too entertaining for us to get really acquainted You ask am I sorry for Sam's being in business. No! I had all my sorrow out about Sam when he gave up being an artist. His life can never be wholly fit, nor ever fail to be full of acquisition. How does he look now? Dear Carrie I wish it was any use to ask you to write at once. Will you see this letter and note rightly delivered for love of

MARGARET.

ALfrS (MH:fMS Am 1086 [9:166]); MsCfr (MH:fMS Am 1086 [9:233]). Published in part in *Memoirs*, 2:307–10, 317–18, 319; Higginson, *MFO*, p. 271; Van Doren, pp. 312–14; and Chevigny, pp. 491–93.

Fuller appears to have begun the letter before Christmas and finished it after. She probably began it in the middle of the month, when she was writing other letters to the United States.

trees always warm in mid-winter] trees ↑ always warm in mid-winter ↓
second and prevailing] second ↑ and prevailing ↓
sure a first object with me] sure ⟨my⟩ ↑ a ↓ first object ↑ with me ↓
children, many] children, ↑ many ↓
Emmanuel. But] Emmanuel. ⟨Emmanuel.⟩ But
I see I] I ↑ see I ↓

1. In her letter to Margaret of 21 May 1849 (MH) Mrs. Fuller said: "I *know* of no prospect of Arthur's being married, I think he would tell me if any existed, but he might not—I have not been present at the marriage of any child of mine yet."

2. Probably a reference to the aria "Ah! quel giorno ognor rammente," which Arsace sings early in act one of *Semiramide*.

3. Leopold II (1797–1870), grand duke of Tuscany, son of Ferdinand III, archduke of Austria, ruled in Florence from 1824 to 1859. Matilde Bonaparte (1820–1904), princess of Westphalia, was the daughter of Jerome Bonaparte. She married Prince Anatoly Nikolaevich Demidov (1813–70). Claude-François Tircuy de Corcelle (1802–92) was an author who became the French envoy to Rome. He worked for French intervention before the siege and advised Oudinot during the Roman surrender (*Dictionnaire de biographie française*); Farini, 4:216). Sorrequer is unidentified.

4. Filippo Brunelleschi (1377?–1446), a Florentine architect, defined the interests of Renaissance architecture. He designed and constructed the dome of Santa Maria del Fiore. His other works include the churches of San Lorenzo and San Spirito (*A Biographical Dictionary of Artists*, ed. Sir Lawrence Gowing [London, 1983]).

5. In one of the most famous American murder cases of the nineteenth century, Dr. John White Webster (1793–1850) was convicted and executed for the murder of Dr. George Parkman (1790–1849), an uncle of the historian. Both men were prominent Boston physicians who had graduated from Harvard and both were well known in the community. Parkman, an early psychologist, had established a small hospital for the insane in Boston. He was also a moneylender and speculator, and he had advanced loans to Webster. The latter was the Irving Professor of chemistry at Harvard, a sociable and well-liked man whom the Fullers knew in the 1820s. From 1842 to 1847 Webster borrowed money from Parkman. Relations between the two grew so bitter that Webster murdered Parkman on 23 November 1849 (*DAB*; Harvard archives; Robert Sullivan, *The Disappearance of Dr. Parkman* [Boston, 1971], pp. 26–31).

INDEX

Adams, Abigail, 65n
Adams, Henry, 173n
Adams, John, 65n
Adams, John Quincy, 58n
Albano, 67–68, 69n
Alcott, A. Bronson, 174, 175n
Allen, Mary, 39–40
Ambarvalia (Burbidge and Clough), 288n
Ames, Joseph Alexander, 62
Ames, Sarah Fisher Clampitt, 62, 159, 181
Andersen, Hans Christian, 181, 185n
Arconati Visconti, Costanza, 14, 49n, 149, 189, 190, 191n, 234, 270n, 279, 280; opinion of Mazzini, 49
—letters to, 49, 69, 73, 192–93, 249–50, 269–70
Arconati Visconti, Giovanni, 269, 270n, 280
Arconati Visconti, Giuseppe, 191n
Arnold, Matthew, 287, 288n
Aspre, Konstantin d', 234n
Assumption and Coronation of the Virgin (Titian), 47
Attila (Verdi), 41
Austria, 97, 173n, 234n; attacks papal states, 97, 229, 244n; revolution in, 8, 59n
Avezzana, Giuseppe, 269n
Azeglio, Massimo Taparelli d', 265

Bacci, Francesco, 136, 137
Banks, James Lenox, 286n
Barberini-Colona, Francesco-Maria, 147, 150n
Barberini Palace, 181, 182n, 188, 189

Baring Bros., 82, 83n
Barker, Anna, 52
Bate, Gerardine, 170n
Beethoven, Ludwig van, 174
Belgioioso, Cristina, 12, 51–52, 54, 228–29, 233
Bellà, Tancredi, 253, 254n
Bells and Pomegranates (Robert Browning), 181, 185n, 189, 204
Bertrand, Count, 44
Bible, 150n, 155n, 187, 188n, 298, 300
Black, Mrs., 233, 268
Black, Charles Christopher, 159, 190
Blanc, Louis, 61n, 67n
Blewitt, Octavian, 191n
Boccaccio, Giovanni, 239
Bologna, 100n
Bonanni, Giuditta, 80, 81, 84, 85, 87, 92, 93, 112, 113, 121, 126, 127, 132, 133
Bonanni, Maria, 80, 81
Bonanni, Nicomedi, 123, 124
Bonaparte, Carlo (Prince Canino), 63n, 268, 269n
Bonaparte, Jerome, 307n
Boott, Francis, 286n
"Bothie of Toper-na-fuosich, The" (Clough), 287, 288n
Bremer, Fredrika, 294, 297
Brisbane, Mr., 185–86
Brisbane, Albert, 187n
Brook Farm, 275, 277n
Brown, Caroline Clements, 233, 234n
Brown, Nicholas, 3d, 230n, 233, 269n
Brown, Shipley & Co., 177, 179–80, 193
Browning, Elizabeth Barrett, 14, 75, 159,

Browning, Elizabeth Barrett (*cont.*)
170, 189, 204, 275, 279, 280, 282, 288n
—letter to, 289–90
Browning, Robert, 14, 149, 159, 170, 181,
185n, 189, 204, 275, 279, 280, 282, 287,
289, 307
—works of: *Bells and Pomegranates*, 181,
185n, 189, 204; *Pippa Passes*, 307
Browning, Robert Wiedeman Barrett
(Pen), 275, 277n, 280, 282
Brownson, Orestes, 174, 175n
Brunelleschi, Filippo, 305, 307n
Brunetti, Angelo (Ciceruacchio), 10, 150n
Brunetti, Luigi, 150n
Bryant, William Cullen, 63n
Burbidge, Thomas, 287, 288n
Bürger, Gottfried August, 75, 76n
Butler, Mr., 63
Byron, George Gordon, Lord, 147, 189,
190n
—works of: *Childe Harold's Pilgrimage*, 147,
150n; *Don Juan*, 190n

Canino, Prince (Carlo Bonaparte), 63n,
268, 269n
Carlyle, Thomas, 5, 232n
Casigliano, duke of (Andrea Corsini), 267,
268n–69n
Casino di Raffaello, 181, 185n
Cass, Lewis, Jr., 13, 229, 230n, 262, 264,
268, 269n, 277
—letters to, 228–29, 231, 242–46, 249,
252, 254–55, 264, 265, 267–68
Cenci, Beatrice, 44, 45n, 181, 182n
Channing, Caroline Sturgis, 46, 47n, 52,
293
Channing, Ellen Fuller, 5, 45n, 51, 68,
103, 186, 187n, 202, 203n, 232
—letters to, 45–47, 206–7, 242, 251–52,
290–93
Channing, Ellery, 45n, 46, 57, 58n, 186,
187n
—works of: *Conversations in Rome*, 46, 47n;
Poems: Second Series, 47n
Channing, Margaret Fuller (Greta), 42, 43,
45n, 46, 103, 206, 293
—letter to, 52–53
Channing, Mary, 279
Channing, Dr. Walter, 186, 187n
Channing, Walter (son), 186, 187n
Channing, Dr. William Ellery, 45n, 65
Channing, William Henry, 41, 45n, 65,
71, 72n, 201
—letters to, 58–59, 155, 205–6, 246–48,
258, 266, 300–301

"Character of the Happy Warrior, The"
(Wordsworth), 154, 155n
Charles Albert, king of Piedmont, 6–11,
13, 59n, 65n, 70n, 74n, 99, 101, 102,
107n, 138, 139, 224n; Fuller's opinion
of, 73, 102n–3n
Childe Harold's Pilgrimage (Byron), 147,
150n
Chopin, Frédéric, 54, 55n
Ciceruacchio (Angelo Brunetti), 10, 150n
Clark, Elijah Pope, 231, 232n, 244
Clark, Sarah Wilby, 232n
Clarke, Anna Huidekoper, 175
Clarke, Herman, 260, 262n
Clarke, James Freeman, 171, 173n
—letter to, 173–75
Clarke, Rebecca Hull, 171, 172
Clarke, Sarah Ann, 173n, 174
—letters to, 171–72, 281–82
Clarke, William, 281, 282
Clements, Louisa Mendum, 234n
Clements, Pierce, 234n
Clésinger, Jean-Baptiste Auguste, 216n
Clough, Arthur Hugh, 236–37, 275, 285,
287
—letter to, 236
Cobden, Richard, 295, 297n
"Cockney School of Poetry" (Lockhart),
190n–91n
Colman, Henry, 61n
—letter to, 60–61
Colman, Mary Harris, 61n
Considérant, Prosper-Victor, 242n
Consuelo (Sand), 42, 45n
Contemporaneo, Il, 62–63
Conversations in Rome (Ellery Channing),
46, 47n
Cook, Clarence Chatham, 65n
Cook, Louisa De Windt, 65
Cooley, Isaac, 195n
Cooper, James Fenimore, 251
Corcelle, Claude-François Tircuy de,
305, 307n
Correggio, 43, 45n
Corsini, Andrea, 267, 268n–69n
Corsini, Tommaso, 268n
Cowper, William, 277
Cranch, Christopher Pearse, 64, 65, 203–
4, 233, 253n
Cranch, Elizabeth De Windt, 65n, 74, 233
—letters to, 64–65, 203–5
Cranch, George William, 65, 203, 204
Cranch, Leonora, 65, 75, 76n, 203, 204
Crane, Abigail, 178, 179n
Crane, Elizabeth Crane, 179n

Crane, Simeon, 179n
Crawford, Louisa Ward, 182, 185n, 194, 200, 204, 207, 211
Crawford, Thomas, 185n, 200, 207, 263
Crispoldi, Marchioness, 148
Cropsey, Jasper Francis, 195n, 204
Cropsey, Maria Cooley, 195, 204
Curtis, George Ticknor, 76n
Curtis, George William, 253n, 288n
—letter to, 274–77
Curtis, George William, Jr., 76n
Curtis, Joseph Story, 76n
Curtis, Mary Story, 75, 76n
Custoza, battle of, 9, 107n

Dante, 273
Davis, George, 40n
Demidov, Anatoly Nikolaevich, 307n
Demidov, Matilde Bonaparte, 305, 307n
Democratie pacifique, La, 242
De Rose, Anna, 39, 40n
De Windt, Louisa, 205
Dichtung und Warheit (Goethe), 198
Dickens, Charles, 210, 211n
Didier, Charles, 192, 193n
Doherty, Hugh, 294, 297n
Domenichino, Il, 196n
Don Juan (Byron), 190n
Dudevant, Solange, 216n
Duomo, 273, 305
Duyckinck, Evert, 63n
Duyckinck, George Long, 63

Edgeworth, Maria, 292, 294n
Eliot, Frances Brock, 179n
Eliot, Thomas Dawes, 179n, 202
Emerson, Charles, 47n
Emerson, Edward Waldo, 64
Emerson, George Barrell, 185n
Emerson, George Samuel, 182, 185n
Emerson, Olivia Buckminster, 185n
Emerson, Ralph Waldo, 5, 6, 15, 46, 54, 55n, 72, 76n, 201, 204, 287, 291, 293; Fuller's opinion of, 86
—letters to, 55, 63–64, 66, 85–86, 187, 239–40
—works of: "Nature," 187, 188n; *Poems*, 204
Emerson, Waldo, 14, 64, 255, 260, 293
Erbeau, Miss: letter to, 281
Erskine, James, 55n
Erskine, Katherine Stirling, 54, 55n
Este, Leonora d', 76n
Eustachio, Saint, 168, 170n

Extraits de lettres de madame la duchesse de Praslin, 61

Fabbri, Odoardo, 100n, 150n
Farini, Luigi, 84n
Farrar, Eliza Rotch, 62, 104, 171, 176, 177–78, 231
Farrar, John, 62
Fenzi, Emanuele, 235n
Ferdinand II, king of Naples, 7, 83, 84n, 92, 93, 136, 137, 154, 227n, 230n, 252
Fitten, Miss, 61
Florence, 14; Fuller's opinion of, 158, 161, 273–74
Fornarina, La (Raphael), 182n
Fourier, Charles, 71, 72n
Frank, Mrs., 233
Frascati, 68
Freeman, Augusta Latilla, 253n
Freeman, James Edwards, 252, 253n
France, 7–8; attacks Rome, 12, 13, 190n, 226–30, 232–42; Republic of, 66, 67n, 190n; revolution in, 54, 58–61, 66, 67n
Fucino, Lake, 103, 105n
Fuligno, Antonietti di, 241
Fuller, Abraham Williams, 48, 70–71, 178, 186
Fuller, Arthur Buckminster, 40, 57, 68, 83, 103, 105n, 160, 178, 187n, 203, 212, 304, 307n
—letter to, 185–86
Fuller, Eliza Rotta, 180, 182n
Fuller, Ellen Crane. *See* Channing, Ellen Fuller
Fuller, Eugene, 57, 58n, 83, 105n, 177, 180, 186, 229, 231, 244, 293, 303
Fuller, Henry Holton, 56, 58n, 82–83
Fuller, Lloyd, 40, 185, 186
Fuller, Margaret: goes to Rieti, 9, 67, 69, 163, 164; health of, 40, 42, 43, 46, 53, 55, 57, 67, 69, 78, 79, 118–20, 134, 135; leaves Rome, 9, 67, 69, 243–45; on letter writing, 180; plans to return to the United States, 177–78, 284, 298–99, 303; pregnancy of, 6, 9, 57, 66
—works of: history of Italian revolution, 73, 74, 82, 213; *Papers on Literature and Art*, 290n, 296–97, 298n; *Woman in the Nineteenth Century*, 61, 65n, 290
Fuller, Margarett Crane, 14, 48, 58, 68, 71, 77, 103, 105n, 151n, 160, 187n, 212, 257, 290, 292–93, 304, 307n
—letters to, 145–50, 176–78, 202–3, 259–62, 298–99
Fuller, Richard Frederick, 14, 40n, 47, 53,

Fuller, Richard Frederick (*cont.*)
58n, 177, 178, 202, 304; Fuller's opinion
of, 39–40, 51
—letters to, 39–40, 48, 49–52, 57–58,
67–68, 81–83, 103–5, 151–52, 160,
179–82, 193–94, 211–14, 229–32,
243–44
Fuller, Sarah Batchelder, 202, 203n
Fuller, Timothy, 57, 58n, 298
Fuller, William Henry, 57, 58n
Fusano, Castle, 59, 60n

Gales, Joseph, Jr., 63n
Galletti, Giuseppe, 151n
Gamage, Edward, 267, 269n
Gamage, Mary Ellise, 269n
Gamage, Samuel, 269n
Gardiner, Clarissa Holbrook, 53n, 206
Gardiner, Henry, 52–53, 68, 103
Garibaldi, Giuseppe, 12, 13, 63n, 209,
211n, 222, 223, 227n, 230n, 233, 238,
243n, 246, 254
Germany, 8, 59n
Gifford, Mary, 72n, 179n, 202
Gioberti, Vincenzo, 9, 11, 13, 69
Giradin, Alexandre de, 45n
Giradin, Emile de, 45n
Goethe, Johann Wolfgang von, 13, 181,
182n, 194, 198, 251, 252n, 269
—works of: *Dichtung und Warheit*, 198;
Italienische Reise, 181, 185n, 252n;
Römische Elegien, 181, 185n; *Wilhelm
Meisters Lehrjahre*, 194, 195n
Gonzaga, Anselmo Guerrieri, 58, 59n
Greeley, Arthur Young (Pickie), 14, 255–
57, 259–60, 262n, 293, 295
Greeley, Horace, 5, 48, 63n, 82, 83n, 90,
91, 97, 103, 104, 177, 295
—letter to, 255–57
Greeley, Mary Young, 83n, 257
Greene, Anna Shaw, 215, 216n
Greene, George Washington, 230n
Greene, William Batchelder, 216n
Greene & Co., 61, 177, 180
Greenough, Elizabeth Gore, 279
Greenough, Frances Boott, 279, 285,
286n, 306
Greenough, Henry, 286n, 287
Greenough, Horatio, 159, 267, 277, 291
Greenough, Louisa Gore, 159
Gregory XVI, pope, 6
Griswold, Rufus, 290n
Grotto Ferrata, 195, 196n
Guadalupe Hidalgo, treaty of, 182n
Guerrazi, Dominico, 154, 155n
Guizot, François-Guillaume, 54n, 150

Hall, Catharine Davis, 277n
Hall, Cornelia Romana, 277
Hall, James, 277n
Handbook for Travellers in Central Italy
(Murray), 189, 191n
Harring, Harro, 290n, 296, 298n
Hawthorne, Nathaniel, 5, 92n
Heath, Frank, 199–200, 233–34
Hedge, Frederic Henry, 54
—letters to, 41, 54–55
Hicks, Thomas, 63, 66n, 91, 92, 145, 199,
205, 279
—letter to, 66
Hill, Ellen Crane, 178, 179n, 202, 203n
Hillard, George Stillman, 61, 68, 103, 206
*History of England from the Accession of
James II* (Macaulay), 287
Hoar, Elizabeth Sherman, 6, 46, 47n, 51,
64, 103, 178, 187, 293, 306
—letters to, 241, 266
Hooker, Elizabeth Winthrop, 76n
Hooker, James C., 75, 76n, 89, 90, 92–96,
105, 106, 130, 131, 179, 204, 263, 285
—letters to, 90–92, 96–97
Hooper, Edward William, 172, 173n
Hooper, Ellen Sturgis, 14, 172, 173n, 175,
186, 189, 193, 210, 217
Hooper, Marian, 172, 173n
Hooper, Robert, 173n, 186
Howe, Julia Ward, 190, 191n, 263n
Howitt, Mary, 185n
Hudson, Radcliff, 191, 192n

Improvisatore (Andersen), 181, 185n
Italienische Reise (Goethe), 181, 185n, 252n
Italy. *See names of individual cities*

Jameson, Anna, 170n
Jesuits, 49, 69
Jesus, 198, 296, 306

Keats, John, 181, 182n, 189, 190n–91n
King, Jane Tuckerman, 159, 160, 172, 285
—letters to, 59–60, 168
Kingdom of Northern Italy, 73, 74n, 107n
Körner, Theodore, 152
Kossuth, Lajos, 295, 297n–98n

Lamartine, Alphonse-Marie-Louis de Prat
de, 61n
Lamennais, Félicité-Robert de, 5, 193n
Last Days of the Republic in Rome, The, 249
Lawrence, Abbott, 247, 248n
Lawrence, Amos, 247, 248n
Lawrence, Saint, 180–81, 182n
Lawrence, William, 247, 248n

Lays of Ancient Rome (Macaulay), 288n
Lenore (Bürger), 75, 76n
Leopold II, grand duke of Tuscany, 7, 14, 234n, 305, 307n
Lesseps, Ferdinand Marie de, 12, 230n, 233, 234n, 238
Lichtenstein, Franz, 97n
Literati, The (Poe), 290n
Lockhart, John Gibson, 190n
Loring, Anna, 40
Loring, Ellis Gray, 159
Loring, George Bailey, 75, 76n
Loring, Louisa, 159
Lorrain, Claude, 181, 185n, 254
Louis Napoleon (Napoleon III), 12, 173n, 188, 190n, 230n
Louis-Philippe, king of France, 7–8, 12, 54n, 59n, 146
Lowell, James Russell, 75
Lunati, Giuseppe, 151n

Macaulay, Thomas Babington, 287, 288n
Macpherson, James, 170n
Macpherson, Robert, 169, 170n, 263
Maestri, Pietro, 169, 170n
Mamiani, Terenzio, 69, 70n, 100n, 151n
Mamora, Alfonso La, 232n
Manin, Daniele, 107n
Manning, Mary Weeks, 104, 105n
Manning, Richard Henry, 104, 105n
Maquay, Mr., 91
Margaret of Antioch, Saint, 296, 298n
Maria Maggiore, 163
Martin, Jacob, 92, 230n
Martin, l'enfant trouvé (Sue), 200
Masi, Luigi, 62, 63n, 153n, 241
Mazzini, Giuseppe, 5, 10–14, 49, 63, 70n, 74n, 149, 152, 153n, 154, 155n, 168, 193n, 201, 202, 204–5, 210, 222, 223, 240, 247, 248n, 269n, 278n, 295; arrives in Rome, 196–98, 201, 202; Fuller's opinion of, 11–12, 152, 198n, 210, 247, 250; writes to Pius IX, 49 —letter to, 196–98
Mazzini, Maria, 196, 198n
Mazzoni, Giuseppe, 155n
Medici, Lorenzo de, 235
Memoir of William Ellery Channing, D.D. (W. H. Channing), 65
Metternich, Klemens Wenzel von, 8, 59n
Michelangelo, 161
Mickiewicz, Adam, 55, 63, 124, 125, 129, 175n; on Fuller, 175n–76n
Milan, 7, 8, 58–59, 65; Austria captures, 102n
Modena, Giacomo, 248n

Modena, Giulia Calame, 247, 248n
Modena, Gustavo, 247, 248n
Modena, Luigia Bernaroli, 248n
Mogliani, Dr., 126, 127, 133–35, 140, 141, 164
Molière (Jean-Baptiste Poquelin), 233
Montanelli, Giuseppe, 73, 74n, 150n, 154, 155n, 163
Monte Mario, 161, 163n
Mozier, Joseph, 91, 92n, 97, 233, 234, 271, 278–81, 285, 290–91
Mozier, Isabella, 285, 286n
Muzzarelli, Carlo Emanuele, 151n, 170n

Nachbarn, Die (Bremer), 297n
Napoleon I, 44, 45n, 155n, 190n
Napoleon III (Louis Napoleon), 12, 173n, 188, 190n, 230n
Nathan, James, 6, 15
National Intelligencer, 63
"Nature" (Emerson), 187, 188n
Neukomm, Sigismund von, 54
Newcomb, Charles King, 78n, 206
—letters to, 76–78, 156–57
Newcomb, Charlotte, 78n
Newcomb, Elizabeth, 78n
Newcomb, Rhoda Mardenbrough, 76, 78n, 156
New-York Daily Tribune, 5, 6, 8–12, 48, 52, 55, 63, 71, 72n, 83n, 104, 214n
New-York Evening Post, 63
Niccolo de' Lapi (d'Azeglio), 265
Niebuhr, Barthold Georg, 160, 161n, 192–93
North American Phalanx, 294, 295, 297n
Novara, battle of, 11, 224n, 232n

Old Curiosity Shop, The (Dickens), 210, 211n
Ombressi, James, 267, 269n
Orioli, Francesco, 69, 70n
Ossoli, Angelo Eugene Philip, 10, 13–14, 111–14, 117, 120–26, 129, 130, 138–44, 163, 164, 166, 167, 208–10, 218–25, 235, 236, 246, 248, 249, 254, 257–61, 264–66, 269–70, 274, 280, 283, 285, 288n, 292–96, 298, 300–302, 305–6
Ossoli, Giovanni Angelo, 5, 6, 9, 10, 12–15, 92n, 96, 161, 169, 234, 244–45, 248, 254, 257, 262–63, 266, 267, 280, 282–83, 285, 299, 304; Fuller's opinion of, 248, 250, 260–62, 270–72, 278, 286–87, 291–92, 300–303
—letters to, 78–81, 84–90, 92–102, 105–45, 163–67, 218–28, 235–37, 253–54
Ostia, 68, 69n

Oudinot, Nicholas-Charles-Victor, 12–13, 227n, 230n, 234n, 238, 307n
Ovid, 103, 105n

Page, Mr., 68, 103
—letter to, 62–63
Papers on Literature and Art (Fuller), 290n, 296–97, 298n
Parent's Assistant (Edgeworth), 294n
Parkman, Francis, 277n
Parkman, George, 306–7
Parsons, Anna Quincy Thaxter, 189, 191n
Peabody, Elizabeth Palmer, 181, 185n
Perkins, Charles Callahan, 195, 200
Phillips, Jonathan, 247, 248n
Phillips, William, 247, 248n
Piacenzia, Giovanna da, 43, 45n
Pianciani, Amalia, 278n
Pianciani, Luigi, 278n
Pianciani, Vincenzo, 278n
Piccinino, Il (Sand), 195, 196n, 215
Pippa Passes (Robert Browning), 307
Pius VII, pope, 154, 155n
Pius IX, pope, 6–15, 49, 62, 63n, 65, 70n, 72, 91–93, 99, 101, 102, 106, 107, 109, 146–47, 149, 150n, 152–54, 171, 173n, 251; allocution of, 9, 65; Fuller's opinion of, 6, 9, 65, 72, 73, 101, 102, 151n, 154; leaves Rome, 10, 158, 159n
Poe, Edgar Allan, 289–90; Fuller's opinion of, 290n
—works of: *Literati*, 290n; *Raven and Other Poems*, 290n; "To One in Paradise," 290n
Poems (Emerson), 204
Poems: Second Series (Ellery Channing), 47n
Poems: Second Series (Lowell), 75, 76n
Poetry (Raphael), 42, 45n
Poniatowski, Prince, 44
Porta Maggiore, 161, 163n
Porzio, Luigi, 241
Poussin, Nicolas, 181, 188
Powers, Hiram, 158, 159n, 174
Pretorian Camp, 181
Prose Writers of Germany (Hedge), 55

Rachel, Élisa Félix, 43–44, 45n, 200
Radetzky, Joseph Wenzel, 7–9, 14, 59n, 100n, 102n, 138, 139, 244n
Radziwill, Princess, 42, 45n
Raphael, 42, 45n, 182n, 200, 254
Raven and Other Poems, The (Poe), 290n
"Reality" (Shelley), 297n
Ricci, Angelo Maria, 254, 255n
Ricci, Anne-Alexanderine-Catherine de, 44, 45n

Ricordi di giovani d'Italia, 193n
Rieti, 199, 208–9, 245–46, 252
Robeson, Andrew, 71, 72n
Robeson, Anna Rodman, 72n
Rome: constitutional assembly of, 168–69, 170n, 179, 188n; Fuller's opinion of, 11, 40, 43, 60, 68, 147, 156, 170, 174, 217, 240; seige of, 12, 13, 190n, 226–30, 232–42, 258
Rome souterraine, La (Didier), 192, 193n
Römische Elegien (Goethe), 181, 185n
Römische Geschichte (Niebuhr), 161n
Rosmini, Antonio, 151n
Rossi, Pelligrino, 10, 146–47, 150n, 153n
Rossini, Giocchino Antonio, 304
Rotch, Ann Waln, 62
—letter to, 61–62
Rotch, Francis, 62
Rotch, Francis Morgan, 191, 192n
Rotch, Maria, 62, 72
—letter to, 191
Rotch, Mary, 14, 72n, 176–77, 178, 179n, 186, 193, 202; death of, 130, 131
—letter to, 70–72
Russell, George Robert, 216n
Russell, Sarah Shaw, 215, 216n
Russell, W., 64

Saint Peter's (Rome), 305
Salasco, treaty of, 9, 74n, 102n, 107n, 224n
Sand, George (Aurore Lucie Dudevant), 5, 45n, 51, 52n, 193n, 215, 216n
—works of: *Consuelo*, 42, 45n; *Piccinino*, 195, 196n, 215
San Lorenzo (Rome), 180
San Lorenzo fuori le Mura (Rome), 161, 163n
Santa Agnese (Rome), 161
Santa Maria Maggiore (Rome), 233
Santissima Trinità de Monti (Rome), 163
Saunders, William Carroll, 230n
Schiller, Johann Christoph Friedrich, 185n
Scott, Walter, 76n, 251
Seaton, William W., 63n
Sebastiani, Altarice-Rosalba, 61
Semiramide (Rossini), 304, 307n
Severin, Dr., 64
Shaw, Coolidge, 72
Shaw, Francis George, 215
Shaw, Pauline Agassiz, 277n
Shaw, Quincy Adams, 275, 277n
Shaw, Sarah Sturgis, letter to, 214–15
Shelley, Percy Bysshe, 297n
Smith, Elizabeth Oakes, 292, 294n
Socialism, 206, 215, 295
Speranza, La, 219, 220

Spring, Herbert Marcus, 295, 297n
Spring, Marcus, 42, 43, 45n, 48, 104, 172
—letters to, 152–53, 201, 294–97
Spring, Rebecca Buffum, 42, 43, 45n, 104, 113, 172, 273
—letter to, 294–97
Sterbini, Pietro, 10, 150n–51n, 153
Stirling, Johanna Wilhelmina, 54
—letter to, 53–54
Stirling, John, 54n
Story, Edith Marion, 47n, 53, 75, 158
Story, Emelyn, 47, 64, 65, 91, 149, 200, 203, 204, 229, 236, 262, 304
—letters to, 74–75, 157–59, 168–70, 188–90, 195, 232–35, 238, 262–63, 279–80, 284–85
Story, Joseph, 47n, 75
Story, William Wetmore, 47, 64, 75, 149, 158, 189, 190, 200, 203, 204, 229, 232–36, 262, 286n, 304
—letters to, 161–63, 286–88
Sturgis, Caroline. *See* Tappan, Caroline Sturgis
Sturgis, William, 160, 161n
Subiaco, 69
Sue, Eugène, 200
Sumner, Henry, 277n
Sumner, Horace, 275–77, 280

Tappan, Caroline Sturgis, 6–7, 14, 46, 75, 78, 159, 160, 161n, 204, 216; marriage of, 41
—letters to, 41–44, 198–200, 207–11, 258–59, 301–7
Tappan, Ellen Sturgis, 204, 205n, 207–8
Tappan, William Aspinwall, 6, 44n, 208, 211
Tartuffe (Molière), 233
Tasso, Torquato, 76n, 251
Terry, Luther, 185n
Théobald, Charles-Laure-Hughes, 61n
Thoreau, Henry David, 5

Titian, 47
Tivoli, 69
"To One in Paradise" (Poe), 290n
Torlonia, Alessandro, 74n
Torlonia, Giovanni, 73, 74n
Torres, Bartolomeo de, 93, 94n
Torres, Ferdinando de, 93, 94n
Triumph of Galatea (Raphael), 181, 182n
Tucker, Martha Robeson, 71, 72n

Vasari, Giorgio, 75, 76n
Verdi, Giuseppe, 41
Victor Emanuel, king of Piedmont, 11, 232n
Villa Albani (Rome), 161, 240
Villa di Raffalo (Rome), 240
Villa Farnesina (Rome), 182n
Villa Ludovisi (Rome), 161
Villa Negroni (Rome), 263
Vinci, Leonardo da, 182n
Völkerbund, Der, 287, 288n

Walewska, Marie, 45n
Walewski, Alexandre, 44, 45n
Ward, Anna Hazard Barker, 174
—letters to, 216–17, 271–74
Ward, Samuel Gray, 200, 216, 217, 307
—letters to, 271–74, 278–79
Webster, John White, 307
Welby, Edgar T., 263n
—letters to, 263, 264
Welles, Adeline Fowle, 48n
Welles, Samuel, 48n
Wetmore, Thomas, 75, 76n, 158, 168, 188, 229, 262
Wilhelm Meisters Lehrjahre (Goethe), 194, 195n
Winckelmann, Johann Joachim, 240
Woman in the Nineteenth Century (Fuller), 61, 65n, 290
Wordsworth, William, 154, 155n

Zeuli, Alfonso, 252, 253n

Library of Congress Cataloging-in-Publication Data
(Revised for vol. 5)

Fuller, Margaret, 1810–1850.
    The letters of Margaret Fuller.

    Includes bibliographies and indexes.
    Contents: v. 1. 1817–38 — v. 2. 1839–41 —
[etc.] — v. 5. 1848–49.
    1. Fuller, Margaret, 1810–1850—Correspondence.
2. Authors, American—19th century—Correspondence.
I. Hudspeth, Robert N.   II. Title.
PS2506.A4   1983   818'.309   [B]   82-22098
ISBN 0-8014-1386-9 (v. 1)